Manasara Series No. II

Indian Architecture

According to Mānasāra-Śilpaśāstra

Prasanna Kumar Acharya

Low Price Publications

2022

First Published 1934

Reprinted in LPP
1995, 2004, 2011, 2022

ISBN 10: 81-7536-348-7
ISBN 13: 978-81-7536-348-9

Published by
Low Price Publications
A-6, Second Floor, Nimri Commercial Centre,
Ashok Vihar Phase-IV, Delhi 110 052 (INDIA)
Tel.: +91 11 47061936
E-mail: info@LPPindia.com
Website: www.LPPindia.com

Printed at
Balaji Offset
Delhi

PRINTED IN INDIA

" What the learned world demand of us in India is to be quite certain of our data, to place the monumental record before them exactly as it now exists, and to interpret it faithfully and literally."

ACKNOWLEDGMENT.

I take this opportunity to offer my respectful thanks to the Government of the United Provinces of Agra and Oudh, to whose generosity I owe the publication of this volume as also my three other books : *A Dictionary of Hindu Architecture, The Mānasāra* (Sanskrit Text) and *The Architecture of Mānasāra* (English Translation of the Text). For the arrangement I am indebted to the distinguished lovers and encouragers of Oriental scholarship, Sir Claude de la Fosse, C.I.E., M.A., D. LITT., the then Director of Public Instruction and the first Vice-Chancellor of the reconstructed Allahabad University, and Dr. F. W. Thomas, the Librarian of India Office, London. For an encouragement I am indebted to Rai Rajeshwar Bali Sahib, O.B.E., the Minister of Education, Kunwar Jagdish Prasad, C.I.E., O.B.E., I.C.S., the Educational (now Chief) Secretary, and Mr. A. H. Mackenzie, M.A., B.Sc., the Director of Public Instruction.

To Dr. Thomas I am, further, grateful for many helpful directions and for procuring for me the available manuscripts and placing at my disposal the books in the India Office Library where I made a special study of the Purāṇas and the Epics. Professor L. D. Barnett, M.A., LITT. D., who was my teacher at University College, London, initiated me to the study of the Āgamas at British Museum, London; he also taught me the various South Indian scripts and helped me with his scholarly instructions for which I am grateful to him. Under the guidance of Professor J. Ph. Vogel, Ph.D., a summary of the Mānasāra was prepared at Leiden University, Holland, and I am grateful to him for his assistance. I am thankful to the authorities of the Government Manuscripts Library, Madras, for permission to use the Library where I studied the available manuscripts on Indian Architecture. To the late lamented Dr. D. B. Spooner, the then Director-General of Archæology, I owe all the facilities to work at the rich Archæological Library at Benmore, Simla, where, at the encouragement of his talented wife, two difficult sections of this volume (III, V) were completed

The first proof was turned out without diacritical marks which were not then available at Government Press. I owe to Mr. H. K. Ghosh, the Manager of the Indian Press, an arrangement by which their chief proof reader, Mr. Ajit Kumar Banerji, put in these marks and has thereby earned my gratitude. To Dr. Meghanath Banerji, a great lover of our ancient store of knowledge and a versatile genius, I owe the revision of the second proof. For many useful suggestions and improvements I am indebted to my esteemed colleague Professor H. N. Randle, M.A., D. PHIL., who very readily and generously took the trouble of going through the whole book at the revision stage of the penultimate proof. To another colleague of mine, Pandit Kshetresh Chandra Chattopadhyaya, M.A., I owe an important reference, among other occasional assistance, recorded under note 1, page 198. I am thankful to one of our research scholars, Pandit Keshoram Pandya, M.A., for selecting most of the words on which I have written notes under the Index.

Last but not least I am pleased to record my grateful thanks to Major W. C. Abel, M.B.E., V.D., lately the Superintendent of Government Press, Allahabad, and to his able successor, Mr. D. W. Crighton, and to their staff for their ever sympathetic and kind treatment towards me and for their patient and careful handling which was necessary in bringing out a volume like this.

SANSKRIT DEPARTMENT,
UNIVERSITY OF ALLAHABAD:
August, 1927.

P. K. ACHARYA.

CONTENTS

Acknowledgment iii

Preface: Connotation of Śilpa-Śāstra and Signification of Mānasāra ... 1

I.—A General Survey: Popularity of Architecture in—

I.—Vedic Literature 5

II.—Buddhist Literature 9

III.—Classical Literature:—

(a) The Epics 17

(b) The Purāṇas 19

(c) The Āgamas 23

(d) Miscellaneous Treatises 29

II.—Śilpa-Śāstras: Summaries and Synopses of—

(a) The Mānasāra 34

(b) The Mayamata Śilpa-Śāstra 89

(c) The Aṁśumad-bheda of Kāśyapa 92

(d) The Viśvakarma-Śilpa 96

(e) The Agastya... 100

(f) The Sanatkumāra-Vāstuśāstra 102

(g) The Śilpa-Śāstra of Maṇḍana 103

(h) The Saṁgraha 106

III.—Position of the Mānasāra in Literature:—

(a) The Types of Buildings... 111

(b) The Measurements 121

(c) The Five Orders 125

(d) The Three Styles 130

IV.—The Mānasāra and Vitruvius Compared:—

(a) The Extent and Popularity 134

(b) Similarity in Number and Titles of chapters 137

(c) Similarity in Training of architects... 137

(d) Similarity in Preliminary chapters 142

(e) Similarity in Town-planning 143

(f) Similarity in Forms, Species and Foundations of Buildings... 147

(g) Similarity in Columns 149

(h) Similarity in division of Compound into five courts .. 154

(i) Similarity in Doors 155

(j) Similarity in Sculptural measures 156

(k) Similarity in Linguistic style 158

(l) Similarity in mysterious Titles 159

V.—Age of the Mānasāra :—
(a) The Bṛihat-saṁhitā 160
(b) The Bhavishya and Matsya Purāṇas 163
(c) The ancient Professors of Architecture 164
(d) Types of buildings and columns 167
(e) The Matsya, Garuḍa and Agni Purāṇas 168
(f) The Artha-śāstra, Kāmandakīya-nīti and Śukra-nīti .. 169
(g) The Daśakumāra-charita 170
(h) The Holal Inscriptions 171
(i) The Sūrya-siddhānta, Līlāvatī and Siddhānta-śiromaṇi ... 172
(j) The ten types of twelve storeyed buildings representing ten provinces... 173
(k) The three styles representing three geographical divisions of India 176
(l) Identification of Nāgara, Vesara and Drāviḍa styles . 180
(m) Division of Royalty into nine classes 181
(n) The extent of Gupta Empire 184
(o) The prevailing Religion... 185
(p) Developments in Literature, Language and fine Arts .. 193
(q) Unfaded memory of Seven Gupta Kings 195
(r) Conclusions 198
Appendix : The Language of the Śilpa-Śāstra 199
General Index 215

PREFACE

THE term *śilpa* means an art, fine or mechanical. It covers some sixty-four such arts. But here *Śilpa-śāstra* is used in the sense of *Vāstu-śāstra*, this latter term being less usual.[1] The literal rendering of *Vāstu-śāstra* would be 'science of architecture,' but a complete *Vāstu-śāstra* deals with more than what is generally understood by architecture. In the *Vāstu-śāstras* the term architecture is taken in its broadest sense and implies what is built or constructed. Thus in the first place it denotes all kinds of buildings, religious, residential, and military; and their auxiliary members and component mouldings. Secondly, it covers town-planning; laying out gardens; constructing market-places including ports and harbours; making roads, bridges, gateways, triumphal arches; digging wells, tanks, trenches, drains, sewers, moats; building enclosure walls, embankments, dams, railings, landing-places, flights of steps for hills and bathing ghāts, and ladders. Thirdly, it connotes articles of furniture such as bedsteads, couches, tables, chairs, thrones, wardrobes, baskets, cages, nests, mills, conveyances, lamps and lamp-posts for streets. It also includes the making of dresses and ornaments such as chains, crowns, head-gear and foot and arm wear. Architecture also includes sculpture and deals with carving of phalli, idols of deities, statues of great personages, images of animals and birds. It is also concerned with such preliminary matters as the selection of site, testing of soil, planning, designing, finding out cardinal points by means of a gnomon, dialling, and astronomical and astrological calculations.

All these matters are systematically treated in the standard work on the subject known as the *Mānasāra*. Under this short title the work has been catalogued and generally referred to. But the complete title, as appears from the seventy colophons of the text, is the

[1] Western scholars like Dr. Burgess have also used the expression *Śilpa-śāstra* in this sense (see *Imperial Gazetteer*, II. 176)

Mānasāra-vāstu-śāstra. Some manuscripts have the title *Mānavasāra.* It is stated on the fly-leaf of some other manuscripts that those manuscripts were copied from a *Śilpa-śāstra* which is apparently meant to be the title of the original work.

The etymological rendering of the word *mānasāra* is 'the essence of measurement,' *sāra* meaning essence and *māna* measurement. It may, however, be rendered by 'the standard measurement' or 'the system of proportion' as has been done by the author of *An Essay on the architecture of the Hindus.*[1] In this sense the full title *Mānasāra-Vāstu-śāstra* would imply a *Vāstu-śāstra* or science of architecture, where the essence of measurement is contained, the standard measurement followed, or the system of proportions embodied.[2]

There is an ambiguity as regards the signification of the title of this standard work. The colophon annexed to each of the seventy chapters contains the expression *Mānasāre Vāstu-śāstre.* This is apparently intended to mean either the *Vāstu-śāstra* by *Mānasāra* or the *Vāstu-śāstra* named *Mānasāra.*[3] In other words, *Mānasāra* would seem to be such a name as may be applied to the author as well as to the work.[4] In a passage in the treatise itself the term *mānasāra* has been used in both these senses.[5] Therein it is held that 'all this is stated to have been compiled by the ancient *Mānasāras.* This great science was formerly revealed by all the gods beginning with the Creator and the King of gods. Having been compiled therefrom, this treatise *Mānasāra* is made

---

[1] Rām Rāz, p. 9 note.

[2] There are several other treatises of which the titles end in *sāra*, meaning essence; for instance, Vedānta-sāra, Jyotis-sāra, Āchāra-sāra, Laghu-śilpa-jyotis-sāra, Śilpa-śāstra-sāra (saṁgraha).

[3] But from the locative use of *mānasāra*, the latter sense seems to be the usual one.

[4] The same ambiguity apparently attaches to titles like Kauṭilīya-artha-śāstra. But the titles like Sanatkumāra-vāstu-śāstra, Maya-śilpa-śāstra, Gārga-saṁhitā or Śukranīti would indicate only the first category.

[5] कृतमिति चाखिलमुक्तं मानसारपुराणैः पितामहेन्द्रप्रमुखैः
समस्तैर्देवैरिदं शास्त्रवरं पुरोदितम् ।
तस्मात्समुद्धृत्य हि मानसारम्
शास्त्रं कृतं लोकहितार्थमेतत् ॥ (LXX, 114-8).

for the benefit of the people'. In this passage the term *mānasāra* is once used in the sense of a generic name (of architects), and secondly as the title of a treatise implying 'the essence of measurement,' which is the etymological rendering of *mānasāra*. This latter sense is explicitly expressed in another passage where it is stated that 'having successively collected in a concise form the essence of measurement from the *śāstra*' this treatise is compiled.[1] The former sense is also substantiated by several other passages. In one place it is stated that 'the treatise, compiled by the sages or professors of architecture called Mānasāras, was named after the sage or architect Mānasāra.'[2] There is yet another ambiguity in this passage, Mānasāra being once a generic name in the plural and in a second place a personal name in the singular. As a generic name it is used in another passage where it is stated that 'there are many Mānasāras.'[3] Then thirty-two sages or professors of architecture are specified by names[4], wherein *māna* or measurement is associated with four names—Māna-sāra, Māna-kalpa, Māna-bodha and Māna-vid. It is not unlikely that the sages or professors, with whose names *māna* or measurement is associated, are intended to be distinguished from the rest as being specialists in 'measuring' which is a very important feature of the science of architecture. It is also used exclusively as a personal name when it is stated 'by all great sages or professors, Mānasāra and others.'[5]

All the available external references to *Mānasāra*, however, point to its being used mostly as a personal name. In the *Daśa-kumāra-charita* of Daṇḍin, Mānasāra is mentioned as the king of Malwa. With him was engaged in war the king Rājahaṁsa of Pāṭaliputra who

---

[1] मानानां सारं संगृह्य शास्त्रं संक्षेपतः क्रमात् । (XXXIII. 2).

[2] मानसार-ऋषीणां कृतं शास्त्रं मानसारमुनिनामकमासीत् । (I. 39).

In this line two epithets, *Ṛishi* and *Muni*, one in the plural and the other in the singular, are applied to the name *Mānasāra*.

[3] मानसारा बहुः श्रुतः । (LXVIII. 11).

[4] See pages 165; 86 note 3.

[5] सकलमुनिवरैर्मानसारादिमुख्यैः । (LXIX. 216).

was the father of Rājavāhana, the chief of the ten princes.[1] In two unpublished inscriptions Mānasāra (? Mānasarpa) occurs as the name of an architect.[2] In the Agni-purāṇa also Mānasāra is mentioned, but its meaning is uncertain.[3] Therein it may be interpreted as implying both the title of a treatise and the name of an author.

The contents of the *Mānasāra*, however, fully justify its unique position as the most representative *silpa-śāstra*. It can also be placed side by side with Vitruvius's work, which is the standard treatise on Roman architecture. No elaborate explanation is perhaps necessary for the justification of the title of this volume. This was originally intended to be an introduction to the *Mānasāra* and to be read along with the First Edition and the English Translation prepared by the present writer. But the study of the whole subject is in its infancy, if not at its birth. So it was found necessary to refer briefly to a few essential things which, though elaborately discussed in the writer's Dictionary, can hardly be included in a mere Introduction to either the Text or the Translation of the *Mānasāra*.

---

[1] मगधनायको मालवेश्वरं प्रत्यग्रसंग्रामघस्मरं समुत्कटमानसारं मानसारं प्रति …………संग्रामाभिलाषेण रोषेण महताविष्टो निर्ययौ।

(Ed. Kale, Bombay, 1917, page 4, para 2, line 3).

राजहंसो मुनिमभाषत—भगवन् मानसारः प्रबलेन दैवबलेन मां निर्जित्य मद्भोग्यं राज्यमनुभवति। (*Ibid.* page 12, para 1, line 3).

अवन्तिसुन्दरी नाम मानसारनन्दिनी……………नगरोपान्तरम्योद्याने विहारोत्कण्ठया मनोभवमर्चन्ती रेमे। (*Ibid.* page 43, para 1 line, 4).

[2] Epigraphist's Report, Madras, 1901, nos. 207, 209. For details see page 130, note 5; page 171, page 176, note 1.

[3] तदूर्ध्वे तु भवेद्वेदी सकण्ठा मानसारकम्। (XLII. 127).

For different readings, and discussion in detail see page 106.

Manu is a puzzling name which is mentioned in the Mānasāra (see pages 88, 162, 163) and associated with architectural treatises. In the Manusaṁhitā (I. 63) mention is made of as many as fourteen Manus. I wonder whether between *Manu* and *Māna* there is some confusion due either to reading, script or something else. It is not difficult to read *Mānasāra* for *Manusāra*. But Mānasāra has already become too well known to admit any possibility of its name being changed, although no sage of that name is discoverable in ancient literature.

I

A GENERAL SURVEY

For civilized people a comfortable residence is as necessary as food and clothes. In fact the standard of civilization seems to be regulated, amongst other things, by durability, scientific plan, æsthetic construction, and successful finish of buildings, religious, residential or military. It is, therefore, not surprising to find references to the art of building in all branches of the literature of a cultured people. For ancient Indian writers, at any rate, architecture seems to have been a very fascinating subject, inasmuch as the Vedic, Buddhist. Epic, Paurāṇic, Āgamic, Historical, Political and even Astronomical literature bear traces of it. Illustrations in detail are hardly necessary. We propose to refer briefly to only the representative branches of literature.

I Vedic Literature

It is needless to say that the details of the art of building were systematically embodied for the first time in the avowedly architectural treatises. They are necessarily missing in non-architectural literature, especially that composed before the growth of the *Vāstu-śāstras*. But casual references to this art go as far back as the oldest existing literature of the world. The Vedic literature before the Sūtra period, however, contains little about the structure of a house.[1] That the people of that time had learnt the art of building and used to reside in constructed houses and not in caves is sufficiently clear, not only from the synonyms for a house[2] but also from the component members of a building, such as doors, pillars, and

[1] Compare *Vedic Index*, by MacDonell and Keith, I. 229-31.

[2] For griha, dhāma or dhāman, pastyā and harmya in the sense of the whole compound, see
Ṛig-veda, III, 53, 6 ; IV, 49,6 ; VIII, 10, 1.
Atharva-veda, VII, 83, 1 ; X, 6, 4.
Aitareya-Brāhmaṇa, VIII, 21.
Vedic Index, p. 229.

cross-beams.[1] "The hymns of the Atharva-veda[2] give some information about the construction of a house, but the details are extremely obscure............. According to Zimmer[3], four pillars (*upamit*) were set up on a good site, and against them beams were leant at an angle as props (*pratimit*). The upright pillars were connected by cross-beams (*parimit*) resting upon them. The roof was formed of ribs of bamboo cane (*vaṁśa*)[4],............ The walls were filled up with grass in bundles (*palada*), and the whole structure was held together by ties of various sorts (*nahana, prāṇāha, saṁdaṁśa, parishvañjalya*)[5]. It was composed of several rooms, ..., and it could be securely shut up." [6]

Atri is stated to have been "thrown into a machine room with a hundred doors, where he was roasted."[7] Vasishṭha desired to have "a three-storeyed dwelling" (*tri-dhātu-śaraṇam*)[8]. Mention is made of a sovereign "who, exercising no oppression, sits down in this substantial and elegant hall built with a thousand pillars[9]," and of residential houses with such pillars as are said to be "vast, comprehensive, and thousand-doored."[10] Mitra and Varuṇa are represented as occupying a great palace with a thousand pillars and a thousand gates.[11] Muir is quite

---

[1] Dvār and dvāra, R. V. I, 13, 6.
A. V. VIII, 3, 22; XIV, 1, 63.
Vājasaneyi-Saṁhitā, XXX, 10.
Śata-patha-Brāhmaṇa, XI, 1, 1, 2; XIV, 3, 1, 13.
Upamit (pillar), R. V. I, 59, 1; IV, 5, 1.
A. V. IX, 3, 1.
Parimit (cross-beam), A. V. IX. 3. 1.
Ibid. page 230.

[2] III, 12, IX, 3. Bloomfield, Hymns of the Atharva-veda, 343, et seq. Weber, Indische Studien, 17, 234, et seq. Whitney, Translation of the Atharva-veda, 525, et seq.

[3] Altindisches Leben, 153.

[4] "It seems likely that, as the ribs were of bamboo and were probably fixed in the ridge, the roof was wagon-headed, like the huts of the Todas at the present day (see illustrations of rivers, *The Todas*, pp. 25, 27, 28, 51), and the rock-cut Chaityas or Assembly halls of the Buddhists in Western India, in some of the earliest of which the wooden ribs of the arched roof are still preserved. See Fergusson, *History of Indian Architecture* II, 135, cf. 126."

[5] A. V. IX, 3, 4, 5.

[6] R. V. VII, 55, 6.

[7] R. V. I, 112, 7. Wilson's R. V. IV, 148.

[8] Ibid. IV, 200.

[9] Ibid. II, 313.

[10] Ibid. IV, 179.

[11] Compare R. V. II, 41, 5; V. 62, 6; VII, 88, 5.
A. V. III, 12; IX, 3, which contains prayers for the stability of a house at the time of its construction.

reasonable when he comments on this by saying that "this is but an exaggerated de cription of a royal residence such as the poet had seen."[1]

The *Śulva-Sūtras*, which are but the supplementary portions of the *Kalpa-Sūtras*, treating of the measurement and construction of the different *Vedis* or altars, furnish us with some interesting structural details of the Agnis, the large altars built of bricks. The construction of these altars, which were required for the great Soma sacrifice, seems to have been based on sound scientific principles and was probably the beginning of religious architecture (temple-building) in India.

These altars could be constructed in different shapes, the earliest enumeration of which is found in the *Taittirīya-Saṁhitā*.[2] Following this enumeration[3], Baudhāana and Āpastamba furnish us with full particulars about the shape of all these different chitis (altars) and the bricks which were employed for their construction. Everyone of these altars was constructed of five layers of bricks, which together came up to the height of the knee; in some cases 10 or 15 layers, and proportionate increase in the height of the altar were prescribed. Every layer in its turn was to consist of two hundred bricks, so that the whole Agni (altar) contained a thousand; the first, third, and fifth layers were divided into two hundred parts in excatly the same manner; a different division was adopted for the second and the fourth, so that one brick was never laid upon another of the same size and form.

---

[1] Muir, *Sanskrit Texts*, V, 455.

Compare R. L. Mitra, *Indo-Aryans*, I, 27: "Pillars, spacious doors and windows, though frequently mentioned, are not decisive indications of the existence of masonry buildings: but bricks could not possibly have originated unless required for such structures, for it would be absurd to suppose that bricks were known, and made, and yet they were never used in the construction of houses."

[2] V, 4, 11.

[3] (i) Chaturaśra-śyena-chit—so called because it resembles the form of a falcon and the bricks out of which it is composed are all square shaped.

(ii) Kaṅka-chit—in the form of a heron (cf. Burnell. Cat. 29. of a carrion kite) is the same as śyena-chit except the two additional feet.

(iii) Alaja-chit—is the same except the additional wings

(iv) Prauga-chit—is an equilateral triangle; and the

(v) Ubhayataḥ-Praugachit—is made up of two such triangles joined at their bases.

(vi) Ratha-chakra-chit—is in the form of a wheel, (i) a massive wheel without spokes, and (ii) a wheel with sixteen spokes.

(vii) Droṇa-chit—is like a vessel or tube, square or circular.

(viii) Parichayya-chit—has a circular outline and is equal to the Rathachakra-chit, differing in the arrangement of bricks which are to be placed in six concentric circles.

(ix) Samūhya-chit—is circular in shape and made of loose earth and bricks.

(x) Kūrma-chit—resembles a tortoise and is of a triangular or circular shape. Cf. Thibaut, *J. A. S. B.*, 1875, part I.

"The first altar covered an area of 7½ *purushas*, which means 7½ squares, each side of which was equal to a *purusha*, i.e., the height of a man with uplifted arms. On each subsequent occasion the area was increased by one square *purusha*. Thus, at the second layer of the altar one square *purusha* was added to the 7½ constituting the first *chiti* (altar), and at the third layer two square *purushas* were added and so on. But the shape of the whole and the relative proportion of each constituent part had to remain unchanged. The area of every *chiti* (altar), whatever its shape might be—falcon, wheel, tortoise, etc.,—had to be equal to 7½ square *purushas*.[1]

Frequent mention is made also of villages, towns and forts,[2] and cities with hundred enclosures or fortifications are referred to[3]. On this Muir remarks that although they are only alluded to as figurative expressions of the means of protection afforded by the gods, they no doubt suggest the idea of forts consisting apparently of a series of concentric walls, as actually existing in the country at that time."[4]

From references like these many scholars are of opinion that the authors of the Vedic literature "were not ignorant of stone forts, walled cities, stone houses, carved stones, and brick edifices."

[1] Thus squares had to be found which would be equal to two or more given squares, or equal to the difference of two given squares; oblongs were turned into squares and squares into oblongs. Triangles were constructed equal to given squares or oblongs and so on. A circle had to be constructed, the area of which might equal as closely as possible that of a given square. See illustrations in *The Pandit*, new series, June, 1876, no. 1, volumes I and IV, 1882; old series, June, 1874, no. 97, volumes IX and X, May, 1876.

[2] R. V. i, 58, 8; 144, 1; ii, 20, 8; iv, 27, 1; 30, 20; viii. 3, 7; 15, 14; 89, 8; 95, 1.

[3] R. V. 1, 166, 8; vii. 15, 14.

[4] Muir, *Sanskrit Texts*, v. 451.

II Buddhist Literature

"In the Buddha's time and in that portion of northern India where the Buddhist influence was most early felt—that is to say, in the districts including and adjoining those now called the United Provinces and Behar"—the arrangements of villages were practically similar. "We nowhere hear of isolated houses. The houses were all together, in a group, separated only by narrow lanes. Immediately adjoining was the sacred grove of trees of the primeval forest .... Beyond this was the wide expanse of cultivated field, usually rice field." Villagers are described as "uniting of their own accord to build mote-hills and rest-houses and reservoirs, to mend the roads between their own and adjacent villages, and even to lay out parks." [1]

The exact details of town-planning are not available. But "we are told of lofty walls, ramparts with buttresses and watch-towers and great gates; the whole surrounded by a moat or even a double moat, one of water and one of mud. But we are nowhere told of the length of the fortifications or of the extent of the space they enclosed. It would seem that we have to think not so much of a large walled city as of a fort surrounded by a number of suburbs ... From the frequent mention of the windows of the great houses opening directly on to the streets or squares it would appear that it was not the custom to have them surrounded by any private grounds. There were, however, no doubt, enclosed spaces behind the fronts of the houses, which latter abutted on the streets" [2]

---

[1] *Buddhist India*, Rhys Davids, 43, 45, 49 : compare *Jat*, 1. 199.

[2] R. D. ibid. pp 65-64.

Cf. The hill fortress, Girivraja, four and a half miles in circumference, is said to have been built by Mahā-Govinda, the architect. Bimbisāra is stated to have built Rājagriha, king's house, which was three miles in circumference. "The stone walls of Girivraja are the oldest extant stone buildings in India." Mention is also made of Ayojjha, Bārāṇasī, Kampilla, Kosāmbī, Madhurā, Mithilā, Sāgala, Sāketa, Sāvatthi, Ujjeni, Vesāli and other cities, of which however few architectural details are given (Vimāna-Vatthu, commentary, p. 82).

Compare *Digh*. XIX, 36 :

दन्तपुरं कालिङ्गानमस्सकानाञ्च पोतनम् ।
माहिस्सती अवन्तीनम् सोवीरानञ्च रोरुकम् ॥
मिथिला च विदेहानम् चम्पा अङ्गेसु मापिता ।
बाराणसी च कासीनम् एते गोविन्द-मापितेति ॥

See Rhys. Davids, ibid. p. 38.

But detached references to individual buildings, as distinct from villages and towns, are found in abundance in the canonical texts as well as the Jātakas. At places it appears as if Buddha were delivering discourses on architecture. As a matter of fact, he enjoined upon his devotees the supervision of building construction as one of the duties of the order.[1] It is stated in one of the early texts that the Bhikkhus were told on a certain occasion by the Blessed One, after the delivery of a religious discourse, with respect to dwellings, thus: 'I allow you O Bhikkhus, abodes of five kinds—*Vihāra*, *Arddhayoga*, *Prāsāda*, *Harmya*, and *Guhā*.'[2]

Buildings are thus divided into five classes. But the details of the distinguishing features are not methodically given in the texts, obviously because these are not architectural treatises.[3]

Vihāras are the well known monasteries or temples of the Buddhists, originally implying halls where the monks met. *Ardhayogas* seem to be a special kind of Bengal buildings, partly religious and partly residential. *Prāsādas* are wholly residential storeyed buildings; *Harmyas* are a larger and more pompous

---

[1] *Chullavagga*, VI. 17, 1; transl. pp. 212-216.

[2] *Vinaya texts*, *Mahavagga*, I 30, 4, p. 173-74; *Chullavagga*, VI. 1, 2, p. 158.

[3] The commentator Buddhaghosha has, however, submitted an explanatory note. *Vihāra* is the well known Buddhist monastery. *Ardhayoga*, which literally means 'half-joining', is stated by this commentator to imply *Suvarṇa-vanga-griha*' or "gold-coloured Bengal house" as rendered by Oldenberg and Rhys Davids. There appear, however, no such houses in Bengal, nor is this class of buildings mentioned in the Śilpa-śāstras. It is clear, however, that these are meant to imply some sort of luxurious buildings of the then Bengal. Regarding *prāsāda* Buddhaghosha simply says that it is a long *Prāsāda*. Rhys Davids has made several conjectures,—"a long storied mansion, or the whole of an upper storey, or the storied buildings." Sir M. M. Williams seems to explain this by "the monks' hall for assembly and confession." *Harmya* is stated to be a *prāsāda* with an upper chamber placed on the topmost storey. The references to the uses of *prāsāda* and *harmya* as found in the Śilpa-śāstras, general Sanskrit literature, and the archæological records will be found in the writer's *Dictionary* under those terms. *Guhā* literally means cave and would seem to refer to underground buildings. One of the Jātakas (*Ummagga*, p. 480) actually contains an elaborate description of an underground palace, and there are the rock cut temples as in the famous Ajanta caves. According to Buddhaghosha these *guhā* buildings are of four kinds, namely, those built of bricks, stone, wood, or earth. Rhys Davids has rendered *silāguhā* by hut made in a rock, and left out the translation of *paṁsu* (Sanskrit *pāṁsu*, meaning sand, dust, or crumbling soil) *guhā*. Buddhaghosha has thus explained the *pañcha-lenāni* under Mahāvagga 1.30.4—

'अड्ढयोगो' ति सुवण्णवङ्गगेहम्। पासादो' ति दीघपासादो। हम्मियान्' ति उपरि आकासतले पतिट्ठितकूटागारो पासादो येव। गुहा' ति इट्ठकगुहा सिलागुहा दारुगुहा पंसुगुहा।

Compare also Oldenberg and Rhys Davids, Vinaya texts, translation, *Mahāvagga*, p. 173, note, also *Chullavagga*, p. 158, note 2.

type of storeyed buildings. *Guhās* seem to be less dignified buildings, originally built underground for middle-class people. The extensiveness of these buildings can be imagined from the length of time devoted to getting a house completely built. Thus, it is stated that "with reference to the work of a small *Vihāra*, it may be given in charge (to an overseer) as a *Navakamma* (new work) for a period of five or six years, that on an *Aḍḍhayoga* for a period of seven or eight years, that on a large *Vihāra* or a *Pāsāda* for ten or twelve years."[1] That the long periods were not idled away will be clear from the following details of houses gathered from the Vinaya texts.[2]

The selection of building sites shows a highly developed good taste. The *ārāma* (rest-house), well fitted for quiet people, is stated to be built "not too far from the town and not too near, convenient for going and for coming, easily accessible for all who wish to visit him, by day not too crowded, by night not exposed to too much noise and alarm . . . . ."[3] The whole compound is enclosed with ramparts (*prākāra*) of three kinds, namely, brick walls, stone walls, and wooden fences, which are again surrounded with bamboo fences, thorn fences, and ditches.[4]

Houses were built comprising "dwelling-rooms and retiring-rooms, and store-rooms, and service halls and halls with fire-places in them, and store-houses, and closets, and cloisters, and halls for exercise, and wells, and sheds for the well, and bath-rooms, and halls attached to the bath-rooms, and ponds, and open-roofed sheds (maṇḍapas)."[5] These buildings are meant to be dwelling houses; so it is stated that "an *upāsaka* (devotee) has built for his own use a residence, a sleeping room, a stable, a tower, a one-peaked building, a shop, a *boutique*, a storeyed house, an attic, a cave, a cell, a store-room, a refectory, a fire-room, a kitchen, a privy, a place to walk in, a house to walk in, a well, a well-house, a *yantra-gṛiha* (which is supposed by Bühler to be 'a bathing place for hot sitting baths'), a *yantra-gṛiha* room, a lotus pond and a pavilion."[6]

The inner chambers are divided into three classes, called *Śivikā-garbha* or square halls, *Nālikā-garbha* or rectangular halls, and *Harmya-garbha* which appears

---

[1] *Chullavagga*, VI. 17, 1 ;(Translation, page 214).

[2] *Chullavagga*, VI. V, etc., and *Mahavagga*.

[3] *Chullavagga*, VI. 4, 8 ; (Translation, page 187).

[4] *Ibid.* VI. 3, 7, 10 ; (Translation, pages 176—7, 187).

[5] *Chullavagga*, VI. 4, 10 ; (Translation, page 189).

[6] *Mahāvagga*, III. 5, 9 ;(Translation, page 304), also III. 5, 6 ; (Translation, page 303).

to be a large dining-hall.[1] The verandahs (*alinda*) seem to have been a special characteristic of these buildings. The Blessed One (Buddha) says, "I allow you, O Bhikkhus, covered terraces, inner verandahs, and over-hanging eaves."[2] The storeyed buildings (*prāsāda*) are stated to be furnished with "a verandah to it, supported on pillars" with capitals of elephant-head.[3]

Details of gates, doors and windows are also elaborate. Gateways are built with rooms and ornamental screen-work over them[4]. And gates are made of stakes interlaced with thorny brakes.[5]

Doors are furnished with "door-posts and lintel, with hollows like a mortar for the door to revolve in, with projections to revolve in those hollows, with rings on the door for the bolt to work along in, with a block of wood fixed into the edge of the door-post, and containing a cavity for the bolt to go into (called the monkey's head), with a pin to secure the bolt by, with a connecting bolt, with a key-hole, with a hole for a string with which the door may be closed, and with a string for that purpose."[6] The windows are stated to be of three kinds according as they are

[1] About the last Buddhaghosha seems to be doubtful and says हम्मियगब्भो ति कुटागारगब्भो मुदगुल्लादनगब्भो वा;—but about the other two terms he is clear: सिविकागब्भो ति चतुरस्सगब्भो; नालिकागब्भो ति वित्थारतो द्विगुणतिगुणायामो दीघगब्भो (*Chullavagga*, VI. 3. 3). But Oldenberg and Rhys Davids seem to have been wholly misled when they translate these last two by "palankeen shaped and quart measure shaped" about the latter of which Indians of even to-day are quite unfamiliar.

[2] *Chullavagga*, VI. 3. 5. (Translation, page 175), commented on by Buddhaghosha: आलिन्दो नाम पमुखं वुच्चति। (Compare *Abhidhānappadīpikā*, verse 218). पघनं नाम यं निक्खमन्ता च पविसन्ता च पादेहि हनन्ति, तस्स विहार द्वारे उभतो कुट्टं निहरित्वा कतपदेसस्स एतं अधिवचनम्, पघानन्न ति पि वुच्चति। पकुट्टन ति मज्झे गब्भस्स समन्ता परियागारो वुच्चति पकुटन्न ति पाठो। ओसरको ति अनालिन्दके वंसं दत्वा ततो दण्डके ओसारेत्वा कतं छादनपमुखं।

[3] Ibid. VI. 14. 1. (Translation, page 208): हत्थिनखकं supported on the frontal globes (*kumbha*) of elephants, says Buddhaghosha.

[4] *Chullavagga*, VI. 4. 10 (Translation, page 189); 3. 10, तोरण of which excellent examples in stone have been found at the Sāñchi and Bharhut Topes, (Translation, page 178).

[5] Ibid. VI. 3. 10, (Translation, page 178).

[6] Ibid. VI. 3. 8, also 2. 1 and 17. 1, (Translation, pages 177, 161, 219). Compare the distinction between कवाट (door proper) and द्वार (doorway or gateway) (Translation, page 160, note 3). The keys are stated to be of three kinds, as they are made of bronze, hard wood or horn (VI. 2. 1; Translation, page 162).

made with railings, lattices, and slips of wood.[1] The shutters are adjustable and can be closed or opened whenever required.[2] Five kinds of roofing are mentioned —brick-roofing, stone-roofing, cement-roofing, straw-roofing, and roofing of leaves.[3] The roof is first covered over with skins(?) and plastered within and without; then follow whitewash, blocking, red-colouring, wreath-work and creeper-work.[4] "The floors were of earth, not of wood, and were restored from time to time by fresh clay or dry cowdung being laid down, and then covered with a whitewash in which sometimes black or red was mixed. From the parallel passage in *Mahāvagga* (I. 25. 15) and *Chullavagga* (VIII. 3. 1), it would seem that the red colouring was used rather for walls, and the black one for floors."[5] It appears, however, that with a view to removing the dampness gravel was spread over the floor.[6]

There were stairs of three kinds, namely, brick stairs, stone stairs, and wooden stairs. And they were furnished with *ālambana-bāhu* or balustrades.[7] A more detailed description of flights of stairs (*sopāna*) is given in the *Mahā-Sudassana Sutta*: "Each of these had a *thambhā*, evidently posts or banisters; *sūchiyo*, apparently cross-bars, let into these banisters; and *uṇhīsaṁ*, either a head-line running along the top of the banisters, or a figure-head at the lower end of such a head-line."[8]

Thus it is clear that very minute details also are mentioned in this literature. The subject, therefore, seems to have been treated in a more than casual manner.

---

[1] *Chullavagga* VI. 2. 2, वेदिका वातपानं which according to Buddhaghosha means चेतिये वेदिकासदिसं, of which वेदिका has been explained by Rhys Davids in his note on *Mahā-Sudassana Sutta*, 1. 60, (see R. D's. *Buddhist Suttas*, page 262). जालवातपानं नाम जालकबद्धं, of which जाल literally means 'net' but corresponds to lattice. R. D. advises to compare Anglo-Indian 'jalousie' (page 162). सालक वातपानं नाम थमूभक वातपानं which "possibly means with slips of wood arranged horizontally as in our Venetian blinds" (page 163). In spite of all these the learned Orientalists, Rhys Davids and Oldenberg, would say that "There were, of course, no windows in our modern sense, but only spaces left in the wall to admit light and air, and covered by lattices of three kinds" (note on Ibid. VIII 2. 2, Translation, page 279).

[2] *Mahāvagga*, I. 25. 18, (Translation, page 160); *Chullavagga*, VIII. 2. 2, (Translation, page 279).

[3] *Chullavagga*, VI. 3. 10, (Translation, page 179). Compare also VI. 3. 8. 3. 3, etc.

[4] Ibid. V. 11. 6, (Translation, page 97); the rendering of the term 'ogumpheti' which also occurs in *Mahāvagga*, V. 11, by 'skins' seems doubtful and unsuitable. Buddhaghosa in his note at the latter place says चगुम्फियन्तोति भित्ति-दण्डकादिसु वेठेत्वा बन्धाति।

[5] Rhys Davids and Oldenberg, note on *Chullavagga*, VI. 20. 2, (Translation, page 218).

[6] Compare *Chullavagga*, V. 14. 5.

[7] *Chullavagga*, V. 11. 6, (Translation, page 96).

[8] *Mahā Sudassana Sutta*, 1. 59. See also R. Davids' '*Buddhist Suttas*', page 262, and compare *Chullavagga*, VI. 3. 3.

"The entrance to the great houses was through a large gateway. To the right and left of the passage-way were the treasury and grain stores. The gateway led into an inner courtyard round which were chambers on the ground-floor. And above these chambers was a flat roof called the *upari-prāsāda tala*, the upper flat surface of the house, where the owner sat, usually under a pavilion which answered the purpose at once of a drawing-room, an office, and a dining-hall."

"In the King's palace there was accommodation also for all the business of the state, and for the numerous retinue and the extensive harem.............. The supplementary buildings included three institutions which are strange to us, and of considerable historical interest."

"We are told several times of a building of seven storeys in height."[1] Professor Rhys Davids seems to be of the opinion that these buildings must have some connection with the seven-storeyed Ziggarats of Chaldæa. "But in India the use to which such seven-storeyed palaces were put was entirely private, and had nothing to do with any worship of the stars." Still he would add that "in this case also the Indians were borrowers of an idea."

"Another sort of building historically interesting were the hot-air baths, described in full in *Vinaya* texts.[2] They were built on an elevated basement faced with brick or stone, with stone stairs leading up to it, and a railing round the verandah. The roof and walls were of wood, covered first with skins, and then with plaster; the lower part only of the wall being faced with bricks. There was an ante-chamber, and a hot-room, and a pool to bathe in. Seats were arranged round a fire-place in the middle of the hot room; and to induce perspiration hot water was poured over the bathers.............."

In the *Dīgha Nikāya*[3] there is a description of "another sort of bath, an open-air bathing tank, with flights of steps leading to it, faced entirely with stone, and ornamented both with flowers and carvings."

---

[1] *Satta-bhumika-pāsāda, Jataka*, 1. 227, 346; 5. 52, 426; 6. 577. R. Davids refers to a building "still standing at Pulasti-pura in Ceylon and the thousand stone pillars on which another was erected at Anurādhāpura," (*Buddhist India*, page 70).

[2] III. 105-110, 297. "After the bath there was shampooing, and then a plunge into the pool." "It is very curious to find," observes Rhys Davids "at this very early date in the Ganges valley a sort of bathing so closely resembling our modern" so-called 'Turkish bath'. "Did the Turks", he asks, "derive this custom from India?" (Ibid. page 74).

[3] *Buddhist Suttas*, translated by R. Davids, (page 262 foll.), who refers to "several ancient baths still to be seen at Anurādhāpura in a fair state of preservation in spite of the more than two thousand years that have elapsed since they were first constructed." (Ibid. page 76).

The Dāgabas or topes were another class of monuments erected in the cemeteries.[1] They were pre-Buddhistic in origin[2] but became very prominent after Buddha. The priestly records, however, ignore these topes, because they were erected "more especially by those who had thrown off their allegiance to the priests, and were desirous to honour the memory of their teachers, who were leaders of thought, or reformers, or philosophers."

"The first step was probably merely to build the cairn more carefully than usual with stones and to cover the outside with fine *chunam* plaster to give a marble-like surface. The next step was to build the cairn of concentric layers of the huge bricks in use at the time, and to surround the whole with a wooden railing."

"Even in the Buddha's time the size of these monuments had already reached very considerable dimensions. The solid dome erected by the Sākiyas over their share of the ashes from the Buddha's funeral pyre must have been about the same height as the dome of the St. Paul's measured from the roof."[3]

From the books referring to the earlier Buddhist period stone seems to have been used only for pillars, walls and stair cases. A palace of stone is once mentioned in a fairy land[4]. According to Rhys Davids, "the superstructure at least, of all dwellings was either of wood-work or brick-work. In either case it was often covered, both internally and externally, with fine chunam plaster-works, and brilliantly painted in fresco, with figures or patterns, four of which have been preserved, namely, wreath-work, creeper-work, fine-ribbon-work and dragon's-tooth-work.[5] When the figures predominated the result is often called a picture-gallery (*chittāgāra*)."[6]

The articles of furniture, which form an important part of the architectural subjects, are also elaborately described in the Buddhist literature. Benches were made long enough to accommodate three persons[7]. The bedstead (*pallanka*) or

---

[1] *Vinaya* texts, 4. 308.

[2] Cf. *White Yajurveda*, chap. 35, and the writer's *Dictionary*.

[3] R. Davids, page 83-4. References to a large number of topes will be found in the writer's *Dictionary* under *stūpa*. Buddhaghosha's enumeration of the parts of a palace also shows the popularity of the subject of architecture in Buddhist literature. "Ayam phasso nāma yathā pāsādam patvā thambho nāma, sesadabhasambbhārānam balavapaccayo tulā saṁghāṭā bhitti pādakuṭa-gopānasipakkhapāsamukhavaṭṭiyo thambhe baddhā thambhe patiṭṭhitā evam eva sahajātasampa-yuttadhamānam balavapaccayo hoti." (*Atthasālini*, para 286, page 107, ed. Müller).

[4] *Jat*, 6.269.

[5] *Vinaya texts*, Translation, 2. 67 ; 4. 47.

[6] R. Davids, page 68.

[7] *Chullavagga*, VI. 18. 2, (Translation, page 308).

divan was a separate piece of furniture.[1] Large couches (*āsandi*) or chairs seem to have been important articles of furniture.[2] Couches covered with canopies are also mentioned.[3] Mention is made of a large variety of chairs, namely, rectangular chair (*āsandako*), arm chair, sofa (*sattaṅgo*), sofa with arms to it, state chair (*bhadda-pīṭham*), cushioned chair (*pīṭhikā*), chair raised on a pedestal *elaka-padaka-pīṭham*), chair with many legs (*āmalaka-vaṇṭika-pīṭham*), leaning board (*phalakam*), cane-bottomed chair (*kochchham*) and straw-bottomed chair. Mention is also made of the litter or sedan-chair.[5]

Valuable carpets, rugs, pillows, curtains, and such other luxurious decorations also are elaborately described. Thus mention is made of "coverlets with long fleece, counterpanes of many colours, woollen coverlets white or marked with thick flowers, mattresses, cotton coverlets dyed with figures of animals, rugs with long hair on one or both sides, carpets inwrought with gold or with silk, large woollen carpets such as the nautch (dancing) girls dance upon, rich elephant housings, horse rugs or carriage rugs, panther or antelope skins, large cushions and crimson cushions."[6] Pillows are of various kinds; they are stated to be of both "the size of a man's head" and half "the size of a man's body." The Buddha allows the Bhikkhus "to comb out the cotton, and make the cotton up into pillows if it be of any of these three kinds, cotton produced on trees, cotton produced on creepers, and cotton produced from *potaki*-grass." [7] The bolsters made for the use of high officials were of five kinds as they were stuffed with wool, cotton cloth, bark, grass or leaves. There were also coverlets for them.[8] The smaller articles like the floor cloth, mosquito curtain, handkerchief and spittoon did not escape the notice of the then house-decorators.[9]

---

[1] Chullavagga, VI. 14.1; VI. 8.1, etc., (Translation, page 209, 197); Mahāvagga, V. 10 3, (Translation, page 27).

[2] Ibid. VI. 14.1, VI. 8. 1, etc., (Translation, page 209, 197); Mahāvagga, V. 10.3, (Translation, page 27). Rhys Davids and Oldenberg render *āsandi* twice by cushions and once by couches, and Childers by 'chairs' (see his Dictionary). It seems to imply Sanskrit *āsana* which means 'a seat.'

[3] *Mahāvagga*, V. 10.3; (Translation, page 27).

[4] *Chullavagga*, VI. 2 4; (Translation, page 165). Renderings are mostly those made by Rhys Davids and Oldenberg depending on Buddhaghosha's note. Compare also *Chullavagga*, VI. 20.2 and VIII. 1.3. *Apassena-phalakam* as a "board to lean up against" is also mentioned in *Mahāvagga*, I. 25, 15, 16. For arm-chair and sofa there seems to be another expression '*apasayam*,' see Buddhaghosha's note on *Chullavagga*, VI. 2. 4.

[5] *Mahāvagga*, V. 10. 2, (Translation, page 27).

[6] *Mahāvagga*, V. 10. 3, (Translation, page 27).

[7] *Chullavagga*, VI. 2. 6, (Translation, page 167); see also IV. 4. 4. and VIII. 1. 3.

[8] Ibid. VI. 2. 7, (Translation, page 168).

[9] Ibid. VI. 20. 1, (Translation, page 219); V. 14. 1, (Translation, page 102); Mahāvagga, VIII. 18. (Translation, page 227), for *chelaka* or handkerchief see also *Chullavagga*, VI. 19 and V. 9. 4.

III.—CLASSICAL LITERATURE

THE EPICS.

The Epics furnish copious description of cities, storeyed buildings, balconies porticos, triumphal arches, enclosing walls, flights of stone masonry steps for tanks and a variety of other structures, all indicative of a flourishing architecture in the country.

The plan of the city of Ayodhyā is strikingly similar to the town-plan given in the *Mānasāra* and other architectural treatises.[1] "The temples (*devāyatana*) in this city (Ayodhyā) were as resplendent as the sky. Its assembly-halls, gardens, and alms-houses (*prapā*) were most elegant; and everywhere were arranged extensive buildings crowded with men and women............ The houses were as mines of gems, and the abodes of the goddess of fortune. The steeples (*śikhara*) of the houses were as resplendent as the crests of mountains and bore hundreds of pavilions (*vimāna*) like the celestial palace of the chief among the Devas. The rooms were full of riches and corn, exquisitely gilt and decorated, and seemed as charming as pictures; and they were so arranged that men could pass from one room to another without perceiving any inequality (in the floor)." [2]

The Mahābhārata contains short but comprehensive accounts of the cities of Dvārakā (III.15), Indraprastha (I. 207, 30f), a floating city (III. 173, 3), Mithilā (III. 207, 7), and others.

In the Sabhā-parvan there are interesting descriptions of some assembly-halls. Maya built an assembly-hall for the Pāṇḍavas (chapter I). A description is given also of the assembly-hall of Indra (chapter VII), of Yama (chapter VIII), of Varuṇa (chapter IX), of Kubera (chapter X), and of Brahman (chapter XI).

A large number of houses were needed for the accommodation of the kings invited to Indraprastha on the occasion of King Yudhishṭhira's royal feast, *Rājasūya*, and the poet describes the lodgings assigned to the guest: "O king, these and many other princes of the middle country (India proper) came to the great ceremonial, *Rājasūya*, of the sons of Pāṇḍu. By order of the virtuous monarch to

[1] See writer's Dictionary under *Nagara*.

[2] Rāmāyaṇa, I. 5, 10-15. Compare also the description of Laṅkā, Laṅkā-kāṇḍa (VI.), 3rd Sarga.

them were assigned dwellings replete with refreshments of every kind, and having by them charming lakes and ranges of ornamental plants..............Those houses were lofty as the peaks of the Kailāśa mountain, most charming in appearance, and provided with excellent furniture. They were surrounded on all sides by well-built high walls of a white colour. The windows were protected by golden lattices and decorated with a profusion of jewellery. The stairs were easy of ascent; the rooms were furnished with commodious seats, and clothing, and garlands; and the whole was redolent with the perfume of the finest agallochum. The houses were white as the goose, bright as the moon, and looked most picturesque even from a distance of four miles. They were free from obstructions, provided with doors of uniform height, but of various quality, and inlaid with numerous metal ornaments, even as the peak of the Himālaya. The princes were refreshed by the very sight of those mansions."[1]

"In the story of Nala, allusion is made to a lofty balcony from which men were seen from a great distance; and in the Rāmāyaṇa, Mantharā ...... looks out from an upper window of the palace to notice the rejoicings of the people in the street on the nomination of Rāma to the Vice-Kingship of Kośala."[2]

"In the city [described in the epics] special palaces existed for the King, the princes, the chief priests, ministers, and military officers. Besides these and humble dwellings (the larger houses being divided into various courts)[3], there were various assembly-halls, courts of justice, and the booths of small traders with goldsmith's shops, and the work-places of other artisans."[4]

"The words *toraṇa*, arched gateway; *harmya*, masonry house; *devāyataṇa*, temple; *sabhā*, assembly hall; *prāsāda*, palace; *śikhara*, steeple; and *vimāna*, pavilion, in the above extract [from the Rāmāyaṇa] are noteworthy. None of them can consistently be applied to huts and thatched houses for which the poets invariably use different words. Prurient fancy may extol and exaggerate, but it never suffices to create names of material objects which the fanciful have never seen or heard of; a Ruskin may amuse himself and his readers by building an imaginary palace in the air,[5] but his ideas are always of the earth, earthly, taken from material objects with which he is familiar."[6]

---

[1] Mahābhārata, B. II. C. 34, As. Soc. Edition, I, page 354.

[2] R. L. Mitra, *Indo-Aryan*, I, page 21.

[3] Compare the Mānasāra, under *Prākāra*, in the writer's Dictionary.
Cf. "These courts have mosaic pavements of gold" (R. VI. 37, 27, 68; Mbh. 1. 185. 20; 11-33 and 34)

[4] Hopkins, *J. A. O. S.*, 13, under *city*.

[5] The Queen of the Air, by John Ruskin, 1869.

[6] Mitra, ibid, pages 23-24.

The Purāṇas generally deal with the subject of architecture in more detail than the classes of literature referred to above. Casual references like those given above from the preceding classes of literature are frequently met with in all the nineteen great Purāṇas.[1] Some nine Purāṇas have, however, treated the subject more systematically, and have materially contributed to the later Śilpa-śāstras themselves. The *Matsay-Purāṇa*, for instance, has eight comprehensive chapters dealing in great detail with architecture and sculpture.[2] In one of these chapters accounts are given of eighteen ancient architects.[3] One chapter is devoted to the column which is the regulator of the whole composition of a building.[4] Columns are divided into five classes, as in the western system, and their component parts into eight mouldings exactly like those of the Græco-Roman orders.[5] Buildings are described in two chapters together with their architectural details, such as plans, measures, classifications, pavilions, halls, storeys, steeples, and cupolas.[6] Some of the building materials are also discussed in a separate chapter.[7] The remaining three chapters are devoted exclusively to sculpture.[8] One of these deals with a very technical subject, namely, the *tālamāna* or proportionate measures of an image[9]; and in the other two the images of the Phallus and its Pedestal are described.

The *Skanda*, which is another early Purāṇa, has devoted three chapters to the subject. One of these refers to the laying out of a large city.[10] In another, mention is made of the construction of a golden hall and three chariots in accordance with the descriptions supplied, and the names of the architects are

---

[1] वायु, स्कन्द (also called कुमार), मत्स्य, विष्णु, भागवत, पद्म, गरुड, अग्नि, ब्रह्म, शिव, नारद, मार्कण्डेय, वराह, वामन, लिङ्ग, कूर्म, ब्रह्माण्ड, ब्रह्मवैवर्त and भविष्य।

[2] Chapters 252, 255, 257, 258, 262, 263, 269 and 270.

[3] See pages 161-62.

[4] Chapter 255—स्तम्भमाननिर्णय।

[5] For details see pages 147, 149, 123.

[6] Chapters 269—(प्रासादलक्षण), and 270 (मण्डपलक्षण)

[7] Chapter, 257, दार्वाहरण।

[8] Chapters 258—(नवताल लक्षण), 262 (पीठिकालक्षण), 263 (लिङ्गलक्षण).

[9] For details see page 81.

[10] माहेश्वरखण्ड, Part II, chapter 25—स्वयं विश्वकर्मद्वारा निर्मापितमहीनगरस्थापनवर्णनम्।

added.[1] The details of the construction of a special pavilion for the wedding of a royal princess is described in another chapter wherein reference is made to the painting also.[2] Sculpture is associated with architecture; but painting is hardly mentioned in these works.

The *Garuda-purāṇa* makes some valuable additions to the contributions of this class of literature to architecture. One of the four chapters devoted to this subject deals systematically with all the three classes of buildings, namely, residential, military and religious, as well as with the laying out of pleasure-gardens and pavilions therein. Thus, in this chapter residential buildings, forts and fortified towns, temples and monasteries are described along with garden-houses.[3] The following chapter treats exclusively of religious buildings.[4] The remaining two chapters are dovoted to sculpture, one dealing with rules regarding the construction of an image and the other with the installation of images in temples.[5]

The *Agni*, among all the Purāṇas, has dilated on the subject at great length. There are sixteen chapters of which one deals with town-planning, two with residential buildings and the remaining thirteen with sculpture. The importance of its contributions to the Śilpa-śāstra lies, however, specially in two things. First, it seems to have been aware of the *Mānasāra*, the standard work on architecture.[6] Secondly, its chapter on town-planning is a real addition to the Purāṇas' contributions to architecture.[7] Temples and residential buildings are described in two chapters.[8] The treatment of sculpture also is unique, and is the most exhaustive of all the

---

[1] वैष्णवखण्ड, Part II, chapter 25—निखिलसाहित्यसम्भारसंग्रहपत्रं श्रुत्वा इन्द्रद्युम्नाज्ञया पद्मनिधिना स्वर्णशालानिर्माणम्। नारदाज्ञया विश्वकर्मणा स्यन्दनत्रयनिर्माणम्। तस्य रथस्य नारदकरेण स्थापनम्। तत्प्रसंगेन रथस्थापनप्रकारविधिवर्णनम्।

[2] माहेश्वरखण्ड, Part 1, chapter 24—हिमालयेन स्वसुताया विवाहार्थं गर्गाचार्यपुरोहितं पुरस्कृत्य विश्वकर्मद्वारा पूर्वमण्डपनिर्माणादिवर्णनम्। विवाहमण्डपे चातुर्येण सर्वदेवताप्रतिकृतिचित्रविन्यासं श्रुत्वा सर्वेषां देवानां शङ्काप्राप्तिः।

[3] Chapter 46—प्रासादारामदुर्गदेवालयमठादिवास्तुमानलक्षणनिरूपणम्।

[4] Chapter 47—प्रासादलिङ्गमण्डपादिशुभवास्तुलक्षणनिरूपणम्।

[5] Chapters 45—शालग्राममूर्तिलक्षणम्, 48—देवानां प्रतिष्ठाविधिः।

[6] Compare, तदूर्ध्वे च भवेद् वेदी सकण्ठा मानसारका। (Chapter 42, verse 16)

तृतीये वेदिका लग्ने सकण्ठो मानसारकः। (Chapter 104, verse 11).

For details see page 166.

[7] Chapter 106—नगरादिवास्तु।

[8] Chapters 42—प्रासादलक्षणकथनम्, and 104—प्रासादलक्षणम्।

For details see page 113.

accounts given in the Purāṇas. It deals with almost all the classes of religious images, both of male and female deities, as well as of those not falling under either of these categories. Thus, of the thirteen chapters on sculpture, one is devoted to the description of the sun-god,[1] one to the ten incarnations of Vishṇu,[2] two others also to Vishṇu under the name of Vāsudeva,[3] one to the guardian angel of the house,[4] one to the goddess of fortune,[5] two to the female deties in general,[6] four to the Phallus and its Pedestal,[7] and the remaining one to the stone gods, Śālagrāma and others.[8]

The *Nārada-purāṇa* practically completes the Purāṇas' contributions to architecture. In a single chapter it describes the construction of pools, wells and tanks as well as temples.[9] The *Liṅga-purāṇa* supplements the contributions by adding an account of the construction of sacrificial pits together with a description of temples and the installation of deities therein.[10]

The *Vāyu*, which is one of the very early Purāṇas, maintains its unique position by dealing with the construction of various temples built upon mountain tops.[11] Examples of these temples are still found on several peaks of the Himālaya and the Vindhya ranges. For the *Brahmāṇḍa-purāṇa* there was very little left to add. In a single chapter it describes the construction of temples and residential buildings.[12]

The *Bhavishya*, apparently a late Purāṇa, has also nothing new to contribute. Three of its chapters are devoted to sculpture.[13] Architecture proper, comprising the description of temples is treated in a single chapter.[14] The most striking

---

[1] Chapter 51—सूर्यादिप्रतिमालक्षणम् ।

[2] Chapter 49—मत्स्यादिदशावतारकथनम् ।

[3] Chapters 44—वासुदेवादिप्रतिमा, and 60—वासुदेवादिप्रतिष्ठाविधिः ।

[4] Chapter 43—प्रासाददेवतास्थापनम् ।

[5] Chapter 62—लक्ष्मीप्रतिमाविधिः ।

[6] Chapters 50—देवीप्रतिमालक्षणम्, and 52—देवीप्रतिमालक्षणम् ।

[7] Chapters 53—लिङ्गलक्षणम्, and 54—लिङ्गमानादिकथनम्, 45—पिण्डिकालक्षणम्, 55—पिण्डिकालक्षणकथनम् ।

[8] Chapter 46—शालग्रामादिमूर्तिलक्षणम् ।

[9] Part I, Chapter 13—देवतायनवापीकूपतडागादिनिर्माणम् ।

[10] Part II, Chapter 45—यागकुण्डविन्यासकथनपूर्वकं सर्वेषां देवानां स्थापनविधिनिरूपणम् ।

[11] Part I, Chapter 39—शैलस्थितविविधदेवालयकीर्तनम् ।

[12] Chapter 7—गृहादिनिर्माणम् ।

[13] The Madhya-parvan, Chapter 12—प्रतिदेवताप्रतिमालक्षणवर्णनम् ।
The Brahma-parvan, Chapters—
131—मूर्तिस्थानम्, 132—प्रतिमामानम् ।

[14] The Brahma-parvan, Chapter 130—प्रासादलक्षणवर्णनम् ।

feature of this Purāṇa is that the number, name and other architectural details of the buildings described in it are identical with the twenty types found in the *Matsya-purāṇa*, and the *Bṛihat-saṁhitā* of Varāhamihira[1].

The *Bṛihat-saṁhitā*, usually classed under the astronomical and astrological treatises, is but a semi-Purāṇa, dealing, as it does, with heterogeneous subjects like the Purāṇas themselves. Its authorship is attributed to Varāhamihira who is supposed to be one of the nine traditional gems in the court of a mythical Vikramāditya[2], and is thus imagined to be a contemporary of Kālidāsa a poet of unrivalled fame In this treatise there are but five chapters devoted to both architecture and sculpture. But the subjects have been treated with a master hand. The chapters open with a definition of the science of architecture, and the author goes on to describe, briefly but succinctly and to the point, the suitable building sites, testing of soil, general plan, comparative measures of storeys and doors, and carvings thereon, and other important parts of a building. The preliminary subjects are described in the opening chapter.[3] Then follows the description of the buildings proper under the same twenty types as in the *Matsya* and *Bhavishya Purāṇas*, the names and details being identical.[4] The preparation of cement is discussed in a separate chapter.[5] One whole chapter is dovoted to the construction of the necessary articles of house-furniture, such as bedsteads, couches, and seats. Quite consistently with his sense of proportion Varāhamihira devotes only one chapter to sculpture, where too the details of images are described in a scientific manner which is distinctly missing in other ancient literature.[7] He is however, accused of being "in the habit of uncritically copying his authorities" and misappropriating their materials. But in his treatise seven architectural authorities are mentioned distinctly.[8]

---

[1] For details see pages 114—118.

[2] For the names of the nine gems, see page 161, note 1.

[3] Chapter 53—वास्तुविद्या ।

[4] Chapter 56—प्रासादलक्षणम् ।

For iuller details, see pages 117, 115, 116.

[5] Chapter 57—वज्रलेपलक्षणम् ।

[6] Chapter 79—शय्यासनलक्षणम् ।

[7] Chapter 58—प्रतिमालक्षणम् ।

[8] गर्ग and मनु (LVI. 30-31), वसिष्ठ (LVIII. 3), भास्कर (LVIII 52), विश्वकर्मन् (LI. 30, नग्नजित् (LVIII, 4, 15) and मय (LI, 29, LVII, 3).

The Āgamas

The term *Āgama* generally implies a traditional doctrine or precept, a sacred writing or scripture and hence the Vedas. But there is a special class of works inculcating the mystical worship of Śiva and Śakti like the *Tantras*: they belong to South India and are known as the *Āgamas*.[1] They are encyclopaedic works like the *Purāṇas*, whose ultimate object is also to discuss the worship of the Triad The *Purāṇas*, however, deal with all the three deities forming the holy Trinity, although Vishṇu has received preference and to his worship fourteen of the Purāṇas are devoted. The *Āgamas*, on the other hand, deal mostly with Siva. Obviously they are intended to represent the *Purāṇas* of South India. These *Āgamas* of *Dākshiṇātya* are in fact more extensive than the *Purāṇas* of *Āryāvarta*. There are as many as twenty-eight recognized *Āgamas*,[2] while the number of the great *Purāṇas* is not more than eighteen or nineteen.[3]

The *Āgamas*, like the *Purāṇas*, incidentally deal with architectural subjects; their contributions to the *Śilpa-śāstra* are, however, more extensive and valuable. Some of the *Āgamas* deal with very technical matters. which are not met with in the *Purāṇas*. Moreover, some *Āgamas* to all intents and purposes are but architectural treatises. The *Kāmikāgama*, for instance, devotes sixty chapters out of a total of seventy-five to architecture and sculpture, and its treatment of the subjects can hardly be surpassed by that of an avowedly architectural treatise. Just like a *Śilpa-śāstra* it begins systematically with the preliminary matters, such as the testing and preparation of soil, selection of sites, scheme of measurement and the finding out of the cardinal points by means of gnomons for the orientation of buildings, and the ground plans. Buildings proper are described under twenty types, just as in the *Matsya* and *Bhavishya Purāṇas*, as well as the *Bṛihat saṁhitā*.

---

[1] Compare the traditional definition of the Āgama :

आगतं पञ्चवक्त्रात्तु गतं च गिरिजानने ।
मतं च वासुदेवस्य तस्मादागममुच्यते ॥

[2] (1) कामिकागम, (2) सुप्रभेदागम, (3) योगजआगम, (4) चिन्त्यागम, (5) कारणागम, (6) अजितागम, (7) दीप्तागम, (8) सूक्ष्मागम, (9) सहस्रागम, (10) अंशुमानागम, (11) विजयागम, (12) निश्वासागम, (13) स्वायंभुवागम, (14) अनिलागम, (15) वीरागम, (16) रौरवागम, (17) मकुटागम, (18) विमलागम, (19) चन्द्रज्ञानागम, (20) बिम्बागम, (21) प्रोद्गीतागम, (22) ललितागम, (23) सिद्धागम, also called वैखानसागम, (24) सन्तानागम, (25) सर्वोक्तागम, (26) परमेश्वरागम, (27) किरणागम, and (28) वातुलागम.

[3] See page 19, note 1.

But, unlike the *Purāṇas*, there is in the *Kāmikāgama* a discussion of architectural matters under some very highly technical classifications, such as the styles, Nāgara, Drāviḍa and Vesara; shapes, masculine, feminine, and neuter; Śuddha, Miśra, and Saṁkīrṇa, depending respectively on a single material, mixture of two materials, and the amalgamation of many materials; Saṁchita, Asaṁchita and Apasaṁchita otherwise known as Sthānaka, Āsana, and Śayana, which, in case of temples, depend on the erect, sitting, and reclining postures of the image[1]. Another very technical matter referred to is *āyādi* formulas so very important in selecting the right proportions.[2] For the close similarity of this *Āgama* with the *Śilpa-śāstras* it is, however, necessary to glance over the following *paṭalas* or chapters together with the corresponding chapters of the standard Śilpa-śāstra, the *Mānasāra*, which is referred to in more detail elsewhere in this volume[3]:

11. Bhū-parīkshā-vidhi—examination of soil (*Mānasāra*, chapter IV, bearing the same title).
12. Praveśa-bali-vidhi—offerings (M. VIII).
13. Bhū-parigraha-vidhi—selection of site (M. V).
14. Bhū-karshaṇa-vidhi—ploughing the site (M. V).
15. Śaṅku-sthāpana-vidhi—gnomons (M. VI).
16. Mānopakaraṇa-vidhi—system of measurement (M. II).
17. Pada-vinyāsa—ground-plan (M. VII).
18. Sūtra-nirmāṇa—making ropes (M. II)
19. Vāstu-deva-bali—offerings to the guardian angel of the house (M. VIII) cf. 12.
20. Grāmādi-lakshaṇa—laying out villages and towns (M. IX, X)
21. Vistārāyāma-lakshaṇa—dimensions (M XI).
22. Āyādi-lakshaṇa—a special kind of architectural and sculptural measurement used in selecting the right proportion (M. LXIV).
24. Daṇḍikā-vidhi—dealing with doors and gateways (M. XXXVIII XXXIX, XXXIII).
25. Vīthi-dvārādi-māna—roads and doors (M. IX, X, XXXIX).
26. Grāmādi-devatā-sthāpana—temples in villages and towns (M. IX, X).
28. Grāmādi-vinyāsa—more details on villages and towns (M. IX, X), cf. 20.
29. Brahma-deva-padādi—more details on ground-plan (M VII). cf. 17.
30. Grāmādi-aṅga-sthāna-nirmāṇa—more details on villages and towns (M. IX, X), cf. 20, 26, 28.

[1] For fuller information, consult the writer's Dictionary under these terms; and also see page 118

[2] For details see the writer's Dictionary under Shaḍvarga; and also see page 192, note 1.

[3] See pages 87 to 91.

31. Garbha-nyāsa—foundations (M. XII).
32. Bāla-sthāpana-vidhi— the installation of Bāla.
33. Grāma-griha-vinyāsa—the arrangement of houses in villages and towns (M IX, X), cf. 20, 26, 28, 30.
34. Vāstu-śānti-vidhi—not mentioned in M.
35. Śālā-lakshaṇa-vidhi—halls, etc. (M. XXXV).
36. Viśesha-lakshaṇa-vidhi—not mentioned in M.
37. Dvi-śālā-lakshaṇa-vidhi—houses with two compartments, in many places in M.
38. Chatuḥ-śālā-lakshaṇa-vidhi—houses with four compartments, not in one place in M.
40. Vardhamāna-śālā-lakshaṇa—more details on Śālās (M. XXXV), cf. 35, 37, 38.
41. Nandyāvarta-vidhi—more details on Śālās (M. XXXV), cf. 35, 37, 38, 40.
42. Svastika-vidhi—more details on Śālās (M. XXXV), cf. 35, 37, 38, 40, 41.
43 Paksha-śālā-vidhi—more details on side-halls or ante-chambers (M. XXXV), cf. 35, 37, 38, 40, 41, 42.
44. Asti(Hasti) śālā-vidhi—more details on Śālās (M. XXXV), cf. 35, 37, 38, 40, 41, 42, 43.
45. Mālikā-lakshaṇa-vidhi—a special kind of buildings (cf. M. XIX to XXX).
46. Lāṅgala-mālikā-vidhi—more details on Mālikā buildings, cf. 45.
47. Maulika-mālikā-vidhi—more details on Mālikā buildings, cf. 45, 46.
48. Padma-mālikā-vidhi—more details on Mālikā buildings, cf. 45, 46, 47.
49. Nāgarādi-vidhi—not separately treated in M.
50. Bhūmi-lamba-vidhi—dimensions of storeys (M. XI).
51. Ādyeshṭaka-vidhāna-vidhi—laying the foundation stone; in many places in M.
52. Upapīṭha-vidhi—pedestals (M. XIII).
53. Pāda-māna-vidhi—pillars (M. XV).
54. Prastara-vidhi—entablatures (M. XVI).
55. Prāsāda-bhūshaṇa-vidhi—the articles of house furniture (M. L).
56. Kaṇṭha-lakshaṇa-vidhi—the neck parts of buildings, in many places in M.
57 Śikhara-lakshaṇa-vidhi—the top parts of buildings, in many places in M.
58. Stūpika-lakshaṇa-vidhi—steeples or domes of buildings, in many places in M.
59. Nālādi-sthāpana-vidhi—construction of waterways and drains, in many places in M.
60. Eka-bhūmyādi-vidhi—buildings of one and more storeys (M. XIX-XXX)
61. Mūrdhni-sthāpana-vidhi—construction of tops of buildings, in many place in M.
62. Liṅga-lakshaṇa-vidhi—the Phallus (M. LII).

63. Aṅkurārpaṇa-vidhi—literally sowing the seed, not separately treated in M.

64. Liṅga-pratishṭhā-vidhi—installation of the Phallus (M. LII).

65. Pratimā-lakshaṇa-vidhi—images (M. LXIV, etc.).

67. Devatā-sthāpana-vidhi—installation of images of deities (M. LI, LIV, LV, LVI, LXIV, etc.).

68. Pratimā-pratishṭhā-vidhi—more details on images, cf. 65, 67.

69. Vimāna-sthāpana-vidhi—buildings (M. XVIII).

70. Maṇḍapa-sthāpana-vidhi—pavilions (M. XXXIV).

71. Prākāra-lakshaṇa-vidhi—courts and enclosures (M. XXXI).

72. Parivāra-sthāpana-vidhi—temples of attendant deities (M. XXXII).

74. Vṛishabha-sthāpana-vidhi—the bull, the riding animal of Śiva (M. LXII).

75. Gopura-sthāpana-vidhi—the construction of gate-houses (M. XXXIII).

The *Karaṇāgama* also devotes much space to architecture and sculpture. There are thirty-seven chapters in this *Āgama*, which deal with these subjects exhaustively. It makes a distinct addition to the *Āgamas*' contributions to the *Śilpa-śāstras*. It contributes two valuable chapters dealing with the details of the nine and ten tāla measures.[1] This is also a highly technical matter concerning sculpture and entirely missing in the *Purāṇas*. This *Āgama* also has close similarities with the *Mānasāra*, which will appear, however imperfectly, from the following list of chapters:

Part I, chapters (paṭalas)—

3. Vāstu-vinyāsa—classification of building-sites (*Mānasāra*, *Vāstu-prakaraṇa*, chapter III).

4. Ādyeshṭaka-vidhi—laying the foundation stone, mentioned in many places in M.

5. Adhishṭhāna-vidhi—bases (M. XIV)

6. Garbha-nyāsa-vidhi—foundations (M. XII).

7. Prāsāda-lakshaṇa-vidhi—buildings (cf. M. XVIII, XIX to XXX).

8. Prākāra-lakshaṇa-vidhi—courts (and enclosures) (*Mānasāra*, bearing same title, chapter XXXI).

9. Liṅga-lakshaṇa-vidhi—the Phallus (M. LII).

10. Mūrdhaleshṭaka-lakshaṇa—ornaments at the topmost parts of buildings.

11. Pratimā-lakshaṇa—images (M. LXIV, LI, LIV to LXII).

12. Strī-māna-daśa-tāla-lakshaṇa—intermediate type of daśa (ten) tāla measurement, used for the images of females (M. LXVI).

---

[1] For details consult the writer's Dictionary under Tālamāna, and see pages 51-53, 84-85.

13. Kapishṭha-daśa-tāla-lakshaṇa —the smallest type of *daśa* (ten) *tāla* measurement (M. LIX).
14. Nava-tālottama-lakshaṇa—the largest type of *nava* (nine) *tāla* measurement (M. LIX).
16. Bali-karma-vidhi—offerings (M. VIII).
19. Mṛit-saṁgrahaṇa-vidhi—collection and preparation of earth (for images).
20. Aṅkurārpaṇa-vidhi—literally sowing the seed
21. Mahābhisheka-vidhi—great coronation or anointing (cf. M. XLIX).
56. Vāstu-homa vidhi—sacrificial offerings in connection with the construction of a house, cf. 16.
59. Liṅga-sthāpana-vidhi—installation of the Phallus (M. LII), cf. 9.
60. Parivāra-sthāpana-vidhi—the temples of the attendant deities (M, XXXII).
61. Bali-pīṭha-pratishṭhā-vidhi—seat of sacrifice.
62. Ratna-liṅga-sthāpana-vidhi—more details on the Phallus, cf. 9, 59.
66. Parivāra-bali—more details on the attendant deities, cf. 60.
88. Bhakta-sthāpana-vidhi—on the images of devotees (M. LIX).
136. Mrit-saṁgrahaṇa—more details on the collection and preparation of soil, cf. 19.

Part II, chapters (paṭalas)—

4. Kīla-parīkshā—the nail at the top.
5. Gopura-vidhāna—gate-houses (M. XXXIII).
6. Maṇḍapa-lakshaṇa—pavilions (M. XXXIV).
7. Pīṭha-lakshaṇa—pedestals (M. XIII, LIII).
8. Śakti-lakshaṇa—female deities (M. LIV).
9. Grāma-śānti-vidhi—villages (M. IX, X).
11. Mṛit-saṁgrahaṇa—more details on soil, cf. part I, 19, 136.
12. Aṅkurārpaṇa—more details on sowing the seed, cf. Part I, 20.
13. Bimba-śuddhi—purification of idols.
14. Kautuka-bandhana—experimental yoking for the purpose of ploughing the building-site (M. V).
15. Nayanonmīlana—chiselling the eyes (M. LXX).
18. Bimba-śuddhi—purification of idols (cf. II, 13).
19. Śayanāropaṇa—bedsteads (M. XLIV).
20. Śiva-liṅga-sthāpana—more details on the Phallus, cf. I, 9, 59.
98. Maṭha-pratishṭhā—monasteries.

The *Suprabhedāgama* has devoted only fifteen chapters to architecture and sculpture. Nor has it any thing new to add to the *Āgamas'* contributions to the *Śilpa-śāstras*. But its unique nature consists in the fact that it has quite successfully summarised all important matters in a comparatively small space,[1] and in respect of brevity, explicitness and precision it surpasses even the *Bṛihat-saṁhitā* of Varāhamihira.[2] This *Āgama* has apparently drawn upon a *Śilpa-śāstra*. Its similarities with the *Mānasāra*, discussed elsewhere in detail[3], may be partly apparent from the following list of its chapters read together with the corresponding portions of the standard *Śilpa-śāstra* :

22. Karaṇādhikāra-lakshaṇa—on the constructive arts, dealing with *ushnīsha* (head gear), *āsana* (seat, chair), *paryaṅka* (bedstead, couch), *siṁhā-sana* (throne), *raṅga* (courtyard, theatre), and *stambha* (column), (*Mānasāra*, XLIX, XLIV, XLV, XLVII, XV, etc.).
23. Grāmādi-lakshaṇa-vidhi—villages and towns (M. IX, X).
26. Taruṇālaya-vidhi—a special kind of building.
27. Prāsāda-vāstu-vidhi—buildings in general (M. XVIII, XIX to XXX).
28. Ādyeshṭaka-vidhi—laying the foundation-stone, mentioned in many places in M.
29. Garbha-nyāsa-vidhi—foundations (M. XII).
30. Aṅguli-lakshaṇa-vidhi—the *aṅgula* (finger-breadth) measurement (cf. M. II, LV).
31. Prāsāda-lakshaṇa-vidhi—more details on buildings, cf. 27.
32. Mūrdhnīshṭaka-vidhi—an ornament on the top-most part of buildings.
33. Liṅga-lakshaṇa—the phallus (M. LII).
34. Sakala-lakshaṇa-vidhi—images of Īśvara and other deities (M. LI to LXIV)
35. Aṅkurārpaṇa-vidhi—sowing the seed.
36. Liṅga-pratishṭhā-vidhi—installation of the phallus (M. LII); cf. 33.
37. Sakala-pratishṭhā-vidhi—installation of the images of Īśvara and other deities, cf. 34.
38. Śakti-pratishṭhā-vidhi—installation of the images of the female deities (M. LIV).
39. Parivāra-vidhi—temples of attendant deities (M. XXXII)
40. Vṛishabha-sthāpana-vidhi—the image of the Bull of Śiva (M. LXII).

The *Vaikhānasāgama* has two chapters on sculpture, one of which deals with the general description of images and the other with the ten-*tāla* measures.[4] The *Aṁśumad-bhedāgama*[5] has a single chapter on the ten-*tāla* measures.[6] Instances like those given above can be culled from the remaining *Āgamas* also; but the multiplication of illustrations is not likely to furnish any new information. It is, however, clear that architecture was a favourite subject for the authors of the *Āgamas* also.

---

[1] See pages 118, 119 [2] See pages 117, 118, 119. [3] See pages 110 -113, 117—119.

[4] पटल (Chapter) 22—प्रतिमालक्षण, 43—उत्तमदशताल।

[5] There is an architectural treatise bearing the title अंशुमद्भेद the authorship of which is attributed to Kāśyapa. Consult the writer's Dictionary, Appendix; and see pages 94 to 97.

[6] पटल (Chapter) 28—उत्तमदशतालविधिः।

Miscellaneous Treatises

The works on royal polity deal with architectural matters in a more than casual way. The Kauṭilīya *Artha-śāstra*, for instance, devotes some seven chapters to the subject, containing a large number of structural details. There are interesting descriptions of forts, fortified cities, town-planning, and military and residential buildings.[1]

The *Śukra-nīti* deals with both architectural and sculptural objects. Rules and structural details are given along with interesting descriptions of forts and fortified towns, of temples and other kinds of buildings, and of various sorts of images.[2] In this treatise sculptural details are more numerous in some respects

---

[1] Chapters 22—जनपद निवेश ।

23—भूमिच्छिद्रविधान ।

24—दुर्गविधान ।

25—दुर्गनिवेश । The last two deal with the laying out of fortified towns and forts.

65—वास्तुक, गृहवास्तुक (residential and military buildings).

66—वास्तुविक्रय, सीमाविवाद, मर्यादास्थापन etc. For full details see the writer's Dictionary under Durga, Nagara, and Grāma.

[2] Chapter IV, Section 4:—

(1) देवमन्दिरनिर्माणव्यवस्था—the construction of temples and other kinds of buildings. For details of royal palaces see the concluding portion of chapter I.

(2) प्रतिमानिर्माणव्यवस्था—images.

(3) मूर्तीनां वाहननिर्माणव्यवस्था—the images of the riding animals of deities.

(4) गणपतिमूर्तिनिर्माणव्यवस्था—the image of Gaṇapati

(5) शक्तिमूर्तिनिर्माणव्यवस्था—images of the female deities.

(6) बालमूर्तिनिर्माणव्यवस्था—images of Bāla (Child Krishṇa).

(7) सप्ततालादिमूर्तिभेदस्य निर्माणव्यवस्था—the images measured in the seven (*sapta*) and other *tāla* measurements.

(8) पैशाचीमूर्तिनिर्माणव्यवस्था—the images of the demonesses.

(9) भग्नप्रतिमास्थापनव्यवस्था—the repair of the damaged images.

(10) उत्सवव्यापारव्यवस्था—Festival in connection with installation of images.

Section 6—

(1) दुर्गनिर्माण—the construction of forts (and fortified towns)

For full details see the writer's Dictionary under *tālamāna*.

than even in the *Śilpa-śāstras*. Repair of broken images, for instance, is an important matter in sculpture, which has been dealt with in detail in this treatise. Another important contribution made by the *Śukra-nīti* to the *Śilpa-śāstras* is the description of the seven-*tāla* measures which are generally applicable, both in India and the West, to well proportioned human figures only.

Avowedly historical works are not numerous in Sanskṛit. Of the two treatises, one is concerned with the reign of a single king and the other with the events of a country covering many reigns. In both these treatises architecture has been given its already well-recognized place.

The *Harsha-charita* is a history of Harshavardhana of Kanauj, during whose reign the famous Chinese traveller Hieun Tsang visited India. In this history it is stated that "the palace had besides the harem always more than three court-yards; the outer one being for people and for state reception, the next inner one for sardars (chiefs or nobles) and the third one for intimate persons only. The palaces were stately buildings, though not of stone. The floors, however, are described as made of shining stones. The columns and walls were ornamented with gold and even precious stones. There was usually a several storeyed building with inner gardens of flower-beds and large fruit trees."[1] Mention is made also of detached buildings like the *Maṇḍapas* or pavilions for the purposes of *sabhā* (council hall), *satra* (inn), *prapā* (drinking-house), and *prāg-vaṁśa*.[2] The useful articles of house furniture, such as thrones (*siṁhāsana*), couches (*śayana*), and *āsandī*, meaning chairs, are also described.[3]

The *Rāja-taraṅgiṇī* of Kalhaṇa, dealing with the history of Kashmir, refers frequently to architectural objects like castles (*Bāṇa-śālā*)[4], monumental buildings (*Chaitya*),[5] and monasteries (*Vihāras*).[6] But in these references very few structural details are to be met with. The references of Kalhaṇa to temples and other buildings also generally lack constructive details.[7] But interesting structural details of some shrines merely referred to in Kalhaṇa's work are elaborated by

---

[1] History of Mediæval India, Vaidya, page 152. See Harsha-charita, pages 215-216, description of the palace of Prabhākara Vardhana of Thāneśvara.

[2] Harsha-charita, page 176:

बहिरुपरचितविकटसभासत्रप्रपाग्वंशमण्डपैः प्रसूतानवेश्मभिः ।

See also ibid, page 187.

[3] H. C. page 108, ibid, 153.

[4] VIII, 1666.

[5] I, 103, 170; III, 380, 381; IV, 200, 204.

[6] I, 93, 94, 98, 103, 140—144, 146, 147, 169, 199, 200; III, 9, 11, 13, 14, 355, 380, 464, 476; IV, 79, 184, 188, 200, 210, 215, 216, 262, 507; VI, 171, 175, 303; VII, 696, 1236; VIII, 246, 248, 2402, 2410, 2417, 2431, 2433, 3343, 3352, 3353.

[7] Compare, e.g., the Śāradā temple (I. 37), Śāradā-sthāna (VIII, 2556, 2706), etc.

Major C. B. Bates in the Gazetteer of Kashmir[1] and have been given in a note by Sir M. A. Stein.[2]

The astrological and astronomical treatises frequently refer to architectural topics, especially those bearing upon auspicious times. In a pamphlet of this class twenty-one things are stated to be observed in connection with building a house.[3] A famous astronomical treatise, the Gárga-saṁhitá, deals with a large number of purely architectural subjects, such as the courts, compounds, compartments, rooms, dimensions, and location of doors.[4]

---

[1] page 339.

[2] "The temple is approached from the lower slope of the hill . . . by an imposing stone staircase . . . which leads up in sixty-three steps to the main entrance of the quadrangular court enclosing the temple. It is about 10 feet wide and rises rather steeply between two flanking walls of massive construction, broken in six steps or flights. The entrance to the court is through a gateway, provided with the usual double porch of Káśmírian architecture."

"The temple, which occupies the centre of the quadrangle, forms a square cella conforming in plan and elevation to the usual features of Káśmír architecture. It is raised on a basement 24 feet square and 5′ 8″ high. The walls of the cella proper recede about 2 feet from the edge of the basement. They are adorned on the north, east and south by trefoil arches and supporting pilasters both projecting in relievo. Below these arches are small trefoil-headed niches covered by double pediments."

"The entrance to the interior of the cella is . . . approached by stairs 5½ feet wide with flanking side walls. There is an open portico in front of the door projecting about 4 feet beyond the pilasters on each side of the doorway. It is supported on the outside by two pillars. . . . The interior of the cella forms a square of 12 feet 3 inches, and has no decoration of any kind."

(Kalhaṇa's Rájataraṅgiṇí, vol. II, notes, page 289 fol.)

[3] आयराशिश्च नक्षत्रं व्ययस्तारांशकस्तथा ।
ग्रहमैत्री राशिमैत्री नातिभेदगणान्वयाः ॥
आधिपत्यं वारलग्ने तिथ्युत्पत्तिस्तथैव च ।
आधिपत्यं वर्णवैरं तथैव योनिवैरकम् ॥
अक्षवैरं स्थिति गांशो लक्षणान्येकविंशतिः ।
कथितानि मुनिश्रेष्ठैः शिल्पविधिर्गृहादिषु ॥

(Laghu-Śilpa-jyotiḥ-sára, verses 3-5).

[4] The manuscript in the Trinity College, Cambridge, is in a mutilated condition. The contents of the first and second chapters, fol. 67—68, are almost illegible. The following are a little better—

(i) वास्तुविद्यायां चतुर्भागभिमागप्रतिमाणविधिः (fol. 60 a).

(ii) मार्गियायां वास्तुविद्यायां चतुःशालाद्विभिशालैकशालाविधिः (fol. 60 a).

(iii) द्वारनिर्देशः (chap. 8, fols. 57 a and 68 b).

द्वारप्रमाणविधिः (fol. 57 b).

द्वारस्तम्भोच्छ्रायः (fol. 60 b).

(iv) गृहप्रवेशः (fol. 68 b).

The more authoritative works like the *Sūrya-siddhānta*,[1] the *Siddhānta-śiromaṇi*[2], and the *Līlāvatī*[3] deal exhaustively with a very technical matter bearing upon architecture, namely, the description of gnomons which were used for finding out cardinal points. The subject is architecturally very important, inasmuch as it refers to the orientation of buildings.[4]

The poetical works of Kālidāsa, Bhavabhūti and others refer occasionally to architectural matters. In the *Vikramorvaśī*, for instance, mention is made of a flight of stairs made like the waves of the Ganges.[5] The *Uttara-Rāma-Charita* refers to an architecturally important matter, namely, cement which is specially described in some *Śilpa-śāstras*.[6] In the same work Nala, the son of the heavenly architect Viśvakarman, is mentioned as an engineer who built the bridge joining India with Ceylon.[7]

Of this class of works, the *Mṛichchhakaṭika* which is a modernized drama, dealing as it does with the ordinary affairs of worldly people, refers very frequently to architectural matters which are too numerous to be included here.[8] A very interesting description of the gateway and as many as eight courtyards into which the whole compound is divided, is given in the fourth Act. This description is further

---

[1] Chapter III, verses 1—4.

[2] Chapter VII, verses 36—40.

[3] Part II, chapter II, section VII.

[4] Compare the writer's Dictionary under *Śaṅku*, and for full details see page 37.

[5] गङ्गातरङ्गस्फटिकमणिसोपान, see also मणिहर्म्य (Kale's ed. 1898, Act. III. page 73).

[6] वज्रलेप, Act III, preceding verse 40.

[7] Act III, verse 45. Compare the *Rāmāyaṇa*, युद्धकाण्ड, chapter 22, verses 41—43. In the *Mānasāra* also Nala is mentioned as an architect, see *Mānasāra*, chapter II.

[8] Act I. गृहदेहली, threshold (verse 17); पक्षद्वारक, side entrance (88; also II. 88; IV. 19?, VI, 209, 211, etc.); चतुःशाला, courtyard (89); प्रासादबालाग्रकपोतपालिका, dovecot on the top palace (52; VIII, 282, 283; IX. 347, 349, 350, 351).

Act II. श्रेष्ठिचत्वर, merchant quarters (88, 180); बहिर्द्वारशाला, outer hall (101, 117) अभ्यन्तरचतुःशाला, inner court (107, 108, 109, VI. 204).

पक्वेष्टक, आमेष्टक, baked and unbaked brick (111).

Act V. प्राकार, fence (177); आरामप्रासादवेदिका, roof of the garden-house (177)

Act VI. प्रतोलीद्वार, main gate (216).

Act IX. व्यवहारमण्डप court of justice (289, 291),

अधिकरणमण्डप, court of justice (289, 302, 305, 307, 320, etc.),

दुर्वाचत्वर, grass lawn (291).

full of architectural details. This reference is specially important owing to the fact that in the *Mānasāra* as well as the *Purāṇas* and the *Āgamas* the compound, however big it may be, is divided into not more than five courts, the fourth of which is technically called *prākāra* in the *Mānasāra*.[1]

Traces of an advanced state of architecture are found also in works like grammars and lexicons. Yāska in his *Nirukta* mentions several words which can be used for masonry houses only.[2] In the later lexicons like the *Amarakosha* lists of several architectural terms are met with.[3] Derivations of words like *bhāskara*, sculptor; *ishṭaka*, brick; *stambha*, pillar; *aṭṭālikā*, edifices are found in Pāṇini's grammar. They no doubt imply the existence of brick and stone buildings in those times.[4]

---

[1] See page 51.

[2] R. L. Mitra, *Indo Aryan*, I, 25–26.

[3] Amarakosha, Section on towns and houses (Chapter II, section ii named *pura-varga*, verses 1–20; pages 116–126, ed. Śivadatta, Bombay, 1915).

[4] Mitra, ibid, I, 19.

II

SILPA-ŚĀSTRAS

A SUMMARY OF THE MĀNASĀRA[1]

CHAPTER I

The table of contents (*Saṁgraha*)

The first verse is an invocation to Brahmā, the Creator of the Universe. In the second verse it is stated that the science of architecture (Vāstu-śāstra) had come down from Śiva, Brahmā and Vishṇu, through Indra, Bṛihaspati, Nārada and all other sages, to the seer (ṛishi) Mānasāra who systematised it.

After this genesis titles of the chapters are given in order. The colophon of the last chapter (named *Nayanonmīlana* in all the complete manuscripts gives the number of the chapter as seventy-one. The manuscript called I, the *codex archetypus* of my text, has made up the number seventy-one by repeating the chapter *Strīmāna-madhyama-daśatāla*; in one place it is numbered 66 and in the second 67. The only explanation of this number 71 for the last chapter is to suppose that the copyists of all complete and independent manuscripts were equally careless in numbering the chapters. This supposition is corroborated by the fact that the contents of the work do not show that any chapter is missing.

The last verse of the first chapter states the reason why the book is named *Mānasāra*, and explains the importance and authority of the work. It is called *Mānasāra* after a sage of that name. And as an authoritative work on art and complete in all respects, it has been accepted by the best among the leading artists.

CHAPTER II

The system of measurement (*Mānopakaraṇa-vidhāna*)

The first part of this chapter gives a mythical genealogy of the artists. From the four faces of Brahmā, the Creator of the Universe, originated in order the

[1] This summary has developed out of a Dissertation, which was accepted by the University of Leiden for the Ph D. degree.

heavenly architect Viśvakarman, Maya, Tvashṭar and Manu. Their four sons are called respectively Sthapati, Sūtragrāhin, Vardhaki and Takshaka. These four evidently represent the progenitors of the four classes of terrestrial artists.

The *sthapati* is highest in rank; he is the master-builder. The *sūtragrāhin* is the *guru* of *vardhaki* and *takshaka*; while the *vardhaki* is the instructor of the *takshaka*.

The *sthapati* must be well-versed in all sciences (*śāstras*). He must know the Vedas. He must have the qualifications of a supreme director (*āchārya*).

The *sūtragrāhin* also should know the Vedas and the Śāstras. He must be an expert draftsman (*rekhājña*).

The *vardhaki* too should have a general knowledge of the Vedas. But the object of his special study is painting (*chitra-karman*).

The *takshaka* must be an expert in his own work, i.e., carpentry.

The second part of this chapter deals with the system of measurement:

The *paramāṇu* or atom is the smallest unit of measurement.

8 *paramāṇus*	=	1 *rathadhūli* (*lit.* car-dust).
8 *rathadhūlis*	=	1 *bālāgra* (*lit.* hair's end).
8 *bālāgras*	=	1 *likshā* (*lit.* a nit).
8 *likshās*	=	1 *yūkā* (*lit.* a louse).
8 *yūkās*	=	1 *yava* (*lit.* a barley corn).
8 *yavas*	=	1 *aṅgula* (*lit.* finger's breadth).

Three kinds of *aṅgulas* are distinguished, the largest of which is made of 8 *yavas*, the intermediate one of 7 *yavas*, and the smallest one of 6 *yavas*.

12 *aṅgulas*	=	1 *vitasti* (span).
2 *vitastis* or 24 *aṅgulas*	=	1 *kishku-hasta* (small cubit).
25 *aṅgulas*	=	1 *prājāpatya-hasta*.
26 ,,	=	1 *dhanurmushṭi-hasta*.
27 ,,	=	1 *dhanurgraha-hasta*.
4 *hastas*	=	1 *dhanus* (bow) or *daṇḍa* (rod).
8 *daṇḍas*	=	1 *rajju* (string).

Directions are given with regard to the use of the four different kinds of cubits (*hasta*) enumerated above. Conveyances (*yāna*) and couches (*śayana*) are said to measured in the cubit of 24 *aṅgulas*, *vimāna* in the cubit of 25 *aṅgulas*, buildings (*vāstu*) in general in the cubit of 26 *aṅgulas*, and villages, etc., in the cubit of 27 *aṅgulas*. The cubit of 24 *aṅgulas* may, however, also be used in measuring all these objects.

In the concluding portion of this chapter directions are given for the preparation of the yard-stick (*hasta*), the rod (*daṇḍa*), and the measuring string (*rajju*). The former two objects should be made of the wood of certain trees, which are enumerated. In the same manner certain fibres are to be used as materials for the rope. The presiding deity of the yard-stick and the rod is Vishṇu, and that of the measuring rope Vāsuki, the king of serpents.

CHAPTERS III, IV, V.

The classification of vāstu (*Vāstu-prakaraṇa*)

Examination of soil (*Bhū-parīkshā*) and Selection of site (*Bhūmi-saṁgraha*)

The first part of the third chapter defines *vāstu* (dwelling or habitation) and divides it into four classes. The place where men and gods reside is called *vāstu*. This includes the ground (*dharā*), the building (*harmya*), the conveyance (*yāna*), and the couch (*paryaṅka*). Of these, the ground is the principal one, for nothing can be built without the ground as a support. The building (*harmya*) includes *prāsāda*, *maṇḍapa*, *sabhā*, *śālā*, *prapā* and (*a*)*raṅga*. The conveyance (*yāna*) includes *ādika*, *syandana*, *śibikā* and *ratha*. The couch (*paryaṅka*) includes *pañjara*, *mañchali*, *mañcha*, *kākāshṭa*, *phalakāsana* and *bāla-paryaṅka*.

The second part of the third chapter as well as the fourth and fifth chapters deal with the same subject, namely the site, on which a village, town, fort, palace, temple, or house, is to be built. The soil is examined with regard to its contour, colour, odour, features (*rūpa*), taste and touch. The level of the ground as well as the characteristic vegetation of the site are also minutely examined.

If a plot of land is found to be satisfactory on all or most of these points, it should be selected for a village, town, fort or house, as the case may be. But even after this selection it would be wise to test the ground in some other ways. A square hole of one cubit deep should be dug on the selected site and be filled with water. After twenty-four hours the chief architect should mark the condition of the water in the hole. If all the water be dried up by this time, the earth must be very bad. But if, on the other hand, there remains some water in the hole, the selected plot of land would be fit for any building purposes.

Another final test is this: a similar hole is dug on the plot and filled up with the earth taken out of it. If this earth fills up the hole exactly, the land is fair; if this earth be not quite enough to fill up the hole the ground must be very bad, but if this earth overfills the hole, the soil must be very good for any building purposes. The import of both tests seems to be that in the former case porous soil is avoided, while in the latter case loose soil is said to be unfit for the construction of a building

After this final selection the ground should be ploughed over. The concluding part of the fifth chapter gives a minute description of the oxen and the plough to be used in ploughing the selected site.

CHAPTER VI

The gnomon (*Śaṅku-sthāpana-vidhāna*)

The object of this chapter is to lay down rules on the principles of dialling and for ascertaining the cardinal points by means of a gnomon.

The gnomon is made of the wood of certain trees. It may be 24, 18, or 12 *aṅgulas* in length, and the width at the base should be respectively 6, 5, and 4 *aṅgulas*. It tapers from the bottom towards the top.

For the purpose of ascertaining the cardinal points, a gnomon of 12, 18, or 24 *aṅgulas* is erected from the centre of a watered place (*salila-sthala*) and a circle is described with the bottom of the gnomon as its centre and with a radius twice its length. Two points are marked where the shadow (of the gnomon) after and before noon meets the circumference of the circle. The line joining these two points is the east-west line. From each of these east and west points a circle is drawn with their distance as radius. The two intersecting points, which are called the head and tail of the fish (*timi*), are the north and the south points. The intermediate regions are found in the same way through the fish formed between the points of the determined quarters.

As regards the principles of dialling, each of the twelve months is divided into three parts of ten days each and the increase and decrease of shadow (*avachchhāyā*) [1] are calculated for these several parts of the different months.

Why the subject of the present chapter is important for architecture is evident from the rules regarding the orientation of buildings. Here it is said that a building should preferably face the east or the north-east, but that it should never be made to face the south-east, as this is considered inauspicious.

The chapter closes with a passing reference to the *khāta-śaṅku* which appears to denote wooden stakes posted in different parts of the foundations made for constructing buildings thereon.

CHAPTER VII

The ground-plan (*Pada-vinyāsa*)

When a site is selected for constructing a village, town or building thereon the ground is divided into different numbers of squares. Thirty-two kinds

[1] Cf. Vitruvius, Book IX, Chap. VIII, "....the principles of dialling and the increase and decrease of the *days* in the different months" (translated by Gwilt).

of such schemes are distinguished by as many different names according to the number of squares into which the whole area is partitioned out. The whole scheme has been arranged in such a manner that in each case the number of partitions represents the square of the serial number. The eighth plot, for instance, which is called Chaṇḍita, comprises a division into sixty-four squares, while by the ninth plot, which bears the technical name of Paramaśādhika, the ground is divided into eighty-one squares.

Each of these squares is assigned to its presiding deity. Some deities, however, are lords of more than one square. The lord of the central square is always Brahmā. Charagī, Vidārikā, Pūtanā and Rākshasī are the presiding deities of the four corners. A detailed description of all the squares of the eighth and the ninth plans is given in the text. Then the forty-four deities, who are enumerated in connection with the Paramaśādhika scheme, are described in the form of as many *dhyānas*. This portion is of some iconographical interest.

Finally, the presiding deity of the site (*vāstu-purusha*), who is described as humpbacked and of crooked-shape, is said to occupy the habitated area (*vāstu*) in such a manner that his limbs cover the several squares or groups of squares which, as set forth in the former part of the chapter, are assigned to and named after various deities. As he is supposed to lie down with his face turned downward, his head being in the central square on the east side (assigned to Sūrya), his right and left hands must be in the partitions of Agni (S. E.) and Iśāna (N. E) respectively, and his right and left feet in those of Nairṛit (S. W.) and Vāyu (N. W.) respectively. The middle part of his body occupies the central portion of the plot, which, as we saw, is assigned to Brahmā.

CHAPTER VIII

The offerings (*Balikarma-vidhāna*)

Different kinds of offerings (*bali*) are prescribed for the various deities enumerated in the preceding chapter, who are supposed to preside over the different partitions of the Paramaśādhika or Maṇḍūka ground-plan. These offerings consist of milk in its various forms, butter, rice and sesame, parched grain (*lāja*), honey and sweetmeat (*modaka*, offered to Sugrīva), incense and lamps, flowers and fruit. Blood is offered to Asura, dried meat to Mṛiga, dried fish to Roga (Disease), and sea-fish to Bhṛiṅgarāja. The four demonesses, namely, Rākshasī, Pūtanā, Vidārī and Charagī, also receive their share, the first-mentioned evil spirit in the shape of meat of goats mixed with blood.

In the bringing of these offerings the master-builder (*sthapati*) takes a leading part.

CHAPTER IX

The village (*Grāmalakshaṇa-vidhāna*)

According to the *Mānasāra*, there is not much difference between a village, a town, and a fort. All are fortified places intended for the residence of people. A town is the extension of a village. A fort is in many cases nothing more than a fortified town, with this difference that a fort is principally meant for purposes of defence, while a village or a town is mainly intended for habitation.

A detailed description of the plan of villages, towns, and forts, and the arrangement of the various buildings which they contain is given in the text.

Villages are divided according to their shapes into eight classes, called *daṇḍaka*, *sarvato-bhadra*, *nandyāvarta*, *padmaka*, *svastika*, *prastara*, *kārmuka* and *chatur-mukha*.

Each village is surrounded by a wall made of brick or stone; beyond this wall there is a ditch broad and deep enough to cause serious obstruction in the event of an attack on the village. There are generally four main gates at the middle of the four sides, and as many at the four corners. Inside the wall there is a large street running all round the village. Besides, there are two other large streets, each of which connects two opposite main gates. They intersect each other at the centre of the village, where a temple or a hall is generally built for the meeting of the villagers. The village is thus divided into four main blocks, each of which is again subdivided into many blocks by streets which are always straight and run from one end to the other of a main block. The two main streets crossing at the centre have houses and foot-paths on one side of the street. The ground-floor of these houses on the main streets consists of shops. The street, which runs round the village, has also houses and foot-paths only on one side. These houses are mainly public buildings, such as schools, libraries, guest-houses, etc. All other streets generally have residential buildings on both sides. The houses high or low are always uniform in make. Drains (*jala-dvāra*, lit. water-passage) follow the slope of the ground. Tanks and ponds are dug in all the inhabited parts, and located where they can conveniently be reached by a large number of inhabitants. The temples of public worship, as well as the public commons, gardens and parks are similarly located. People of the same caste or profession are generally housed in the same quarter.

The partition of the quarters among the various sects cannot be said to be quite impartial. The best quarters are generally reserved for the Brahmins and the architects. Such partiality to the artists is not met elsewhere in Sanskrit literature. The quarters of the Buddhists and the Jains are described in a few lines. The habitations of the Chaṇḍālas, as well as the places for cremation are located outside the village-wall, in the north-west in particular. The temples of fearful deities, such as Chāmuṇḍā, are also placed outside the wall.

CHAPTER X

Towns [and Forts] (*Nagara-vidhāna*)

As stated above, a town is a large village. According to the *Mānasāra*, it appears that the dimensions of the smallest town-unit are 100×200 *daṇḍas*; the largest town-unit is 7,200×14,400 *daṇḍas*. A town may be situated from east to west or from north to south according to the position it occupies. There should be one to twelve large streets in a town. It should be built near a river or a mountain and should have facilities for trade and commerce with the foreigner (*dvīpāntara-vartin*). Like a village, it should have walls, ditches and gates drains, parks, commons, shops, exchanges, temples, guest-houses, colleges. etc. For purposes of military defence, the towns are generally well fortified.

Towns are divided into eight classes : *rājadhānī*, *nagara*, *pura*, *nagarī*, *kheṭa*, *kharvaṭa*, *kubjaka*, and *pattana*. The distinction between them is slight, the general description given above being applicable to all. But it may be noted that the city called *pattana* is a big commercial port. It is situated on the banks of the sea or a river, and is always engaged in exchange and commerce with foreigners who deal specially in jewels, silk clothes and perfumes, etc., imported from other countries (*dvīpāntara*).

Forts are first divided into eight classes, called *śibira*, *vāhinī-mukha*, *sthānīya*, *droṇaka*, *saṁviddha* or *vardhaka*, *kolaka*, *nigama*, and *skandhāvāra*. There is a further division of these forts according to their position. They are known as mountain fort (*giri-durga*), forest fort (*vana-durga*), water-fort (*jala-durga*) chariot fort (*ratha-durga*), gods' fort (*deva-durga*), marsh fort (*paṅka-durga*) and mixed fort (*miśra-durga*).

The mountain fort is subdivided into three classes, according as it is built on the top of the mountain, in the valley, or on the mountain-slope.

All these forts are surrounded with strong walls and ditches. The wall is made of brick, stone and similar materials. It is at least 12 cubits in height and its thickness at the base is at least 6 cubits It is provided with watch-towers.

CHAPTER XI

The dimensions of buildings of various storeys (*Bhūmilamba-vidhāna*)

The name of this chapter is 'Bhūmilamba,' which literally means the height of the storey. The *Kāmikagāma* (*paṭala* 50, verse 1) defines this name, Bhūmilamba, thus: "*Chatur-aṁśādi-saṁsthānaṁ bhūmi-lambam iti smṛitam.*" The chapters on the subject, in both the works, *Mānasāra* and *Kāmikāagma*, deal with the measurement of length, breadth, and height of buildings of one to twelve storeys.

The various shapes of buildings are mentioned in the opening lines of the chapter. They may be square, rectangular, round, octagonal, or oval. Buildings of all kinds, such as the *vimāna* or temple, the *harmya* or palace, the *gopura* or gate-house, the *śālā* or hall, the *maṇḍapa* or pavilion, and the *veśman* (residential houses generally) should have one of these five shapes.

Buildings are again divided into four classes—*jāti*, *chhanda*, *vikalpa* or *saṁkalpa*, and *ābhāsa*—which are frequently referred to in the subsequent chapters. These four classes seem to have different characteristics in different cases.

The proportion between height and width is expressed by five technical names, *śāntika*, *paushṭika*, *pārshṇika* (sometimes called *jayada*), *adbhuta*, and *sarvakāmika*. When the height of a building or idol is 2¼ times of its width, it is called *śāntika*, the *paushṭika* height is twice the width, the *pārshṇika* or *jayada* height is 1¾ of the width, the *adbhuta* height is 1½ of the width, and the *sarvakāmika* height is 1¼ of the width. This proportion of height and width is not, however, strictly followed all through. There is a slight variation in some cases. But the proportions given above are the most common. The measurement of length, breadth and height is invariably divided into three types: large, intermediate, and small. The *śāntika* and the *paushṭika* heights are prescribed for the large type of measurement, the *pārshṇika* or *jayada* for the intermediate type, and the *adbhuta* and the *sarvakāmika* for the small type.

Five series of length and five series of breadth are prescribed here for each of the several classes of buildings of one to twelve storeys. But in some subsequent chapters as many as nine alternatives of length or breadth are prescribed for one and the same object.

The five series of breadth in the small type of one-storeyed buildings are 2, 4, 6, 8 and 10 cubits, and the five series of length are 3, 5, 7, 9 and 11 cubits. In the intermediate type the five series of breadth are 5, 7, 9, 11 and 13 cubits, and the five series of length 6, 8, 10, 12 and 14 cubits. In the large type, the five series of breadth are 6, 8, 10, 12 and 14 cubits, and the five lengths are 7, 9, 11, 13 and 15 cubits.

All the classes of buildings of one to twelve storeys are in this way measured separately. The dimensions of the twelve-storeyed building in its three types are given briefly.[1] In the small type they are 35, 37, 39, 41, 43 cubits, in the intermediate type 36, 38, 40, 42, 44 cubits, and in the large type, 37, 39, 41, 43, 45 cubits. These are the fifteen kinds of *Vipula*, and the height should be as before.

These are the measurements in the *jāti* class of buildings. Three-fourths, half and one-fourth of these are prescribed for the *chhanda*, the *vikalpa* and the *ābhāsa* classes respectively.

The concluding part of this chapter prescribes the number of storeys allowed in edifices according to the social status of their occupants. In the first instance reference is made to the various classes of kings[2], of whom the one highest in rank, namely, the *chakravartin* or universal monarch, is said to inhabit a palace of five to twelve storeys. The residence of the heir-apparent (*yuvarāja*), as well as those belonging to the chief feudatories (*sāmanta-pramukhya*), should have one to three storeys.

CHAPTER XII

The foundation (*Garbhanyāsa-vidhāna*)

The foundation is classified under three heads, namely, for buildings, for villages, etc., and for tanks, etc. The last named foundation is meant for a cistern, well or tank (*vāpī-kūpa-taṭāka*), etc.

The depth of the excavation (*garbha-bhājana*) in case of a village, a town or a fort (*grāma, nagara, pura, pattana, kharvaṭa, koshṭha, kola,* etc.) is stated to be of five kinds, and varies in accordance with the size of the construction. Similarly for a building or a well suitable depth of the excavation is prescribed.

The foundation of buildings is further divided into two classes as it may belong to temples or to human dwellings. Of temples, those of Vishṇu and Brahmā are dealt with, and the others are said to be like these.

---

[1] The description of these dimensions is much clearer in the *Kāmikāgama* (*paṭala* 50). According to this work, the width of a twelve-storeyed building is 70 cubits and the height 100 cubits. It expressly states (*śloka* 33) that it is never desirable that buildings should be larger than 77 cubits in height and 70 cubits in width.

[2] Cf below, chapter XLI. In the present passage only six out of the nine classes are mentioned, the *maṇḍaleśa*, *paṭṭadhara* and *pārshṇika* having been omitted.

For human dwellings there are four classes of foundations according to the caste of the occupier, Brāhmaṇa, Kshatriya, Vaiśya or Śūdra. In the laying of a foundation ritualistic prescriptions play a prominent part, the actual process apparently being the same in all cases.

The depth of the excavation is equal to the height of the basement. The four corners and sides, built of brick or stone, are equal. The cavity is filled with water, and ten kinds of earth, such as earth taken from an anthill, from a crab-cave, etc., are placed at the bottom.

Portions of certain plants are then deposited on the four sides: the root of the blue lotus (*utpala-kāṇḍa*) to the east, the root of the white lotus (*kumuda-kāṇḍa*) to the south, *saugandhi* (a kind of fragrant grass) to the north, and some other plant to the west. Above these are to be placed grains of ten kinds of cereals, to wit, *śāli* (rice) to the north-east, *vrīhi* (rice) to the east, *kodrava* (paspalum scrobiculatum) to the south-east, *kaṅgu* (panicum italicum) to the south, *mudga* (phaseolus mungo) to the south-west, *māsha* (phaseolus radiatus) to the west, *kulattha* (dolichos uniflorus) to the north-west and *tila* (sesamum indicum) to the north.

The twelve kinds of breadth and length of the excavation to suit buildings of one to twelve storeys are respectively 3, 5, 7, 9, 11, 13, 15, 17, 19, 21, 23, 25 *aṅgulas*; and 4, 6, 8, 10, 12, 14, 16, 18, 20, 22, 24, 26 *aṅgulas*. And its height should be equal to the breadth, or less by [illegible] or [illegible] of the breadth.

The concluding lines of this chapter deal with the measurement of bricks, with which buildings of one to twelve storeys are preferably built, and also with the ceremonies in connection with the laying of the foundation-stone (lit. first brick, *prathameshṭaka*). The breadth of a brick may be from 7 to 29 or 30 *aṅgulas*. The length is greater than the breadth by [illegible], [illegible], or [illegible]; or is twice of the breadth. The thickness should be half of the breadth.

CHAPTER XIII

The pedestal (*Upapīṭha-vidhāna*)

The opening lines of the chapter describe the height of the pedestal as compared with the base. This height is said to be of nine kinds, which are worked out by nine proportions. Five of them are those expressed by the technical terms *śāntika*, *paushṭika*, *jayada*, *adbhuta* and *sarvakāmikā* ([illegible], [illegible], [illegible], [illegible] and [illegible]). Rām Rāz on the authority of a Tamil manuscript says that the height of the pedestal is to be reckoned from one-quarter to six times of the height of the base.

The next topic of this chapter refers to the measurement of the projections (*nirgama*) of pedestals. The height of the pedestal is divided into 3, 4, 5, 6, 7, 8, 9, 10, 11, 12, 13, 14 or 15 equal parts ; of these 1, 2, 3, 4, 5, 6, 7 or 8 are given to the projection. The nine kinds of projection are 1 1¼, 1½, 1¾, 2, 2¼, 2½, 2¾ and 3 *hastas*. The projections may be 1, 1½, 2, 2½, 3, 3½, 4, 5, 6, 7, 8, or 9 *daṇḍas*.

After this, the pedestals are divided into three classes known as *vedi-bhadra*, *prati-bhadra*, and *mañcha-bhadra*. Each of these is subdivided into four types. The measures of the mouldings of each of these twelve kinds of pedestals are given in detail.

The remaining portion of the chapter contains the names and measurement of the various mouldings which are to be employed in each of the twelve kinds of pedestal.

CHAPTER XIV

The base (*Adhishṭhāna-vidhāna*)

The heights of the bases are of twelve kinds, beginning at 30 *aṅgulas* and ending at 4 *hastas*, the increment being by 6 *aṅgulas*. These twelve heights are used respectively in twelve different storeys one above the other. The heights of the bases are said to be 4 *hastas* in the houses of the Brāhmaṇas, 3 *hastas* in those of the Kshatriyas, 2 *hastas* in those of the Vaiśyas and 1 *hasta* in the houses of the Śūdras.

Some sixty-four bases are described under nineteen different types called *pāda-bandha*, *uraga-bandha*, *pratikrama*, *kumuda-bandha*, *padma-kesara*, *push-pa-pushkala*, *śrī-bandha*, *mañcha-bandha*, *śreṇi-bandha*, *padma-bandha*, *kum-bha-bandha* (or *kalaśa-bandha*), *vapra-bandha*, *vajra-bandha*, *śrī-bhoga*, *ratna-bandha*, *paṭṭa-bandha*, *kukshi-bandha*, *kampa-bandha*, and *śrīkānta*. Of each of the bases the mouldings and ornaments are described in detail.

CHAPTER XV

The pillar (*Stambha-lakshaṇa-vidhāna*)

The opening lines divide the subject matter into five heads, namely, the measurement of pillars, their shapes, their ornaments and mouldings, the collection of wood for the purpose of making pillars, which may, however, be made of stone, and the ceremonial and process of erecting pillars.

The height of a pillar is measured from above the base to below the *uttara*, or above the pedestal from the *janman* to the *uttara*. The height of a pillar, in other words, is measured from the plinth up to the lowest member of the entablature, so as to include the capital. In an important passage in the Kāśyapa, quoted by Rām Rāz, it is stated that the measurement may also be taken from the cimbia of the shaft, exclusive of the base.

The height of a pillar is twice, one-and-a-half times or one-and-a-quarter times that of its base, or the height of the pillar begins at $2\frac{1}{2}$ *hastas* and ends at 8 *hastas*, the increment being by 6 *aṅgulas* or $\frac{1}{4}$ *hasta*. But according to Kāśyapa, the height of the pillar may be 3 times that of the base; or 6 or 8 times that of the pedestal. The width (diameter) of a pillar may be $\frac{1}{6}$, $\frac{1}{7}$, $\frac{1}{8}$, $\frac{1}{9}$ or $\frac{1}{10}$ of its height, or $\frac{1}{3}$, $\frac{1}{4}$ or $\frac{1}{5}$ of the height if it be a pilaster (*kuḍya-stambha*). The width of the pilaster, according to the *Mānasāra*, is 3, 4, 5 or 6 *mātras* (*aṅgulas*), and twice, thrice or four times of these should be the width of the *kampa*. The height of a pillar being divided into 12, 11, 10, 9 or 8 parts, the one of these parts may be the breadth of the pillar, and at the top it is diminished by one-fourth.

The column admits of different shapes. A square pillar is called *brahma-kānta*. An octagonal one is called *vishṇu-kānta*. A sixteen-sided or circular one is known as *rudra-kānta*. A pentagonal one is called *śivakānta*, and the hexagonal one *skanda-kānta*. These shapes are stated to be uniform from bottom to top. But the base may be quadrangular.

With respect to dimensions and ornaments the five kinds of columns—*brahma-kānta*, *vishṇu-kānta*, *rudra-kānta*, *śiva-kānta*, and *skanda-kānta*—are called *chitra-karṇa*, *padma-kānta*, *chitra-kumbha*, *pālikā-stambha*, and *kumbha-stambha*. A sixth one, *koshṭha-stambha*, in the latter division, is stated to be two-sided, and is the same as the *kuḍya-stambha* or pilaster.

It should be noticed that the former set of five names refers to the shapes of the shafts, whilst the latter set of five names is based on the shapes of the capitals, but in the detailed description both the capital and shaft are included.

Some special kinds of pillars are also described, such as *Chitra-karṇa*, *Padma-kānta*, *Chitra-kumbha*, *Vīra-kaṇṭha*, *Pālikā-stambha*, *Kumbha-stambha* and *Koshṭha-stambha*. Then follow the description and measurement of the mouldings of the pillars.

Columns, when in rows, must be in a straight line. "The intercolumnation may be two, three, four or five diameters; it is measured in three ways, 1st, from the inner extremity of the base of one pillar to that of another; 2nd, from the centre of the two pillars; and 3rd, from the outer extremities of the pillars including the two bases." There seems to be no fixed intercolumnation. This has been left to the discretion of architects who are, however, required to be particularly careful with regard to beauty and utility.

Minor pillars should be proportionate to the main pillar. A main pillar with one minor pillar (*upapāda*) is called *eka-kānta*, with two minor pillars *dvikānta*, and with three minor pillars *tri-kānta*. A main pillar with four minor pillars is called *brahma-kānta*, with five *śiva-kānta*, with six *skanda-kānta*, and with eight minor pillars, it is called *vishṇu-kānta*.

There is a long description of the collection of wood for purposes of pillars. The details seem to indicate that at the time when the *Mānasāra* was composed, wood was frequently used for making columns; stone pillars are also mentioned, but pillars made of brick alone are not particularly dealt with. It is, however, stated that stone, brick and wood were used for making different parts of a column. The square *ādhāra* or base of a stone pillar, it is stated, should be made of stone, and that of the wooden pillar of wood. But at the end of the next chapter, it is added that all the parts of a column should be made of stone (*śilā*), wood (*dāru*) or brick (*ishṭaka*). In the middle of the same chapter the use of these three materials is elaborately discussed. The pillars, etc., are called *śuddha* (pure) when made of one material, *miśra* (mixed) when made of two materials, and *saṁkīrṇa* (amalgamated) when made of all the three (or more) materials.

The concluding part of this chapter deals with ceremonies in connection with erecting columns. They are essentially ritualistic. It is directed that the column should be posted (*veśayet*) at the side of a *maṇḍapa* or pavilion.

CHAPTER XVI

The entablature (*Prastara-vidhāna*)

The height of the entablature (*prastara*), as compared with that of the base (*adhishṭhāna*), is of six kinds. The height of the former may be equal to that of the latter, or less by ¼, or greater by ¼, ½ or ¾; or it may be twice; or, in cubit (*hasta*) measurement these six kinds of height of the entablature begin at 7 cubits and end at 4½ cubits, the decrement being by ½ cubit. These six kinds of entablatures are respectively used in the houses of the gods, the Brahmins, the kings (or Kshatriyas), the crown-princes (*yuvarāja*), the Vaiśyas and the Śūdras.

The height of the entablature is said to be ½ or ¾ of, or equal to, that of the pillar (*pāda*), or greater by ¼, ½ or ¾. Yet another set of six heights is described. The height of the pillar being divided into eight parts, seven, six, five, four, three or two parts may be assigned to that of the entablature.

The greater portion of the chapter is devoted to an enumeration of the various mouldings and the measurement of each of the eight different kinds of entablatures.

In this chapter the roofing (*prachchhādana*) of buildings is described. It is stated that a brick-built building may be furnished with a wooden roof, and that the roofs of stone buildings should also be built of stone.

CHAPTER XVII

Wood-joinery (*Sandhikarma-vidhāna*)

The definition of the name (*sandhikarman*) of the chapter is given in the opening lines. The joining of pieces of wood for buildings is called *sandhi-karman*. Several kinds of wood-joining are described in detail. It would be impossible to give here a resumé. But it may be noted that wood was very largely used in constructing houses of various kinds; some parts of pillars too were made of wood, as has already been pointed out. Doors were mostly made of wood. The same was the case with couches, cars, chairs, etc.

The wood-joining is of various kinds and forms. Pieces of wood are said to be joined in such a way as to make the *nandyāvarta*, *svastika*, *sarvato-bhadra* and such other shapes. Some kinds of wood are strictly forbidden to be joined with some others. Fresh timber, it is stated, should under no circumstances be joined with seasoned wood.

CHAPTER XVIII

The general description of buildings (*Vimāna-vidhāna*)

The contents of the chapter are divided into the following headings: the classification of the *vimānas* of one to twelve storeys; the three styles of architecture; the characteristic features of the *stūpikā* or pinnacle, the *stūpi-kīla* or pinnacle staff, the *lupā*, and the *mukha-bhadra*; and the ceremonies of fixing the pinnacle staff.

The description begins with the making of the foundation; but this subject has already been dealt with in the 12th chapter.

The classification of *vimānas* of one to twelve storeys is elaborately described here, their absolute dimensions having already been given in the 11th chapter called *Bhūmilamba-vidhāna*. Each of the twelve classes is subdivided into three types, according to their size—large, intermediate and small. Whilst the width of the small type of one-storeyed building is 1, 2, 3, 4, 5, or 6 parts, it should be 5, 6, or 7 parts in the intermediate type, and 6, 7, or 8 parts in the large type. These 'parts' appear to be the partitions of the façade bordered by two pilasters (*pāda*).

The three styles of architecture are called *nāgara*, *drāviḍa* and *vesara* which are apparently geographical names. The distinguishing feature seems to be the general shape of the *śikhara*.

In the third place the measurement and mouldings of the pinnacle (*stūpi* or *stūpikā*) are given in detail. The height of the *stūpi* is one cubit (*hasta*) in the houses of the Śūdras, two cubits in those of the Vaiśyas, two cubits and a half in the houses of the crown-princes (*yuvarāja*), three cubits in the houses of the kings (*kshatriya*), three cubits and a half in the houses of the Brāhmaṇas, and four cubits in the houses of the gods, that is, in temples.

Building materials are then discussed. Four kinds of material are distinctly mentioned: stone, brick, wood, and iron (*lauha*).

Buildings are made of one, two, three or all four of these materials, but preference is given to the use of one material alone. With regard to materials, buildings are divided into three classes, namely, *śuddha* (pure) made of one material alone, *miśra* (mixed) made of two materials and *saṁkīrṇa* (amalgamated) made of three or more materials.

The term *stūpi-kīla* literally means the nail or pin of the *stūpi*. Its form is described clearly. It is quadrangular at the base, octagonal at the middle, circular at the top, and tapering gradually from bottom to top. The width at the top is one *aṅgula*.

Then two more architectural members are described, namely, the *lupā* and the *mukha-bhadra*. The former is explained by Rām Rāz[1] as "a sloping and a projecting member of the entablature, representing a continued pent roof. It is made below the cupola [*śikhara*], and its ends are placed as if it were suspended from the architrave, and reaching the stalk of the lotus below."

The *mukha-bhadra*, or front tabernacle according to the same author,[2] indicates an ornamental niche, which occupies a central position in the façade of the building.

The chapter concludes with a description of the ceremonies in connection with fixing the *stūpi-kīla*.

CHAPTER XIX

The one-storeyed building (*Ekabhūmi-vidhāna*)[3]

The chapter opens with various classifications of buildings. They are first divided into four classes called *jāti*, *chhanda*, *vikalpa*, and *ābhāsa*. Here they are considered with regard to their measurement. The *jāti* class is said to be

[1] Rām Rāz, *Essay*, p. 52, footnote 2.
[2] *Ibidem*, pp. 51 f.
[3] Cf. *ibidem* pp. 49–58; plate XXI

measured in the *pūrva-hasta*, the first kind of cubit, i.e., the cubit of 24 *aṅgulas*. The *chhanda* is measured in $\frac{3}{4}$ cubit, the *vikalpa* in $\frac{1}{2}$ of this (?), and the *ābhāsa* in $\frac{1}{2}$ cubit or span.

A further classification is into *sthānaka*, *āsana* and *śayana*, which are also called respectively, *saṁchita*, *asaṁchita* and *apasaṁchita*. This classification also refers to measurement. In the *sthānaka* class the measurement of the height is considered, in the *āsana* the breadth is taken into consideration, and in the *śayana* the width is measured. It should be noted that these three classes, namely, *sthānaka*, *āsana*, and *śayana*, have a further signification with regard to the object of worship. In the *sthānaka* buildings the idol is in an erect posture, in the *āsana* buildings in a sitting posture, and in the *śayana* buildings in a recumbent posture.

A third classification refers to the shape Buildings are classed as masculine (*purusha*) when they are equiangular or circular, and as feminine when they are rectangular. Male deities are installed in masculine temples, and female deities in feminine temples. It is added, however, that the images of the latter may be placed in masculine temples too.

After this introduction comes the description of one-storeyed buildings. The absolute measurement is referred to in the the chapter called *Bhūmi-lamba* (dimensions of storeys). The comparative measurement and plan are described here at great length. The whole height of the building is divided into a certain number of equal parts which are distributed in a happy proportion amongst the different members, namely, the base, the pillar, the entablature, the neck, the dome and the pinnacle. Similarly the length of the entire temple is divided into a certain number of equal parts which are also distributed amongst various rooms and halls, namely, the *garbha-gṛiha* or shrine, the *antarāla* or anteroom and the *maṇḍapa* or pavilion. These component parts of the building are described in detail in subsequent chapters, as also the gate-houses (*gopura*), courts (*prākāra*) and such other architectural members as doors, windows, arches, and so forth. In the present chapter a detailed account is given of the water-channed (*nāla*), which is meant to be an outlet for the water.

The eight kinds of one-storeyed buildings are known as *jayantika*, *bhoga*, *śrīviśāla*, *svasti-bandhana*, *śrīkara*, *hasti-pṛishṭha*, *skandhatāra*, and *keśara*.

The concluding portion of this chapter as well as of the next eleven chapters are devoted to an enumeration of the various deities with whose images the doors and walls of buildings should be decorated.

The Buddhist and Jain temples, dealt with in only two lines, are directed to be similarly built, with this difference that in these temples the images of the Buddhist and Jain gods should be installed instead of the images of the Brāhmanas,

CHAPTERS XX—XXX

Buildings of two to twelve storeys.[1]

The contents of these eleven chapters of the *Mānasāra* may be conveniently summarised together. They deal respectively with two-storeyed (*dvi-tala*), three-storeyed (*tri-tala*), four-storeyed (*chatus-tala*), five-storeyed (*pañcha-tala*), six-storeyed (*shaṭ-tala*), seven-storeyed (*sapta-tala*), eight-storeyed (*ashṭa-tala*), nine-storeyed (*nava-tala*), ten-storeyed (*daśa-tala*), eleven-storeyed (*ekādaśa-tala*), and twelve-storeyed (*dvādaśa-tala*) buildings. In each of these chapters we find a classification of the peculiar kind of edifice under discussion followed by an account of certain details, in particular the location of the divine images with which the walls are decorated. Thus the buildings of two storeys are divided into eight classes which are called *śrīkara*, *vijaya*, *siddha*, *paushṭika*, *śāntika*, *adbhuta* (also *prabhūtaka*), *svastika*, and *pushkala*. Those of three storeys are likewise divided into eight classes, called *śrīkānta*, *āsana*, *sukhālaya*, *keśara*, *kamalāṅga*, *brahma-kānta*, *meru-kānta*, and *kailāśa*. The same eight-fold division is found in connection with the four-storeyed buildings; here the names are *vishṇu-kānta*, *chatur-mukha*, *sadā-śiva*, *rudra-kānta*, *īśvara-kānta*, *mañcha-kānta*, *vedi-kānta*, and *indra-kānta*. The eight classes of the five-storeyed buildings are called *airāvata*, *bhūta-kānta*, *viśva-kānta*, *mūrti-kānta*, *yama-kānta*, *griha-kānta*, *yajña-kānta* and *brahma-kānta*. In the case of the buildings of six storeys there are no less than thirteen classes, the technical names of which are *padma-kānta*, *kāntāra*, *sundara* *upakānta*, *kamala*, *ratna-kānta*, *vipulāṅka*, *jyotish-kānta*, *sarorūha*, *vipulākriti*, *svasti-kānta*, *nandyāvarta*, and *ikshu-kānta*. The seven-storeyed buildings are divided into eight kinds—*puṇḍarīka* *śrīkānta*, *śrībhoga*, *dhāraṇa*, *pañjara*, *āśramāgāra*, *harmya-kānta*, and *hima-kānta*. The eight classes of eight storeyed buildings are called *bhū-kānta*, *bhūpa-kānta*, *svarga-kānta*, *mahākānta* *jana-kānta*, *tapas kānta*, *satya-kānta*, and *deva-kānta*. Those of nine storeys are divided into seven kinds—*saura-kānta*, *raurava*, *chaṇḍita*, *bhūshaṇa*, *vivrita*, *supratikānta*, and *viśva-kānta*, of which the first four represent the small type of nine-storeyed buildings, the next two the intermediate type, and the last one the large type. The ten-storeyed buildings are divided into six classes which are named *bhū-kānta*, *chandra-kānta*, *bhavana-kānta*, *antariksha-kānta*, *megha-kānta*, and *abja-kānta*. Buildings of eleven storeys admit of six varieties—*śambhu-kānta*, *īśa-kānta*, *chakra-kānta*, *yama-kānta*, *vajra-kānta*, and *akra-kānta*. Finally, buildings of twelve storeys are divided into ten kinds—*pāñchāla*, *drāviḍa*, *madhya kānta*, *kāliṅga-kānta*, *virāṭa*, *kerala*, *vaṁśa-kānta*

[1] Rām Rāz, *Essay*, pp. 53-57, see plates XXII—XXXIV.

māgadha-kānta, *janaka-kānta* and *gurjara* (*sphūrjaka*). It deserves notice that in this instance the terms by which the classes are designated are apparently geographical names.

In chapter XXX we find, moreover, an elaborate account of staircases (*sopāna*).

CHAPTER XXXI

The courts (*Prākāra-vidhāna*)

The chapter begins with the announcement that five kinds of *prākāra* buildings will be described in connection with *bali* (offerings), *parivāra* (attendant deities), *śobhā* (beauty), and *rakshaṇa* (defence).

But the main object of the chapter is evidently to describe the various courts into which the whole compound is divided. The description of five such courts is given. The first or innermost court is called the *antar-maṇḍala*. The second is known as *anta-nihāra* and the third as *madhyama-hāra*. The fourth court is technically named *prākāra*. The fifth and last one is known as the *mahāmaryādā* or 'the extreme boundary.' As the title of the chapter indicates, the greater part of it describes only the fourth court. Here it may be briefly observed that this *prākāra* is also divided into the *jāti*, *chhanda*, *vikalpa*, *ābhāsa* and *kāmya* classes. Under each class a number of buildings (*śālā*) is exhaustively described. A further classification (*saṅkīrṇa*, etc.) is made with regard to the materials of which the *prākāra* buildings are made. These materials are the same as in other cases, namely, stone, brick and timber.

The shrines of the attendant deities (*parivārā-vimāna*) and the gate-houses (*gopuras*) are very briefly described in conclusion, the next two chapters being entirely devoted to a special treatment of these two subjects.

CHAPTER XXXII

The attendant deities (*Parivāra-vidhāna*)

The temples of these deities are directed to be built round the *prākāra*. At the eight cardinal points of the innermost or the first court, the temples of a group of eight deities are built. Groups of sixteen and thirty-two deities are located in the second and the third courts respectively. Between the third and the fifth courts is said to be a special pavilion. After an elaborate description of the location of temples for each of the deities of the three groups, the attendant deities of Vishṇu are described in detail.

With regard to the family of Vishṇu, it may be pointed out that it also includes the same three groups of eight, sixteen and thirty-two deities. The second group relating to Vishṇu includes Buddha too. The well known ten incarnations of Vishṇu, except the *Matsya* (fish) and the *Kūrma* (tortoise) are included in the third group.

The temples of the Bauddhas and Jainas, it is expressly stated, should be constructed according to the rules of their own *Śāstras*.

It should be noticed that the description of the temples intended for so many deities does not contain any measurements, etc. The text is solely occupied with the location of these temples or deities in the compound. But a considerable portion of the chapter is devoted to the description of *maṇḍapas* for such purposes as bathing, sleeping, assemblies, performances of musicians and dancing girls, and stabling of cows and horses.

CHAPTER XXXIII

The gate-house (*Gopura-vidhāna*)[1]

Gate-houses (*gopura*) are built in front of each of the five courts into which the whole compound is divided. The *gopura* belonging to the first court (*antar-maṇḍala*) is technically called the *dvāra-śobhā* or 'the beauty of the gate'[2]; that belonging to the second court is known as *dvāra-śālā* or gate-house. The gate-house of the third court is called *dvāra-prāsāda*, and that of the fourth court (*prākāra*) has the name of *dvāra-harmya*. The gate-house of the fifth or outermost court (*mahāmaryādā*) is known as *mahāgopura* or the great gate house.

Each of these five classes of gate-houses is subdivided again into three kinds—the small, the intermediate, and the large. Gate-houses are exhaustively described under these fifteen kinds. They are further divided into ten classes with regard to the number of architectural members designated as *śikhara* (domes), *stūpikā* (pinnacle), *gala-kūṭa* (neck-peak), and *kshudra-nāsī* (vestibule). A *gopura* is thus technically called *śribhoga* when its *śikhā* is like a *śālā*, and it has a circular surrounding *stūpikā*, and is furnished with a *gala-kūṭa*, four *kshudra-nāsis*, and eight *mahānāsis*. The remaining nine classes are called respectively *śrīviśāla*, *vishṇu-kānta*, *indra-kānta*, *brahma-kānta*, *skanda-kānta*, *śikhara* and *saumya-kānta*. The names of two of these ten classes are evidently missing.

The fifteen kinds of gate-houses referred to above may have one to sixteen or seventeen storeys. But the details of those of one to five storeys only are given, others being left to the discretion of the artists and stated to be built in the same way as those described so minutely.

---

[1] Rām Rāz, *Essay*, pp. 58—61; plates XXXVI—XLII.

[2] This term in Prākrit form (*duārasohā*) occurs in the *Mṛichchhakaṭika* (ed. Stenzler), p. 72, 1, 13, in the description of Vasantasena's palace (Act V) which is divided into seven courts.

The measurements, both absolute and comparative, of length, breadth and height of each storey belonging to each of the fifteen kinds of gate-houses are described at great length. The ornaments and mouldings of each storey are also given in detail. The *garbha-gṛiha* (cella or sanctum) as well as all other rooms together with their different parts, such as pillars, entablatures, walls, roofs, floors, doors, windows, etc., are exhaustively discussed.

The measurements, etc., of the gate-houses are discussed in comparison with those of the main buildings also. Then follows a lengthy description of their solid (*ghana*) and hollow (*aghana*) parts. The description of some interior members is also included in this section.

The chapter closes with an interesting description of windows, not only for gate-houses, but also for other kinds of buildings, both religious and residential. The general plan of windows seems to be this: a post or pillar is fixed in the middle to which are attached two perforated screens (*jālaka* and *phalakā*). These admit of various patterns represented by the following names, by which they are classed with regard to their shapes, *nāga-bandha*, *valli*, *gavāksha* (cow's eye), *kuñjarāksha* (elephant's eye), *svastika*, *sarvato-bhadra*, *nandyāvarta*, and *pushpa-bandha* (bouquet or bunch of flowers). They are decorated with floral and foliated ornaments, as well as with decorative devices in imitation of jewels. The measurement of length, breadth and thickness is entirely left to the discretion of the artist. But it is stated in conclusion that according to some authorities the width of the windows for gate-houses varies from 1½ to 5 cubits (*hasta*), the increment being by six *aṅgulas*.

CHAPTER XXXIV

The maṇḍapa (*Maṇḍapa-vidhāna*)

The term *maṇḍapa* generally means a temple, pavilion, bower, shed or open hall. But the word has been used in three technical senses in this chapter. It is used to imply a house in the country, etc., or built on the sea-shore or the bank of a river, tank, or lake; secondly, it is used to imply all the detached buildings in a compound which is generally divided into five courts. But in the most general sense, it implies various sorts of rooms in a temple or residential building; for the greater part of this long chapter is devoted to a description of these rooms.

After an account of the architectural members indicated by the technical terms *bhitti*, *alinda* and *prapā*, follows the lengthy description of *maṇḍapas*. Seven *maṇḍapas* are said to be built in front of the *prāsāda* or the main edifice They are technically called *himaja*, *nishādaja*, *vijaya*, *mālyaja*, *pāriyātra*, *gandha-mādana* and *hema-kūṭa* respectively. The first is said to be used for the purpose of a bath-room, the second for a study, library or school (*adhyayana*), and so forth. Various parts of these buildings, such as walls, roofs, floors, verandas, court-yards, doors, windows, columns, etc., are described in detail. Besides these seven, various other classes of *maṇḍapas* are also described exhaustively. Their technical names together with the main purposes for which they are built may be given here.

The *meruja maṇḍapa* is used as a library-room, the *vijaya* for marriage ceremonies, the *padmaka* as a temple-kitchen, the *sicha* as an ordinary kitchen, the *padma* for collecting flowers, the *bhadra* for a water-reservoir, store-house, etc the *śiva* for unhusking corn, the *veda* for an assembly-hall, the *kula-dhāraṇa* for storing perfumes, the *sukhāṅga* for a guest-house, the *dārva* for an elephant's stable, and the *kauśika* for a horse-stable, the *saukhyaka* and others built on the banks of the sea, river, lake, etc., are meant for purposes of pilgrimage, and the *jayāla* and others for summer residence. The plan, ornaments, etc. of each of these various classes are described in detail.

The chapter closes with a description of the forms of *maṇḍapas*. Those of temples and of the houses of the Brāhmaṇas should have the *jāti* shape, the *chhanda* shape is given to the *maṇḍapas* of the Kshatriyas, the *vikalpa* shape to those of the Vaiśyas, and the *ābhāsa* shape to those of the Śūdras. But according to some, these four classes are also said to be based on the form of the *bhadra* or front tabernacle.

The *maṇḍapas* of two faces are called *daṇḍaka* and those of three faces *svastika*; but the latter may also have the *lāṅgala* or plough shape. The *maṇḍapas* of four faces are known as *chatur-mukha*, those of five faces as *sarvato-bhadra* and those of six faces as *maulika*.

A short description of *maṇḍapas* in villages or towns is given at the end. Their principal members are said to be the *lupā*, *prastara*, *prachchhādana*, *sabhā* and *kūṭa*, etc. *Maṇḍapas* are also built on the roadside and elsewhere.

All classes of *maṇḍapas* mentioned above are described separately, according as they may belong to a temple or to the houses of the Brāhmaṇas, the Kshatriyas the Vaiśyas and the Śūdras respectively.

CHAPTER XXXV

The Śālā (*Śālā-vidhāna*)

The distinction between the *śālā*, the *maṇḍapa*, and the *gṛiha*, to each of which, a separate chapter is devoted, is not quite clear. The three terms are used more or less in the same sense, to imply houses in general. All of them consist of the same parts and are used for similar purposes. In the compounds *go-śālā* (cowshed), *aśva-śālā* (horse stable), *pāṭha-śālā* (college or school), etc., the word *śālā* indicates a detached building ; while in *pāka-śālā* (kitchen), etc., it may imply a hall or room. In the present chapter *śālā* is used mostly in the sense of temples and of residential buildings for Brāhmaṇas, Kshatriyas, Vaiśyas and Śūdras.

Like villages, *śālās* are first divided into the same six classes of *daṇḍuka*, *svastika*., *maulika*, *chatur-mukha*, *sarvato-bhadra*, and *vardhamāna*. Some of these with a fixed number of halls are said to be temples, while others varying in the number of rooms are meant for the residence of people of different castes. A distinction is made with regard to the number of storeys they should be furnished with. The maximum number of storeys a *śālā* has is twelve. The various storeys of all these *śālās* are described in detail. Eleven alternative breadths, eleven lengths, and five heights, are given to each *śālā*. It should be observed that the width is generally the standard of measurement in Indian architecture ; the length and the height being in most cases determined in comparison with the breadth. The height is described here by the general formulas indicated by the five technical names, *śāntika*, *paushṇika*, *jayada*, *dhanada* (in other places *sarva-kāmika*), and *adbhuta*. Many alternatives in measurement are, however, modified by the rules of *āyādi-shaḍ-varga*, as in all other places.

The plan and characteristics of the six classes of *śālās*, both religious and residential, are described in detail. The various parts, mouldings and ornaments of a *śālā* are the same as those of an ordinary house. Columns, walls, roofs, floors, domes, doors, windows, staircases, arches, arcades, etc., are minutely described.

A special feature of the present chapter is the consideration of the times and season proper for the building of a *śālā*. Certain months and seasons are stated to be quite unsuitable for this purpose. Astrological and ritualistic considerations form another peculiarity of this chapter. Some classes of *śālās* are said to suit particular people born under the influence of certain planets and stars.

The chapter closes with an account of the rules of *shaḍ-varga* as applied to *śālās*, and with an enumeration of the various parts of a *śālā*.

CHAPTER XXXVI

The location and measurement of houses (*Gṛiha-māna sthāna-vinyāsa*)

The main object of the chapter is to describe the arrangement and situation houses in the compound. The breadth of a house is said to be of five kinds, namely, from two or three *daṇḍas* to ten or eleven *daṇḍas*, the increment being by two *daṇḍas*. The length may be equal to twice the breadth. Houses are stated to be built in a village, town, port (*pattana*), *kheṭaka*, grove, or hermitage, near a hill or mountain, or on the bank of a river, etc.

In the 34th chapter various sorts of *maṇḍapas* have been stated to be located in different parts of the five courts into which the whole compound of a temple is divided. In the present chapter, structures intended for various purposes are located in the different squares into which an inhabited area is divided according to the *parama-śādhika* plan described in the 7th chapter called *Pada-vinyāsa*

The *Brahma-sthāna* or the central square is stated to be unfit for a residential building. The temple of the family god is generally built in this part. Round this are constructed the dwelling houses for the master of the family, his wife and children, and servants, sheds for cows, horses, poultry, etc., the kitchen and dining hall, etc., rooms for guests, for reading or study, for the daily sacrifices of the upper caste-people, for amusements and music, for the dancing girls, and for all other domestic purposes. The arrangement of these different structures is, however, slightly different according to the caste and social position of the family. But the general plan of the dwelling houses for a family is the same in all cases.

CHAPTER XXXVII

The first entry into the house (*Gṛiha-pravesa-vidhāna*)

The ceremonies in connection with the opening of and first entry into a house are described in detail. An auspicious day and moment, and the worship and sacrifice in this connection, are still usually observed in India. The masters of the ceremonies are stated to be the *sthapati* and the *sthāpaka*. They lead the procession in circumambulating the village and the compound before the ceremonial entry into the house. The head of the family and his consort are usually the chief figures in these affairs. After completing the worship and sacrifice, a prayer is offered to the guardian angel of the house (*Gṛiha-Lakshmī*) to confer male offspring, wealth, and long life, on the master of the house.[1] After the solemn entrance into the house has been performed, the householder should feed the Brāhmaṇas, and present the architects and their followers with rich gifts.

CHAPTER XXXVIII

The location of doors (*Dvāra-sthāna*)

Doors and gates have already been described on various occasions. Two separate chapters are now devoted to the arrangement, location, measurement and ornamentation of doors to be used in all kinds of buildings. Such a special description

---

[1] The *mantra* to be recited runs:

हे लक्ष्मोः गृहकर्तारं पुत्रपौत्रधनादिभिः ।
संपूर्ण कुरु चायुष्यं प्रार्थयामि नमस्तुते ॥

of windows has already been noted at the end of the 33rd chapter on gate houses (*gopura*).

It is stated in this chapter that four main doors are constructed on the four sides of all kinds of buildings of gods and men. In most cases four smaller doors are also made at the four corners. Many other smaller doors are prescribed in the intervening spaces. Drains (*jala-dvāra*) are made underneath the house.

The main doors are always furnished with a flight of steps. In many buildings, the entrance-door is made, not at the middle of the frontage, but on either side of it. But in some houses they may be made in the middle of the front wall. In the case of kitchens, in particular, the main doors must be at the middle of the wall.

It is also stated expressly that where it is inconvenient to make so many smaller doors, as prescribed here, they should be replaced by windows.

The materials with which doors are constructed are mainly timber; but stone is used in some exceptional cases.

CHAPTER XXXIX

The measurements of doors (*Dvāra-māna-vidhāna*)

The common rule is that the height of a door should be twice its breadth. But various alternative measurements are also given. The height of the larger doors may vary from 1½ cubits (*hasta*) to 7 cubits, the increment being by 6 *aṅgulas*. The height of the smaller doors varies from one cubit to three cubits, the increment being by 3 *aṅgulas*. In the former case, therefore, we have twenty-three, in the latter seventeen, varieties of dimensions.

These dimensions are prescribed for doors in the *jāti* class of buildings. But other measurements are given for doors in houses of the *chhanda*, *vikalpa* and *ābhāsa* classes. The alternative dimensions are modified by the application of the *shaḍ-varga* formulas.

The door-posts and other parts of the door are then described at great length. Doors are generally double but single doors are also mentioned.

Doors are profusely decorated with foliated and floral ornaments. The images of Gaṇeśa, Sarasvatī and other deities should be carved over the entrance.

CHAPTER XL

The royal palace (*Rāja-gṛiha-vidhāna*)

Palaces are divided into nine classes with regard to their size, according as they may belong to a king of any of the nine classes enumerated in the next chapter Each class of palaces, whether of a *chakravartin*, *mahārāja*, *narendra*, *maṇḍaleśa*, etc., admits of nine sizes. For each of the nine main classes it is further laid down, that they should consist of a certain number of halls (*śālā*). Thus the palace of the *chakravartin*, universal monarch or emperor, should have from one to seven halls; that of the *adhirāja* (or *mahārāja*) from one to six halls; that of the *narendra* from one to five halls, and so forth.

Then the location of the various palace buildings is minutely described on the basis of the *Paramaśādhika* plan explained in the 7th chapter called *Pada-vinyāsa*.

The *Brahma-pīṭha* is installed in the *Brahma-sthāna*, the square in the centre. The main palace of each of the nine classes of kings is then located in certain of the remaining squares—Indra, Varuṇa, Yama, Pushpadanta, etc. Among the other palace buildings enumerated we find mention of the residences of the queens, the princesses, and the private council-hall.

Other buildings, which are necessary adjuncts to the dwelling of an Indian king, are the coronation pavilion (*abhishekādi-maṇḍapa*), the arsenal (*āyudhālaya*), the store-house (*vastu-nikshepa-maṇḍapa*), the house for keeping ornaments (*bhūshaṇālaya*), the dining-hall (*bhojana-maṇḍapa*), the kitchen (*pachanālaya*), the flower pavilion (*pushpa-maṇḍapa*), the baths (*majjanālaya*), the bed-chamber (*śayanālaya*) and several others. These all belong to the inner part (*antaḥ-śālā*) of the palace.

In the outer part (*bahiḥ-śālā*) are situated the residences of the crown prince (*yuvarāja*), of the family priest (*purohita*), of the ministers and others, likewise the hall of public audience (*āsthāna-maṇḍapa*), temples, etc.

Pleasure-gardens, flower-gardens, groves, tanks, etc., are assigned their proper places. Stables for horses, elephants, and cow-sheds, etc., are generally made near the main gate. Other animals, which are kept within the royal enclosure, are rams, cocks, deer and antelopes, monkeys, tigers, and peacocks. Pavilions to witness ram-fights and cock-fights (*mesha-yuddhārtha-maṇḍapa*, *kukkuṭa-yuddha-maṇḍapa*) are specially mentioned. The jail (*kārāgāra*) is located in a rather out-of-the-way place, such as the *Bhṛiśa* or the *Antariksha* part. At the end of the chapter it is stated that for the rest the arrangement is left to the choice of the king and to the discretion of the architects.

CHAPTER XLI-XLII

Royal courts and characteristics of kings (*Rājāṅga-lakshaṇa*, *Bhupāla-lakshaṇa*)

These two chapters deal with the royal courts, the classification of kings, the qualities which are required in a good ruler, and so forth.

Kings are divided, in descending progression of rank, into nine classes namely, *chakravartin*, *mahārāja* (or *adhirāja*), *mahendra* (or *narendra*), *pārshṇika*, *paṭṭadhara*, *maṇḍaleśa*, *paṭṭabhāj*, *prāhāraka*, and *astragrāhin*.

The opening and closing lines of chapter XLI describe the general qualifications of all kings. They should know philosophy and religion and must be learned in all the Śāstras, and in the political, military, civil and moral laws. They should be haughty (*uddhata*), gracious (*lalita*) and generous (*udātta*) in their behaviour. They should have the direct knowledge of and control over the subordinate kings and ministers. They should themselves be great warriors and wise in all matters. The treasury should always be kept full and they should themselves be religious and of strict morals. They should be the protectors of their subjects. They should possess peace of mind, love of fame, good taste in matters of art, and fondness for music (*Gāndharva śāstra*).

Then it is stated of each of the nine classes of kings what should be the number of his horses, elephants, soldiers, women and queens. The *astragrāhin*, for instance, who is least in rank, is said to possess 500 horses, 500 elephants, an army of 50,000 soldiers, 500 female attendants and one queen (*mahishī*). The *prāhāraka*, who follows next, has 600 horses, 600 elephants, 100,000 soldiers, 700 beautiful women and two queens. The highest figures are reached in the case of the *chakravartin* or universal monarch.

Chapter XLII begins with the classification of kings mentioned above. The extent of their kingdoms and some special characteristics of each of the nine classes of kings are then described. The empire of the *chakravartin* reaches as far as the four oceans (*chatuḥ-sāgara*) He is the suzerain of all subordinate kings. He is strict in his judgment of right and wrong, but protects the people with kindness and mercy. He is famous and the most fortunate of all. The next king (*mahārāja* or *adhirāja*) is the lord of seven kingdoms. He has the six principal kingly qualities (*guṇa*), the six strengths (*bala*), and the three powers (*śakti*).[1] He is also versed in politics (*nīti*). He is born either in the Solar or in the Lunar race. The remaining seven classes of kings are similarly described.

---

[1] The six 'qualities' (*guṇa*) of a king are found in *Manu*, VII, 160:

सन्धिं च विग्रहं चैव यानमासनमेव च ।
द्वैधीभावं संश्रयं च षड्गुणांश्चिन्तयेत्सदा ॥

"Let him [the king] constantly think of the six measures of royal policy (*guṇa*), viz., alliance, war, marching, halting, dividing the army, and seeking protection." (Bühler, *S. B. E.* XXV, p 241). But according to another source the six *guṇas* or qualities of a king are valour, energy, firmness, ability, liberality and majesty. The three royal powers (*śakti*) are found in the *Amarakosha* 2, 8, 1, 19—*śaktayas tisraḥ prabhāvotsāha mantrajāḥ*, "the three powers come forth from majesty, energy and good counsel."

A point of great historical interest in this passage is that royalty is no longer the monopoly of the Kshatriyas. A king may belong to any of the four castes—the Brāhmaṇas, the Kshatriyas, the Vaiśyas, and even the Śūdras. The *prāhāraka* is expressly stated to belong to any of the four castes.

The nine kinds of crowns, which pertain to these nine classes of kings, are then described. This subject, however, is more elaborately treated in the 49th chapter (*Abhisheka-lakshaṇa*). Next comes the description of the nine kinds of thrones used by the nine classes of kings. Here other royal insignia, particularly the white umbrella (*dhavala-chhattra*) and the chowrie or fly-whisk made of the yak's tail (*chāmara*) are also mentioned. Thrones, it will be noticed, are fully dealt with in the 45th chapter (*Siṁhāsana-lakshaṇa-vidhāna*).

The next point of importance is the rate of royal revenue. The *chakravartin* takes only one-tenth of the produce as his share. The *mahārāja* takes one-sixth, the *narendra* one-fifth, the *pārshṇika* one-quarter, the *paṭṭadhara* one-third; the exact proportions of the other kings' shares are not given. No tax should be illegally imposed. Punishment and fines should be legal and moderate. The temples, as well as the Brāhmaṇas, the hermits and similar people should be supported by the state.

At the end of the chapter it is stated that this description of kings is made on the authority of the *Vedas*, the *Purāṇas*, and the *Śāstras*.

CHAPTER XLIII

Cars and chariots (*Ratha-lakshaṇa-vidhāna*)

Cars and chariots are constructed for the ceremonial and ordinary use of gods, Brāhmaṇas and kings, as well as for war and other purposes. The wheels and other parts of cars, their shapes, their measurements, their ornamentations and mouldings are described in order.

The chapter begins with a minute description of the wheel, the most important part of the car. It is always circular, and is furnished with a strong tyre of similar shape. All its parts, together with their measurements, are described in detail—the *kukshi* (navel, *lit.* belly), *aksha* (axle), *śikhā* or *danta* (axle-band), *chhidra* (hole) and the *kīla* (axle-bolt, linch-pin), etc. Particular trees yielding timber for the wheel are enumerated. On a double support (called *ādhāra* and *upādhāra*), which rests on the axles, is raised a lofty structure which is provided with balconies (*bhadra*) and profusely decorated. It may have as many as nine storeys, the height of each upper storey being smaller than that of the one just preceding. The exact proportion is not given.

The forms of cars are next discussed. With regard to their shapes, cars are divided into seven classes—*nabhasvān-bhadraka*, *prabhañjanab-hadraka*, *nivāta-bhadraka*, *pavana-bhadraka*, *pṛishada-bhadraka*, *indraka* (or *chandraka*)-*bhadraka*, and *anila-bhadraka*. The first of these is square, the second hexagonal, the third should have two *bhadras*, and the fourth, three *bhadras*; the fifth and the sixth should have ten *bhadras*, and the last one should be furnished with twelve *bhadras*.

The description of the different shapes of cars is rather confusing. According to another classification given here the square cars are called *nāgara*, the octagonal ones *drāviḍa*, the circular ones *vesara*, the hexagonal ones *andhra* (*randhra* ?), and the oval ones *kāliṅga*.

These cars, in accordance with the different purposes referred to above, have various kinds of wheels and other members. Thus a fighting car has three wheels, the car for mock-fighting has four wheels, one for ordinary festivals (*nityotsava*) has five wheels, one for special festivals (*mahotsava*) may have six, seven, eight, nine or ten wheels. In the same manner the number of *vedis* (platforms) varies according to the special purpose for which a car is to be used.

Thus it is stated that the chariot of the universal monarch (*sārvabhauma*), should have one to nine *vedikās*, that of the *mahārāja* one to seven *vedikās*, that of the *narendra* one to five *vedikās*, and so forth. The cars of Vishṇu and Śiva should consist of one to nine *vedikās*, those of Buddhist and Jain deities one to seven *vedikās*, and in the case of other gods the number should be four, or one to five.

These cars should be decorated with peacock's feathers, chowries, arches (*toraṇa*), little bells, bright mirrors, fans and garlands. There should also be carved images of various deities, particularly on the upper part of the structure, while the basement is adorned with representations of lions, elephants and crocodiles (*hari-kari-makara-rūpaiḥ*), with foliated ornamentation and with figures of dancers (*nāṭaka*), *bhūtas* and *yakshas*.

CHAPTER XLIV

Couches (*Śayana-vidhāna*)

Couches are meant for the use of deities, the twice-born and members of other castes. They are said to be of two kinds, the small (*bāla-paryaṅka*) and the large (*paryaṅka*), the one being distinguished from the other by its size alone.

The measurement and various parts of the two kinds of couches are described separately. The width of the *bāla-paryaṅka* may vary from 11 to 25 *aṅgulas*, the increment being by 2 *aṅgulas*. This makes eight varieties. The *paryaṅka* proper admits of nine varieties, as they may be from 21 to 37 *aṅgulas* in width with increments of 2 *aṅgulas*.

It may be pointed out that they are generally furnished with four legs, and castors are attached to the legs so that they may easily be moved from one place to another. The legs of royal couches should be decorated with lions. The roportion of breadth to length shows that couches are generally rectangular in shape.

Special mention is made of swings suspended from four chains, which are said to be used by the gods, the Brāhmaṇas, the Kshatriyas, etc.

The material of which couches and seats (*āsana*) are constructed is the wood of certain trees. For the legs special kinds of timber are recommended.

CHAPTER XLV

Thrones (*Siṁhāsana-lakshaṇa-vidhāna*)

The expression *siṁhāsana* implies a seat marked with a lion. This lion-seat or throne is made for the use of deities and kings. Royal thrones are divided into four classes. The *prathamāsana* is said to be fit for the first (*prathama* coronation, the *maṅgala* throne for the coronation called *maṅgala*. The *vīra*. throne for the *vīra*-coronation, and the *vijaya* throne for the *vijaya*-coronation What is evidently meant is that these four thrones are employed for the four successive stages of the coronation of one and the same king.

As for the deities, the *nityārchana* throne, as the name indicates, is used for daily worship, the *nityotsava* throne for ordinary festivities, the *viśeshārchana* throne for special worship; and the *mahotsava* throne for great festivals.

Next comes a further division of thrones into ten kinds. An account of the general plan as well as the measurements of the various parts of them is given in detail. They are technically called—*padmāsana*, *padma-keśara*, *padma-bhadra*, *śrībhadra*, *śrīviśāla*, *śrībandha*, *śrīmukha*, *bhadrāsana*, *padma-bandha* and *pāda-bandha* Nine kinds of dimensions are given to each of the above mentioned thrones. But the right proportion in each case should be selected by the application of the rules of *shaḍ-varga*.

Of the ten kinds, the first, *padmāsana*, is used as the throne for Śiva or Vishṇu, the *padma-keśara* for the [other] gods and for the *chakravartin*, the *padma-bhadra* for the *adhirāja* (i. e.. the *mahārāja*); the *śrībhadra* is suitable for the *adhirāja* and the *narendra*, the *śrīviśāla* for the *narendra* and the *pārshṇika*, the *śrībandha* for the *pārshṇika* and the *paṭṭadhara*, the *trimukha* for the *maṇḍaleśa*, the *bhadrāsana* for the *paṭṭabhāj*, the *padma-bandha* for the *prāharaka*, and the *pāda-bandha* throne for the *astragrāhin*. It is expressly stated that lion-shaped legs should not be made for the throne of the last class of kings. But in the case of all other kings, the thrones are marked with lions and furnished with six legs. They are generally placed facing the east. But the thrones of deities should face the four quarters.

At the end of the chapter the author says that the 'thrones of Vishṇu, Rudra, Jinaka, Indra, and all the [other] prominent gods, and also of the kings have thus been described.' It should be noticed that in the description itself no reference whatever is made to thrones of the Buddhist or Jain deities as the term Jinaka would seem to imply.

CHAPTER XLVI

Arches (*Toraṇa-vidhāna*)

The *toraṇa* or arch is stated to be an ornament for the thrones (*āsana*) of gods and kings. It is supported on dwarf pillars (*aṅghri*) which rest on the pedestal (*pīṭha*) of the image. The arch admits of various shapes. It may be circular triangular, crescent-shaped, bow-shaped or of any other suitable form. Directions for making these arches, as well as the measurements of their constituent parts are given in detail. With regard to their ornamentations, arches are divided into four kinds, technically called *patra-toraṇa* (foliated arch, *pushpa-toraṇa* (floral arch), *ratna-toraṇa* (jewelled arch), and *chitra-toraṇa* (ornamental arch).

The various ornaments of arches are then described in detail. The top of the *toraṇa* should be decorated with figures of the heavenly musicians, Tumburu and Nārada, while *makaras* (crocodiles) are placed at the sides. The arch is supported by leogryphs (*vyāli*) which are placed on both sides of the pillars. For the rest the *patra-toraṇa*, as the name indicates, is mainly adorned with foliated ornament the *pushpa-toraṇa* with flowers, and the *ratna-toraṇa* with jewels. Among the other decorative devices mentioned we find the effigies of different classes of semi-divine beings, such as *yakshas*, *vidyādharas*, *kinnaras* and *kinnarīs*. At the end of the chapter it is said that arches may also be made without any ornamentation (*chitra-hīna*).

CHAPTER XLVII

The Theatre (*Madhyaraṅga-vidhāna*)

In the first verse we meet with the expression *mukta-prapāṅga* which appears to be used in the same sense as *madhya-raṅga*. It is provided with dwarf pillars or pilasters (*aṅghri-pāda*), and consists of various other members (*masūraka*, *vedi*, *mañcha*, *kuṭṭima*, *upapīṭha*, etc.), and is decorated with *uttaras*, *vājanas*, *mushṭi-bandhas* and *lupās*. It should be furnished with four *bhadras* (or with one *bhadra*) and with eight or sixteen *kshudra-nāsis*. The upper portion is adorned with figures of leogryphs (*vyāli*) and crocodiles (*makara*). From the last but one verse of the chapter it is evident that there must be a close connection between the *mukta-prapāṅga*, on the one hand, and the *siṁhāsana*, the *makara-torana* and the *kalpa-vṛiksha*, on the other hand, the latter three subjects being discussed in the two immediately preceding and the following chapters.

From this verse it will be seen that the materials to be used for the *mukta-prapāṅga*, etc., are wood, stone, brick (terra-cotta ?) and various kinds of metal (*loha*, literally iron).

CHAPTER XLVIII

The ornamental tree (*Kalpa-vṛiksha-vidhāna*)

The name of the chapter is *Kalpa-vṛiksha* which literally means a mythical tree granting all wishes or, in other words, an all-productive tree. But here it is undoubtedly a decorative device surmounting a seat (*āsana*) or throne It is also mentioned in connection with the *mukta-prapāṅga*, the *maṇḍapa* and the *makara-toraṇa*.

The minute description and measurement of the various parts of the tree are given. Its trunk (*pāda*) is wound with a serpent, with expanded five-fold hood. The measurements of the snake, of its hood, and of its tail are described in detail. The number of branches as well as their size varies according to the special purpose of the throne, for the decoration of which the tree is meant. The tree is beautifully decorated with creepers, leaves, and flowers of various colours and forms. Jewels and garlands of pearls are inserted in suitable places. The figures of deities, *siddhas*, *vidyādharas*, monkeys, etc., are placed in the intervals between the branches.

Many other particulars regarding this ornamental tree are left to the discretion of the artist.

CHAPTER XLIX

Crowns and coronation (*Abhisheka-lakshaṇa-vidhāna*)

The chapter is divided into two parts: the first part describes the crowns of gods and kings, and the second deals with the ceremonies of the coronation of kings.

The chapter opens very unusually with the description of the lavish presents to be made to the architects. These gifts consist, among other things, of girls, wealth, land, houses, and servants, both male and female.

After this introduction there follows an enumeration of the various head-dresses used by gods and kings, namely, *jaṭā*, *mauli*, *kirīṭa*, *karaṇḍa*, *śirastraka*, *kuṇḍala* (*kuntala*?), *keśa-bandha*, *dhammilla*, *alaka*, *chūḍā*, *makuṭa* and *paṭṭa* (turban).

Of these the last-mentioned is subdivided into three kinds, called foliated, jewelled, and floral turbans (*patra-paṭṭa*, *ratna-paṭṭa*, and *pushpa-paṭṭa*).

The *jaṭā* (matted hair) and the *mukuṭa* (lit. diadem) are said to suit Brahmā and Śiva. The *kirīṭa* and *mukuṭa* are suited to Nārāyaṇa (i.e., Vishṇu). Other minor gods wear the *karaṇḍa* and *mukuṭa*. The love-goddess, Rati (Manonmanī), wears a *jaṭā*, *mauli*, *maṇḍala* or *kuṇḍala*. Sarasvatī and Sāvitrī put on a *keśa-bandha* and a *kuṇḍala*. All the female deities may wear a *karaṇḍa* or *mukuṭa*.

Among the kings, the *chakravartin* (*sārvabhauma*) and the *adhirāja* wear the *kirīṭa*. The *narendra* puts on a *karaṇḍa*, and the *pārshṇika* a *śirastraka*. But the *chakravartin* and other kings may wear a *karaṇḍa* or *mukuṭa*. The *patra-paṭṭa* is suited to the *paṭṭa-dhara*, the *ratna-paṭṭa* to the *pārshṇika*, the *pushpa-paṭṭa* to the *paṭṭabhāj*, and the *pushpa-mālya* (flower wreath) to the *prāhāraka* and the *astragrāha*.

The *kuṇḍala* (or *kuntala*) and *mukuṭa* are prescribed for the queen of a *chakravartin*, the *keśabandha* for the queens of an *adhirāja* and a *narendra*, the *dhammilla* and *kumuda-kuntala* for the queens of a *pārshṇika*, a *paṭṭadhara*, a *maṇḍaleśa* or a *paṭṭabhāj*, and the *alaka* and *chūḍā* for the queens of a *prāhāraka* and a *astragrāha*.

The height of a crown varies with the importance of the divine or royal bearers; it is set forth at considerable length. Next is described in detail the number of gold pieces and precious jewels in the crowns worn by the kings of various ranks and by their consorts. The forms of these crowns are then described.

The second part of the chapter deals with the royal coronation (*abhisheka*). In the coronation ceremonies of the *chakravartin* and other kings, four stages are prescribed, which are called *prathama* (here called *prāpta*), *maṅgala*, *vīra*, and *vijaya*. In this matter, too, the architects take a leading part. The *sthapati*, the *sthāpaka*, and the Brahmin priest perform the *aṅkurārpaṇa* and all other ceremonies ending with the *adhivāsana*. Afterwards the king is anointed with various auspicious substances. This is the *abhisheka* proper. The king is then adorned with the royal robes, the sacred thread, and various ornaments, and led to the coronation hall (*abhisheka-maṇḍapa*) which is furnished with the *madhya-raṅga*, the royal thrones, the wish-yielding-tree (*kalpavṛiksha*), the ornamental arch (*toraṇa*), and other emblems of empire.[1] The king and the queen take their places side by side on their thrones, the queen being on the left side of the king. The crown is held by the leading priests (*purohita-purogāḥ*); but it is actually placed on the king's head by the *sthapati* and the two *sthāpakas* at an auspicious moment during the pronouncement of *svasti* and other auspicious sounds. After this the king is garlanded, anointed, and besprinkled with various substances of good augury. Then the king mounts an elephant and circumambulates the city amidst acclamations of felicity. On the occasion of the entry into the palace a curious ceremony takes place in order to determine the success awaiting the new king, as well as the future prosperity of the kingdom. Various auspicious and inauspicious things are arranged in a hall in the palace. The king is led there blind-folded and has to pick up anything he chooses. The thing thus picked up by the blind-folded king points to the prosperity of the people and victory of the king, or the opposite.

'If the rice-porridge or rice be touched [by him], there will be an increase of rice. If the heap of corn is touched by the [royal] hand, there will be plenty of food (*subhiksha*). If gold and other precious metals be touched, it indicates that the subjects will prosper. If the sword or other weapons be touched, it bespeaks the king's prowess. It would be unfortunate for the whole kingdom, if any inauspicious things be touched by the king.'

The chapter closes with a recapitulation of the four forms of coronation, the directions as to the conduct of the ceremonial regal procession, and a reference to the authorities (*Vedas* and *Purāṇas*) under which the coronation ceremonies are prescribed.

CHAPTER L

The ornaments of the body and articles of furniture (*Bhūshaṇa-lakshaṇa-vidhāna*)

In the first verse it is announced that the chapter is devoted to a description of the ornaments of gods and kings. But in reality only the first part of

---

[1] Cf. HULTZSCH, *South Indian Inscriptions*, Vol. 1, p. 64, ll. 23—25, where in an Eastern Chalukya grant the *makaratoraṇa* is mentioned among the royal insignia. Professor HULTZSCH quotes SANDERSON'S *Canarese Dictionary*, where the word is explained as 'an honorary wreath or string of flowers, etc., raised upon poles and carried in front of one, as an emblem of distinction.'

the chapter deals with ornaments proper, and the remaining portion deals with certain miscellaneous articles of furniture, such as lamp-posts, fans, mirrors, swings, and so forth.

The first part is called 'ornaments of the body' (*aṅga-bhūshaṇa*), and the second 'external ornaments' (*bahir-bhūshaṇa*).

Ornaments proper are here divided into four classes, namely, *patra-kalpa*, *chitra-kalpa*, *ratna-kalpa*, and *miśrita*. All these are suited to the deities. The emperor or universal monarch (*chakravartin*, *sārvabhauma*) can put on all these ornaments excepting the *patra-kalpa*. The *adhirāja* and *narendra* can wear both the *ratna-kalpa* and the *miśrita*. The *miśra-kalpa* is prescribed for all other kings.

The *patra-kalpa* ornaments are so called, because they show foliated decoration. The *chitra-kalpa* kind consists of floral and foliated designs, precious stones, and *nāṭaka*. The *ratna-kalpa* variety is made of flowers and jewels. The *miśra-kalpa* decoration consists of leaves and jewels, and, in short, a mixture of all others. These four kinds, it should be observed, are specially made for the images of gods and kings only.

The following is a list of the personal ornaments mentioned in the course of the chapter:

Kirīṭa—a diadem, a crown.
Śiro-vibhūshaṇa—a head-ornament.
Chūḍāmaṇi—a crest-jewel.
Kuṇḍala—an ear-ring.
Tāṭaṅka (or *tāḍaṅka*)—a kind of ear-ornament.
Makara-bhūshaṇa—an ear-pendant decorated with *makaras* (*makarāṅkita-kuṇḍala*).
Kaṅkaṇa—a bracelet.
Keyūra, *kaṭaka*—an armlet worn on the upper-arm.
Valaya—an armlet worn round the upper-arm (*bāhumūle*) or on the fore-arm (*prakoshṭha*).
Maṇi-bandha-kalāpa[1]—a jewelled ornament worn on the fore-arm.
Kiṅkiṇī-valaya—a bracelet (or anklet) fitted with little bells.
Aṅgulīyaka—a finger-ring.
Ratnāṅgulīyaka—a jewelled finger-ring.

[1] Cf. *mukta-kalāpa* (*Kumāra-sambhava* I, 48).

Hāra[1] } a string of pearls worn round the neck.
Ardha-hāra }

Mālā—a garland or necklace hanging down from both shoulders.

Vana-mālā—a garland of wild flowers (?).

Nakshatra-mālā[2]—a necklace of 27 pearls.

Dāman—a garland or string worn round the shoulders.

Stana-sūtra } a cord or chain worn round the breasts.
Suvarṇa-sūtra }

Pura-sūtra—a cord or chain worn round the chest.

Udara-bandha—a girdle worn round the waist.

Kaṭi-sūtra—a cord or chain worn round the loins.

Mekhalā—a girdle, a belt.

Suvarna-kañchuka- a golden cuirass (or bodice?).

Nūpura—an anklet.

Valaya—a bracelet.

Pāda-jāla-bhūshaṇa—a net-like ornament worn on the feet.[3]

The following articles, which are reckoned to belong to the 'external' ornaments (*bahirbhūshaṇa*), are described in great detail: (1) the *dīpa-daṇḍa* (lamp-post); (2) the *vyajana* (fan); (3) the *darpaṇa* (mirror); (4) the *mañjūshā* (basket, chest, box); (5) the *dolā* (swing or palanquin); (6) the *tulā* (balance) of kings; and (7) the *pañjara* (cage), *nīḍa* (nest) for domestic animals and birds.

The lamp posts (*dīpa-daṇḍa*)[4] are of two kinds, the stationary, placed in front of the house, and the movable. The former are made of wood, iron or stone, the latter of wood or iron. They may be square, octagonal, or circular in shape. The *vedikā* (platform) or the pedestal at the bottom of these is generally shaped like a lotus. Lamp-posts generally taper from the bottom upwards. Various other parts and also the mouldings of lamp-posts are described in detail. Their measurements are also given.

---

[1] According to *Bṛihat-saṁhitā*, LXXXII, 32, a chain of 108 strings is styled a *hāra* and a chain of 64 strings an *ardhahāra*. KERN's *Verspr. Geschr.* vol. II, p. 101.

[2] A *nakshatramālā* (lit. a star-cluster) consists of 27 pearls in accordance with the number of *nakshatras* or lunar mansions. Cf. *Bṛihat-saṁhitā*, LXXXII, 34

[3] A few more terms of uncertain meaning are mentioned, namely: *viśeshika* (=*tilaka*?), *bālapaṭṭa*, *chūlikā*, *pārimā*, *keśahūṭaka* and *mallikā*.

[4] In literature we find the evidently synonymous expression *dīpavṛiksha* (*lit.* lamp-tree). *Mahābh.* XII, 7204; XIV, 1787. *Rām.* (ed. GORRESIO) II, 5, 18; *Buddhacharita* (ed. COWELL), V, 44. Monumental lamp pillars of stone, now-a-days designated by the name of *dīpdān*, are found especially in the South of India. Cf. FERGUSSON, *History of Indian and Eastern Architecture*, Revised edition, vol. I, pp. 347 sq. and II, 81.

The fan-post (*vyajana-daṇḍa*) as well as the fan itself is described in a like manner. These posts are made of timber or iron, but the fans appear to be made of leather.

Nine alternative measurements are prescribed for the mirror, namely, from 5 (or 6) *aṅgulas* up to 21 (or 22) *aṅgulas*. Mirrors should be quite circular (*suvṛitta*) with the edge a little raised. The surface must be perfectly bright, the rim being decorated with linear ornament (*rekhā*) and the reverse with the figures of Lakshmī and others. An account of the various parts is given in detail.

Three kinds of *mañjūshas* are described in detail. They are made of either timber or iron, and are square, rectangular or circular in shape. They generally consist of one, two or three compartments or chambers (*koshṭha*). The *parṇa-mañjūshā* looks like a box or trunk. The *taila* (oil) *mañjūsha* is apparently a receptacle for oil. It does not differ from the other, except in its greater height. The third kind is called *vastra-mañjūshā* and is easily identified with a wardrobe or linen-chest. Its breadth is said to vary from one to three cubits, the height and length being proportionate to the breadth.

The word *dolā* means both a swing and a palanquin. But as the description opens with the statement that the height of the post or pillar (*pāda*) varies from three to eight cubits, there can be little doubt that the passage refers to a swing. We may assume that the *phalaka*, which is repeatedly mentioned in this connection, must be the swing-board. The swing is said to be used by both gods and men.

The balance[1] consists of the horizontal balancing rod or beam, the strings by which the scale pans are suspended, and the scale pans themselves. The two pans are made of iron, the rod of timber or iron, and the *jihvā* (lit tongue) and the *toraṇa* (lit. arch) are always made of iron. The various parts of the balance are described minutely together with their measurements.

A large portion of the chapter is devoted to a description of cages (*pañjara*). A number of birds and other animals are enumerated, and the size

[1] From the description given in the text it may be conjectured that 'the royal balance' in question was meant to be used by kings in performing the ceremony of having themselves weighed against gold and precious stones which were afterwards distributed among the Brāhmaṇas. This ceremony, known as *tulā-purusha-dāna*, was performed on certain special occasions, such as the coronation, or on the day of a solar or lunar eclipse, or on New Year's day. Cf. A. H. LONGHURST, The *tulā-purusha-dāna monument at Hampi*. *Annual Report Archaeological Survey of India* for 1912—13, pp. 142 sqq., plates LXXXIV.

of the cage in which they are kept is given, the measurements admitting in each instance of nine different varieties. The following is a complete list:—

	Size of cage	Increment
Mṛiga-nābhi-biḍāla (musk cat?) ...	1—2 *hastas*	3 *aṅgulas*.
Suka (parrot)	9—23 *aṅgulas* [1]	2 ..
Chātaka (rains-cuckoo or cuculus melanoleucus)	7—23 ..	2 ,,
Chakora (partridge or perdix rufa) ...	7—23 ,,	2 ,,
Marāla (a crow-phesant, ? a goose or duck)	7—23 ,,	2 ,,
Pārāvata (turtle dove)	7—23 ,,	2 ,,
Nīlakaṇṭha (roller)	25—73 ,,	6 ,,
Kuñjarīya (ground-man)... ...	5—21 ,,	2 ,,
Khañjarīṭa (?)	7—23 ,,	2 ,,
Kukkuṭa (cock)	15—31 ,,	2 ,,
Kulāla (phasianus gallus) ...	15—31 ,,	2 ,,
Nakula (mongoose, viverra ichneumon)	11—27 ,,	2 ,,
Tittiri (francolin partridge) ...	7—23 ,,	2 ,,
Godhāra (?)	9—25 ,,	2 ,,
Vyāghra (tiger)	1½—3½ *hastas*	6 ,,

CHAPTER LI

The Triad (*Trimūrti-lakshaṇa-vidhāna*)

The Indian Triad, to which the title of the chapter refers, consists of the three great gods, Brahmā, Vishṇu and Śiva. The chapter may be divided into two parts. The first part deals with the materials (*dravya*) of which the idols of all other deities as well as of these three are made. The second part describes the external features of the Triad.

The materials for making idols are nine, namely, gold, silver, copper (*tāmra*), stone, wood, *sudhā* (stucco, also mortar and plaster), *śarkarā* (*lit.* gravel or grit), *ābhāsa* (marble) and earth (terra-cotta). All the materials enumerated are well known except *ābhāsa*, of which a special description is given.

Ābhāsa is subdivided into three kinds, called *chitra*, *ardha-chitra*, and *ābhāsa* proper. If it is perfectly transparent (*sarvāṅga-dṛiśyamāna*, *lit*, which can be completely seen through) it is called *chitra*; if only half transparent, it is known as *ardha-chitra*; and in case it is partially (*lit.* one fourth) transparent,

[1] Evidently there is a mistake here in the figures, which would yield only eight varieties of size. Another mistake seems to the size of cages, which in many cases is absurdly small.

it is called *ābhāsa* proper. This description, however, does not help us to identify *ābhāsa* with any certainty. It may have some affinity to crystal, but the latter has been referred to elsewhere by its own common name, *sphaṭika*. The ordinary meaning of the word *ābhāsa* is splendour, light, transparency. It implies undoubtedly a transparent substance. I am inclined to think that it may refer to some particular and more or less transparent variety of marble (alabaster ?), of which various other kinds, such as white, black, red, yellow, etc., are described in the next chapter in connection with the materials of which the *pīṭha* or *yoni* part of the phallus (*liṅga*) of Śiva is made.

The second part begins with an account of the different classes of images. An idol may be stationary (*sthāvara*) or movable (*jaṅgama*); erect, sitting or recumbent. The movable images are used especially on the occasion of festivals. The three or four poses (*bhaṅga*), called *ābhaṅga*, *samabhaṅga*, and *tribhaṅga*, are discussed more fully at the end of chapter LXVII.

The remaining portion of the chapter is devoted to a minute description of the images of Brahmā, Vishṇu and Śiva, the three gods constituting the *Trimūrti*.

Brahmā should have four arms and four faces. He should wear a diadem and the matted hair of an ascetic (*jaṭā-mukuṭa-maṇḍita*). Two of his hands should be in the gift-bestowing (*varada*) and refuge-granting (*abhaya*) attitudes. The four attributes held in his hands are the water-pot (*kuṇḍika*), the rosary (*aksha-mālā*), and the large and small sacrificial ladles (*sruk-sruva*). The various ornaments, with which his body is to be adorned, are described in great detail. As to his clothes, he is said to wear a strip of bark (*chīra*) and an upper garment (*uttarīya*). His whole body should be of golden colour. Brahmā is accompanied by his two Śaktis (female energies), the goddesses Sarasvatī and Sāvitrī, standing to his right and left respectively.

Vishṇu is also four-armed (*chatur-bhuja*), but has one head. His head-gear is the diadem called *kirīṭa*. He wears a yellow garment, while the colour of his body is dark blue (*śyāma*). His chest is adorned with the symbol called *śrīvatsa*. Two of his hands are in the gift-bestowing and refuge-granting attitudes. His attributes are the lotus-flower, the mace (*gadā*), the discus (*chakra*), and the conch-shell called *Pāñchajanya*. Among the numerous ornaments which bedeck his limbs, special mention is made of the graceful garland of wild flowers (*vana-mālā*) which hangs down by both his legs. At the back of his head there is an ornamental nimbus (*śiraś-chakra*, lit., a head-disc). Vishṇu is likewise attended by two goddesses (*Śakti*), apparently Lakshmī and Bhū-devī (the Earth-goddess).

Śiva, the third member of the Triad, is four-armed and is, moreover, distinguished by a third eye, which is placed in the middle of his fore-head. Like Brahmā, he wears the matted hair of the ascetic. The figure of Gaṅgā (the river personified) as well as the crescent are inserted in his head-dress, the latter on the left side. On the left side of his neck there is the mark of the deadly poison *kālakūta*. His dress consists of a tiger-skin reaching down to the knees, and a waist-cloth. His complexion is said to be red.[1] Two of his hands are in the attitude of granting a boon (*vara*) and of conferring security (*abhaya*). In the remaining two hands he holds an antelope (*hariṇa*) and a tabor or hand-drum.[2] Śiva is accompanied by the goddess Pārvatī who keeps standing or seated on his left side.

Images of the three members of the triad are said to be measured in the largest type of the *daśa-tāla* measurement and those of their consorts in the middle type. The particulars of these two types of measurement are not discussed here, but reserved for an elaborate treatment in two separate chapters.

The pedestals are also dealt with in a separate chapter. Here it is very briefly stated that the pedestals of the triad should be of the *padma-pīṭha* or the *mahā-pīṭha* kind, and be furnished with a *prapā* (canal), a *toraṇa* (ornamental arch), and *kalpa-vṛiksha* (ornamental tree).

The chapter closes with a statement that the particulars not mentioned here with regard to the making of these idols, should be supplied according to the rules of the *Śāstras*.

CHAPTER LII

The Phallus (*Liṅga-vidhāna*)[3]

Various classifications of phalli are given. They are classified first into, six heads—*śaiva*, *pāśupata*, *kāla-mukha*, *mahāvrata*, *vāma*, and *bhairava*; secondly into four—*samakarṇa*, *vardhamāna*, *śivāṅka*, and *svastika*, fit to be worshipped by Brāhmaṇas, Kshatriyas, Vaiśyas, and Śūdras respectively; thirdly into four with regard to height —*jāti*, *chhanda*, *vikalpa*, and *ābhāsa*; fourthly into

---

[1] Elsewhere the complexion of Śiva is stated to be white.

[2] The name of the second attribute which occurs also in the iconographic portion of the 7th chapter, appears to be *ḍhakkā*. But this word usually indicates a large kettle-drum, whereas the tabor which is one of Śiva's emblems is called *ḍamaru*.

[3] The phallus worship is very popular in India: this is unmistakably proved by the fact that the number of *liṅgas* or phalli in India is estimated at thirty millions of which the best known are Viśveśvara at Benares, Somanātha in Gujarāt, Mahākāla at Ujjayinī, etc.

three types, with regard to width—*nāgara*, *drāviḍa*, and *vesara*; fifthly into four—*daivika*, *mānusha*, *gāṇava*, and *ārsha*, the four together being called *svayambhū*[1] or *udbhūta*; sixthly into two — *ātmārtha* (for one's own worship), and *parārtha* (*lit.* for others, for public worship); again into two-*ekaliṅga* (single), and *bahu-liṅga* (phalli in a group); or into many kinds—*vajra*, *suvarṇa*, etc., with regard to the material; and lastly into two—*kshaṇika* (for temporary worship) as contrasted with the permanent *liṅga*. All these kinds of phalli are described at great length. Various alternative measurements are prescribed for each of them. In some cases as many as thirty-six alternative heights are suggested. But in most cases their number is nine. The nine alternative heights of the phallus are determined in some cases by a comparison with different parts of the body of the worshipper (*yajamāna*). The height of the phallus may reach the worshipper's sex-organ, navel, heart, breast, arm-joint (*bāhu-sīmānta*), chin, nose, eye, or be equal to his full length. Another comparative measurement is given with regard to the *garbha-gṛiha* (the cella of the temple in which the phallus is enshrined). Various absolute measurements also are given in some cases. These measurements vary according to the four classes, *jāti*, *chhanda*, *vikalpa*, and *ābhāsa*, mentioned above. In the *jāti* class the height may vary from 1 to 9 cubits (*hasta*), the increment being 1 *hasta*. The *chhanda* class admits of nine varieties, namely, from ¾ to 6¾ cubits, the increment in this case being ¾ *hasta*. In the third class (*vikalpa*) the height varies from 1 to 4½ *hastas* with increments of ½ *hasta*, and in the fourth class (*ābhāsa*) from ¼ to 2¼ *hastas* with increments of ¼ *hasta*. Thus each of the four said classes admits of nine varieties of height. The breadth of the phallus is in like manner discussed at great length. The impracticability of so many alternative measurements is, however, removed by the application of the rules of *āyādi-shaḍvarga*, which are described in detail at the end of the chapter.

The second part deals with the *pīṭha* which is the stand upon which the phallus proper is placed. The *praṇāla* (*lit.* canal, drain) or *yoni-dvāra*, and all other parts of the *pīṭha* are described in detail, together with their measurements. The same subject is discussed in greater detail in the next chapter. The general appearance of a phallus is well-known; the *Mānasāra* does not deviate much from it. The *mūla* or the lower part, technically called *Brahma-bhāga*, says our author, is square (*chatur-asra*, lit., four-cornered), whereas the middle part, called *Vishṇu-bhāga*, is octagonal (*ashṭāgrābha*), and the upper part, called *Śiva-bhāga*, is round.

[1] The term *svayambhū* (self-existent, self-created) indicates natural objects of worship. Such *svayambhū-liṅgas* are even to this day worshipped at several *tīrthas* of Kāśmīr. Cf. *Kalhaṇa's Rājataraṅgiṇī*, a chronicle of the kings of Kāśmīr, translated by M. A. STEIN, vol. I. p. 22 (note I, 113).

But these shapes of the three parts may be interchanged in some cases. The top is sometimes shaped like a bud (*kuḍmala*) or a leaf (*pattra*).[1]

The phallus proper and the *pīṭha* are generally made of the same material. But when they are made of very precious substances, such as jewels, gold, etc., the material of the two may differ. The *pīṭha* is mostly made of marbles of various colours such as white, red, yellow, black, etc. Precious stones are inserted in the different parts of the phallus.

The chapter closes with an account of the various fruits to be derived from phallus worship, and of the formulas of the *āyādi-shaḍvarga*.

CHAPTER LIII

The Pedestal of the Phallus (*Pīṭha-lakshaṇa-vidhāna*)

It has been pointed out in the previous chapter that the *pīṭha*[2] forms the *yoni* or the lower part of the phallus. The *pīṭha* must match the phallus of which it forms the lower member. There must, consequently, be as many kinds of *pīṭhas* as there are of the phalli. But the mouldings of the *pīṭha* are described under four classes, technically called, *bhadra-pīṭha*, *trībhadra*, *śrīviśāla*, and *upapīṭha*. The principal parts of the *pīṭha* are the *nāla* (*lit.* canal), the *jala-dhārā* (*lit.* drain), the *ghṛita-vāri*, the *nimna*, and the *paṭṭikā*. These are, it may be observed, the various parts of which an ordinary *yoni* (female organ) is formed. The name of the principal mouldings are the following: *prathama* or *janman*, *padma*, *kshepaṇa*, *kandhara*, *kampa*, *ūrdhva-padma*, *vājana*, *ghṛita-vāri*, and *vṛitta-kumbha*.

A minute description and measurement of all these and other mouldings of *pīṭhas* of various kinds are given in detail. With regard to their shape, the *pīṭhas*, like the phalli (and, in fact, all other architectural and sculptural objects), are divided into three types, *nāgara*, *drāviḍa*, and *vesara*. The *pīṭhas* of the *nāgara* class are said to be square, those of the *drāviḍa* type are octagonal, and the *vesara* ones are round (*vṛitta*).

CHAPTER LIV

The female deities (*Śakti-lakshaṇa-vidhāna*)

The following female deities are specially described: Sarasvatī, the goddess of learning; Sāvitrī; Lakshmī the goddess of wealth or fortune; Mahī, the

[1] A variant reading gives *chhattra* (an umbrella).

[2] The term *pīṭha* means a stool, seat, chair, throne, pedestal, an altar. The well-known fifty-one *Pīṭha-sthānas* are the sacred spots where the parts of the body of Satī (Pārvatī), the consort of Śiva, fell after she had been cut to pieces by the discus of Vishṇu. As the *liṅga* or phallus symbolically represents Śiva, so the *pīṭha* does his consort Pārvatī.

earth-goddess; Manonmanī, the goddess of love; Durgā; and the the Seven Mothers (*Sapta-mātṛi*) collectively so called. Of these, Lakshmī is distinguished into Mahā- (or the great) Lakshmī, and Sāmānyā (the ordinary) Lakshmī, the latter being installed in all the family chapels. The Seven Mothers consist of Vārāhī, Kaumārī, Chāmuṇḍā, Bhairavī, Māhendrī, Vaishṇavī, and Brahmāṇī. These seven goddesses are measured in the *nava-tāla* system, and all other female deities in the *daśa-tāla* system. The details of those measurements are discussed in two separate chapters, wherein the comparative measurements of the several parts of the various limbs of the body are given. It may be pointed out here that according to the *daśa-tāla* system the whole length of the body is ten times the face, while in the *nava-tāla*, it is nine times, and hence in the *ashṭa-tāla* it should be eight times the face, and so forth.

The characteristic attributes and poses, and the ornaments, decorations, etc., of each of these female deities are described in detail.

The goddess Sarasvatī is represented as seated on a lotus-seat. Her complexion is white like crystal. She is four-armed; in her two right hands she holds a *saṁdarśa*[1] and a rosary (*aksha-mālā*), and in her two left hands a book (*pustaka*) and a water-pot (*kuṇḍika*). There exists, however, also a two-handed variety of the Sarasvatī image. Her ornaments, which are described in detail, include ear-pendants of the type called *grāha-kuṇḍala* (*makara-kuṇḍala*).

Sāvitrī, who is seated on a lotus-seat to the left of Brahmā, may be white and red (*śveta-rakta*) or dark blue (*śyāma*). She has two arms and two eyes, in other words, she assumes a purely human shape. She holds a blue lotus-flower (*utpala*) in her right hand, while her left hand is stretched out in the pose of granting a boon (*vara*). Sāvitrī too is adorned with various ornaments.

Lakshmī, the goddess of good fortune, looks benign (*prasanna-vadanā*); her complexion is like pure gold. She has four arms. Her upper right hand is raised in the attitude of granting security (*abhaya*), and in her other right hand she holds either a red lotus flower (*padma*) or a rosary. The attributes held in her left hands are a tabor or hand-drum (*ḍiṇḍima*) and a blue or red lotus flower. As befits the goddess of luck, she is bedecked with gorgeous ornaments and jewels.

In contradistinction with 'the Great Lakshmī' (Mahā-Lakshmī) thus described, the 'ordinary' Lakshmī is said to have only two hands in each of which she holds a red lotus flower (*rakta-padma*). Her distinguishing feature is that she is placed between two elephants with uplifted trunks. A brief account is given about representations of Lakshmī as the spouse of Vishṇu.

---

[1] Should we read it *ādarśa* (mirror)? The regular attribute of Sarasvatī, however, is the lute (*vīṇā*).

The Earth-goddess (*Mahī-śakti*), who is placed on the other side of Vishṇu, is said to be two-armed and two eyed. In her right hand she holds a blue lotus (*utpala*); with her left hand she indicates the granting of a gift. She has a dark blue (*śyāma*) complexion and wears *makara* ear-rings.

Durgā, also called Gaurī and Pārvatī, the consort of Śiva, is two-armed. She holds a blue lotus in her right hand and her left hand is in the pose of granting a gift (*vara*). She is distinguished by all the marks of female beauty and is profusely adorned with ornaments. She has a dark blue (*śyāma*) complexion and wears yellow garments. She is placed to the left of Śiva, or of his symbol, the *liṅga*.

Manonmanī, the goddess of love, is four-armed and three-eyed. Strange to say, her hair-dress is said to be the matted hair (*jaṭā*) of an ascetic. Two of her hands are in the attitude of assuming protection (*abhaya*) and of granting a boon (*vara*). In each of the two other hands she holds a lotus-flower. Her complexion is red and white (*śveta-rakta*) or dark blue (*śyāma*). It appears that this Śakti also is reckoned as belonging to the retinue of Śiva, in whose temple she is worshipped.

Finally, the Seven Mothers are described. In general these Śaktis have the same emblems and distinguishing features as their male counterparts. Brahmāṇī and Rudrāṇī, for instance, who are the Śaktis of Brahmā and Rudra (or Śiva) respectively wear the matted hair of the ascetics. Brahmāṇi has four faces and four hands, in two of which she holds a rosary (*aksha-mālā*) and a water-pot (*kuṇḍika*). Rudrāṇī has a white complexion, her attributes are the antelope (*hariṇa*) and the noose (*pāśa*). Vaishṇavī and Vārāhī, who are both Śaktis of Vishṇu, are distinguished by a dark blue (*śyāma*) complexion and hold the discus (*chakra*) and conch-shell (*śaṅkha*), which are the well-known emblems of Vishṇu. Vārāhī has a boar's head.

The chapter closes with a very brief reference to the plumb-lines which are more fully treated in a separate chapter.

CHAPTER LV

The Jain Images (*Jaina-lakshaṇa-vidhāna*)

The opening lines describe in detail the various kinds of measurements used in Indian sculpture.

The linear measurement is divided into six kinds, *māna*, *pramāṇa*, *parimāṇa*, *lamba-māna*, *unmāna*, and *upamāna*.

The measurement from the foot to the top of the head is called *māna* which is in fact nothing but height. *Pramāṇa* is the measurement of breadth (*vistāra*);

parimāṇa is the measurement of girth or circumference (*paritaḥ*); *lamba-māna* is the measurement along the plumb-line or the line drawn perpendicularly through the different parts of the body, the *māna* or the measurement of the height being determined by the surface of the body; *unmāna* is the measurement of thickness (*nimna*) or diameter; and *upamāna* is the measurement of interspace (*antara*), such as that between the two feet of an image; this measurement is evidently taken from one plumb line to another.

The primary measurement (*ādi-māna*) refers to comparative measurement and is divided into nine kinds. The height of an image is determined 1st, by comparing it with the breadth (*tāra*) of the whole temple (*harmya*); 2ndly, with the height of the cella or sanctum (*garbha-gṛiha*); 3rdly, with the height of the door (*dvāra-māna*); 4thly, with the measurement of the base (*adhishṭhāna*); 5thly, by expressing it in *hastas*; 6thly, in the *tāla* system; 7thly, in *aṅgulas*; 8thly, by comparing it with the height of the worshipper; and 9thly, with the height of the riding-animal (*vāhana*) or with the height of the principal idol (*mūla-bera*).

Absolute measurement in cubits (*hasta*), etc., is given in the case of many architectural and sculptural objects.

The *aṅgula* (lit. finger) measurement has reference to both comparative and absolute measurements. Three kinds of *aṅgulas* are expressly distinguished, and a fourth *aṅgula* is added later.

(*a*) The *berāṅgula* is the measurement taken by the *aṅgula* or finger of the main idol.

(*b*) The *mānāṅgula* refers to the ordinary absolute measurement in *aṅgulas*, one *aṅgula* being equal to eight *yavas* (barley grains) or ¾ of an English inch.

(*c*) The *mātrāṅgula* is the measurement determined by the length of the digit and the width of the middle finger in the right hand of the master (*kartṛi*).

(*d*) Another kind of *aṅgula* measurement is determined by dividing the whole length of the body of an image into a number of equal parts each of which is called a *deha-labdhāṅgula* or simply *dehāṅgula*. In the last sense, *aṅgula* is used to mean simply a part. Thus both *aṅgula* and part (*aṁśa*) are indiscriminately used throughout the work. If the length, etc., of a building or image is divided into a number of equal parts for some special purpose, each of them is called *aṅgula* or *aṁśa* indiscriminately. This lack of discrimination has been very confusing in many places, rendering it extremely hard to distinguish an absolute measurement from a comparative one.

The height of the image is determined by comparing it with the height of the worshipper (*yajamāna*). It may be of nine kinds, according as it extends from the foot of the worshipper to his sex-organ, navel, heart, breast, arms, chin, tip of the nose, hair limit (on the forehead), or to his full height. The *tālamāna* admits of many varieties: the ten *tāla* measurements vary from one *tāla* to ten *tāla*; each of these is again divided into three types, the *uttama* or the largest, the *madhyama* or the intermediate, and the *adhama* or the smallest. Thus an image is of the *daśa-tāla* measurement when its whole length is equal to ten times the face inclusive of head. In the largest type of the *daśa-tāla* system, the whole length is divided into 124 equal parts which are proportionately distributed over the different limbs of the body; in the intermediate type, the whole length is divided into 120 equal parts, and in the smallest type, into 116 equal parts. In the *nava-tāla* system, the whole length would be nine times the face, in the *ashṭa-tāla*, eight times, and so forth. Several of these *tāla* measures are described in detail in the subsequent chapters.

The varieties of the alternative measurements in each case are simplified by the application of the rules of *āyādi-shaḍ-varga*.

The main object of the chapter, namely, the description of the Jain deities, is thus submerged in a lengthy discussion of the various measurements used both in architecture and sculpture.

Like all other idols, the images of Jain deities too may be stationary or movable; they may be in the erect or in the sitting posture. They have a purely human shape, and wear neither robes nor ornaments. On the chest the *śrīvatsa* symbol is marked in gold. They are placed on a throne decorated with the *makara-toraṇa*, and the ornamental tree (*kalpa-vṛiksha*), and are attended by Nārada and other sages, by Yakshas, Vidyādharas, Siddhas, Nāgendras, and Lokapālas, etc. All these attendants, it should be observed, are also known as Hindu deities.

The twenty-four Tîrthaṅkaras or Jain saints, are referred to but not specified.[1]

CHAPTER LVI

The Buddhist images (*Bauddha-lakshaṇa-vidhāna*)

The account of these images too is very meagre. Evidently the author had in mind solely effigies of Buddha, not of other Buddhist deities. This is clear from his description. These figures, he says, which may be either erect or in the sitting posture, are placed on a throne (*siṁhāsana*) and are distinguished by the *aśvattha* tree as well as by the *kalpa-vṛiksha* or mythic wonder-tree. The latter, as we have seen, is represented in connection with other divine beings as well, but

[1] Cf. James Burgess, *Digambara Jaina Iconography*, *Indian Antiquary*, vol. XXXII, pp. 459 sqq., for the full list of the Jain Saints; see also the writer's Dictionary of Hindu Architecture,

the *aśvattha* or ficus religiosa is characteristic of Buddha, as the Bodhi-tree under which he attained enlightenment (*Bodhi*) belongs to that species. Another peculiar mark of Buddha, which has been duly noted by the author, is the *ushṇīsha* or protuberance of the skull (*ushṇīshojjvala-maulika*).[1] For the rest the appearance of Buddha is purely human. He has a full face, a long nose, smiling eyes and elongated ears. His body is fleshy, his chest broad, his belly round and his arms long. He wears a yellow garment (*pītāmbara-dhara*) and his complexion is white. Like other idols, the Buddha images are made of wood, stone or iron (*loha*). They are measured according to the largest type of the *daśa-tāla* system.

CHAPTER LVII

Images of sages (*Muni-lakshaṇa-vidhāna*)

The seven well-known patriarchs or sages (*ṛishi* or *muni*) are taken to illustrate the three varieties of the *tāla* measurement. They are Agastya, Kāśyapa, Bhṛigu, Vasishṭha, Bhārgava, Viśvāmitra, and Bharadvāja.

Agastya is bright blue (*śyāma*) in colour, Kāśyapa yellow (*pīta*), Bhṛigu dark or black (*kṛishṇa*), Vasishṭha red (*rakta*), Bhārgava brownish (*piṅgala*), Viśvāmitra red (*rakta*), and Bharadvāja yellow (*hāridra*, lit. turmeric-coloured). They are represented in a purely human shape, being 'two-armed and two-eyed'; they wear yellow garments and the sacred thread (*yajña-sūtra*) and are distinguished by the matted hair of the ascetics (*jaṭājūṭa*). In their two hands they hold a staff (*daṇḍa*) and a book (*pustaka*). Of Agastya who is mentioned first among the seven sages, it is stated particularly that he is corpulent (*bṛihat-kukshi*) and hump-backed (*kubjākāra*).

Of these seven sages, Agastya is measured in the seven-*tāla*, Kāśyapa and Bhṛigu in the eight-*tāla*, and the rest in the nine-*tāla*. The details of these three *tāla* measurements are given subsequently.

In the *sapta* or seven-*tāla* measurement, the whole length of the image is seven times the height of the face which is generally twelve *aṅgulas* (9 inches) in the Indian system. This length is divided into $12 \times 7 = 84$ equal parts, of which the proportional distribution among the different limbs is explained at great length.

In the *ashṭa* or eight-*tāla* system, the whole length is similarly divided into 96 equal parts, and in the nine-*tāla* into 108 equal parts.

---

[1] The *ūrṇā* or mark between the brows, which is another distinguishing feature of Buddha, is not noticed in the course of this description.

CHAPTER LVIII

Images of Yakshas, Vidyādharas, etc., (*Yaksha-vidyādhara-vidhāna*)

The present chapter deals briefly with four classes of semi-divine beings, namely, Yakshas, Vidyādharas, Gandharvas, and Kinnaras. They are said to have two arms and two eyes, in other words, they assume a purely human appearance. They are adorned with the crown known by the name of *karaṇḍa*. The colour of the Yakshas is stated to be dark blue (*śyāma*) and yellow (*pīta*), that of the Vidyādharas dark red (*śyāma-rakta*) and yellow. The images both of the Yakshas and the Vidyādharas are measured according to the *nava-tāla* system. The Yakshas are distinguished from the Rākshasas, the latter being evil spirits, while the former are regarded as supernatural beings of a benevolent and inoffensive disposition. The Yakshas act as attendants (*anuchara*) and chowry-bearers of the gods. The Vidyādharas are a kind of fairies possessed of magical power. Here apparently they are described as Atlantes. The Gandharvas are celestial choirs, and celebrated as musicians.

The description of the Kinnaras is contained in a Mālini stanza at the end of the chapter. "The legs are like those of an animal, the upper part of the body is like that of a man, the face is like that of Garuḍa (the bird of Vishṇu) and the arms are provided with wings. He is adorned with a diadem and a red lotus, has the beautiful hue of a flower, and holds a lute (*vīṇā*). These are the characteristic features of the Kinnara."[1]

CHAPTER LIX

Images of devotees (*Bhakta-lakshaṇa-vidhāna*).

Devotees are divided into four classes according to the four stages of holiness, and are called *sālokya*, *sāmīpya*, *sārūpya*, and *sayujya*.[2] *Sālokya* is the result of devotion (*bhakti*), knowledge (*jñāna*) and renunciation (*vairāgya*). Knowledge combined with renunciation leads to *sāmīpya*. *Sārupya* is produced in the worshipper by meditation alone, and *sāyujya* is attained by the true knowledge (of God).

The images of the *sālokya* class of worshippers are measured in the largest type of the *nava-tāla* system, in which the whole length is divided into 112(?) equal parts. Those of the *sāmīpya* class are measured in the smallest type of the

---

[1] It may be noticed that the body of the *kinnara* is a combination of the bodies of a man, an animal and a bird.

[2] The *sālokyādi-chatushṭaya* is also mentioned in the *Bhāgavata-purāṇa*, IX, 4, 67. The literal meaning of the four terms in question is: dwelling in the same world (*viz.*, as the deity), dwelling in the vicinity (of the deity), being in conformity (with the deity), and being united (with the deity)

daśa-tāla system, in which the whole length is divided into 116 equal parts. Those of the *sārūpya* class are measured in the intermediate type of the *daśa-tāla* system, in which the whole length is divided into 120 equal parts. And the figures of the *sārūpya* class are measured in the largest type of the *daśa-tāla* system, in which the whole length is divided into 124 equal parts.

The first two systems, namely, the largest type of the *nava-tāla* and the smallest type of the *daśa-tāla*, are minutely described in this chapter. The other two systems, that is, the intermediate and the largest types of the *daśa-tāla*, are treated subsequently in two separate chapters.

CHAPTER LX

Riding animals of the Gods: the Goose (*Vāhana-vidhāne Haṁsa-lakshaṇa*)

The chapter opens with the announcement that the *vāhanas* of the Triad (*Trimūrti*) will now be described. But only one of them, namely, the Goose (*haṁsa*), is described in this chapter, the other three, the Garuḍa, the Bull, and the Lion being described in the next three chapters. In these four chapters, the term *vāhana* is used to designate the various animals and birds used by the gods and goddesses for riding.

The goose is the *vāhana* of Brahmā. The limbs of the goose are said to be measured in the largest type of the *dvi-tāla* system. The details of this system are described minutely. The Goose is white all over, with red legs and golden beak.

The chapter closes with the statement that rows of geese should be beautifully carved or painted in the temples of the gods and in the mansions of Brahmins and kings: they are figured on the entablature (*prastara*), on the upper part of the *uttara*, on the *kuṭa*, *nīḍa*, and *grīvā* (neck).

CHAPTER LXI

The Garuḍa (*Garuḍa-māna-vidhāna*)[1]

The chapter opens with a lengthy discussion on the application of the rules of *āyādi-shaḍ-varga* in order to reconcile various comparative measurements suggested for the Garuḍa and other riding animals of the gods.

[1] The Garuḍa is a mythical bird, the sovereign of the feathered tribes and the enemy of the Serpent (*Nāga*) race. There is a tradition that Garuḍa is the son of Kāśyapa and Vinatā. Hence the metronymic 'Vainateya' by which he is often designated. The myth of the birth of Garuḍa is told in the *Mahābhārata*, *Ādi-parva*, chapter 16.

Garuḍa is the *vāhana* of Vishṇu. His limbs are measured in the *nava-tāla* system, the details of which are given in a previous chapter. He is figured in an erect or sitting posture, and as meditating on Vishṇu with joined palms. The arrangement of his various limbs and their colour, etc., are described at great length. The Garuḍa is figured partly as a human creature and partly as a bird. He is provided with feathers, with wings painted in five colours, and with a beak (*tuṇḍa*); but, on the other hand, the description refers to his arms (*prakoshṭha*), his ears and hair (*keśa*). He wears various ornaments (*sarvālaṅkāra-saṁyukta*) including a diadem of the kind called *karaṇḍa* (*lit.*, a basket) and is gorgeously painted in a great variety of colours. He is described as being of a terrific appearance (*ugradṛiś*). His worship is stated to be conducive to the destruction of the enemy (*śatru-nāśa*).

CHAPTER LXII

The Bull (*Vṛishabha-lakshaṇa-vidhāna*)

The bull Nandin[1] is the animal of Śiva. Its image, which may be either recumbent or erect, is placed facing the Śiva temple on a pedestal (*pīṭha*), either inside the shrine, or in a pavilion (*maṇḍapa*) in front of the temple, or at the door. It is not measured in any *tāla* system. Various absolute and comparative measurements are prescribed. Its height, for instance, may be equal to the height of the idol (of Śiva), or up to its ears or arms, or the height may be from one cubit to nine cubits, or equal to three-fourths or one half of the height of the door of the temple. The bull Nandin is made either solid or hollow, of iron (*lohaja*), stone, wood, *ābhāsa* (marble), *ratna* (precious stone), *sudhā* (stucco), baked clay (terra-cotta ?) and *śarkarā* (grit).

The description and measurements of the various limbs of the bull are given in great detail. From the description it would appear that the bull of Śiva is white in colour except the four legs, the hoofs, and the ears, which are red. He is covered with a tiger-skin and wears not only garlands round the neck but even foot-rings or anklets (*nūpura*).

---

[1] The image of the bull Nandin is regularly found in front of temples dedicated to Śiva. A well-known example is the colossal recumbent bull, placed opposite the famous *vimāna* of Tanjore. It is hewn out of one block of black granite and measures 16 feet in length and 13 feet in height. A remarkable bronze Nandin, which is found at Brāhmor (Chambā) in the Western Himālaya and which, on the evidence of an inscription, may be assigned to the seventh century A. D., is illustrated in the *Antiquities of Chamba State* (*Archaeological Survey of India*, New Imp. Series, vol. XXXVI, Part I plate X).

CHAPTER LXIII

The Lion (*Siṁha-lakshaṇa-vidhāna*)

The lion is the last of the four divine *vāhanas*, to which a chapter is devoted.[1]

As in the case of the bull, the image of the lion is not measured in any *tāla* system. The absolute measurements of the various parts of the lion, expressed in *aṅgulas*, are enumerated. The lion is made in an erect, sitting or recumbent posture. His tail is generally equal to his height. His four legs are like those of the tiger. His colour is white, but his mane should be red. The shape of his nails and teeth is compared to that of the crescent (*bāla-chandra, ardha-chandra*).

CHAPTER LXIV

The image (*Pratimā-vidhāna*)

This chapter, which is missing in all the manuscripts but one, opens with the announcement that herein will briefly be described the measurements from head to foot of the sixteen attendant deities of the Vishṇu temple. It will be remembered that in the 32nd chapter on 'attendant deities' (*Parivāra-vidhāna*) groups of eight, ten, sixteen and thirty-two deities have been mentioned, who are stated to occupy subsidiary shrines in the compound of a large Vishṇu temple.

But the contents of the chapter, in reality, do not expressly describe any of the groups of deities in question. The first part deals with the various kinds of comparative measurements already discussed at the beginning of the 55th chapter on the Jain deities. The second part elaborately describes the rules of the *āyādi-shaḍ-varga*, which have been repeatedly mentioned whenever a variety of measurements was suggested for any particular object.

The comparative measurement is distinguished into twelve kinds, according as it is compared with the phallus, the main Vishṇu image, the width of the sanctum (*garbha-griha*), the breadth of the main temple (*harmya, prāsāda*), the door, *vaṁsa*, basement, pillar; or is based on cubit (*hasta*) measurement, *tāla*-measurement, the measurement of the worshipper, and *aṅgula* measurement.

---

[1] At the beginning of the chapter (and again in the concluding verse) the lion is loosely indicated as 'the riding animal of the gods' (*devānāṁ vāhanam*). It is, however, well known that the lion (or the tiger) is more particularly the animal of Pārvatī, the consort of Śiva. It is hardly necessary to point out that of the other deities, both male and female, each, as a rule, has his or her own *vāhana*, e.g., Kārttikeya the pea-cock, Gaṇeśa the mouse, Indra the elephant, Yama the buffalo, Sūrya a chariot drawn by seven horses, Varuṇa a crocodile (*makara*), Kubera a man (whence his epithet *nara-vāhana*), etc.

The *aṅgula* is further distinguished, as already pointed out, into three kinds, namely, *liṅga* or *berāṅgula*, the *mānāṅgula*, *viz.*, *aṅgula* of eight *yavas* or ¾ inch, and the *dehalabdha-aṅgula*, *viz.*, one of the equal parts into which the whole length of an image is divided. The measurement obtained from a comparison with the height of the main idol or the worshipper is of nine kinds, as it may reach the full length (of the idol or the worshipper), his eyes, nostrils, chin, arms, breast, heart, navel, and sex-organ.

Other measurements obtained from a comparison with the phallus and various parts of the temple, such as the door, the pillar, etc., admit of many varieties and proportions.

CHAPTER LXV

The largest type of the daśa-tāla measurement (*Daśa-tāla vidhāna*)

In this system the whole length of an image is divided into 124 equal parts, which are proportionately distributed over the different parts of the body from head to foot. The measurement of breadth, etc., of the various limbs is not included in these 124 parts. The measurement of the hand, etc., is also excluded. All the numerous parts of the body are minutely described. Such minute measurement as that of the finger-digit, the interspace between two toes, etc., has not escaped the notice of the author of the *Mānasāra*.

CHAPTER LXVI

The intermediate type of the daśa-tāla measurement (*Madhyama-daśa-tāla-vidhāna*)

The female deities of the higher order are generally measured in this system. The whole height of the image is divided into 120 equal parts which are proportionately distributed over the various parts of the body from head to foot. The details are minutely described.

The face is taken as the standard of the *tāla* measurement, and is generally twelve *aṅgulas* or about nine inches in length. The face is stated to be of oval shape (*kukkuṭāṇḍa-samākāra*, lit., 'shaped like the egg of a hen'). The eye-brow is shaped like the bow (*chāpākāra*), the eyes like a fish (*matsyākāra*), the nose like the sesame flower (*tilapushpākṛiti*), and the nostrils (*puṭa*) like a bean (*nishpāva-bīja*).

According to both Indian and European canons, a well proportioned male human figure is equal to eight times (*ashṭa-tāla*) the length of the face, and a female human figure is seven and a half times the length of the face. " The other rules arrived at by the Indian artist do not appear to be divergent from those evolved by the European artist, and if in Indian sculpture the results are not good in some instances, it is the fault of the artist and not attributable to the guide book."[1]

CHAPTER LXVII

The plumb-lines (*Pralamba-lakshaṇa-vidhāna*)

The plumb-lines, as has already been pointed out, are lines drawn through the body of an image in order to find out accurately the perpendicular and the horizontal measurements of the different parts of the body.

This is done by means of an instrument, called *pralamba-phalaka*, which is a square plank of four, three, two, or one *aṅgula* in thickness, with the sides equal to three-fourths or one-half of the length of the image. Another plank of the same size is used as the stool on which the image is placed. The first mentioned plank (*pralamba-phalaka*) is fixed to the crown of the head of the image. The planks are kept parallel to each other. Holes are made in the upper plank, wherefrom are suspended strings at the other end of which are attached small balls of iron or stone. The number of holes and strings suspended from them, by which the plumb-lines are determined, varies from five to eleven, according to the different postures and poses of the image. The five principal plumb-lines consist of one drawn from the centre of the upper plank corresponding to the crown of the head, and four on the four sides of the body. Two other lines drawn adjoining the right and left sides of the face make the number seven. Another two lines drawn on the right and left sides of the back of the head make the number nine, and two lines drawn from the two arm-pits make the total of the lines eleven.

The line drawn from the crown of the head (*śikhā-maṇi*, lit., crest jewel) passes by the diadem and the head-dress, the middle of the forehead, the eye-brows, the nose, the chin, the neck, the chest (*hṛidaya*), the navel, the sex-organ, the thighs, between the knees, the ankles (*nalakas*), the heels, the soles of the feet and the two big toes. This is evidently drawn along the surface of the body in a perfectly erect or straight posture of the image. The other plumb-lines too touch different parts of the body; but they are not particularly mentioned here.

Very minutely are described the comparative and the absolute measurements of the perpendicular distance between different parts of the body by a plumb-line, as well as the horizontal distance from one line to another. The distance, say, between the two big toes, is said to be eight *aṅgulas*. The variation of these measurements in different postures and poses is carefully considered.

---

[1] T. A. Gopinath Rao, *Elements of Hindu Iconography*.

The three postures of images, namely, erect or standing (*sthānaka*), sitting (*āsana*) and recumbent (*śayana*), are frequently mentioned in the *Mānasāra*.[1]

In the present chapter a special reference is made to the three *bhaṅgas* or poses which are distinguished in Indian sculpture. They are known as *sama-bhaṅga* or equipoise, *ābhaṅga* or a slight flexion, *ati-bhaṅga* or an excessive flexion, and *tri-bhaṅga* or of three flexions.[2]

CHAPTER LXVIII

The first casting of the image (*Madhūchchhishṭa-vidhāna*)

The chapter opens with an enumeration of the names of phalli and ascetics (*muni*), as well as of architects,[3] but the subject proper is the casting of an image in wax (*madhūchchhishṭa*). The *sthapati* and the *sthāpaka* prepare the wax, but the manner of its preparation is not expressly described. All kinds of images, temporary or permanent, stationary or movable, are moulded in wax. The process appears to be this. Some part of the image is covered with a thin copper-leaf (*tāmra-patra*) and the wax is laid on two or three *aṅgulas* deep. *Mulikā* (?) is spread above the part covered with wax. The idol is heated after it has been besmeared. If the master likes, the smearing may be done with melted iron too. One half of the image, which is not covered with earth, is washed in water. The process is repeated several times. If any of the minor limbs be lost through this process, the image should be furnished with it again

---

[1] Each of these three, of course, admits of a variety. The sitting posture (*āsana*) is in particular distinguished into various forms in Indian literature and sculpture, such as the *padmāsana*, *bhadrāsana*, *vajrāsana*, *vīrāsana*, *svastikāsana*, *yogāsana*, etc. In some books, even eighty-four postures are enumerated. These manners of sitting form part of the eight-fold observances of ascetics.

[2] The expression *tri-bhaṅga* (and *tri-bhaṅgin*) is applied to Kṛishṇa in his aspect of the divine cow-herd (Gopāla) playing the reed-pipe. Cf. *Een onbekend Indisch tooneelstuk* (*Gopālakeli-chandrikā*) Tekst met inleiding door W. CALAND. (Verhand. Kon. Akad. v Wetensch. te Amsterdam N. R. Dl. XVII, No. 3. Amsterdam 1917, p. 46, l. 1 (*marakata-vibhaṅgojjvala-tri-bhaṅgāṅga-gopālena*) and p. 124, l 32 (*tri-bhaṅgin*).

[3] The six kinds of phalli (*jyotir-liṅga*) enumerated here are: *śaiva*, *pāśupata*, *kālamukha*, *mahāvrata*, *vāmana* and *bhairava*. Cf. above, where the fifth class is called *vāma*. The names of the *munis* are Agastya, Kāśyapa, Bhṛigu, Gautama, Bhārgava, Gālaya (? Gārga), etc., cf. above. The expert authorities on architecture are the following: Viśvakarman, Viśveśa, Viśvasāra, Prabodhaka, Vṛita, Maya, Tvashṭar, Manu, Nala, Mānavin, Mānakalpa, Mānasāra, Prashṭar, Mānabodha, Viśvabodha, Naya, Ādisāra, Viśāla, Viśvakāśyapa, Vāstubodha, Mahātantra, Vāstuvidyāpati, Parāśarīyaka, Kālayūpa, Chaitya, Chitraka, Āvarya, Sādhakasāra-saṁhitā, Bhānu, Indra, Lokajña, and Saura.

after having been heated. But if the head or the middle of the body (*madhya-kāya*) be damaged, the whole image should be changed. If the master does not approve of the image, it should be recast. The whole process in its different stages has to be attended by many ritualistic ceremonies.

In other texts the process of casting an image is much more clearly described:

"If images have to be cast in metal, the wax must first be melted and poured (out of the mould) and all defects removed with cloth."[1]

"If the images be required to be made of earth, rods (of metal or wood) must be (inserted in them), if of metal, they must first be prepared well in wax."[2]

"If an image is to be made of metal, it must first be made of wax, and then coated with earth; gold and other metals are purified and cast into (the mould) and a complete image is thus obtained by capable workmen."[3]

"In regard to bronze images," says Mr. Rao,[4] "it is believed by some that India could not have known the *cire perdue* method of making metal images earlier than about the 10th century, A.D., and that India must have therefore borrowed it from Europe. That the art of casting metals in wax moulds is much earlier in India can be shewn in more ways than one." In support of his assertion, Mr. Rao cites the three above mentioned quotations.

CHAPTER LXIX

The defects of the limbs (*Aṅga-dūshaṇa-vidhāna*)

The chapter opens with the announcement that it will describe the evil consequences of a defective construction of buildings, which threaten the king, the kingdom, and the maker. It is laid down that no part of a building should be larger or smaller than what is prescribed. But nothing is further stated about the defects themselves. Nor are images separately mentioned. The penalties for defective construction are enumerated with regard to the different architectural members, such as doors, staircases, columns, walls, domes, spires, etc. Thus, it is stated that, if the altar (*vedikā*) be too small, the master will lose his eye-sight; if the pinnacle (*stūpikā*) be too large or too small, the people will be afflicted with poverty; if the columns be too large or too small, the family of the master will be exterminated, and so forth.

No such penalties, however, are mentioned for defects in sculptural objects.

---

[1] *Karaṇāgama*, II. V. 41.

[2] *Suprabhedāgama*, XXXIV. 21.

[3] *Vishṇu-saṁhitā*, *paṭala*, 14.

[4] *Elements of Hindu Iconography*.

CHAPTER LXX

The chiselling of the eye (*Nayanonmīlana-lakshaṇa-vidhāna*)

When the Indian sculptor has carved a divine image, the ceremony of chiselling (*lit.*, opening) the eyes of the idol is the final function, by which it is, as it were, imparted with eye-sight and rendered fit to be worshipped. The custom is quite ritualistic, although it is stated here that it should be carried out by the architect. The ceremonies consist in the worshipping of different deities, in performing the sacrifice with the holy fire, and in the *ratna-śuddhi* (*lit.*, purifying the jewel), etc.

The setting of precious stones in the different parts of the phallus, and in the images of the deities is also described in the present chapter.

This last chapter of the work closes with the statement that this science of architecture and sculpture was originally described by Brahmā, Indra and all the other gods, and that the *Mānasāra* has been complied on the basis of these authorities.

It will be noticed that of the seventy chapters of the *Mānasāra* the first eight are introductory, the next forty-two deal with architectural matters, and the last twenty are devoted to sculpture. In the introductory chapters full accounts are given of such preliminary matters as the table of contents, the system of measurement, the necessary training and qualifications of the different classes of architects, the selection of site, testing of soil, planning, designing, dialling, finding out cardinal points, and astronomical and astrological calculations. Next are given all the architectural details of various kinds of villages, towns and forts; joinery, dimensions and foundations of buildings; pillars and their component parts such as pedestals, bases, shafts and entablatures; storeys varying from one to twelve in ordinary buildings and to seventeen in gate-houses; compounds and courts of edifices, their gate-houses, their attached and detached buildings, their compartments halls and chambers, their doors, windows and the openings, their courtyards, quadrangles, and arches; royal courts, palaces, thrones and crowns; cars, chariots and other conveyances; articles of furniture such as bedsteads, couches, tables, chairs, wardrobes, baskets, cages, mills, lamps; dresses and garments; and ornaments such as chains, armlets, head-gear and foot wear. In the concluding portion are given the sculptural details of idols of deities of the Hindus, the Buddhists and the Jains, statues of great personages, and images of animals and birds.[1]

Thus it may be concluded that as a standard work on architecture in the widest sense of the term, the *Mānasāra* is perfectly complete and methodical in all respects.

---

[1] See pp. 1, 137—156.

The Mayamata Silpa-Śāstra

The next well-known Śilpa-śāstra is the Mayamata attributed to one Gannamāchārya.[1]

A detailed summary of this work is not necessary. The following list of thirty-six chapters placed side by side with the similar chapters of the *Mānasārā* will show that in respect of the titles of chapters, their sequence and contents the *Mayamata* and the *Mānasāra* are identical.[2]

(1) Saṁgrahādhyāya—table of contents—*Mānasārā*, chapter I.

(2) Vāstu-prakāra—classification of architectural subjects—*Mānasāra*,[3] chapters IV, V.

(3) Bhū-parikshā—testing of soil, *Mānusāra*, chapters IV, V.

(4) Bhū-parigraha—testing of soil, *Mānasāra*, chapters IV, V.

(5) Mānopakaraṇa—materials (system) of measurement, M. II.

(6) Dik-parichchheda—chapter on finding out cardinal points, M. VI.

(7) Pada-devatā-vinyāsa—ground plan, M. VII.

(8) Bali-karma-vidhāna—offerings to gods, M. VIII.

(9) Grāma-vinyāsa—villages, M. IX.

(10) Nagara-vidhāna—town-planning, M. X.

(11) Bhū-lamba-vidhāna—dimensions of storeys, M. XI.

(12) Garbha nyāsa-vidhāna—foundations, M. XII.

(13) Upapiṭha-vidhāna—pedestals, M. XIII.

(14) Adhishṭhāna-vidhāna—bases, M. XIV.

(15) Pāda-pramāṇa-dravya-saṁgraha—columns, M. XV.

(16) Prastara-prakaraṇa—entablatures, M. XVI.

(17) Sandhi-karma-vidhāna—(wood) joinery, M. XV.

(18) Śikhara-karana-bhavana-samāpti-vidhāna—making the finials and finishing the building, M. XVIII.

(19) Eka-bhūmi-vidhāna—one-storeyed buildings, M. XIX.

(20) Dvi-bhūmi vidhāna—two-storeyed buildings, M. XX.

---

[1] Oriental Manuscripts Library, Madras, Catalogue, volume XXII, no. 13088; also 13084—13089 Compare the colophon इति गन्नमाचार्यविरचितायां (१) मयमते शिल्पशास्त्रे ।

[2] The edition of the Mayamata by M. M. Gaṇapati Śāstri contains only the first thirty-four chapters. Besides it does not seem to have made use of the manuscripts mentioned elsewhere. But there is reference to three other manuscripts in this edition.

[3] The Mānasāra has 'Mānopakaraṇa' for chapter II, which is placed in chapter V of the Mayamata.

(21) Tri-bhūmi-vidhāna—three-storeyed buildings, M. XXI.

(22) Bahu-bhūmi-vidhāna[1]—buildings of more than three storeys, M. XXII—XXX.

(23) Prākāra-parivāra—courts, and temples therein of the attendant deities; in the *Mānasāra* these two subjects are treated in two chapters, XXXI, XXXII.

(24) Gopura-vidhāna—gate-houses, M. XXXIII.

(25) Maṇḍapa-vidhāna—pavilions, M. XXXIV.

(26) Śālā-vidhāna—halls, M. XXXV.

(27) Gṛiha-mānādhikāra[2]—(location and) measurement of houses, M. XXXVI

(28) Gṛiha-praveśa—first entry into a newly built house (opening or house-warming ceremony), M. XXXVII.

(29) Rāja-veśma-vidhāna—royal palaces, M. XL.

(30) Dvāra-vidhāna—doors; in the Mānasāra this subject is described in two chapters, XXXVIII, XXXIX.

(31) Yānādhikāra—conveyances, M. II, XLIII.

(32) Yāna-śayanādhikāra—cars and chariots, couches and bedsteads, M. XLIV, XLV.

Sculptural subjects are abridged in only four chapters:

(33) Liṅga-lakshaṇa—the Phallus, M. LII.

(34) Pīṭha-lakshaṇa—the Pedestal of the Phallus, M LIII.

(35) Anukarma-vidhāna—minor works on sculpture, LI, LIV, LV, LXIII, LXV, LXX.

(36) Pratimā-lakshaṇa—images in general, M. LXIV.

It should be noticed that in respect of the titles of chapters, their sequence except in one instance, and contents and method of treatment, the *Mayamata* runs exactly like the *Mānasāra*, step by step. It is hardly necessary to point out that in chapter 22 of the former the chapters XXII—XXX of the latter are abridged, to the great relief of readers. So also chapter 30 of the former is an abridgement of chapters XXXVIII, XXXIX of the latter. Chapters XLI (royal courts) and XLII (characteristics of kings) of the *Mānasāra*, which have very little use in an architectural treatise, have been prudently omitted in the *Mayamata*. Chapters XLV to L of the *Mānasāra*, which deal respectively with thrones, arches, theatres, ornamental trees, crowns, ornaments and articles of house furniture, are left out in the *Mayamata*, apparently as matters of detail.

Sculpture is said to be the hand-maid of architecture. This statement, in its restricted sense, is however appropriate only to religious architecture, that is,

[1] Compare Śāstri, ibid, where *Chatur-bhūmyādi* is added at the beginning.

[2] Compare Śāstri, ibid, where it is read *chatur-griha-vidhāna*.

temple-building. But in a treatise which is concerned with all sorts of buildings—religious, residential, military—undue space and preference for sculpture have been economically avoided in the *Mayamata*. In this treatise, as has already been pointed out, sculpture dealing with the Phallus, Pīṭha, images and minor matters, is described in four chapters, while in the *Mānasāra* nearly two-thirds of the whole book, comprising twenty chapters, is given to these subjects; and in the *Aṁśumad-bheda* of Kāśyapa to be discussed presently, which is avowedly a sculptural treatise, nearly half the space, comprising chapters 46 to 84, is devoted to matters of sculptural detail.

It does not, therefore, seem unreasonable to suppose that in the compilation of the treatise named *Mayamata*, whether by Gunnamāchārya as stated in the colophon, of Ms. no. 13038, Oriental Manuscripts Libary, Madras. Catalogue, volume XXII, page 8763) or by some body else, the *Mānasāra* has been largely drawn upon.

In consideration of the fact that with the *Mayamata* (Ms. no. 13037, fol. 218*a*) the *Mānasāra* (1*a*) has become mixed, I am further led to believe that the manuscript of the *Mayamata* in the Madras Oriental Library seems to be an abridgement of the *Mānasāra*.

The fact that one Mayamata is included in the list of thirty-two authorities mentioned in the *Mānasāra* itself does not present much difficulty in accepting this view. Mayamata, like Manu (or Mānasāra), is apparently a generic name, and the treatise catalogued under the title *Mayamata-vāstu-śāstra* need not necessarily be ascribed to the authority mentioned in the *Mānasāra*.

The Aṁśumad-bheda of Kāśyapa

This is another well known treatise on architecture and about the next largest in size to the *Mānasāra*. There is also a striking similarity between the *Aṁśumad-bheda* and the *Mānasāra* as will be shewn by the following lists of chapters of these treatises:

(1) Karshaṇa—ploughing of the selected site, *Mānasāra*, chapter V.

(2) Prāsāda-vāstu—classification of buildings, *Mānasāra*, chapter III.

(3) Vāstu-homa—sacrificial offerings to the presiding deity of the site, *Mānasāra*, chapter VIII.

(4) Prathameshṭaka-vidhi—laying the foundations; in the *Mānasāra* this subject is dealt with in several places and not in a separate chapter.

(5) Upapīṭha-vidhāna—pedestals, *Mānasāra*, chapter XIII.

(6) Adhishṭhāna-vidhi—bases, M. XIV.

(7) Nāla-lakshaṇa,—canals; in the *Mānasāra* this subject is referred to in several places and not in a separate chapter.

(8) Stambha-lakshaṇa—columns, M. XV.

(9) Phalaka-lakshaṇa—planks, M. LXVII.

(10) Vedikā-lakshaṇa—platforms, railings; in the *Mānasāra* this is described in many places.

(11) Jālaka-lakshaṇa—perforated windows, M. XXXIII (concluding portion).

(12) Toraṇa-lakshaṇa—arches, M. XLVI.

(13) Vritta-sphuṭita-lakshaṇa—in the *Mānasāra* this is not described in a separate chapter.

(14) Stambha-toraṇa-vidhi—arches upon columns, M. XII.

(15) Kumbha-tala-lakshaṇa—capitals of columns; this also is not described in any one chapter in the *Mānasāra*, but is referred to in many places.

(16) Vṛitta-sphuṭita-lakshaṇa—same as chapter 13.

(17) Dvāra-lakshaṇa—doors, M. XXXVIII, XXXIX.

(18) Kampa-dvāra-lakshaṇa—a special door, M. XXXVIII, XXXIX.

(19) Prastara-lakshaṇa—entablatures, M. XVI.

(20) Gala-vidhāna—necks; this is also not described in any one chapter in the *Mānasāra*.

(21) Śikhara-lakshaṇa—top, finials; in the *Mānasāra*, this also is referred to in many places.

(22) Nāsikā—noses, wings; in the *Mānasāra* this is described in several places.
(23) Mānopakaraṇa—system of measurement, same title in M. II.
(24) Māna-sūtrādi-lakshaṇa—measuring strings, M. II.
(25) Nagarādi-vidhi—towns, etc., M. X.
(26) Garbha-nyāsa-vidhi—foundations, etc., M. XII.
(27) Eka-tala-vidhāna—one-storeyed buildings, M. XIX.
(28–30) Dvi-chaturtha-tala-vidhāna—two to four-storeyed buildings, M. XX—XXII.
(31) Kūṭādi-lakshaṇa—finials, in the *Mānasāra* referred to in many places.
(32—39) Pañcha-bhānu-bhūmi-vidhāna—five to twelve-storeyed buildings, M. XXIII—XXX.
(40) Trayodaśa-tala-vidhāna—thirteen-storeyed buildings, and
(41) Shoḍaśa-bhūmi-vidhāna—sixteen-storeyed buildings, subjects of these two chapters (40, 41) are dealt with in M. XXXIII.
(42) Mūrdheshṭaka-vidhi—the brick at the top; in the *Mānasāra* referred to in many places.
(43) Prākāra-lakshaṇa—courts, M. XXXI.
(44) Maṇṭa(-ḍa)pa-lakshaṇa—pavilions, M. XXXIV.
(45) Gopura-lakshaṇa—gate-houses, M. XXXIII.

The remaining portion of this treatise, except the last two chapters on villages, deals with sculpture more elaborately than in the *Mānasāra*. It will be noticed that the purely architectural topics are more exhaustively described in the *Mānasāra*.

(46) Sapta-mātṛikā-lakshaṇa—the seven mothers (female images), M. LXIV.
(47) Vināyaka-lakshaṇa—image of Vināyaka or Gaṇeśa; not specified in the *Mānasāra*, but see chap. LVII, XLI.
(48) Parivāra-vidhi—images of attendant deities, M. XXXII
(49) Liṅga-lakshaṇoddhāra—unearthing the phallus, cf. M. LII.
(50) Uttama-daśa-tāla-purusha-māna—the largest type of ten-tāla measure as applied to male deities, M. LXV.
(51) Madhyama-daśa-tāla-purusha-māna—the intermediate type of the ten tāla measure as applied to male deities, M. LXVI, LXI.
(52) Uttama-nava tāla—the largest type of the nine-tāla measure, M. LVII, XLI.
(53) Madhyama-nava-tāla—intermediate type of the nine-tāla measure, M. LVII, XLI.
(54) Adhama-nava-tāla—the smallest type of the nine-tāla measure, M. ibid.
(55) Ashta-tāla—the eight-tāla measure, M. LVII.

(56) Sapta-tāla—the seven-tāla measure, M. LVII.
(57) Pīṭha-lakshaṇoddhāra—the pedestal of the phallus, M. LIII.
(58) Sakala-sthāpana-vidi—the installation of the images of Iśvara and three other deities, M. LI.
(59) Sukhāsana
(60) Sukhāsana } —posture of an image, M. LXVII.
(61) Chandra-śekhara-mūrti-lakshaṇa—the image of Chandraśekhara (Śiva), M. LI.
(62) Vṛisha-vāhana-mūrti-lakshana—the image of the bull, the riding animal of Śiva, M. LXII.
(63) Nṛitta-mūrti-lakshaṇa—the image of dancing (Śiva), M. LI.
(64) Gaṅgādhara-mūrti-lakshaṇa—the image of the Ganges-bearing Śiva, M. LI.
(65) Tripura-mūrti-lakshaṇa—the image of Śiva in the pose of killing Tripura (demon), M. LI.
(66) Kalyāṇa-sundara-lakshaṇa—the image of Kalyāṇa-sundara, M. LI.
(67) Ardha-nārīśvara-lakshaṇa—the image of Śiva combined with his consort Pārvatī, M. LI.
(68) Gajaha-mūrti-lakshaṇa—the image of Gajaha (?Gaṇeśa).
(69) Pāśupata-mūrti-lakshaṇa—the image of Pāśupata (Śiva), M. LI.
(70) Kaṅkāla-mūrti-lakshaṇa—the image of a skeleton, M. not specified.
(71) Haryardha-Hara-lakshaṇa—the combined image of Vishṇu and Śiva—M. LI.
(72) Bhikshāṭana-mūrti-lakshaṇa—the image of Śiva in the pose of a beggar.
(73) Chaṇḍeshānugraha, M. not specified.
(74) Dakshiṇā-mūrti-lakshaṇa—the image of Dakshiṇā, M. not specified.
(75) Kālaha-mūrti-lakshaṇa—the image of Kālaha, M. not specified.
(76) Liṅgodbhava-lakshaṇa—revelation of the phallus, M. LII.
(77) Vṛiksha-saṁgrahaṇa—collection of wood, M. XV.
(78) Śūla-lakshana—the pike, M. not specified.
(79) Śūla-pāṇi-lakshaṇa—the image of Śūlapāni (Śiva), M. LI.
(80) Rajju-bandha-lakshaṇa—binding of rope.
(81) Mṛit-saṁskāra-lakshaṇa—the process of casting images in earth, referred to in many places in the *Mānasāra*.
(82) Kalka-saṁskāra-lakshaṇa—preparation of mixtures.
(83) Varṇa-saṁskāra-lakshaṇa—preparation of colours.
(84) Varṇa-lepana-medhya-lakshaṇa.

The contents of chapters 78-84 are referred to in several places in the *Mānasāra*.

(85) Grāmādi-lakshaṇa } villages, M. IX.
(86) Grāma-lakshaṇa }

In this treatise architecture proper is treated in the first forty-five and the last two chapters. These forty-seven chapters are similar in many respects to the first fifty chapters of the *Mānasāra*. The *Aṁśumad-bheda* deals much more elaborately with sculptural objects in thirty-nine chapters in place of some twenty chapters of the *Mānasāra*. But purely architectural topics are more exhaustively described in the *Mānasāra* which seems in any case to have largely influenced the other work in these matters.

THE VIŚVAKARMA-ŚILPA

The most popular treatise on architecture is naturally the one attributed to Viśvakarman, the heavenly architect. There seems to have been more than one title to this work: one is called the *Viśvakarma-Prakāśa* or *Viśvakarma-Vāstu-śāstra*; another is called the *Viśvakarmīya-Śilpa*, apparently the same as the *Viśvakarmīya-Śilpa-śāstra*.[1] The one designated as *Viśvakarma-Prakāśa* or *Viśvakarma-Vāstu-śāstra* deals with directions on the building of houses, the making of roads, tanks, etc. The treatise contains thirteen chapters in which the following topics are dealt with:

(1) Maṅgalācharaṇa— auspicious preliminaries (benediction).
(2) Vāstu-purushotpatti-varṇanam—the origin of the presiding deity of the house.
(3) Bhūmi-lakshṇa - soil, *Mānasāra*, II, III.
(4) Gṛiha-praveśa— first entry into the house or house-warming, M. XXXVII.
(5) Khanana-vidhi - digging (ploughing) the soil, M. V.
(6) Svapna-vidhi—dreams.
(7) Bhūmi-phalam—fruit of soil, M. IV, V.
(8) Gṛihārambhe samaya-vidhi—auspicious time for beginning a building, M. includes this in many places.
(9) Dhvajādhyāya-phalāni—flags.
(10) Āya-vyayāṁśādīnāṁ phalāni, M. LII, XXXIX, IX, XXX, LXIV, LV.
(11) Gṛiha-madhye devādīnāṁ sthāpana-nirṇaya—installation of gods in temples, M. in many places.
(12) Dhruvādi-gṛiha-bheda, M. not specified.
(13) Dvāra-mānāni— measurements of doors, M XXXIX.
(14) Stambha-pramāṇāni—columns, M. XV.
(15) Gṛihāṇāṁ śālā-nirṇaya—halls of houses, M. XXXV.
(16) Gṛihārambha-kāla nirṇaya—almost the same as (8).
(17) Gṛihārambhe lagna-kuṇḍalistha-graha-phalāni, M. not specified.
(18) Śayyā-mandira-bhavana-sumana-sudbārādi-gṛihāṇāṁ lakshaṇāni (see below the comparisons of the Purāṇas and Āgamas), referred to in many places in M.

---

[1] Egg. Catalogue, page 1129. A treatise bearing the same title was published by the Venkaṭeśvara Press, Bombay, in Saṁvat 1952, Śaka, 1817, another at Benares in 1888. The same treatise is stated to have been translated into Bhāshā under the title 'Pālārāma Vilāsa' by Mukula Śaktidhara Śarmā, at Lucknow in 1896.

In the Oriental Mss. Lib. Madras, there is a Ms. bearing the title 'Viśvakarmiyam-Śilpa-Śāstram' (see Catalogue vol. XXI no. 13057).

(19) Pādukā-upānaha-mañchādīnāṁ māna-lakshaṇa—measurement of foot wear, shoes, couches, etc., referred to in many places in M.

(20) Śaṅku-śilā-nyāsa-nirṇaya—finding out the cardinal points, etc., by means of a gnomon, M. VI.

(21) Vāstu-deha-lakshaṇāni-pūjanaṁ-bali-dāna—offerings, M. VIII.

(22) Śilā-nyāsa—referred to in many places in M.

(23) Prāsāda-vidhāna—buildings, described in many places in M.

(24) Śilpa-vyāsa, M. not specified.

(25) Prāsāda-nirṇaya, M. XIX—XXX.

(26) Pīṭhikā-lakshaṇa—pedestals (of the phallus), M. LIII, XIII.

(27) Maṇḍapa—pavilions, M. XXXIV.

(28) Dvāra-lakshaṇa—doors, M. XXXVIII, XXXIX.

(29) Vāpi-kūpa-taḍāgodyāna-kriyā—making of tanks, wells, pools, gardens, referred to in many places in M.

(30) Dāru-chchhedana-vidhi—cutting wood, M. XV

(31) Gṛiha-praveśa-nirṇaya—almost the same as (4), M. XXXVI.

(32) Gṛiha-praveśa-kāla-śuddhi, M. XXXVII.

(33) Śayyāsana-dolikādīnāṁ lakshaṇa—bedsteads, seats, palanquins (?hammocks), almost the same as (18).

(34) Durga-nirṇaya—forts and fortified cities, M. X.

(35) Śalya-jñānaṁ, śalyoddhāra—semi-astrological topics, referred to in many places in M.

(36) Nāgara-saṁbandhi-rāja-gṛihādīnāṁ nirṇaya—the palaces in cities, M. XLI.

It should be noticed that most of these topics of this version of Viśvakarman refer to non-architectural and chiefly astrological matters. It is also worth notice that this treatise leaves out sculptural topics altogether.

The *Viśvakarmīya-śilpa*[1], apparently the same as is mentioned in Rājendralāla Mitra's notices of Sanskrit manuscripts, is a Nāgari copy made in

[1] In Rājā Dr. Rājendralāla Mitra's "Notices of sanskrit Mss." (Vol. II, no 781, p. 142).

Of the other version, Viśvakarmīya-Śilpa-Śāstra, the Madras Ms. noted above, which was copied by Niṭla Sūrappa on Saturday, the 5th day of the bright fortnight of the Āśvija month in the year Jaya, contains a statement referring to Viśvakarmā's debt to Brahmā, Indra, Maya, Bhārgava, Aṅgirasa, Dhruva, Gautama, Gārgeya, Manu, Vyāsa, and Bhṛigu. Agastya is also referred to.

It is stated to have been founded on the revelation of Viśvakarman and traced back successively to Bṛihadratha, Parāśara and Śambhu. In the Mānasāra the origin of the science is attributed to Śiva, Brahmā and Vishṇu, and through Indra, Bṛihaspati, Nārada and others it was revealed to Mānasāra; Viśvakarman, Maya, Tvashṭar, and Manu represent the heavenly architects, and Sthapati, Sūtragrāhin, Vardhaki and Takshaka form the guild of modern architects; but there are thiry-two other architectural authorities mentioned in the Mānasāra.

1872 from an original written in the Hala-Kānādī character, the older codex being in the library of the Rājā of Tanjore. "None of the Mss. examined by Mr. Burnell is perfect or even tolerably correct. This treatise is apparently a compilation, as it is written in the Tāntric style, having Śiva for its narrator." The contents are classified under the following seventeen chapters:

(1) Viśvakarmotpattiḥ karma-viśesha-bhedena vyavahṛita-takshaka-varddhakyādi-śabda-vyutpattiś cha—origin of Viśvakarman, derivation of the words takshaka, vardhaki, etc., M. II.

(2) Satyādi-yuga-jāta-narochchatā-pramāṇaṁ, yajñīya-kāshṭhena prastareṇa vā deva-pratimā-nirmāṇe mānādi—height of man in different ages of the world, wood and stone for the construction of images.

(3) Takshakasya garbhādhānādi-saṁskāra-kathanaṁ, garbhotpatti-kathanādi cha—sacraments for sculptors and carpenters.

(4) Śiva-liṅgādi-pratishṭhārthaṁ sabhā-nirmāṇādi—halls for the installation of Śiva's phallus and other gods, M. LII.

(5) Graha-pratimā-nirmāṇa-pramāṇaṁ, liṅga-pīṭha-nirmāṇa-pramāṇādi cha—proportions of images of the planets and phalli.

(6) Ratha-nirmāṇa-vidhi-kathanam—cars and chariots, M. XLIII.

(7) Ratha-pratishṭhā-vidhiḥ—consecration of cars, M. XLIII.

(8) Brāhmī-Māheśvaryādīnaṁ svarūpādi-varṇādi—characteristics of Brāhmī, Māheśvarī and other goddesses.

(9) Yajñopavīta-lakshaṇam—Brahmanical sacred thread.

(10) Suvarṇa-rajata-mañjyādi-nirmita-yajñopavīta-kathanaṁ, dig-bhedena deva-sthāpana-prakārādi, meru-dakshiṇa-sthita-hema-śilā-kathanādi cha—sacred thread of gold, silver, mañjī fibre, the cardinal points at which images of gods and goddesses are to be installed; qualities of (the stone-god called) Hema-śila (lit., golden stone) to be found to the south of the Meru mountain.

(11) Lakshmī-Brāhmī-Māheśvaryādi-devīndrādi-dik-pāla-grahādi-mūrti-nirmāṇa-prakāraḥ—images of Lakshmī, Brāhmī, Māheśvarī and other goddesses, of Indra, Dikpāla (quarter-masters), planets and other gods.

(12, 13) Mukuṭa-kirīṭa-jaṭā-mukuṭādi-nirmāṇa-prakārādi—crowns, crests and head-gear, M. XLIX.

(14) Sthāvarāsthāvara-siṁhāsana-nirmāṇa-prakārādi, Punar viśeshena kirīṭa-lalāṭa-paṭṭikādi-nirmāṇa-prakāraḥ, Devatāyā mandirasya cha jīrṇoddhāra-prakāraḥ—movable and fixed thrones for images; crests, crowns, bands and other head-gear; repairs of temples, M. XLII, XLV.

(15) Liṅga-mūrti-mandira-dvārādi-kathana—proportions of doors of temples to Phalli, M. XXXVIII, XXXIX, LXIV.

(16) Pratimā-mūrti-mandira-dvārādi-kathana—proportions of doors of temples to (other) images, M. XXXVIII, XXXIX.

(17) Vighneśa-mūrti-mandirādi-nirmāṇādi-vidhi—temples for the images of Vighneśa and other matters.

This portion of the treatise of Viśvakarman is chiefly sculptural. The treatment of the subject is in detail, although not so elaborate as in the *Aṁśumad-bheda* of Kāśyapa. I am inclined to think that the two versions form in fact the complete treatise attributed to Viśvakarman.

We have seen that Viśvakarman refers to the authority of Mayamata[1]. If this Mayamata be the same person as the author of the *Mayamata* discussed above, and there seem reasons to think so, Viśvakarman might have been indebted to the *Mānasāra* through Mayamata, if not directly. Even the brief comparison of the two treatises given above may serve to indicate that there may have been such a relation of indebtedness between the *Viśvakarma-śilpa* and the *Mānasāra*.

---

1 See note 1, page 97.

The Āgastya

Agastya is a name frequently cited, we have seen above, as an authority on architecture. Unfortunately the manuscripts discovered are incomplete and devoted solely to sculpture. One of the manuscripts bearing the title *Agastya-Sakalādhikāra* contains the following chapters.

(1) Māna-saṁgraha—system of measurement, *Mānasāra* II, LV.
(2) Uttama-daśa-tāla—large type of the ten-tāla measure, M. LXV.
(3) Madhyama-daśa-tāla—intermediate type of the ten-tāla measure, M. LVI.
(4) Adhama-daśa-tāla—small type of the ten-tāla measure, M. XLI.
(5) Pratimā-lakshaṇa—general rules on images, M. LXIV.
(6) Vṛishabha-vāhana-lakshana—bull, the riding animal of Śiva, M. LXII.
(7) Naṭeśvara-vidhi—image of Naṭeśvara (dancing Śiva), M. LI.
(8) Shoḍaśa-pratimā-lakshaṇa—sixteen images, M. LXIV.
(9) Dāru-saṁgraha—collection of wood, cf. M. XV.
(10) Mṛit-saṁskāra—preparing earth for images.
(11) Varṇa-saṁskāra—preparation of colours.

In a Madras manuscript the following topics are described[1]:

(1) Māna-saṁgrahà-viśesha—specially on measures, M. II, LV.
(2) Uttama-daśa-tāla—large type of the ten-tāla, M. LXV.
(3) Madhyama-daśa-tāla—intermediate type of the ten-tāla, M. LXVI.
(4) Somāskanda-lakshaṇa—image of Soma and Skanda, M. not specified.
(5) Chandra-śekhara-lakshaṇa—image of Śiva, M. LI.
(6) Vṛishabha-vāhana-lakshaṇa—image of the bull, M. LXII.

Chapters 7 to 13 seem to be missing. It is not clear whether or not the following 7—14 (which numbers are not found in the compilation) are to be attributed to Agastya.

(7) Tripurāntaka-lakshana—image of Śiva, cf M. LI
(8) Kalyāṇa-sundara-lakshaṇa—image of Kalyāna-Sundara.
(9) Ardha-nārīśvara-lakshana—image of Śiva, M. LI
(10) Pāśupata-lakshaṇa—image of Śiva, M. LI.
(11) Bhikshāṭana-lakshaṇa—image of Śiva as a beggar, M. not specified.
(12) Chaṇḍeśānugraha-lakshaṇa—image of Śiva, M. LI.
(13) Dakshiṇā-mūrti-lakshaṇa—image of Dakshiṇā.

[1] In the Oriental Mss. Lib., Madras, there are two fragmentary Mss. ascribed to Agastya (Cat. vol. XXII, nos. 13046, 13047). They deal with astrological matters bearing upon architecture. In the same library (Cat. vol. XXII no. 13068) there is a large Ms. of 420 pages of 25 lines to a page of paper 13¼" 8; two large portions of this compilation are ascribed to Agastya.

(14) Kāla-dahana-lakshaṇa—image of Śiva(?).

All these refer to the images of Śiva described in M. LI.

(15-18) Apparently missing.

(19) Pratimā-lakshaṇa—images, M. LXIV.

In another portion of the compilation the following chapters are numbered as shewn in parallel column:

(20) (8) Upapīṭha-vidhāna—pedestal (for image), M. XIII, LIII.

(21) (9) Śula-māna-vidhāna measurement of pikes for images.

(22) (10) Rajju-bandha-saṁskāra-vidhi—making ropes, M.II.

(23) (11) Varṇa-saṁskāra—preparation of colours.

(24) (12) Akshi-mokshaṇa—chiselling the eye, M. LXX.

We have seen above that Agastya is mentioned together with Maya as one of the authorities, on which Viśvakarma's treatise is based. Agastya was, therefore, presumably known to Viśvakarman. Owing to the incomplete nature of Agastya's extant works the connection of Agastya with Mayamata and with the *Mānasāra* is not clear at present. It is true, however, that several chapters of Agastya are strikingly similar to, if not taken from, the corresponding chapters of the *Mānasāra*.

The Sanat-kumāra-Vāstu-śāstra

Another authority frequently referred to is Sanat-kumāra. There are several fragmentary manuscripts of his treatise. But they are incomplete[1]. In one of the manuscripts the following subjects are dealt with[2] :

(1) Gṛiha-saṁsthāpana—construction of houses, M. XXXVI.

(2) Nakshatra-graha-yoga-vidhi—constellation of planets and stars (in determining the auspicious times) in connection with the building of houses.

(3) Graha-lagna-vidhi—almost the same as (2).

(4) Taru-tantra-vidhi—on trees (wood, for building houses with).

(5) Bhū-parīkshā-vidhi—examination of soil, M. IV, V.

(6) Nakshatra-tithi-vāra-śuddhi—on auspicious time.

(7) Nakshatra-lagna-phala-dvāra-bandha-śubha-sthāna-nirṇaya—ascertaining auspicious time and place (in constructing doors).

(8) Gṛiha-praveśana—first entry into the newly-built house, M. XXXVII.

This treatise of Sanat-kumāra is stated to have been based on the works of Brahman, Śakra, Yama, Bhārgava, Āṅgirasa, Maya, Gautama, Gārgya, Manu, Vyāsa, Bhṛigu, Viśvakarman and others

The same list is differently given in another manuscript (no. 13064), where Śakra is replaced by Chandra and Maya is omitted.

But in other manuscripts (nos. 13062, 13068) Śakra is not replaced by Chandra although Maya is omitted.

As we have seen above, Viśvakarman acknowledges his debt to Maya. And Sanat-kumāra mentions Viśvakarman as his authority; it is, therefore, not unlikely that of these lists the first one, which contains Maya, is correct. And if the view that Maya is indebted to the *Mānasāra* be accepted on the grounds discussed above, it would be easy to infer that Sanat-kumāra may be also indebted, directly or indirectly, to the *Mānasāra*.

---

[1] Egg. III. 3151, 2680; Oppert, vol. I, no. 3289, page 580. In the Oriental Manuscripts Library, Madras, there are nine manuscripts (Cat. vol. XXII, nos. 13060—13068).

[2] Madras manuscripts, no. 13060.

THE ŚILPA-ŚĀSTRA OF MAṆḌANA

The treatise of Maṇḍana, otherwise called Rāja-vallabha-Maṇḍana, Sūtradhāra-Maṇḍana, and also perhaps Bhūpati-vallabha, is unique in a sense. He seems to be a historical person. He is stated to have been "in the employ of king Kumbha-karṇa of Medapāṭha and the husband of Mirābai." According to Tod, king Kumbha ruled over the country of Mewar from 1419 to 1469 A. D.[1] This treatise bears the titles *Śilpa-śāstra*, *Vāstu-śāstra*, and also *Prāsāda-Maṇḍana-Vāstu-śāstra*.[2] It deals with the architectural disposition of houses, palaces and temples in the following fourteen chapters :

(1) Miśraka-lakshaṇa.

(2) Vāstu-lakshaṇa—characteristics and classification of architectural objects, *Mānasāra*, III.

(3) Āyādi-lakshaṇa—architectural formulas of measurement, M. LXVI.

(4) Prākāra-yantra—vāpi-kūpa-taḍāga-lakshaṇa—courts, machines, tanks, wells, pools, described in several places in M.

(5) Rāja-gṛiha-niveśādi-lakshaṇa—opening the royal palaces, M. XL, XXXVII.

The 28th verse (*śloka*) of this chapter (5) mentions the *Matsya-Purāṇa* as an authority on the subject.

(6) Eka-śālā-dvi-śālā-gṛiha-lakshaṇa—houses with one and two halls (compartments), described in many places in M.

(7) Dvi-śālā-tri-śālā-chatuḥ-śālā-gṛiha-lakshaṇa—houses with two, three and four halls, described in many places in M.

(8) Śayana-siṁhāsana-chhatra-gavāksha-sabhāshṭaka-vedika-chatushṭaya-dipa-lakhshana—bedsteads or couches, thrones, umbrellas, windows, eight-councils, four-platforms, and lamps, apparently an abridged collection of several subjects described in M. XLIV, XLV, XXXIII, etc.

(9) Rāja-gṛihādi-lakshaṇa—royal palaces, M. XL.

(10) (Māpita)-Kshetrādbhūta-lakshaṇa.

---

[1] Bhandarkar's Report, ibid., 1882-83, page 37.

[2] Egg. 3142, 1291 ; 3147, 2253.

Apparently one of these Mss. is published with some diagrams by Bhārati at Baroda, 1891.

Five other manuscripts are ascribed to Maṇḍana, (i) Vāstu-Maṇḍana, (ii) Vāstu-Mañjari, (iii) Vāstu sāra, (iv) Rūpa-Maṇḍana, and (v) Āpa-tattva.

(11) Dina-śuddhi-gṛiha-niveśa-gṛiha-praveśa-vivāha-muhūrta-lakshaṇa—auspicious times with regard to beginnging the construction and entry into the house, and the wedding.

(12) Gochara-dina-rātri-māna-svarodaya-kūṭa-chakra-matṛikā-lakhshaṇa—astronomical calculations bearing upon architecture (house).

(13) Jyotisha-lakshaṇa—astrology (astronomy).

(14) Śakuna-lakshaṇa—auspicious signs.

The manuscript bearing the title *Prāsāda-Maṇḍana-Vāstu-śāstra* by Sūtradhāra Maṇḍana (Egg. 3147, 2253) contains the following eight chapters, which, except the first one, are apparently in continuation of the 14 chapters stated above:

(1) Miśra-kalaśa.

(15) (2) Āyatanādhikāra—buildings (temples).

(16) (3) Bhitti-pīṭha-maṇḍ[ap]a-vāra[dvāra]-garbha-gṛiha-udumbara-pramāṇa—walls, pedestals, open courts, doors, shrines, etc., M. XIII, XXXIV, XXXVIII, XXXIX, etc.

(17) (4) Pramāṇa-dṛishṭi-pa(ā)da-sthāna-śikhara-kalaśa-lakshaṇa—measures, sight (perspective, pillars, finials, towers, M. II, XV, etc.

(18) (5) Rājyādi-prāsādādhikāra—royal kingdoms, palaces, etc., M. XL, XLI, XLII, etc.

(19) (6) Keśaryādi-prāsāda-jāti-lakshaṇa, pañcha-kshetra-pañcha-chatvāriṁśan-meru-lakshaṇādhyāya—Keśari and other classes of buildings, forty-five types of buildings beginning with Meru; compare M. XVIII, XIX—XXX, and see comparison of the *Mānasāra* with the Purāṇas and the Āgamas discussed below (page 118f).

(20) (7) Maṇḍapa-bālāṅka-sambaraṇādhikāra—open courts, M. XXXIV.

(21) (8) Jīrṇoddhāra-bhinna-dosha-sthāvara-pratishṭhā, Sūtradhāra-pūjā, Jina-pratishṭha-vāstu-purusha-vinyāsa—repairing and other defects, consecration of movable images, offerings to architects (carpenters), consecration of Jain images, description of the presiding deity of the house, M. LXIX, II, VIII, LV, VII, etc.

As has already been suggested, these two parts of Maṇḍana's treatise, in some respects, seem to be two overlapping portions of one work. Other treatises ascribed to Maṇḍana are fragmentary and useless for any attempt to combine the several portions into a complete whole. The important points of this historical treatise are well worth notice. First its date is pretty certain, secondly it mentions the *Matsya-Purāṇa*, and lastly it contains a list of forty-five buildings, classified under five headings, bearing titles and giving details which correspond exactly with the lists and titles discovered in many important treatises.[1]

Another point of importance is the fact that many of its chapters contain matters which are in fact different topics and have been more logically described under different headings in the *Mānasāra* and other works. It is, therefore, likely that Maṇḍana's work is more or less a compilation from many sources.

---

[1] The *Agni-Purāṇa*, the *Garuḍa-Purāṇa*; also the *Matsya-Purāṇa*, the *Bhavishya-Purāṇa*, the *Bṛihat-saṁhitā* as well as the *Kāmikāgama*, the *Suprabhedāgama* and the *Mānasāra* (see under section III. pp. 110—120).

The Saṁgraha

This work is avowedly a compilation (*saṁgraha*). It bears the title *Śilpa-saṁgraha*, and to our great relief it expressly mentions the sources it has been compiled from.[1] In fact several of the architectural treatises compared above and many more not mentioned here are evidently compilations, although the authors have not acknowledged their debt, nor even mentioned the sources drawn upon. This point is convincingly illustrated in the following instance.

The following chapters in the order found in the manuscript are ascribed to—

I. —Mānasāra :

Under 7, Gomukha-lakshaṇa—under this heading there is no separate chapter in the eleven manuscripts of the *Mānasāra* so far known to exist.

(13) Upapīṭha-lakshaṇa—pedestals, (M. XIII).

Under 15, Vṛishabha-lakshaṇa—image of the bull, the riding animal of Śiva, (M. LXII).

II.—Mayamata :

Under 6, Dik-parichchheda—the cardinal points.

(28) Maṇḍapa-vidhāna—open courts.

(9) Grāma-vinyāsa—villages.

(20) Eka-bhūmi-rodhana—one storeyed buildings.

Under 36, Sthapati-lakshaṇa—characteristics and qualifications of the architect.

(24) Gopura-vidhāna—gate houses.

(13) Upapīṭha-vidhāna—pedestals.

(1) Adhishṭhāna-vidhāna—bases.

(20) Dvi-bhūmi-vidhāna—two-storeyed buildings.

Under 20, Tri-bhūmi-vidhāna—three-storeyed buildings.

III.—Kāśyapa :

Under 7, Prastara-lakshaṇa—entablatures.

„ „ Adhishṭhāna-paṭala—bases.

„ „ Nāla-pramāṇotsedhālaṅkaraṇa—drains and canals.

Under 24, Dakshiṇā-mūrti-paṭala - image of the goddess Dakshiṇā.

Under 22, Nṛitta-lakshaṇa—image of dancing Śiva.

---

[1] Oriental Manuscripts Library, Madras, Cat. vol. XXII, no. 13058. It comprises 429 pages of 25 lines to a page of paper 13¼″ × 8″

IV.—Viśvakarman :

Under 6, Gopura-lakshaṇa—gate-houses.

Under 36, Śayana-lakshaṇa—bedsteads and couches.

(86) Sthapati-lakshaṇa—characteristics and qualifications of the architect.

(14) Āyādi-sampad-artha-vidhāna—the formula of Āya, etc.

V.—Agastya :

Under 1, Māna-saṁgraha-viśesha—system of measurement.

Under 2, Uttama-daśa-tāla—the large type of the ten-tāla measure.

Under 3, Madhyama-daśa-tāla—the intermediate type of the ten-tāla measure.

Under 4, Soma-skanda-lakshaṇa—image of Soma and Skanda.

Under 5, Chandra-śekhara-lakshaṇa—image of Śiva.

Under 6, Vṛisha-vāhana-lakshaṇa—image of the bull, the riding animal of Śiva.

It is not known for certain whether or not the following, under 6 and 19, are to be ascribed to Agastya.

Under 6, Tripurāntaka-lakshaṇa—image of Śiva.

„ „ Kalyāṇa-sundara-lakshaṇa—image of Kalyāṇa-Sundara.

„ „ Ardha-nārīśvara-lakshaṇa—image of Śiva.

„ „ Pāśupata-lakshaṇa—image of Śiva.

„ „ Bhikshāṭana-lakshaṇa—image of Śiva.

„ „ Chaṇḍeśānugraha-lakshaṇa—image of Śiva.

„ „ Dakshiṇā-mūrti-lakshaṇa—image of Dakshiṇā.

„ „ Kāla-dahana-lakshaṇa—image of Śiva.

Under 19, Pratimā-lakshaṇa—images in general.

(3) Upapīṭha-vidhāna—pedestal.

(9) Śūla-māna-vidhāna—pikes.

(10) Rajju-bandha-saṁskāra-vidhi—preparation of ropes.

(11) Varṇa-saṁskāra—preparation of colours.

(12) Akshi-mokshaṇa—chiselling the eyes of an image.

VI.—Bhṛigu :

Under 7, Ratha-nirmāṇa—construction of chariots.

VII.—Paulastya :

Under 22, Dakshiṇā-mūrti-nirmāṇa—the image of that deity.

VIII.—Nārada :

Under 14, Kṛishṇa-lakshaṇa—image of Kṛishṇa.

IX.—Nārāyaṇa:

Under 20, Rāma-Lakshmaṇa—the images of Rāma and Lakshmaṇa

X.—Maushalya:

Under 7, Ratha lakshaṇa chariots.

XI.—Sesha-bhāshya:

Under 36, title missing.

Under 22, Ekatāla-vidhāna—one storeyed buildings.

XII.—Chitra-sāra:

Under 14, title missing.

(7) Pratimāsāra (?).

XIII.—Sārasvata:

Under 28, Chaṇḍeśvara-vidhāna—the image of Chaṇḍeśvera.

(28) Garuḍa-lakshaṇa-paṭala—the image of the garuḍa bird; Rāma-Lakshmaṇa-paṭala—the images of Rāma and Lakshmaṇa. (The term 'paṭala' usually used in the Āgamas, indicates that these chapters may have been borrowed from some Āgamas).

Under 20, Gopura-māna—gate-houses.

(1) Māna-saṁgrahādi—the system of measurement.

XIV.—Viśva-sāra:

Under 20, Aśva-māna-vidhi—image of the horse.

" " Vīra-bhadra-lakshaṇa—image of Vīrabhadra.

" " Skandha—image of Skanda.

" " Tripurī—image of Tripurī.

" " Pratimādi—images, etc.

XV.—Chitra-jñāna:

Under 20, Dhvaja-daṇḍa-paṭa-lakshaṇa—flag, staff and banner.

" " Jīrṇoddhāra—repairs.

XVI.—Kapiñjala-saṁhitā:

Under 20, Garuḍa-lakshaṇa—image of the Garuḍa bird.

XVII.—Kaumudī:

Under 29, Pratimā-lakshaṇa—images in general.

XVIII.—Brahma-śilpa:

Under 15, Śayana-lakshaṇa—bedsteads and couches.

XIX.—Brahma-yāmala :

Under 5, Chāmuṇḍī-dhyāna—characteristics of the demoness Chāmuṇḍī.

Under 20, Daśāvatāra-lakshaṇa—images of the ten incarnations of Vishṇu.

XX.—Dīpta-tantra :

Under 16, Liṅga-lakshaṇa—Phallus

XXI.—Dīpti-sāra :

Under 8, Gopura-lakshaṇa—gate-houses.

Of these, it will be noticed, numbers one to five refer to treatises discussed above, six to ten refer to authors whose treatises are not mentioned here, and the rest refer to treatises and not to their authors. In fact it is practically impossible to trace the authors of these latter treatises, as is the case with several others dealing with architecture and cognate arts.

The brief sketch of this compilation as well as the other illustrative *Śilpa-Śāstras* presented above incidentally substantiate two theories. Most of the architectural treatises, whether or not ascribed to an author, historical or mythical, are but compilations. Some of these have actually acknowledged the sources drawn upon while others have not. This practice of misappropriating somebody else's property is prominently shown in works like the *Purāṇas* and the *Āgamas*, which in most cases are undeniably huge compilations gathered together from various sources dealing with heterogenous subjects. The second theory is that the *Mānasāra*, though itself a compilation, because the author seems to have consulted some thirty-two authorities on architecture, appears to be the standard work on the subject, inasmuch as it is the most complete, scientific, and probably the oldest extant record. This last impression is, further, strengthened by comparison of the *Mānasāra* with the architectural portions of the *Purāṇas*, the *Āgamas* and the *Bṛihat-saṁhitā* in detail.[1]

---

[1] See section III, pp 110—133.

III

POSITION OF THE MĀNASĀRA IN LITERATURE

With a view to ascertaining the position of the *Mānasāra* in relation to the non-architectural literature it will be necessary to discuss the points of similarity in detail. It is, however, practicable, in an article like this, to take into consideration only the architectural portions of works which deal with the subject specially. For the purpose of an elaborate treatment, we propose to compare the *Mānasāra* with the *Agni-Purāṇa*, the *Garuḍa-Purāṇa*, the *Matsya-Purāṇa*, the *Bhavishya-Purāṇa*, the *Bṛihat-saṁhitā*, the *Kāmikāgama*, and the *Suprabhedāgama*.

It has been pointed out at the outset that architecture comprises a variety of subjects. But it cannot be denied that the fundamental business of the architect is with buildings, residential, religious, and military. It appears to be a fashion among many peoples of the past as of the present to designate individual buildings by proper names with or without a meaning.[1] It seems to have been a custom among the ancient Hindu architects to describe buildings under some such names. In the eight treatises we have proposed to compare in detail, we find buildings bearing proper names classified and described in the following way.

1. In the *Mānasāra*, the main buildings are described in some thirteen chapters.[2] Their common features from bottom to top are given under storeys varying from one to twelve. They are also classified under styles—Nāgara, Vesara, and Drāviḍa—chiefly in accordance with the shape of the topmost part[3]; under sizes[4]; as Śuddha, Miśra, and Saṁkīrṇa in accordance with the materials of which they are built[5]; under Jāti, Chhanda, Vikalpa, and Ābhāsa

---

[1] Compare, for instance, Whitehall, Guildhall, Mansion House, Cosy Corner, Gordon Castle, Benmore, Barnes Castle, Svastika, Vijaya, Vipulāṅka, Indra-kānta, Chatur-mukha, Pāñchāla, Drāviḍa Kamalā-Bhavana, Chitta-Viśrāma, etc.

[2] Chapters XVIII to XXX, see the summary of contents in the preceding section under XVIII.

[3] For details of these styles, see the writer's Dictionary under Nāgara.

[4] Large, intermediate and small.

[5] (a) Śuddha or pure, made of one material (brick, iron or wood).
(b) Miśra or mixed, made of two materials.
(c) Saṁkīrṇa or amalgamated, made of three or more materials. M. XVIII, 133–143

in accordance with the various lengths of the cubit with which the buildings are measured[1]; under Sthānaka, Āsana, and Śayana, which are otherwise called Saṁchita, Asaṁchita, and Apasaṁchita respectively[2]; and under shapes, Puṁliṅga (masculine), Strīliṅga (feminine)[3], and Napuṁsaka (neuter).

The details of the ninety-eight types of buildings described according to the number of storeys are given below. The numerical figures on the left indicate the serial numbers, and those on the right refer to the lines or verses of the chapters:

I. The eight kinds of single storeyed buildings with their characteristic features, chapter XIX—(1) Vaijayāntika, with round spire (*śirsha*), pinnacle (*śiraḥ*), and neck (*grīvā*) (line 166); (2) Bhoga has *karṇa* or ears (187); (3) Śrīviśāla has the *bhadra* or front tabernacle in it (168); (4) Svastibandha has octangonal finial (*śirsha*) (169); (5) Śrīkara has quadrangular *śikhara* or steeple (170); (6) Hastiprishṭha has oval steeple (171); (7) Skandatāra has hexagonal spire and neck (172); (8) Keśara has the front tabernacles in the centre of the side-towers at the corners of the roof, and its nose, head, and neck are round or quadrangular (173–175).[4]

II. The eight kinds of two storeyed buildings, chapter XX (The general features are the same in all the eight kinds; the distinction lies in the different proportions given to the component parts from above the ground floor to the top):

(9) Śrīkara (lines 94, 2–9); (10) Vijaya (94, 10–15); (11) Siddha (94, 16–18); (12) Paushṭika (94, 19–25); (13) Antika (94, 25–27); (14) Adbhuta (94, 28–33); (15) Svastika (95, 34–41); and (16) Pushkala (94, 42–43). The projection, the general description, and the carvings on the doors, when these buildings are used as temples, are given (44–93, 96–116).[5]

III. The eight kinds of three-storeyed buildings, chapter XXI:

(The general features and characteristic marks are similar to those of two-storeyed buildings).

(17) Śrīkānta (lines 2–11); (18) Āsana (12–21); (19) Sukhālaya (22–30); (20) Kesara (31–32); (21) Kamalāṅga (33–38); (22) Brahmakānta (39–40); (23) Merukānta (41–49); and (24) Kailāśa (50–52).[6]

---

[1] M. XIX, 2–6.

[2] Referring respectively to height, breadth, and length, ibid 7–9, 10–11. The three latter sets also refer to the postures of the idols in case of temples, namely, erect, sitting, and recumbent.

[3] Equiangular and rectangular respectively. But in case of temples, the former contains the male deities while the latter may contain both female and male deities, ibid 14-17. For the neuter class see the Kāmikāgama below.

[4] For further details see the writer's Dictionary under ekabhūmi.

[5], [6] For further details see the writer's Dictionary under dvitala, and tritala.

The general features, characteristic marks and other details of the following kinds are similar to those of the two-and three-storeyed buildings.

IV. The eight kinds of four-storeyed buildings, chapter XXII :

(25) Vishṇukānta (lines 3—12); (26) Chaturmukha (13—24); (27) Sadāśiva (25-33); (28) Rudrakānta (34—43); (29) Īśvarakānta (44—46); (30) Mañchakānta (47—57); (31) Vedikānta (58—59); and (32) Indrakānta (60—88).[1]

V. The eight kinds of five-storeyed buildings, chapter XXIII :

(33) Airāvata (lines 3—12); (34) Bhūtakānta (13—15); (35) Viśvakānta (16—18); (36) Mūrtikānta (19—24); (37) Yamakānta (25—29), (38) Gṛihakānta (30—33); (39) Yajñakānta (33—40); and (40) Brahmakānta (41—42).[2]

VI. The thirteen kinds of six-storeyed buildings, chapter XXIV :

(41) Padmakānta (lines 3—12); (42) Kāntāra (13—14); (43) Sundara (15), (44) Upakānta (16); (45) Kamala (17—18); (46) Ratnakānta (19); (47) Vipulāṅka (20); (48) Jyoti(sh)kānta (50); (49) Saroruha; 50) Vipulākṛitika (53); (51) Svastikānta (53); (52) Nandyāvarta (54); and (53) Ikshukānta (55).[3]

VII. The eight kinds of seven-storeyed buildings, chapter XXV :

(54) Puṇḍarīka (lines 3—23); (55) Śrīkānta (24); (56) Śrībhoga (25; (57) Dhāraṇa (26); (58) Pañjara (27); (59) Āśramāgāra (28); (60) Harmyakānta (29); and (61) Himakānta (30).[4]

VIII. The eight kinds of eight-storeyed buildings, chapter XXVI :

(62) Bhūkānta (lines 3—21); (63) Bhūpakānta (22—28); (64) Svargakānta (29—34); (65) Mahākānta (35—39); (66) Janakānta (40); (67) Tapa(s)kānta (41—42); (68) Satyakānta (43—45); and (69) Devakānta (46—47).[5]

IX. The seven kinds of nine-storeyed buildings, chapter XXVII :

(70) Saurakānta (lines 5—9); (71) Raurava (10); (72) Chaṇḍita (11—12); (73) Bhūshaṇa (13—14); (74) Vivṛata (20—22); (75) Supratikānta 23—26); and (76) Viśvakānta (27—33).[6]

X. The six kinds of ten-storeyed buildings, chapter XXVIII :

(77) Bhūkānta (lines 6—8); (78) Chandrakānta (6—8); (79) Bhavanakānta (9—13); (80) Antarikshakānta (14—15); (81) Meghakānta (16—17); and 82) Abjakānta (18).[7]

XI. The six kinds of eleven storeyed buildings, chapter XXIX :

(83) Śambhukānta (lines 3—7); (84) Īśakānta (8—0); (85) Chakrakānta (10—14); (86) Yamakānta (15-17); (87) Vajrakānta (18-24); and (88) Akrakānta (24—33).[8]

1, 2, 3, 4, 5, 6, 7, 8. For further details, see the writer's Dictionary under chatustala, pañchatala, shaṭtala, saptatala, ashṭatala, navatala, daśatala, and ekādaśatala.

XII. The ten kinds of twelve-storeyed buildings, chapter XXX : (89) Pāñchāla (lines 6 16) ; (90) Drāviḍa (8—10) ; (91) Madhyakānta (11—14); (92) Kāliṅgakānta (14—16) ; (93) Varāṭa (Virāṭa?) (17—27) ; (94) Kerala (28—30) ; (95) Vaṁśakānta (31—32) ; (96) Māgadhakānta (33—34) ; (97) Jana(ka)kānta (33—36) ; and (98) Sphūrjaka(Gurjaraka) (7, 37—84 ; description of the twelfth storey).[1]

2. *Agni-Purāṇa*, chapter 42, V. 1—9 (general plan), 10 25 (plan with reference to the idol), chapter 104, V. 1—11, 22—34 (further general plan), 11—21 (names, classes, shapes, and description of forty-five kinds of temples).

Five divisions depending on five shapes (plans), and each including nine kinds of temples (chapter 104, V 11—13):

I. Vairāja—quadrangular (square)—includes (1) Meru, (2) Mandara, (3) Vimāna, (4) Bhadra, (5) Sarvatobhadra, (6) Charuka (in the Kāmikāgama, XXXV 87, 91 : Ruchaka), (7) Nandika, (8) Nandi varddhaṇa, and (9) Śrīvatsa, (chapter 104, V. 14, 15).

II. Pushpaka—rectangular—includes (10) Ba(Va)labhī, (11) Gṛiharāja, (12) Śālāgṛiha or Śālāmandira, (13) Viśāla, (14) Sama, (15) Brahma-mandira, (16) Bhavana or Bhuvana, (17) Prabhava, and (18) Śivikā-veśma, (chapter 104, V. 16,17).

III. Kailāśa—round—includes (19) Balaya (Valaya), (20) Dundubhi, (21) Padma, (22) Mahā-padmaka, (23) Varddhanī, (26) Kalaśa, and (27) Svavṛiksha, (chapter 104, V. 17—18).

IV. Maṇika—oval (vṛittāyata)—includes (28) Gaja, (29) Vṛishabha, (30) Haṁsa, (31) Garutman, (32) Ṛikshanāyaka, (33) Bhūshaṇa, (34) Bhūdhara, (35) Śrījaya, and (36) Prithivī-dhara, (chapter 104, V. 19—20)

V. Trivishṭapa—octagonal—includes (37) Vajra, (38) Chakra, (39) Svastika, (40) Vajra-svastika, (41) Chitra, (42) Svastika-khaḍga, (43) Gadā, (44) Śrīkaṇṭha, and (45) Vijaya, (chapter 104, V. 20—21).

3. *Garuḍa-Purāṇa* (chapter 47) has exactly the same general plan (V. 1—20, 32—47), five shapes, five classes (V. 21—23), and forty-five kinds of buildings (V. 24—32), but the wording is not identical. The fourth class is read Mālikā (V. 21) in the general description but the name 'Maṇika' (V. 30) is given later on :

I. Vairāja—square (V. 21—22)—includes the same 9 kinds ; but (7) Nandika is read as Nandana, and (6) Charuka is correctly read as Ruchaka, (V. 24—25).

---

[1] These ten kinds are named, it should be noticed, after the historic places, well marked in the ancient geography of India, which cover the whole length and breadth of the continent.

The topography of these places is described elsewhere (pp. 173 174). For the architectural details of these buildings see the writer's Dictionary under these ten terms. The description of the twelfth storey is given under Dvādaśatala.

II. Pushpaka—rectangular (V. 22—23)—includes nine kinds, where (10) Valabhī is correctly spelt, (13) Viśāla is read as Vimāna, which is apparently a mistake in the *Garuḍa-Purāṇa* because (3) Vimāna is a kind of building included in the square (I) Vairāja class. But the reading of class (II) seems better in the *Garuḍa-Purāṇa*, which may be quoted: (10) Valabhī, (11) Griharāja, (12) Śālāgṛiha, (13) Mandira, (14) Viśāla (text has 'Vimāna'), (15) Brahma-mandira, (16) Bhavana, (17) Uttambha, and (18) Śibikā (for Śivikā)-veśma, (V. 26—27).

III. Kailāśa—round (V 21—23)—has nine kinds, again perhaps with better readings: (19) Valaya, (20) Dundubhi, (21) Padma, (22) Mahāpadma, (23) Mukulī (in place of Varddhanī), (24) Ushṇīshī, (25) Śaṅkha, (26) Kalaśa, and (27) Guvā-vṛiksha, (V. 28—29).

IV. Maṇika—oval (V. 30)—has nine kinds, of which (31) (32), and (33) are read as Garuḍa, Siṁha and Bhūmukha respectively, (V. 29—30).

V. Trivishṭapa—octagonal (V. 21, 23)—has nine kinds, readings again seem better here: (37) Vaira, (38) Chakra, (39) Mushṭika (preceded by Babhru, V. 31), (40) Vakra, (41) Svastika, (42) Khaḍga, (43) Gadā, (44) Śrīvṛiksha, and (45) Vijaya, (V. 31—32).

4. The *Matsya-Purāṇa* chapter 269:

The description of the general plan (verses 1—7)[1] is followed by that of the special plan (verses 8—20).

---

[1] एवं वास्तुबलिं कृत्वा भजेत् षोडशभागिकम् ।
तस्य मध्ये चतुर्भिस्तु भागैर्गर्भं तु कारयेत् ॥ १ ॥
भागद्वादशकं सार्धं ततस्तु परिकल्पयेत् ।
चतुर्दिक्षु तथा ज्ञेयं निर्गमं तु ततो बुधैः ॥ २ ॥
चतुर्भागेन भित्तीनामुच्छ्रयः स्यात् प्रमाणतः ।
द्विगुणः शिखरोच्छ्रायो भित्त्युच्छ्रायप्रमाणतः ॥ ३ ॥
शिखरार्धस्य चार्धेन विधेया तु प्रदक्षिणा ।
गर्भसूत्रद्वयं चाग्रे विस्तारे मण्डलस्य तु ॥ ४ ॥
आयतः स्यात् त्रिभिर्भागैर्भद्रयुक्तः सुशोभनः ।
पञ्चभागेन संभज्य गर्भमानं विचक्षणः ॥ ५ ॥
भागमेकं गृहीत्वा तु प्राग्ग्रीवं कल्पयेद्बुधः ।
गर्भसूत्रसमं भागादग्रतो मुखमण्डपः ॥ ६ ॥
एतत् सामान्यमुद्दिष्टं प्रासादस्य च लक्षणम् ।

The names (V. 28—30), description of architectural details (V. 31—46), measures (47—51) and division (53—54) of twenty types of buildings :

(1) Meru has 100 cupolas (*śriṅga*), 16 storeys (*bhūmika*), many variegated steeples (*śikhara*), and is 50 cubits broad (V. 28, 31, 53); (2) Mandara has 12 storeys, many steeples and faces, and is 45 cubits broad (V. 28, 37, 47, 53); (3) Kailāśa has 9 storeys, (many steeples and faces), and is 40 cubits broad (V. 32, 47, 53); (4) Vimāna-chchhanda has 8 storeys, many steeples and faces (*ānana*), and is 34 cubits broad (V. 25, 32, 33, 47, 53); (5) Nandi-vardhana has 7 storeys, and is 32 cubits broad (V. 29, 33, 48, 53); (6) Nandana has 7 storeys, and is furnished with *vishāṇa* or horns, and is 30 cubits broad (V. 29, 33, 48, 53); (7) Sarvatobhadra has 5 storeys, 16 corners with various shapes, is furnished with art-galleries (*chitraśālā*), and is 30 cubits broad (V. 29, 34, 35, 48, 53); (8) Vallabhi-chchhandaka has 5 storeys, many steeples and faces, and is 16 cubits broad (V. 35, 50, 53); (9) Vṛisha should resemble the height and length of the bull, be round and without corners, should have 5 cupolas, 2 storeys, and should be 4 cubits broad at the central hall (V. 30, 36, 44, 45, 53); (10) Siṁha resembles the lion and is 16 cubits broad is adorned with the famous *chandraśālā* (top rooms, gable-windows), and by the width of the front neck 6 storeys high (V. 29, 36, 40, 49, 53); (11) Gaja resembles the elephant, and is 16 cubits broad, and has many

---

सामान्यमपरं तद्वत्प्रासादं शृणुत द्विजा ।
त्रिभागं कारयेत् क्षेत्रं यत्र तिष्ठन्ति देवताः ॥ २१ ॥
रथाङ्कस्तेन मानेन बाह्यभागविनिर्गतः ।
नेमिपादेन विस्तीर्णा प्रासादस्य समन्ततः ॥ २२ ॥
गर्भंतु द्विगुणं कुर्यात्तस्य मानं भवेदिह ।
स एव भित्तेरुत्सेधो द्विगुणः शिखरो मतः ॥ २३ ॥
प्राग्ग्रीवः पञ्चभागेन निष्कासस्तस्य चोच्यते ।
कारयेत् सुषिरं तद्वत्प्राकारस्य विभागतः ॥ २४ ॥
प्राग्ग्रीवं पञ्चभागेन निष्कासेन विशेषतः ।
कुर्याद्वा पञ्चभागेन प्राग्ग्रीवं कर्णमूलतः ॥ २५ ॥
स्थापयेत् कलशं तत्र गर्भान्ते द्वारमूलतः ।
एवं तु त्रिविधं कुर्याज्ज्येष्ठमध्यकनीयसम् ॥ २६ ॥
लिङ्गमानानुभेदेन रूपभेदेन वा पुनः ।
एते समासतः प्रोक्ता नामतः शृणुताधुना ॥ २७ ॥
तथा मेर्वादयः सप्त ज्येष्ठलिङ्गे शुभावहाः ।
श्रीवृक्षकादयश्चाष्टौ मध्यमस्य प्रकीर्तिताः ॥ ५३ ॥
तथा हंसादयः पञ्च कन्यसे शुभदा मताः ॥ ५४ ॥

chandaśālās or top rooms (V. 36, 41, 49, 53); (12) Kumbha resembles the water-jar, has 9 storeys, 5 cupolas (*aṇḍas*), and is 16 cubits broad (V. 37, 49, 53); (13) Samudraka has 16 sides around, 2 *chandaśālās* (top rooms) at the two sides, 2 storeys (V. 38, 53); (14) Padma has 3 storeys, 16 corners, a variegated steeple, and is 20 cubits broad (V. 30 39, 49, 53); (15) Garuda has the *gṛihārāja* (?) around, 7 storeys, 3 top rooms, and is 8 cubits broad, and there should be 86 (?) compartments (bhūmikā, lit., storeys, V. 42) all around the outside (V. 41, 43, 51). There is a similar Garuḍa-building with 10 storeys and a second Padmaka-building with 2 storeys more (? 12 storeys, V. 43); (16) Haṁsa is 10 cubits broad (36, 51); (17) Vartula is 20 cubits broad (V. 29, 49, 53). No special description is given of the remaining: (18) Chaturaśra (four-cornered, V. 28, 53); (19) Ashṭāśra (eight-cornered, V. 29, 53); (20) Shoḍaśāsra (sixteen-cornered, V. 29, 53).[1]

Similar types of buildings are described almost in the same way in both the *Bhavishya-Purāṇa* and the *Bṛihat-saṁhitā*.

5. The *Bhavishya-Purāṇa*, chapter 130, names (V. 23—26), description of the architectural details and measures (V. 27—35) of the twenty kinds of buildings (same as in the *Bṛihat-saṁhitā*, see below):
   (1) Meru, 39 cubits high and 32 cubits broad, has 12 storeys, various windows (*kuhara*), and four gateways (V. 27).
   (2) Mandara, 30 cubits broad, and has 10 storeys (V. 28).
   (3) Kailāśa, 28 cubits broad, has steeples and 8 storeys (V. 28).
   The description of the following is clearer in the *Bṛihat-saṁhitā*, quoted below; the names may be given here:
   (4) Vimāna with latticed windows (V. 29).
   (5) Nandana (V. 29).
   (6) Samudga (V. 30), Samudra (V. 24) as in the *Bṛihat-saṁhitā* (LVI. 28, 5).
   (7) Padma (V. 30).
   (8) Garuḍa (V. 31).
   (9) Nandi-vardhana (V. 28, Naṁdī, V. 31).
   (10) Kuñjara (V. 32).
   (11) Gṛiharāja (V. 32), *Bṛihat-saṁhitā* (LVI. 25) has 'Guharāja.'
   (12) Vṛisha (V. 33).
   (13) Haṁsa (V. 33).
   (14) Ghaṭa (V. 33).
   (15) Sarvatobhadra (V. 34).
   (16) Siṁha (V. 35).

[1] Compare the three divisions of these buildings according to sizes.

(17) Vṛitta (as in the *Bṛihat-saṁhitā*, LVI, 29, 49); but here (V. 33) it reads Vṛisha like (12), which is apparently a mistake (see V. 30).

No special description is given of the remaining :

(18) Chatushkoṇa (four-cornered V. 25), *Matsya-Purāṇa* (chapter 269, V. 28, 53) has Chaturaśra ; and *Bṛihat-saṁhitā* (VI. 28) has Chaturasra.

(19) Ashṭāśra (octangular, V. 25).

(20) Shoḍaśāśra (sixteen-cornered, V. 25).

Varāhamihira seems to have taken these from an earlier Purāṇa and improved them in the *Bṛihat-saṁhitā*.

6. The *Bṛihat-saṁhitā*, LVI. 1—19:

The religious merits acquired by building temples (V. 1—2); suitable sites—in the garden, wood, banks of rivers, (seas), tanks (V. 3—8); ground (V. 9); general plan (V. 10); situation of doors (V. 10); comparative measures of length, breadth and height (V. 11), of the adytum (garbha, V. 12), of the doors and their different parts (V. 12—14); carvings on the door (V. 15); comparative measures of the idol, pedestal, and door (V. 16); the heights of storeys (V. 29—30).

This is followed by a classification (V. 17—19) and an account of the architectural details (V. 20—28) of the same twenty kinds of temples (prāsāda) as are given in the *Matsya-Purāṇa* and the *Bhavishya-Purāṇa*. The names of these buildings are given below, details being almost the same as in the Purāṇas :

(1) Meru (V. 20).
(2) Mandara (V. 21).
(3) Kailāśa (V. 21).
(4) Vimāna-(chchhanda) (V. 17—22).
(5) Nandana (V. 22).
(6) Samudga (V. 23).
(7) Padma (V. 23).
(8) Garuḍa (V. 24).
(9) Nandivardhana (V. 24).
(10) Kuñjara (V. 25).
(11) Guharāja (V. 25).
(12) Vṛisha (V. 26).
(13) Haṁsa (V. 26).
(14) Ghaṭa (V. 26).
(15) Sarvatobhadra (V. 27).
(16) Siṁha (V. 28).
(17) Vṛitta (V. 18—28).

(18) Chatush-koṇa (V. 18—28).
(19) Ashṭāsra (V. 18—28).
(20) Shoḍaśāsra (V. 18—28).

7. The *Kāmikāgama*, paṭala LV[1]:

The four classes:

Jāti (V. 128), Chhanda (V. 129), Vikalpa (130), and Ābhāsa (130).

Paṭala XLV:

Further classifications:

(1) Saṁchita, Apasaṁchita, and Upasaṁchita (V 6).
(2) Nāgara (6,12,13), Drāviḍa (6,14,15), and Vesara (7, 16—18).
(3) Jāti (7, 19), Chhanda (7—20), and Vikalpa (7—20).
(4) Śuddha (7, 21). Miśra (7, 22), and Saṁkīrṇa (7, 22).
(5) Puṁ-liṅga or masculine, also called Saṁchita (8, 9), Strī-liṅga or feminine (9, 10), and Napuṁsaka or neuter (11).

This class (5) does not refer (like the *Mānasāra*) to the sexes of the deities. Here they appear more like residential buildings: their characteristic features are determined by architectural details. The distinguishing marks of the divisions in the other four classes (1 to 4) are similar to those of the *Mānasāra* noticed above.

In Paṭala XXXV, Śālās, in almost the sense of Prāsāda, are divided into five classes: Sarvatobhadra (87, 88), Varddhamāna (87, 88), Svastika (87, 89), Nandyāvarta (87, 90), and Charuka (87, 91).

Their technical names[2]:

(1) Sindhuka (XLV, 23—28); (2) Sampūrṇa (29—30); (3) Merukūṭa (31); (4) Kshema (32—34); (5) Śiva (35—38); (6) Harmya (39—40); (7) Saumya (40); (8) Viśāla (41); (9) Sarvakalyāṇa (43—49); (10) Vijaya (50); (11) Bhadra (51); (12) Raṅgamukha (52); (13) Alpa (53—54); (14) Koṇa (55—58); (15) Geya (58*a*—59); (16) Sāra (60); (17) Pushkara (61, 63); (18) Adbhuta (61*a*); (19) Saṁkīrṇa (62); and (20) Daṇḍa (64).

8. The *Suprabhedāgama*, Paṭala XXXI (named Prāsāda):

Three styles of temples—Nāgara, Drāviḍa, and Vesara (38—39).

Different kinds of temples—(1) Kailāśa, (2) Mandara, (3) Meru, (4) Himavat, (5) Nishadha (also called Nīlaparvata, Mahendra), (6) Nalīnaka, (7) Pralīnaka, (8) Nandyāvarta, (9) Śrīvarta (? Śrīpada), and (10) Parvata, (40—52).

---

[1] This Paṭala refers to the description of a single building and its component parts. So also does the Paṭala XLV (see under Mālikā); it is named Mālikā-(lakshaṇa) and does not mean anything but Prāsāda: Cf. Prāsāda-vyāsa-dīrghochchā proktā *prāsāda-mālikā* (11, 4).

[2] For further details see the writer's Dictionary under these terms and Mālikā.

Maṇḍapas are first divided into four classes:

Deva-maṇḍapa, Snapana (bath)-maṇḍapa, Brisha (bull, nandin)-maṇḍapa, and Nritta (music)-maṇḍapa (96—97, 98—99); and further classified under epithets, Nandavritta, Śriyāvritta, Virāsana, Jayabhadra, Nandyāvarta, Maṇibhadra, and Viśāla (100—104).

The attention of readers is invited to the lists of the buildings described in the eight works under observation.

The list in the *Mānasāra* contains in 12 classes (storeys) 98 types of buildings; the *Agni-Purāṇa* has in 5 classes (or divisions) 45 types, the *Garuḍa-Purāṇa* also has in the same 5 classes (or divisions) the same 45 types; the *Matsya-Purāṇa* has in 3 divisions 20 types, the *Bhavishya-Purāṇa* has left out the broader divisions but contains the 20 types; the *Brihat-saṁhitā* in the very same way contains the 20 types; the *Kāmikāgama* has in 3 divisions (of various kinds) 20 types; and the *Suprabhedāgama* has left out all the minor divisions but preserves the most important one, namely, the 3 styles (Nāgara, Vesara, Drāviḍa), which comprise 10 types of buildings.

The various broader divisions, such as Śuddha, Saṁchita, Sthānaka, Jāti, Puṁliṅga, etc., we have seen in the *Mānasāra*, are repeated in the same terms and same sense in the *Āgamas*. The most important division into the styles—the Nāgara, Vesara and Drāviḍa—is also preserved intact in the latter works. These are purely architectural divisions, and they are not taken into consideration in the non-architectural treatises like the *Purāṇas* and the *Brihat-saṁhitā*. Even the broadest division into storeys, under which the *Mānasāra* describes the buildings in 12 or 13 chapters, has lost its prominence in the latter works.

Thus the *Mānasāra* has the largest number of the types, namely, 98. The *Agni-Purāṇa* and the *Garuḍa-Purāṇa* have 45 types each. The *Matsya-Purāṇa*, the *Bhavishya-Purāṇa*, the *Brihat-saṁhitā*, and the *Kāmikāgama* have 20 types each. The *Suprabhedāgama* has the smallest number of types, namely, 10.

The technical names of these types of buildings are, as we have seen above, common in many cases. We have also seen that in some instances the architectural details are identical. The lists of the *Agni-Purāṇa* and the *Garuḍa-Purāṇa* on the one hand, and the *Matsya-Purāṇa*, the *Bhavishya-Purāṇa* and the *Brihat-saṁhitā*, on the other, are strikingly similar. Of the works containing the lists of 20 types, the *Brihat-saṁhitā* has the best description. But in respect of brevity, explicitness and precision, the *Suprabhedāgama*, which contains the smallest number of types, surpasses all. And it happens that the smaller the types the better the description.

The common names of the types, the identity of their details, and the similarity in the description may not be accidental. The grades in the linguistic style and in the explicitness and precision of the description do not seem unconnected. And the variations in the number of types of buildings treated in these works may not also be meaningless. But before hazarding an opinion it will be better to compare some of the other important points of similarity between the *Mānasāra* and the architectural portions of the other works.

Amongst others, the three crucial features in architecture, at least so far as these ancient records are concerned, seem to be the measurement, the orders or columns, and the styles. Similarities in these respects are hardly accidental and may be ascribed to a common origin.

Measurements

(*A*) The linear measurement is divided into six kinds[1]:

(1) Māna, (2) Pramāṇa, (3) Parimāṇa, (4) Lamba-māna,

(5) Unmāna, and (6) Upamāna (M. LV. 3—9).

References to these measurements are met with also in non-architectural treatises, like the *Matsya-Purāṇa* (chapter 258, V 16), the *Suprabhedāgama* (paṭala, XXXIV. 35), as well as in the *Bimbamāna* (British Museum, Mss. 658, 5292, verse 9),

(*B*) The primary measurement (ādimāna) refers to comparative measurements and is divided into nine kinds:

The height of an image is determined by comparing it with the

(1) breadth of the main temple,

(2) height of the adytum,

(3) length of the door,

(4) measurement of the basement,

(5) cubit,

(6) tāla,

(7) aṅgula,

(8) height of the worshipper, and

(9) height of the riding animal (M. LV. 10—15).

Each of the measurements is again divided into nine kinds (M. LV. 22).

Under (1), (2), (3), (4), the proportions naturally vary on various occasions but the general methods are similar in these treatises; compare, for instances the *Suprabhedāgama* (XXXI 1—15).

The aṅgula (finger breadth) and the hasta (cubit), (5), 7), measures are in fact of the same class. The finger breadth, equivalent to ¾ inch, is perhaps the earliest unit of measurement invented by human brain. Though not liable

[1] Measurement from the foot to the top of the head is called Māna (which is nothing but height).

Pramāṇa is the measurement of breadth.

Parimāṇa is the measurement of width or circumference (pariṭaḥ).

Lambamāna is the measurement by the plumb-lines or the lines drawn perpendicularly through different parts of the body, the māna or the measurement of height being taken by the surface of the body.

Unmāna is the measurement of thickness (nimna) or diameter.

Upamāna is the measurement of interspace (antara), such as that between the two feet of an image.

Parimāna, unmāna and māna are also mentioned in the Śukra-nīti (I. 310), but their meanings are not quite clear.

to being lost in the course of time, it has its own defects, namely, the finger of two persons is hardly of equal breadth, and the finger of a person is liable to change owing to various natural causes. Apparently with a view to avoiding these defects finger-breadth is ascertained by the measures of certain other objects, atom, car-dust, hair-end, nit, louse, and barley-corn.[1] The largest size of finger breadth is stated to be equal to eight barley corns, the intermediate seven barley corns, and the smallest six barley corns. Again, for the same purpose, this standard measure is divided into three kinds—mānāṅgula, mātrāṅgula, and dehalabdhāṅgula. Of these, mānāṅgula, which is equal to eight barley corns, is meant to be the unit proper. Mātrāṅgula is the measure taken by the middle finger of the master who makes an image (or a building), dehalabdhāṅgula is the measure equal to one of the equal parts into which the whole height of a statue is divided for sculptural measurement.[2]

This aṅgula measure is practically the same in almost all the Indian works bearing upon measurement, for instance—

(1) Mānasāra (II 40—45, 46—47, 48—52, 53—64, LXIV, 49—53, etc.).
(2) Bṛihat-saṁhitā (LVIII, 1—2).
(3) Siddhānta-śiromaṇi, ed. Bāpūdeva (p. 52).
(4) Rāja-vallabha-Maṇḍana, ed. Bhārati (Introduction).
(5) Brahmāṇḍa-Purāṇa (part I, section 2, chapter VII).
(6) Matsya-Purāṇa (chapter 258, verses 17—18).
(7) Vāstu-vidyā, ed. Gaṇapati Śāstri (I, 3—5f).
(8) Bimba-māna (Ms. British Museum, no. 558, 5292, verse 9f.)
(9) Suprabhedāgama (XX. 1—9, 10 – 16, 20—26, etc.).
(10) Kauṭiliya-Artha-śāstra, ed. Shama Śastri (p. 106); compare also
(11) Manu-saṁhitā (VIII. 271).
(12) Rāmāyaṇa (VI. 20,22).
(13) Śata-patha-Brāhmaṇa (X, 2, 13, III. 5, 4, 5).
(14) Aitareya-Brāhmaṇa (VIII. 5).
(15) Chhāndogya-Upanishad (V, 18, 1, etc.).
(16) Śulva-Sūtra of Baudhāyana (J. R. A. S. 1912, 231 – 233, notes 1, 2).

---

[1] 8 atoms = 1 car-dust.
8 car-dusts = 1 hair-end.
8 hair-ends = 1 nit.
8 nits = 1 louse.
8 lice = 1 barley corn.
8 barley corns = 1 aṅgula

[2] For further details see the writer's Dictionary under aṅgula.

The *tāla*-māna (under 6) is a sculptural measure. The length of face inclusive of head is taken as the unit of measurement.[1] But it seems more convenient to have the particular span, namely, the distance between the tips of the fully stretched thumb and middle finger, which is technically called *tāla*, as the unit.[2] It admits of many varieties: ten *tāla* measures are mentioned in the Mānasāra[3], while the Bimba-māna has reference to twelve kinds[4]. Each of these ten or twelve varieties is again divided into three types, namely, uttama or large, madhyama or intermediate, and adhama or small. Thus an image is of the ten (daśa) *tāla* measure when its whole length is ten times the face. In the large type of the ten *tāla* system, however, the whole length is divided into 124 equal parts which are proportionately distributed over the different parts of the body; in the intermediate type the whole length is divided into 120 equal parts, and in the small type into 116 equal parts. In the nine (nava) *tāla* system, the whole length would be nine times the face, in the eight (ashṭa) *tāla* eight times, and so forth.

The principle of the *tāla* measure is fundamentally the same in all the works dealing with the subject, although certain differences in matters of detail are noticed, compare, for instance,—

(1) Mānasāra (LX, 6—35, LVII, LIX, 14—64; 67—100; LXVI. 2—78; LXV, 2—179).
(2) Bimbamāna (verses 17—72, 91—138, and appendix X).
(3) Suprabhedāgama (XXXIV, 30—34; XXX, 31—40).
(4) Bṛihat-saṁhitā (LVIII, 4).
(5) Aṁśumadbheda of Kāśyapa (fol. 251, Eg. 3148, 3012).
(6) Bramhāṇḍa-Purāṇa (Part I, Anusaṁga-pāda, VII. 97).
(7) Matsya-Purāṇa (chapter 258, verse 19).

The details of the *tāla* measures from the following authorities are given by Mr. Rao[5]:

(8) Śilpa-ratna.
(9) Aṁśumad-bhedāgama.
(10) Kā(?ki)raṇāgama.
(11) Vaikhānasāgama.
(12) Kāmikāgama.

---

[1] Matsya Purṇā, chapter 258, verse 19.
Mukhamānena kartavyā sarvāvayava-kalpanā.

[2] Aṁśumadbheda of Kāśyapa, fol. 251. (Ms. Egg. 3148, 3012).

[3] One to ten tāla (M. LX. 6—35, etc.).

[4] One to twelve tāla (Appendix).

[5] Elements of Hindu Iconography by T. A. Gopīnāth Rāo, Appendix B, pp. 9—28.

Another exclusively sculptural measure is that mentioned under (8), (9), namely, the height of an image is compared with the height of the worshipper (yajamāna), and the height of the riding animal (vāhana) is compared with the height of the main idol. Each of these admits of nine varieties. The height of an image may be equal to the full height of its worshipper, and may extend up to his hair-limit on the forehead (sometimes it is stated to be the eye-line), nose-tip, chin, arm-limit (to the shoulder), breast, heart, navel, and sex-organ. The height of the riding animal is in the same manner compared with the height of the main idol.[1]

Corresponding to the abovementioned sculptural measures there are exclusively architectural measures also.

The architectural *gaṇya a-māna*[2] or the comparative heights of the component members of a structure corresponds to the sculptural *tāla*-māna or the comparative heights of the component limbs of a statue.

The *ghana-māna* or the measurement by the exterior, and the *aghana-māna* or the measurement by the interior, of a structure is also exclusively architectural.[3]

In another architectural measure the height of a structure is compared with its breadth. It admits of five proportions, technically called, Śāntika, Paushṭika, Jayada, Sarva-kāmika or Dhanada, and Adbhuta, the height being respectively equal to breadth, 1¼, 1½, 1¾, and twice of the breadth.[4]

These latter items, highly technical and extremely minute in detail, are found in no other treatises under observation than the *Mānasāra*. Thus in respect of at least purely architectural and sculptural measurement the *Mānasāra*, of all these works, should occupy the first place.

---

[1] Mānasāra, LV. 80—88 etc.

[2] See the writer's Dictionary, and compare the Mānasāra, XXVII, 86—40; XXIX, 85—88; XXXIII, 184—145, 216—117, 248, XLV, 86, 97—101; LIII, 29—84; XIII, 36—40, etc.

[3] See the writer's Dictionary, sub voce.

[4] See the writer's Dictionary, under *Utsedha*.

When a large number of absolute measures are prescribed for the one and the same object, the right proportion is selected by the test of six formulas technically called, āya, vyaya, ṛiksha, yoni, vāra, and tithi or aṁśa (see details in the writer's Dictionary under Shaḍ-varga).

The Five Orders

Like the five Græco-Roman orders, Doric, Ionic, Corinthian, Tuscan and Composite, columns in ancient India also were divided into five main orders or classes. In the *Mānasāra* [1] they are called Brahma-kānta[2], Vishṇu-kānta, Rudra-kānta, Śiva-kānta, and Skanda-kānta. These divisions are based on the general shapes of columns. With respect to dimensions and ornaments the five orders are called Chitra-karṇa, Padma-kānta, Chitra-skambha, Pālikā-stambha, and Kumbhastambha. A sixth variety in the latter division is pilaster and not pillar proper, and is called Koshṭha-stambha and Kuḍya-stambha [3].

Among the *Purāṇas*, these details are very clear only in the *Matsya-Purāṇa*. In this *Purāṇa*[4] as well as in the *Bṛihat-saṁhitā*[5] the five orders are called Ruchaka, Vajra, Dvi-vajra, Pralīnaka, and Vṛitta.

Of the *Āgamas*[6], the *Suprabhedāgama* contains the essential details. The names of the five orders according to this Āgama [7] are Śrī-kara, Chandra-kānta, Saumukhya, Priya-darsana, and Śubhaṅkarī; the last one is stated to be the Indian composite order, being compound of Saumukhya and Priya-darśana, just as the Græco-Roman composite order is a compound of Corinthian and Ionic.

Between the European and the Indian columns, however, there is obviously a striking point of difference. Of the Græco-Roman orders, the five names have been left unchanged, while in India the names of the five orders have varied in various treatises referred to above. It is true, all the same, that the criteria of divisions are essentially the same in the *Mānasāra*, the *Āgamas*, the *Purāṇas*, and the *Bṛihat-saṁhitā*[8]. We have also seen above that the *Mānasāra* contains two sets of names of the five orders, one set referring like the *Āgamas*, the *Purāṇas*, and the *Bṛihat-saṁhitā*, to the shapes of the columns, or more precisely the shafts, while the other refers mostly to the capitals. The works other than the *Vāstu-śāstras*

---

[1] Chapter XV, 20—23, 31, 39, 40, 73, 204.

[2] Also mentioned in Corpus Inscriptionum Indicarum, volume III, p 252, 253; Epigraphia Indica, XII, p. 212, 216; V. 151.

[3] Mānasāra, XV, 84.

[4] Matsya-Purāṇa, chapter 255, 1—6.

[5] Bṛihat-saṁhitā, VIII 27—30; also J. R. A. S. (N. S). VI, p. 285, notes 1, 2.

[6] See, for instance, the Kāmikāgama, Paṭala XXXV, 24—25, 161, LV. 208, etc.

[7] Suprabhedāgama, Paṭala, XXXI, 65—67.

[8] See references given above, and for further details consult the writer's Dictionary under *stambha*.

as represented by the *Mānasāra* have not kept this distinction clear. What we can reasonably infer from this as regards the mutual relation of these treatises will be further elucidated by a consideration of the component parts of the column. The question of variation of the names of the five orders in the Indian works can perhaps be explained. While in Europe the origin of the names of the five orders is traced to historical geography,[1] in India the names were based on the shapes of columns. And as the Indians are comparatively religious and poetical rather than historical in temperament and imagination, they chose mythological and poetical names according to the spirit of the times when these various works were composed. Thus in the *Mānasāra*, we see the orders bearing the names of mythological deities, Brahmā, Vishṇu, Rudra, Śiva, and Skanda; as well as called *Chitra-karṇa* (variegated ears), *Padma-kānta* (graceful like lotus), *Chitra-skambha* (of variegated shaft), *Pālikā-stambha* (edged like a measuring pot), and *Kumbha-stambha* (of jug-shaped capital); while in the *Āgama*, they bear highly poetical names—*Śrī-kara* (beautifying), *Chandra-kānta* (graceful like the moon), *Saumukhya* (of very charming face), *Priya-darśana* (sight-pleasing), *Śubhaṅkarī* (auspicious), and in the *Purāṇas* and the *Bṛihat-saṁhitā*, they are called *Ruchaka* (beautiful, pleasing), *Vajra* (club, hence lasting), *Dvi-vajra* (doubly lasting), *Pralīnaka* (firmly attached, hence a pilaster), and *Vṛitta* (round, hence solid and dignified).

With regard to the names and the functions of the component parts of the column the variation is a little less marked. But these subservient parts, called mouldings and common to all orders, vary in number. Thus in the *Mānasāra*, which of almost all the treatises deals separately and exhaustively with the pedestal, the base, and the entablature, mention is made in connection with the pillar, of five mouldings[2] apparently of the shaft, namely, *bodhikā*, *mushṭi-bandha*, *phalakā*, *tāṭikā*, and *ghaṭa*. The *Suprabhedāgama* describes two sets of seven mouldings,[3] one set referring to the column of the main building and the other to that of the pavilion—*daṇḍa*, *maṇḍi*, *kaṇṭha*, *kumbha*, *phalakā*, *vīra-kaṇṭha* and *potikā*; and *bodhikā*, *uttara*, *vājana*, *mūrdhikā*, *tulā*, *jayanti*, and *tala*. These increasing number of mouldings have reached the significant number of eight in the *Matsya-Purāṇa*, the *Bṛihat-saṁhitā* and the *Kiraṇa-tantrā*, and bears the

[1] Doric is derived from the species of columns first seen in the cities of Doria (Vitruvius, IV. 1). That species of which the Ionians (inhabitants of Ionia) were the inventors has received the appellation of Ionic (ibid). Callimachus constructed columns after the model of the tomb in the country about Corinth, hence this species is called Corinthian (ibid). The other two orders, Tuscan and Composite, are of Italian or Roman origin. The Tuscan order has reference to the country of Tuscany, formerly called, Etruria, in Italy (Gwilt encyclopædia of architecture, article 178).

[2] Mānasāra, XLVII, 16—18.

[3] Suprabhedāgama, Paṭala, XXXI, 56—60, 107—108.

very same eight names[1], to wit, *vāhana*, *ghaṭa*, *padma*, *uttoroshṭha*, *bāhulya*, *bhāra* (or *hāra*), *tulā*, and *upatulā*.

The significance of the number eight referred to above lies in the fact that the component parts of the Græco-Roman orders also are eight in number[2], and like the five orders themselves, their names are always the same ever since their introduction, though most of them have been given more than one name. They are called, (1) the ovolo, echinus or quarter round; (2) the talon, ogée or reversed cyma; (3) the cyma, cyma-recta or cyma-tium; (4) the torus; (5) the scotia or trochilos; (6) the cavetto, mouth or hollow; (7) the astragal; and (8) the fillet, listel or annulet.

The *Mānasāra* refers to five mouldings; the *Suprabhedāgama* describes seven; and the *Matsya-Purāṇa*, the *Bṛihata-saṁhitā*, and *Kiraṇa tantra*, each, makes mention of eight mouldings. But if the very large number of mouldings[3], described in the *Mānasāra* in connection with the pedestal, the base, and the entablature, be also taken into account, the *Mānasāra* will certainly exceed all other treatises under notice. Thus in the *Mānasāra* we can detect the following mouldings,—(1) abja, ambuja, padma or saroruha (cyma); (2) antara, antarita, antarāla or antarika (fillet), (3) aṅghri; (4) aṁśu; (5) argala; (6) ādhāra; (7) āliṅga; (8) āsana; (9) bhadra; (10) bodhikā; (11) dala; (12) dhārā-(kumbha); (13) gala, grīva, kaṇṭha or kandhara (dado); (14) ghaṭa; (15) gopāna-(ka); (16) hāra (bead); (17) janman (plinth); (18) kapota; (19) kampa, kampana (fillet); (20) karṇa; (21) kumbha; (22) kumuda (torus or astragal); (23) kendra; (24) kshepaṇa, (25) mushṭi-bandha; (26) mūla; (27) mṛiṇāla or mṛiṇālikā; (28) nāṭaka; (29) nāsī; (30) nimna (drip); (31) paṭṭa or paṭṭikā (fillet); (32) prati or pratika; (33) prati-vakra; (34) prati-vājana; (35) prati-bandha; (36) pratima; (37) pāduka; (38) prastara; (39) phalakā; (40) ratna, compounded with kampa, paṭṭa, and vapra; (41) tāṭikā;

[1] Matsya-Purāṇa, chap. 255, 1—6f; Bṛihat-saṁhitā, VIII, 29—30; Kiraṇa-tantra, J. R. A. S. (N.S.) VI. 285, notes 1, 2 p.

[2] See figures 867—874 and article 2532, Gwilt, Encyclopædia of Architecture; Glossary of architectural terms, Plate XXXIV.

[3] See the writer's Dictionary, under *upapīṭha*, *adhishṭhāna* and *prastara*.

[4] There are mouldings which bear a large number of names or synonyms, e.g.,

(i) Kapota, prastara, mañcha, prachchhādana, gopāna, vitāna valabhī and matta-vāraṇa.
(ii) Prati-prastara, prati-vājana, anvanta, avasāna, vidhāna and vidhānaka.
(iii) Prati-rūpa, dalākāra, vijana, vājana, kshepaṇa, vetra, paṭṭa, uttara, paṭṭikā, kampa, trika, maṇḍa and antarita.
(iv) Tulā-daṇḍa, jayanti and phalakā.
(v) Kapota, vakra-hasta, lūpā, gopānaka and chandra.
(vi) Saṁgraha, mushṭi-bandha, maddala, udbṛita-hasta, valabbī and dhāraṇa.
(vii) Nāṭaka, anta, mṛiṇālikā, vallikā, chitrāṅga and kulikāṅghrika
(viii) Uttara, vājana, ādhāra, ādheya, śayana, udbṛita, mūrdhaka, mahā-tauli and svavaṁśaka.

(42) tuṅga ; (43) uttara (fillet) ; (44) upāna (plinth) ; (45) vapra or vapraka ; (46) valabha or valabhī ; and (47) vājana (fillet).

There are a number of compound mouldings also, such as, Kampa-karṇa. Karṇa-padma, Kshudra-kampa, Kshudra-padma, Kshepanāmbuja, Mahāmbuja, Padma-kampa, Ratna-kampa, Ratna-paṭṭa, Ratna-vapra, Vajra-paṭṭa, etc.

Again, of all these treatises, only the *Mānasāra* and the *Āgamas* refer to certain highly technical and purely architectural matters. Thus in the *Mānasāra* we find the measurements and other details of sixty-four variety of bases divided into nineteen classes[1], called (1) Pāda-bandha, (2) Uraga-bandha, (3) Prati-krama, (4) Kumuda-bandha, (5) Padma-kesara, (6) Pushpa-pushkala, (7) Śrī-bandha, (8) Mañcha-bandha, (9) Śreṇī-bandha, (10) Padma-bandha, (11) Kumbha-bandha, (12) Vapra-bandha, (13) Vajra-bandha, (14) Śrī-bhoga, (15) Ratna-bandha, (16) Paṭṭa-bandha, (17) Kukshi-bandha, (18) Kampa-bandha, and (19) Śrī-kānta.

In the *Suprabhedāgama* only four classes[2] of bases are mentioned, namely, Padma-bandha, Chāru-bandha, Pāda-bandha, and Prati-krama. The *Kāmikāgama* has only the general description of the base.[3]

In the *Mānasāra* sixteen types of pedestals are described in detail under three classes[4], namely, Vedi-bhadra, Prati-bhadra, and Mañcha-bhadra.

Only scanty information of the pedestal is found in the *Kāmikāgama*[5], the *Suprabhedāgama*[6], and a Tamil version of the *Mayamata*.[7]

As regards the entablature, various mouldings and their measurements are described under eight classes in the *Mānasāra*[8]. The *Kāmikāgama*[9], the *Suprabhedāgama*[10] and the *Vāstu-vidyā*[11] have only briefly referred to the general description of the entablature.

The comparative measurements of the column proper and the pedestal, the base, and the entablature, are also given in more detail in the *Mānasāra* than in the *Āgamas* and some of the architectural treatises.[12]

---

[1] Mānasāra, XIV, 11–387. See details in the writer's Dictionary under *adhiṣṭhāna.*

[2] Suprabhedāgama, XXXI. 17 f.

[3] Kāmikāgama, XXXV, 22, 33, 114, 116, 122 ; LV. 102.

[4] Mānasāra, XIII, 37 –127. See details in the writer's Dictionary, under *upapīṭha.*

[5] Paṭala, XXXV, 115, 122.

[6] Paṭala, XXXI, 12.

[7] Essay on the Architecture of the Hindus, Rām Rāz, pp. 28, 26.

[8] Chapter XVI, 22—119. See details in the writer's Dictionary under *prastara.*

[9] XXXV, 27—29 ; LIV. 1—4, 7—8, 9—46, 47.

[10] XXXI, 68—71, 72 –74.

[11] Ed. Gaṇapati Śāstrī, IX. 23, 26.

[12] See details in the writer's Dictionary under *stambha, upapīṭha, adhiṣṭhāna and prastara.*

Thus in respect of the names of columns, the number of their subservient parts called mouldings, and also the base, the pedestal and the entablature, as well as their comparative measurements, the *Mānasāra* will always occupy the first place among all the treatises under observation.

The Three Styles

The style is also a technical and purely architectural subject. Thus it is not dealt with in the *Purāṇas*, not to speak of the epics or other poetical works where, as shown above, casual references to architecture and sculpture are met with. In some of the epigraphical documents and the *Bṛihat-saṁhitā* mention of the styles is occasionally made. The *Āgamas* contain a little more detail, while in the *Mānasāra* the subject is exhaustively treated.

The Nāgara, Vesara, and Drāviḍa are the three broad styles distinguished in the *Mānasāra*.[1] They are applied to both architecture[2] and sculpture[3]. With reference to the construction of cars or chariots a fourth style is mentioned[4]. This is called Randhra, which seems to be a corrupt form of Andhra. In an epigraphical record[5], Kaliṅga is mentioned as a distinct style of architecture. But if the identification of Vesara with Telugu or Tri-Kaliṅga be accepted, the Kaliṅga and the Andhra would be the two branches of the Vesara style. In the case of twelve-storeyed buildings, which are the most magnificent and imposing edifices as described, twelve special types, not necessarily the styles, of residential dwellings are also mentioned in the *Mānasāra*[6]. All these names are geographical, implying the twelve provinces into which the then India was divided architecturally, if not also politically. And these types are distinctly based on geographical divisions, in exactly the same way as the three styles, the Nāgara, Vesara and Drāviḍa, as also the two branches of the Vesara, the Kāliṅga and Āndhra, are based. The

---

[1] Mānasāra, XVIII, 92--104. The Nāgara style is distinguished by its quadrangular shape, the Vesara by its octagonal or hexagonal shape, and the Drāviḍa by its round shape (p. 176, note 1). For details, see p. 176 f. and the writer's Dictionary under *Nāgara*.

[2] Mānasāra, LIII, 53-54. XXI, 72-78. XXVI, 76. XLIII, 124-125, etc.

[3] Mānasāra, LII, 78, 100. LIII, 46-47, etc.

[4] Mānasāra, XLIII, 124-125.

[5] In the record itself it is, however, stated that the Nāgara, Vesara, Drāviḍa, and Kāliṅga are four types, not styles, of buildings (An inscription on the capital of a pillar in the Amriteśvara temple at Holal; Government of Madras, G. O. no. 1260, August, 1915, Progress Report of the Assistant Superintendent for Epigraphy, Southern Circle, 1914-15, page 90).

[6] Pāñchāla, Drāviḍa, Madhyakānta, Kāliṅga, Va(Vi)rāṭa, Kerala, Vaṁśaka, Māgadha, Janaka and Sphū(Gur)jaka (Mānasāra, XXX, 5 - 7). We have seen in the previous section, 98 kinds of mansions are described in the Mānasāra. In the above mentioned Holal inscription a reference is made to 64 kinds of mansions.

Græco-Roman orders, on which the European styles of architecture are mainly based, are also but geographical names.[1]

In the *Kāmikāgama*, as well as in the *Suprabhedāgama*, frequent references to the three broad styles, the Nāgara, Vesara, and Drāviḍa, are made[2].

The distinguishing features of these styles are practically exactly the same in all the three works, namely, the *Mānasāra*, the *Kāmikāgāma*, and the *Suprabhedagama*[3]. The Āndhra and the Kāliṅga branches of the Vesara style are not mentioned in the *Āgamas*. But we have seen that the *Kāmikāgama*, like the *Matsya-Purāṇa*, the *Bhavishya-Purāṇa*, and the *Bṛihat-saṁhitā*, describes twenty kinds of mansions, while the *Suprabhedāgama* has reference to ten kinds. These varieties of buildings, as also the sixty-four kinds mentioned in the Hoḷal inscription, and the ninety-eight kinds described in the *Mānasāra*, do not, however, represent the styles which fall only under three broad divisions, namely, the Nāgara, Vesara and Drāviḍa.

In the *Bṛihat-saṁhitā*[4], a clear mention is made only of the Drāviḍa style in regard to the measurement of the face, although the other styles may be said to have been implied. It is stated that according to one's own aṅgula (finger's breadth) the face (of an image) should be twelve aṅgulas (nine inches) broad and long; but as stated by the architect Nagnajit the face should be twelve aṅgulas long and fourteen aṅgulas broad in the Drāviḍa style. Obviously, therefore, the former measurement refers to other existing styles or those which are not specified here.

In regard to the styles also, then, the *Mānasāra* must be undoubtedly given the first place amongst all these works which for the purpose of the present item of comparison comprise practically the *Āgamas*.

In the light of all these facts—merely to deal with the question in its aspects as they concern the *Mānasāra*—it seems to me impossible to resist the following conclusion. There appears to have been a relation of indebtedness between the *Mānasāra* and the other works, both architectural and non-architectural. Except in a few instances noted above, it is, however, difficult to state definitely that the *Mānasāra* is the debtor or creditor to this or that work in respect of this or that matter. Most of the difficulties, it is needless to observe, hinge upon the chronology which is the irritating point in the Sanskrit literature. If the chronology of

---

[1] See page 126 and foot-note 1.

[2] Kāmikāgama, LXV, 6-7, 12—18, etc.; Suprabhedāgama, XXXI, 37—39, etc.

[3] For details see the writer's Dictionary under *Nāgara*.

[4] Chapter LVIII, 4.

the works discussed above were definitely known, it would have been easier to assume that the works earlier than the *Mānasāra* had been known to its author and those later than the *Mānasāra* had been influenced by it. Except in cases of support by archæological records, epigraphical or non-epigraphical, the dates assigned to Sanskrit works are mostly but provisional. I have discussed elsewhere the available materials and the reasons which have induced me provisionally to place the *Mānasāra* somewhere in the fifth to seventh century of the Christian era. In view of the essential points of comparison and the accepted chronology of the works which have been critically studied by scholars, I should say that the *Bṛihat-saṁhitā* and the later Āgamic and Paurāṇic works, in respect of architectural and sculptural matters, as well as most of the avowedly architectural manus ripts, are debtors to the *Mānasāra*, while it is a debtor itself in respect of the same matters to the Vedic and the early Epic works as also to the early polytechnical treatises (like the *Kauṭilīya-Artha-śāstra* and the *Kāmandakīya*), and to the avowedly architectural works of the thirty-two authorities mentioned in the *Mānasāra*, which might have existed till its own time. Besides, it cannot but have been based on the actual observation and measurement of extant architectural and sculptural objects; in this matter lies the special importance of the *Mānasāra*.

An objection may be raised here. It is possible that those works which are stated above to have been debtors to the *Mānasāra* might have been influenced directly by those which are asserted to have been the creditors to the *Mānasāra*. Such an objection, however, can be easily disposed of. The *Mānasāra*, in whichever period of history it is finally placed, has become a standard work on architecture and sculpture, because we have seen, first, it is the largest of its kind, secondly, its treatment of the subjects is most exhaustive, and thirdly, in it the subject-matter has been scientifically classified and systematised And when there is a standard work existing, it is natural and highly probable that those who treat the subject rather casually or less exhaustively, should draw upon it instead of going to the original sources except in some special instances. For the ordinary meanings or synonyms of a word we generally consult a standard dictionary, rather than attempt to trace the history, phonology, morphology, and semasiology of the word. An analogical instance may perhaps make the point clearer. Pāṇini's grammar makes mention of some nineteen pre-existing grammatical works, and it has been placed by later scholars somewhere in the fourth or third century of the pre-Christian era. Like the works on rhetoric and prosody, grammars cannot be prepared without consulting the existing literature, because the sole business of these works is to generalise certain regulating features of literature. The methods of the pioneers of law books, as well as the grammar, the *Alaṅkāra Śāstra*, and the *Silpa-Śāstra*, must have been inductive. Pāṇini, as he acknowledges generously, has been indebted to his predecessors; it is also clear from his work that he himself has consulted the preceding Vedic and post-Vedic literature. It is true that grammars have been prepared after Pāṇini also. But when Pāṇini's grammar reached the status of a standard work, his rules and regulations were naturally followed in the later literature. The later grammarians also must have been influenced by Pāṇini. In the field of grammar and literature Pāṇini's grammar is, therefore, the regulating and controlling standard work. In the same way, and more clearly and significantly, it seems to me, the *Mānasāra* occupies a unique position in literature, both architectural and non-architectural.

IV

THE MĀNASĀRA AND VITRUVIUS

As has already been pointed out in the Preface, the name Mānasāra is of ambiguous significance. It is, however, clear from the preceding chapters that the text bearing the title *Mānasāra* is a standard treatise on Indian Architecture. It is divided into seventy chapters each bearing a distinct title. In 1834 in his Essay on the architecture of the Hindus, Rām Rāz referred to the first few chapters of the *Mānasāra* from a single fragmentary manuscript to which he had access. Since then several manuscripts have been discovered; but owing to some serious difficulties stated in the Preface nobody had made any attemp to deal with this huge text in any way for a period of 80 years till the present writer undertook in 1914 to edit it for the first time. This, the first, edition is based on all the eleven available manuscripts which are written in five different scripts in a language branded as "barbarous Sanskrit." Figures, sketches, or illustrations of any kind are absolutely wanting in all these manuscripts.

Vitruvius is the name of Roman architect. His treatise, on which in a sense European architecture is bassed, seems to have been composed twenty-five years before the Christian era. "The materals for a life of Vitruvius are only to be found in his own treatise. Among the ancient authors he is merely mentioned by Pliny as one of those writers from whom he compiled; and by Frontinus, in his treatise on Aqueducts, as the first who introduced the Quinarain measure."

The title of Vitruvius's treatise is lost, if it originally had one. The editio princeps, printed at Rome, in or about 1486, bears no title. The unique position of this treatise is, however, sufficiently clear from the fact that since its first appearance in the fifteenth century there have been till 1807 forty-two editions of the work, practically in all the European languages. There are seventeen editions in Latin, eleven in Italian, two in Spanish, six in French, four in German, and two in English[1]. It is divided into ten books, which too do not bear any titles. Each

---

[1] See Gwilt, XV—XXV, for fuller details of the following:—

Latin editions—

1486—Editio princeps printed at Rome by George Herolt begins without title—'Sulpitius lectori salutem.' Poleans says "there are but few errors in this edition."

book contains a number of chapters varying from seven to twenty-two. The chapters also have not any proper titles. The treatise deals with both civil

---

1496—Printed at Florence. According to Fabricus the orthography of this edition is more correct than in the preceding one.

1497—The name of the editor does not appear. With a few slight variations this is little more than a reprint of the Florence edition. In this the chapters of the first book are differently divided from those of the two former editions.

1511—This is the first illustrated edition. It contains many wood blocks and figures. Jocundus (the editor) altered the text of the two former editions in many places.

1513—The figures in this edition are the same as in the preceding, but considerably reduced and more imperfectly kept.

1522—This is a reprint of the preceding edition with the same blocks for the figures.

1523—This was probably edited by Will. Hayon of Lyons. This is a counterpart of the Giunta edition. Some of its figures are taken from the first Italian edition of 1521 which is noticed herein after.

1543—The text is nearly the same as that of Jocundus The figures of the wood-blocks are partly borrowed from the Giunta edition and partly from the Italian edition of 1521.

1550—The text is the same as that of the 1543 edition. But it contains notes of Philander which were first published at Rome in 1544.

1552 — 'Philander himself superintended this edition, chiefly following the Giunta text, which he collated with several Mss. The wood-blocks are better than in any preceding edition."

1567—Darbaro in this seems to have mostly followed Philander's edition of 1552.

1586—Harwood says that "the editor of this edition was Jo. Tornaesious junior, and that it is more correct, though less elegant than that produced by the father in 1552."

1649—With commentary of Meibomius on those chapters relating to musical notation. This was the best edition of the author produced at that time. "De Laet professes to follow the text of Philander's edition; but neither was this accurately done, nor were the notes of Philander, nor the Lexicon of Baldus given entire, as the title would import."

1758—By Marchese Berardo Galiani at Naples with an Italian version noticed under the Italian editions. Harwood says that this is "a fair and valuable edition."

1800—The text of this edition is of little value. Nor its plates well executed. It has no notes appended but it contains the glossary in five languages.

1807—It contains notes.

1807—In the same year another edition was published. The second and third volumes are devoted to commentaries on the text. In contains, however, no plates. "This is the best edition of the author which has appeared."

Italian editions—

1521—This is one of the earliest and rare version of Vitruvius. It was translated with the assistance of Benedict Jovius by Cæsar Cæsarianus who was one of the architects of the Cathedral of Milan. One of the plates contains a plan and two sections of this Cathedral.

1524—This is a repetition of the preceding edition but without the notes of Cæsar Cæsarianus.

1535—This is copied from the preceding edition, but the Index is not quite so copious.

1536—A translation of the first five Books. Perugia.

1556—With Barbaro's commentary.

and military architecture. The rules respecting military engines, "now incomprehensible, but doubtless in his time sufficiently clear," are laid down in the last book. The treatment of civil architecture includes both temples and residential buildings. "That he should have met with opposition from his brethren is quite consonant with later experience, for the rabble of ignorant builders, and artisans, and draftsmen are of the same class as those that flourished subsequently to Vitruvius." From this remark of Gwilt it appears that Vitruvius was induced to "write his treatise with a view to assisting the uneducated professional architects" who, like those of India, depended solely on the knowledge handed down to them from their equally uneducated forefathers.

'Certain points of similarity between the *Mānasāra* and the treatise of Vitruvius are so striking that they raise a presumption that the two works are in some way dependent on each other.' This thesis[1] is proposed to be illustrated in this section

---

1567—With Barbaro's commentary.
1584—Similar to the preceding edition.
1629—Very similar to the preceding edition.
1641—Little differing from the preceding.
1758—In Napoli, accompanied with the Latin text.
1790—Another edition by Galiani, similar to the preceding, but without the Latin text.

Spanish editions—
1602—Without plates.
1787—Large folio with plates.

French editions—
1547—First version in French, Jan Martin, Paris.
1572—A reprint of the preceding, Cavellat, Paris.
1618—Printed from the two preceding editions by Jean de Tournes at Geneva.
1673—Translated by Perrault. Figures are numerous and well executed.
1684—With plates, best of Perrault's editions.
1816—With plates. Bruxelles.

German editions—
1548—With plates on wood-blocks cut by Erard Schaen.
1575—A repetition of the preceding. Basil.
1614—Another repetition with a little different title.
1796—With a life of Vitruvius in the first volume. This edition contains many illustrations of the author.

English editions—
1771—Translated from the original Latin by Newton, London.
1791.—Second volume with many plates.
It exhibits defective knowledge of Latin, but the notes are good.
Latterly a portion was translated by Wilkins
After Joseph Gwilt's translation there have been several others in English.

[1] Submitted as such to Leiden University by the present writer.

Practically seven-tenths of both the works is avowedly architectural.

Out of the seventy chapters of the *Mānasāra* the first fifty deal with architecture proper, and out of the ten books of Vitruvius the first seven deal with the same subjects.

The remaining twenty chapters of the former are devoted to sculpture, and the remaining three books of the latter deal mostly with war instruments, machines, and engines. Of the similar seven tenths in both the works, the names of many chapters, and the contents too in most instances, are the same.

The *Mānasāra* opens, following the usual custom, with a prayer to the Creator Brahmā and touches upon the origin and development of the science of architecture, from Śiva, Brahmā, and Vishnu, through Indra, Bṛihaspati, and Nārada, to the class of Ṛishis called Mānasāra, and concludes the introduction with a list of the chapters.

Vitruvius too opens with a prayer to his patron, Cæsar, and acknowledging his obligations to Cæsar's father and sister, concludes with a proposal to give an account of the magnificent edifices Cæsar had built, and to develop all the principles of the art.

The next chapter (II) in the *Mānasāra* deals with two distinct subjects, the system of measurement (*mānopakaraṇa*) and the requisite qualifications of an architect (*Śilpi-lakshaṇa*).

The corresponding chapter is marked I instead of II by Vitruvius, because the preceding chapter goes without any numbering, as it is called Introduction. This, the present, chapter deals exactly like the corresponding chapter in the *Mānasāra* with two distinct subjects under the heads, 'what architecture is' and 'of the education of an architect.' The former of these two subjects has again been treated in the following chapter, namely, III, of the *Mānasāra*, and is noticed below. The striking similarity in the training demanded of the architect by the two authorities may be noticed here.

According to Vitruvius "an architect should be ingenious, and apt in the acquisition of knowledge. He should be a good writer, a skilful draftsman, versed in geometry and optics, expert at figures, acquainted with history, informed on the principles of natural and moral philosophy, somewhat of a musician, not ignorant of the sciences both of law and physic, nor of the motions, laws and relations to each other, of the heavenly bodies." The absolute necessity for these qualifications has been very satisfactorily elaborated by Vitruvius.

In the *Mānasāra*, artists are first divided into four classes. Together they form the guild of architects, each an expert in his own department but possessing a general knowledge of the science of architecture as a whole. They consist of the chief architect (*Sthapati*), the draftsman or the designer (*Sūtra-grāhin*), the painter (*Vardhaki*), and the joiner (*Sūtra-dhāra*).

According to the *Mānasāra* the chief architect is expected to be well versed in all the sciences. He must possess a knowledge of all the Vedas and all the Śāstras. He must be proficient in law, mathematics, history, geography, painting, draftsmanship, mechanics, and deep "in the ocean of the science of architecture." He must be very learned, meritorious, patient, and dexterous, a champion, of large experience, of industrious habits, and of noble descent, full of resource and capable of application to all kinds of work. He must possess a wide outlook, bold temperament, and self-control. He must be above committing errors. He must have a good name and be faithful to his employers (lit., friends). He must be endowed with all the qualifications of a supreme managing director. He must not be deformed or have any disease or disability ; he must also be free from the seven vices, namely, hunting, gambling, day-dreaming, blackmailing, addiction to women, etc.

A similar set of qualifications is also demanded of each of the other three artists ; but the *Sūtragrāhin* is expected to possess an expert knowledge of draftsmanship, the *Vardhaki* of painting, and the *Sūtradhāra* of carpentry.

The utility or the possibility of so many attainments in a single person has not been expressly discussed in the *Mānasāra*. But Vitruvius has submitted an interesting explanation.

It is familiar to every body that for success in any profession in life one must be clever, industrious, honest and generous. It is also easily understood that an architect, who has got to do both manual and brain work, must not be deformed and must be free from any disease or disability.

According to Vitruvius he is required to be a good writer also, because an architect is to commit to writing his observations and experience, in order to assist his memory. Drawing is employed in representing the forms of his designs. Geometry, which forms a part of mathematics, affords much aid to the architect ; to it he owes the use of the right line and circle, the level and the square, whereby his delineations of buildings on plane surfaces are greatly facilitated. Arithmetic estimates the cost, and aids in the measurement of the works ; this, assisted by the laws of geometry, determines those abstruse questions wherein the different proportions of some parts to others are involved. The science of optics enables him to introduce with judgement the requisite quantity of light according to the aspect. Unless acquainted with history, he will be unable to account for the use of many ornaments, which he may have occasion to inroduce. For history the expression *puraṇa* is used in Indian literature and it implies mythology or mythological stories which are as a rule depicted in the buildings of a nation, There are, however, other uses of history for an architect.

"Moral philosophy," says Vitruvius, "will teach the architect to be above meanness in his dealings and to avoid arrogance, and will make him just, compliant and faithful to his employer; and what is of the highest importance, it will prevent avarice gaining an ascendancy over him; for he should not be occupied with the thoughts of filling his coffers, nor with the desire of grasping everything in the shape of gain, but by the gravity of his manners and a good character, should be careful to preserve his dignity." These precepts of moral philosophy are prescribed by our Indian authorities almost in the same terms. We have seen above that the architect is required to be of noble descent, pious and compassionate. He must not be malicious or spiteful. He must be content and free from greed. He must be truthful and possess self-control. He must be above the seven vices. He must be faithful to his employer. He must not have excessive desire for gain. He must be of good behaviour and generous enough to forgive his rivals.

"The doctrine of physic is necessary to him in the solution of various problems, as for instance, in the conduct of water, whose natural force, in its meandering and expansion over flat countries, is often such as to require restraints, which none know to apply but those who are acquainted with the laws of nature." This matter too has been more exhaustively discussed in various chapters of the *Mānasāra*.

"Music assists him in the use of harmonic and mathematical proportion." In these matters, the *Mānasāra* is rather too elaborate; in most individual cases, nine proportions have been suggested and the selection of the right proportion and harmony has been made dependent on the application of the six formulas which are treated in a very technical manner based on mathematics. According to Vitruvius, music is moreover absolutely necessary in adjusting the force of the balistae, catapultae, and scorpions, in whose frames are holes for the passage of the homotona, which are strained by gut-ropes attached to windlasses worked by hand-spikes. Unless these ropes are equally extended, which only a nice ear can discover by their sound when struck, the bent arms of the engine do not give an equal impetus when disengaged, and the strings, therefore, not being in equal states of tension, prevent the direct flight of the weapon. A knowledge of music is especially useful to the architect in building theatres, lecture rooms, and such other halls where the spread of sound is taken into particular consideration. Both Vitruvius and the *Mānasāra* are equally enthusiastic in speaking about it. The former, further, says that the architect "would, moreover, be at a loss in constructing hydraulic and other engines if ignorant of music." "Skill in physic enables him to ascertain the salubrity of different tracts of country, and to determine the variation of climates, for the air and water of different situations being matters of highest importance, no building will be healthy without attention to those points."

A very elaborate account of the selection of sites and the examination of soil is given in the *Mānasāra* and other architectural treatises[1]. The salubrity of the tracts is minutely ascertained with reference to the site where a village, town, fort, palace, temple or dwelling house is to be built. The soil is examined with regard to its contour, colour, odour, features, taste, and touch. The level of the ground as well as the characteristic vegetation of the site, as pointed out above, are also minutely examined.

"Law should be an object of his study, especially those parts of it which relate to party-walls, to the free course and discharge of the eaves' waters, to the regulations of cesspools and sewage, and to window lights. The laws of sewage require his particular attention, so that he may prevent his employers from being involved in law-suits when the building is finished. Contracts, also, for the execution of the works, should be drawn up with care and precision, because, when without legal flaws, neither party will be able to take advantage of the other."

Law, as explained by Vitruvius, is not mentioned in so many words in the list of accomplishments given in the Vāstu-śāstras quoted above. But most elaborate instructions are given in the Arthaśāstra and other treatises on party-walls, the sewage system, and on windows and other openings.[2]

"Astronomy instructs him in the points of the heavens, the laws of the celestial bodies, the equinoxes, solstices, and courses of the stars; all of which should be well understood in the construction and proportions of clocks." In the Vāstu-śāstras dialling is an important subject; but astronomy, which is always mixed up with astrology, has been drawn upon particularly with regard to the auspicious moment invariably observed in almost all matters.

Vitruvius has added an explanatory note on the expression 'all sciences' of which the architect is required to have sufficient knowledge. This explanation will indeed throw a clear light upon a similar expression, *sarva-śāstra*, used by the Indian authorities. But for the following note of Vitruvius, we might have taken the term *sarva-śāstra* as an exaggeration, which is very often found in Sanskrit literature to imply nothing more than a general knowledge.

"Perhaps, to the uninformed mind," begins Vitruvius, "it may appear unaccountable that a man should be able to retain in his memory such a variety of learning; but the close alliance with each other, of the different branches of science, will explain the difficulty. For as a body is composed of various concordant members, so does the whole circle of learning consist in one harmonious system."

[1] Bṛihat-saṁhitā, Gārga, Viśvak, Kāśyapa, Vāstu-ratnāvali, Vaśishṭha-saṁhitā, Vāstu-pradīpa, Nārada, Gṛiha-kārikā, Bhṛigu, Śilpa-dīpaka, Bhavishya-Purāṇa.
See quotations from these works under *Bhū-parīkshā* in the writer's Dictionary.

[2] See the writer's Dictionary under *Jaladvāra* and *Vātāyana*.

'On this account, Pythius, the architect of the noble temple of Minerva at Priene says, in his commentaries, that an architect should have that perfect knowledge of each art and science, which is not even acquired by the professors of any one in particular.' This seemed rather too much to Vitruvius, so he asks "how can it be expected that an architect should equal Aristarchus as a grammarian, yet should he not (*sic*) be ignorant of grammar. In music, though it be evident he need not equal Aristoxenus, yet he should know something of it. Though he need not exceed, as Apelles, in painting, nor as Myron or Polycletus, in sculpture, yet he should have attained some proficiency in these arts."

"Thus also, in the other sciences," concludes Vitruvius, "it is not important that pre-eminence in each be gained; but he must not, however, be ignorant of the general principles of each. For in such a variety of matters, it cannot be supposed that the same person can arrive at excellence in each, since to be aware of their several niceties and bearings, cannot fall within his power . . . . Wherefore Pythius seems to have been in error, forgetting that art consists in practice and theory. Theory is common to, and may be known by all, but the result of practice occurs to the artist in his own art only. The physician and musician are each obliged to have some regard to the beating of the pulse, and the motion of the feet, but who would apply to the latter to heal a wound or cure a malady? So, without the aid of the former, the musician affects the ears of his audience by modulations upon his instrument. The astronomer and musician delight in similar proportions, for the positions of the stars, which are quartile and trine, answer to a fourth and fifth in harmony. . . . . Throughout the whole range of art, there are many incidents common to all. Practice alone can lead to excellence in any one. That architect, therefore, is sufficiently educated, whose general knowledge enables him to give his opinion on any branch when required to do so. Those unto whom nature has been so bountiful that they are at once geometricians, astronomers, musicians, and skilled in many other arts go beyond what is required of the architect."

Further observations are perhaps unnecessary with a view to reiterating the striking similarities between the *Mānasāra* and Vitruvius on this point. This series of similarities between the injunctions of the two standard works on such an important matter as the training of the architect, the very soul of architecture, seem to have been due to something more than mere coincidence.

The next chapter (III) in the *Mānasāra*, called *Vāstu-prakaraṇa*, defines *vāstu* or habitation and divides it into four classes, ground, building, conveyance, and couch (*dharā*, *harma*, *yāna*, and *paryaṅka*).

Chapter (IV), called *Bhū-parīkshā* or examination of soil, deals with the site where a village, town, fort, palace, temple, or dwelling is to be built, and examines the soil thereof with regard to contour, colour, odour, features, taste, touch; the elevation of the ground; and the luxuriance of certain plants, trees, and grasses.

Chapter (V), called *Bhūmi-saṁgraha* or selection of site, deals further with the soil before it is finally selected for a building site.

The next chapter (VI) considers the orientation of buildings, and recommends that a building should preferably face the east or north-east, and never the south-east. Reasons have not been discussed fully, beyond stating that this is auspicious or that is inauspicious. Incidentally, the principles, mechanics, and details of dialling have been exhaustively discussed.

The following chapter (VII) discusses the design or division of the site selected for a village, town, or house, into a number of plots. Thirty-two schemes are distinguished, each of which is divided into squares of various numbers.

Following the usual custom, this introductory section concludes with a chapter (VIII) on offerings to various deities. In this matter too the chief architect takes a leading part.

The corresponding chapter (II) of Vitruvius is called, "Of those things on which architecture depends." It deals with the fitness (ordinatio) and arrangement (dispositio), also proportion, uniformity, consistency and economy, and is divisible into three heads, ichnography, orthography and scenography, which considered together constitute design.

The next chapter (III) is called, "Of the different branches (building, dialling, and mechanics) of architecture," and the chapter following (IV) is named, "Of the choice of healthy situation," which deals with the climatic conditions and elevation of the building site as well as with its aspects or orientation. Unlike in the *Mānasāra* the consideration of fogs, rains, heat and cold, which are peculiarities of the European countries, has been given prominence here. The explanations of aspects recommended are satisfactory. "A city on the sea-side," it is stated, "exposed to the south or west will be insalubrious; for in summer mornings, a city thus placed would be hot, at noon it would be scorched. A city also with a western aspect would even at sunrise be warm, at noon hot, and in the evening of a burning temperature. Hence the constitution of the inhabitants of such places, from such continual and excessive changes of the air, would be much vitiated." After citing opinions of physicians and others and supporting by illustrations, it is further stated "When, therefore, a city is built in a marshy situation near the sea coast, with a northern, north-eastern, or eastern aspect, on a marsh whose level is higher than the shore of the sea, the site is not altogether improper; for by means of sewers the waters may be discharged into the sea; and at those times, when violently agitated by storms, the sea swells and runs up the sewers, it mixes with the water of the marsh and prevents the generation of marshy insects; it also soon destroys such as are passing from the higher level, by the saltness of its water to which they are unaccustomed." The frequent mention of the sea-side, it is needless to point out, is due to the situation of the prominent Italian cities on the sea-shore, and of Rome, in particular, which was the object of special study to Vitruvius.

Vitruvius has also elaborately treated the subject of dialling in as many as four chapters (Book IX, chapters, I, II, VIII, IX)

In this matter of dialling, as in many others, Vitruvius of course differs in certain details from the *Mānasāra*. For instance, regarding the principles of dialling each of the twelve months is, in the *Mānasāra* (VII), divided into three parts of ten days each and the increase and decrease of shadow are calculated in these several parts of the different months. Vitruvius (Book IX, chapter VIII) on the other hand discusses "the principles of dialling and the increase and decrease of the *days*," not the *shadow* thereof, in the different months.

In both these works, therefore, this introductory section comprises exactly eight chapters, which bear similar titles and deal with the same subjects practically in the same way.

Town-planning is the next topic treated in both the works, and it covers exactly two chapters both in Vitruvius (Book I, chapters VI, VII), as well as in the *Mānasāra* (chapters IX, X).

The *Mānasāra* describes the subject under two heads, *Grāma-lakshaṇa* and *Nagara-vidhāna*, and three categories, village, town and fort. Villages are divided into eight classes, called *daṇḍaka, sarvatobhadra, nandyāvarta, padmaka, svastika, prastara, kārmuka,* and *chaturmukha*; each of these, as the names indicate, represents a particular design and lay-out. Towns are also divided into eight classes: *rājadhānī, nagara, pura, nagarī, kheṭa, kharvaṭa, kubjaka* and *pattana*. These refer more to the situation and distribution of buildings than to their shapes or designs.

Forts are first divided into eight classes: *śibira, vāhinīmukha, sthānīya, droṇaka, saṁviddha* or *vardhaka, kolaka, nigama,* and *skandāvāra* According to their situation, they are further classified into mountain fort (*vana-durga*), water fort (*jala-durga*), chariot fort (*ratha-durga*), gods' fort (*deva-durga*), clay fort (*paṅka-durga*), and mixed fort (*miśra-durga*). The mountain fort is sub-divided into three classes, according as it is built on the top of the mountain, in the valley, or on the mountain slope.

According to the *Mānasāra* there is, however, not much difference between a village, a town and a fort. The town is the extension of a village. And the fort is in many cases nothing more than a fortified town. There seems to be only this difference that a fort is chiefly meant for purposes of defence, while a village or town is mainly intended for habitation and commerce. But the village scheme seems, all the same, to have originated from the plan of the military camp.

Each village is surrounded by a wall made of brick or stone. It is supported by ramparts Beyond this wall there is a ditch, broad and deep enough to cause serious obstruction in the event of an attack on the village. There are generally four main gates at the middle of the four sides, and as many at the four corners. Inside the wall there is a large street running all round the village. Besides, there are two other large streets, each of which connects two opposite main gates. They intersect at the centre of the village, where a public temple or hall is generally built in which the villagers may meet. The village is thus divided into four main blocks, each of which is again subdivided into many blocks by streets which are always straight, and which run from one end to the other of a main block. The two main streets crossing at the centre have houses only on one side facing the street. The ground flour of these houses on the main streets consists of shops. The street which runs round the village also has houses only on one side. These houses are mainly public buildings, such as schools, colleges, libraries, guest-houses, liquor saloons. All other streets generally have residential buildings on both sides. The houses, high or low, are always uniform in make The drains and sewers are made towards the slope of the village. Tanks and ponds are dug in all the inhabited parts and located in such quarters as can conveniently be reached by a large number of inhabitants. The temples of public worship, as well as the public commons, gardens, and parks are similarly located. People of the same caste or profession are generally housed in the same quarter. The habitation of the dead body burners (*chaṇḍālas*) as well as the places for cremation are located outside the village wall to the north-west in particular. The temples of fearful deities, such as Chāmuṇḍā, are also located outside the wall.

A town may be situated from east to west or from north to south according to the position it occupies There should be one to twelve large streets in a town. It should be built near a river or a mountain, and should have facilities for trade and commerce with foreigners. It should be furnished with walls, moats, ditches, gates, drains, parks, commons shops, exchanges, temples, guest houses, colleges, etc. The king and his court usually reside in a town, and traders and forum are essential element in its population.

Forts are also surrounded with strong walls and large and deep ditches. The wall is made of brick, stone. and similar lasting materials. It is at least eighteen feet in height and its thickness at the base is at least nine feet. The wall is provided with watch-towers.

Fortified cities are specially honoured with the residences of the king, the princes, priests, ministers, and military officers. There are also humbler dwellings as well as courts of justice, arsenals, traders' booths, shops, work-houses for artisans, various assembly halls, dancing halls, liquor saloons, and gambling halls.

According to Vitruvius (Book I, chapter V)—

"When we are satisfied with the spot fixed on for the site of the city, as well as in respect of the goodness of the air, as of the abundant supply of provisions for the support of the population, the communications by good roads, and river or sea navigation for the transport of merchandise,[1] we should take into consideration the method of constructing the walls and the towers of the city. From the exterior face of the wall, towers must be projected from which an approaching enemy may be annoyed by weapons; from the ambrasures of those towns, right and left, an easy approach to the wall must be provided against; indeed they should be surrounded by uneven ground, and the roads leading to the gates should be winding and turned to the left from the gates. By this arrangement the right sides of the attacking troops, which are not covered by their shields, will be open to the weapons of the besieged."

"The thickness of the walls should be sufficient for two armed men to pass each other with ease. The walls ought to be tied, from front to rear, with many pieces of charred olive wood; by which means the two faces, thus connected, will endure for ages . . . ."

"The distance between each tower should exceed an arrows's flight . . . . The walls will be intercepted by the lower parts of the towers where they occur, leaving an interval equal to the width of the tower, which space the tower will consequently occupy. The towers should be made either round or polygonal. A square tower is a bad form on account of its being easily fractured at the quoins by the battering ram; whereas the circular tower has this advantage, that when battered, the pieces of masonry whereof it is composed being cuneiform, cannot be driven in towards their centre without displacing the whole mass. Nothing tends more to the security of walls and towers, than backing them with walls or terraces; it counteracts the effects of rams as well as of undermining . . . ."

"In the construction of ramparts, very wide and deep trenches are to be first excavated, the bottom of which must be still further dug out for receiving the foundation of the wall. This must be of sufficient thickness to resist the

---

[1] Compare (Chāṇakya's saying)—धनिकः श्रोत्रियो राजा नदी वैद्यश्च पञ्चमः ।
पञ्च यत्र न विद्यन्ते तत्र वासं न कारयेत् ॥

pressure of the earth against it. Then, according to the space requisite for drawing up the cohorts in military order on the ramparts, another wall is to be built within the former, towards the city. The outer and inner walls are then to be connected by cross walls, disposed on the plan after the manner of the teeth of a comb or a saw, so as to divide the pressure of the filling-in earth into many and less forces, and thus prevent the walls from being thrust out." The materials are stated to be "what are found on the spot, such as square stones, flint, rubble stones, burnt or unburnt bricks." (Book I, chapter V).

"The plan of the city should not be square, nor formed with acute angles, but polygonal, so that the motions of the enemy may be open to observation." (Book I, chapter V).

"The lanes and streets (of which no details are given) of the city should be set out, the choice of sites for the convenience and use of the state remains to be decided on; for sacred edifices, for the forum, and for other public buildings. If the place adjoin the sea, the forum should be seated close to the harbour; if inland, it should be in the centre of the town. The temples of the gods, protectors of the city, as those of Jupiter, Juno, and Minerva, should be on some eminence which commands a view of the greater part of the city. The temple of Mercury should be either in the forum or, as also the temple of Isis and Serapis, in the great public square; those of Apollo and Father Bacchus near the theatre. If there be neither amphitheatre nor gymnasium, the temple of Hercules should be near the circus. The temple of Mars should be out of the city, in the neighbouring country, that of Venus near to the gate. According to the revelations of the Hetrurian Haruspices, the temples of Venus, Vulcan and Mars should be so placed that those of the first be not in the way of contaminating the matrons and youth with the influence of lust; that those of Vulcan be away from the city, which would consequently be freed from the danger of fire, the divinity presiding over that element being drawn away by the rites and sacrifices performing in his temple. The temple of Mars should be also out of the city, that no armed frays may disturb the peace of the citizens, and that this divinity may, moreover, be ready to preserve them from their enemies and the perils of war. The temple of Ceres shall be in a solitary spot out of the city, to which the public are not necessarily led but for the purpose of sacrificing to her. This spot is to be reverenced, with religious awe and solemnity of demeanour, by those whose affairs lead them to visit it." (Book I, chapter VII).

It should be observed that in the *Mānasāra* eight distinctive plans of villages, and some twenty-five varieties of commercial cities and military forts have been described with all details. In town-planning, the Indian authority has recommended almost all the suitable designs, square, rectangular, and polygonal.

But Vitruvius recommends only the polygonal. In the matter of the disposition of temples within the city wall and outside, the two authorities very strikingly correspond. In both the treatises the fear-inspiring deities are similarly located outside the city wall.

The following seven chapters (XI—XVII) in the *Mānasāra* serve the purpose of a preamble to the subsequent chapters dealing with buildings.[1]

The first of these (XI) is named, *Bhūmi-lamba* or height of storey, in the *Mānasāra*. It is defined in the *Kāmikāgama* as the dimensions of the four sides. The contents of the chapter in the *Mānasāra* describe in detail the measurement of length, breadth and height of buildings of one to twelve storeys, assigned to persons of different ranks. The five forms, namely, square, rectangular, round, octagonal and oval, are prescribed for buildings of different classes, *jati*, *chhanda*, *vikalpa* and *ābhāsa*. These shapes are equally applicable to religious, military and residential buildings. A palace of five to twelve storeys is stated to suit the emperor or the universal monarch, highest in rank among the nine classes of kings. Residences of one to three storeys are assigned to the heir apparent and the chief feudatories, and so on.

The title of the corresponding chapter of Vitruvius (Book VI, chapter VIII) is more significant. It is called, "Forms of houses suited to different ranks of persons." As in the *Mānasāra* buildings are divided exactly into five classes, though the criteria of classification are different. It is stated (Book III, chapter II) that "there are five species of temples, whose names are, Pycnostylos, that is, thick set with columns; Systylos, in which the columns are not so close; Diastylos, where they are still wider apart; Aræostylos, when placed more distant from each other...... ; Eustylos, when the intercolumnation......is of the best proprotion." "The conditions of temples are distinguished," it is further stated (Book III, chapter I), "by their different forms. First, that known by the appellation In Antis, then the Prostylos, Peripteros, Pseudodipteros, Dipteros and Hypaethros." "Circular temples are constructed, of which some are Monopteral,......others are called Peripteral." (Book IV, chapter VIII).

As regards the distribution of buildings it is stated (Book IV, chapter III) that "temples of the Doric order are erected to Minerva, Mars and Hercules; on account of whose valour, their temple should be of masculine proportions, and without delicate ornament. The character of the Corinthian order seems more appropriate to Venus, Flora, Proserpine, and Nymphs of Fountains: because

[1] Of these seven preliminary chapters the twelfth, on foundation (*garbha-nyāsa*), should have been in the place of the eleventh which treats of dimensions of buildings (*bhūmi-lamba*), as in Vitruvius's treatise.

its slenderness, elegance and richness, and its ornamental leaves surmounted by volutes seem to bear an analogy to their dispositions. A medium between these two is chosen for temples to Juno, Diana, Bacchus, and other similar deities, which should be of the Ionic order, tempered between the severity of the Doric and the slenderness and delicacy of the Corinthian order." (Book I, chapter II). As regards secular buildings, it is laid down that "the houses of bankers and receivers of the revenue may be more commodious and elegant than those of persons of middling condition in life. For advocates and men of literature, houses ought to be still handsomer and more spacious, to suit the reception of persons on consultations. But for nobles, who in bearing honours, and discharging the duties of the magistracy, must have much intercourse with the citizens, princely vestibules must be provided, lofty atria, and spacious peristylia, groves, and extensive walks, finished in a magnificent style..........If, therefore, houses are erected, thus adapted to the different classes of society......there will be nothing to reprehend, for they will be suitable to their destination."......"I have thus described," concludes Vitruvius, " the proportions of town residences as I promised. I shall now proceed to those of houses in the country." (Book VI, chapter VIII).

It is needless to point out that the subject matter of this chapter is virtually the same in both the authorities. The small differences are due to the local conditions and requirements of the two different countries.

The next chapter (XII), called *Garbha-nyāsa* in the *Mānasāra*, deals with the foundations whereupon buildings, villages and tanks are built. The foundation is excavated in the ground best suited for a structure to the depth of a man's height with uplifted arms. It is laid down that the bottom of the pit thus excavated must be rocky or watery, in other words, it must reach rock or water. It implies that the best soil for receiving foundation, when it is not erected on water, is rock, gravel or closely pressed sandy earth.

The depth of the foundation-cave is equal to the height of the basement. The four corners and sides, built of brick or stone, are equal. This cave is filled with water and ten kinds of earth; thus the earth from an ant-hill, a crab-hole, etc., is placed at the bottom, and closely pressed and hardened by means of wooden hammers shaped like the elephant's foot. Portions of certain plants are then deposited on the four sides, the root of the blue-lotus to the east, the root of the white-lotus to the south, and so on. Upon these are placed grains of ten kinds of cereals such as *phaseolus mungo, phaseolus radiatus, dolichos uniflorus, sesamum indicum*, and so on. The vault is built thereon, the details of which need hardly be repeated here. Upon such 'strong' foundations, the strength whereof varies according to the weights of the buildings above, various structures are constructed.

"When we are satisfied," says Vitruvius (Book I, chapter V), "with the spot fixed on for the site of the city......their foundations should be carried down to a solid bottom, if such can be found, and should be built thereon of such thickness as may be necessary for the proper support of that part of the wall which stands above the natural level of the ground. They should be of the soundest workmanship and materials, and of greater thickness than the walls above." Importance of solid ground is emphasised and it is again stated (Book III, chapter III) "if solid ground can be come to, the foundations should go down to it and into it, according to the magnitude of the work, and the substruction be built up as solid as possible. Above the ground of the foundation, the wall should be one-half thicker than the column it is to receive, so that the lower parts which carry the greatest weight, may be stronger than the upper part......Nor must the mouldings of the bases of the columns project beyond the solid. Thus, also, should be regulated the thickness of all walls above ground. The intervals between the foundations brought up under the columns, should be either rammed down hard, or arched, so as to prevent the foundation piers from swerving. If solid ground cannot be come to, and the ground be loose or marshy, the place must be excavated, cleared, and either older olive, or oak piles, previously charred, must be driven with a machine, as close to each other as possible, and the intervals between the piles, filled with charcoal. The heaviest foundations may be laid on such a base."

These details are also strikingly similar in both the authorities; and this similarity seems to be due to some thing more than mere coincidence.

The next four chapters (XIII—XVI) in the *Mānasāra* deal with the column and its different parts, the pedestal, base, shaft and entablature, and their various mouldings. Vitruvius also treats the subject in exactly four chapters (Book III, chapter III, Book IV, chapters I—III). But the titles of the chapters are a little different; they are named in the *Manasara*, *upapiṭha* or pedestal (XIII), *adhishṭhāna* or base (XIV), *stambha* or shaft (XV), and *prastara* or entablature (XVI); and Vitruvius calls them, 'columns and their ornaments' (Book III, chapter III), 'origin of the three sorts of columns and the Corinthian capital' (Book IV, chapter I), 'ornaments of columns' (ibid, chapter II), and 'Doric proportions' (ibid, chapter III).

'Vitruvius, in the Doric, Corinthian, and Tuscan orders, makes no mention of pedestals, and in the Ionic order he seems to consider them rather as a necessary part in the construction of a temple than as belonging to the order itself' (cf. Book V, chapter VII). In the *Mānasāra* twelve kinds of pedestals are described with detailed measurements of the various mouldings of each pedestal. A comparison of these with similar details of pedestals, quoted in full in the writer's Dictionary from European authorities other than Vitruvius, makes it clear that the Indian pedestals surpass the Græco-Roman pedestals in variety, beauty of proportion and the richness of ornaments.

As regards the base also there is in the *Mānasāra* a larger variety of types, sixty-four in number, described in detail with their mouldings and ornaments. A comparison of the details gathered together in the writer's Dictionary will show that the Indian bases and pedestals are made more systematically and afford a greater variety of proportions than those of the Græco-Roman orders. In European orders the forms and dimensions of both base and pedestal are fixed by invariable rules with respect to the orders in which they are employed, while in the Indian orders the choice is left to the option of the architects.

There are, however, more similarities between the Indian and the Græco-Roman entablatures, consisting of four parts, the capital, architrave, frieze and cornice. "But the massiveness of the Indian entablature offers a striking contrast to the lightness of the Grecian." This is shewn by a comparison of details, given in the writer's Dictionary, of eight kinds of Indian and some five kinds of Græco-Roman entablatures.

But the point to be clear about is whether or not there is some fundamental resemblance between the Indian and the Græco-Roman column as a whole. This is a crucial point; because the column in a building is stated by authorities to be the regulator of the whole composition; and it is the one feature of the ancient architecture, which 'illustrates its rise and progress as well as its perfection and weakness.'

Like the five Græco-Roman orders, called Doric, Ionic, Corinthan, Tuscan, and Composite, columns in ancient India were also divided into five classes or orders. In the *Mānasāra* they are called *Brahma-kānta*, *Vishṇu-kānta*, *Rudra-kānta*, *Śiva-kānta*, and *Skanda-kānta*. These divisions are based on the general shapes. With respect to dimensions and ornaments they are called *Chitra-karṇa*, *Padma-kānta*, *Chitra-stambha*, *Pālikā-stambha*, and *Kumbha-stambha*.

In the *Matsya-Purāṇa*, the *Bṛihat-saṁhitā*, and the *Kiraṇa-tantra* they are called *Ruchaka*, *Vajra*, *Dvi-vajra*, *Pralīnaka*, and *Vṛitta*. In he *Suprabhedagama* the names of the five orders are *Śrī-kara*, *Chandra-kānta*, *Saumukhya*, *Priya-darśana*, and *Śubhankarī*. This last one is expressly stated to be the Indian composite order, being a compound (miśrita) of *Saumukhya* and *Priya-darśana*, exactly like the Græco-Roman Composite order which is a compound of Corinthian and Ionic.[1]

---

[1] For references see page 125 and the foot notes, and the writer's Dictionary under stambha.

Between the European and the Indian columns, there is a point of difference. In the Græco-Roman orders, the names of the five orders do not vary while in India the names of the five orders have varied in various treatises referred to above. It is true, all the same, that the criteria of divisions are essentially the same in all these authorities. The variation of the names of the five orders can perhaps be explained. The names of the Græco-Roman orders, according to Vitruvius and other European authorities referred to in the Encyclopædia of Architecture by Gwilt, are geographical[1].

In India, on the other hand, the names of the orders were based on the shapes of the columns. And as the Indians are comparatively more religious and sentimental than critical in temperament and imagination, they chose mythological and poetical names according to the spirit of the times, when these various works were composed. Thus in the *Mānasāra* we see the orders bearing the names of mythological deities, Brahmā, Vishṇu, Rudra, Śiva, and Skanda; as well as the poetical names like *Chitra-karṇa* (variegated ear), *Chitra-skambha* (variegated capital), *Padma-kānta* (graceful like lotus), *Kumbha-stambha* (of jug-shaped capital), and *Pālikā-stambha* (shaped like a measuring pot). In the *Āgama*, the names are more poetical: *Śrīkara* (beautifying), *Chandra-kānta* (graceful like the moon), *Saumukhya* (of a charming face), and *Subhaṅkarī* (auspicious). In the *Purāṇa*, the *Bṛihat-saṁhitā*, and the *Kiraṇa-tantra*, the names combine beauty and utility—*Ruchaka* (pleasing), *Vṛitta* (round and dignified), *Vajra* (beautiful and solid like the club), *Dvi-vajra* (doubly so), and *Pralīnaka* (firmly attached).

With regard to the names and functions of the component parts of the column the variation is a little less marked. The number of these subservient parts, called mouldings and common to all orders, is very significant. Thus in the *Mānasāra*, which, of almost all the treatises, deals separately and exhaustively with the pedestal, the base, the column or shaft, and the entablature, mention is made, in connection with the pillar, of five mouldings apparently of the shaft. They are called *bodhikā*, *mushṭi-bandha*, *phalakā*, *tāṭikā*, and *ghaṭa*. But the total number of mouldings, when the base, pedestal, and entablature are also taken into consideration, is forty-seven. The *Suprabhedāgama* describes two sets of seven mouldings, one set referring to the column of the main building and the other to that of the pavilion. They are called respectively *daṇḍa*, *maṇḍi*, *kaṇṭha*, *kumbha*, *phalakā*, *vīra-kaṇṭha* and *potikā*; and *bodhikā*, *uttara*, *vājana*, *mūradhikā*, *tulā* *jayantī* and *tala*.

[1] See page 126, note 1. The contents of the four following paras are referred to in more detail elsewhere in this book (p. 125 f); their repetition here is felt unavoidably necessary.

This increasing number of mouldings has reached the significant number of eight in the *Matsya-Purāṇa*, the *Bṛihat-saṁhitā* and the *Kiraṇa-tantra*, and bears the very same eight names—*vāhana*, *ghaṭa*, *padma*, *uttaroshṭha*, *bāhulya*, *hāra*, *tulā*, and *upa-tulā*.

The component mouldings of the Græco-Roman orders are also exactly eight in number, and like the five orders themselves their names have remained invariable ever since their introduction, though most of them have been given more than one name. They are called (1) the ovolo, echinus or quarter round; (2) the talon, ogée, or reversed cyma; (3) the cyma, cyma-recta, or cymatium; (4) the torus; (5) the scotia or trochilos; (6) the cavetto, mouth, or hollow; (7) the astragal, and (8) the fillet, listel, or annulet.

Some of the eight mouldings of the Indian order can be identified, with a reasonable certainty, with the corresponding mouldings of the Græco-Roman order. *Padma*, for instance, implies lotus (petal), and cyma also suggests the same thing. *Uttaroshṭha*, literally the lower lip, and the cavetto, mouth or hollow are apparently the same. *Hāra*, meaning chain, seems to imply the same object as the torus, bead or astragal. *Ghaṭa* means a pot; it may correspond to the ogee, talon or reversed cyma. *Vāhana* is that which supports anything, and the abacus also serves the same purpose; so they may correspond to each other. *Tulā* and *upa-tulā* otherwise called *vājana* and *uttara* seem to correspond to the fillet, listel or annulet.

The proportionate measurement of the columns is another important point of comparison. The details are discussed in the writer's Dictionary. The first Indian sort is six diameters high, the second seven diameters, the third eight diameters, the fourth nine diameters, and the fifth ten diameters high.

"Concerning the proportions of columns," says Râm Rāz (page 38), "the second sort of column in the Hindu arthitecture may be compared with the Tuscan, the third with the Doric, the fourth with the Ionic, and the fifth with the Corinthian or Composite pillar." He further adds that "there are other columns in the Indian architecture, not only one diameter lower than the Tuscan, but one to two diameters higher than the Composite." The same is also the case with the European columns. "The orders and their several characters and qualities," says Gwilt (2538), "do not merely appear in the fixed species of columns into which they have been subdivided, but are distributed throughout the edifices to which they are applied."

"Both the Indian and Grecian columns are diminished gradually in their diameter from the base to the summit of the shaft, a practice which has never been observed in the Egyptian; on the contrary, a diametrically opposite rule has been observed in their shafts, which are made narrower at the bottom than at the top. . . The proportion in which the diminution at the top of the columns of the two former (Indian and Græco-Roman) is made seems to have been regulated by the same principle, though not by the same rule. The general rule adopted by the Hindu architects in this respect is that the thickness at the bottom, being divided into as many parts as there are diameters in the whole height of the column, one of these parts is invariably diminished at the top; but in the Grecian and Roman architecture, the diameter of the upper part of the shaft, in a column of fifteen feet in height, is made one-sixth less than its thickness at the base; and in a column of fifty feet, the diminution is one-eighth. The higher the columns are, the less they diminish, because the apparent diminution of the diameter in columns of the same proportion is always greater according to their height, and this principle is supposed to have been discovered with greater scientific skill, and is adduced as one of the proofs of the highly refined taste of the Greeks: but we observe that precepts derived from the same principle have been taught and practised in India from time immemorial."

The point at issue is not the actual identification. The striking similarities in the names of the mouldings, like *padma* or cyma, *hāra* or bead, or in the names of orders like the *Miśrita* or Composite, may sometimes be attributed to inexplicable coincidence. But in view of other striking similarities between Vitruvius and the *Mānasāra*, such as the classification of orders into exactly five, and the division of subservient parts, called mouldings, common to all the orders, into eight, and also the proportionate measurement varying equally from six to ten diameters, and tapering almost in the same way, there would seem to have been something more substantial than mere coincidence. An influence, direct or indirect, of the one upon the other, seems highly probable. I venture to think, further, that there might have been a relation of indebtedness between the two authorities.

The concluding chapter (XVII) of this section in the *Mānasāra* deals with joinery. No separate treatment has been accorded by Vitruvius to this subject.

The next chapter (XVIII) in the *Mānasāra* is a summary of details concerning buildings of various storeys and kinds described in chapters XIX—XXX. The following chapters, XXXI—XXXVI, deal with attached buildings of various descriptions and requirements. Chapter XXXVII refers to the first entry into a newly-built house. Doors are separately described in two chapters, XXXVIII—XXXIX; so also the royal palaces and courts are described in chapters XL—XLII. Cars and chariots, couches and thrones are treated in the next three chapters, XLIII XLV. Arches are separately described in chapter XLVI, so also the theatre (*Madhya-raṅga*) is treated in chapter XLVII. And this architectural portion of the *Mānasāra* ends with the description of ornamental tree (chapter XLVIII), crowns (chapter XLIX), and ornaments and articles of furniture (chapter L)[1].

---

[1] For more details see pages 47—70.

The sculptural portion of the work (chapters LI—LXX) deals with the art of carving and measuring images. This portion practically comprises illustrations of the *tāla* measures. Vitruvius, as we shall show presently, has not treated the subject separately; he has mixed it up with the architectural description.

With regard to these subjects the comparison between the *Mānasāra* and Vitruvius need not be lengthy. Both these authorities in matters of detail must necessarily differ from each other even if one were translated from the other, because the local conditions and national requirements are entirely different regarding not only residential buildings but also temples. On the broad lines of methods and principles, however, the comparison can be briefly continued in the expectation of fruitful results.

Thus, in the *Mānasāra*, the whole compound of the house is divided into five courts (chapter XXXI), each of which is furnished with a gate-house (chapter XXXIII), and a large number of detached buildings are also built within each court (chapters XXXII, XXXVI, XIX—XXX).

Vitruvius also divides the compound into exactly five courts, which are, however, not used simultaneously (Book VI, chapters III—VII). "There are," says Vitruvius, "five species of courts, which receive their names from their forms. The Tuscan, the Corinthian, the Tetrastylon (with four columns), the Displuviatum (open at the top), and the Testudinatum (roofed)." In the *Mānasāra* also, it should be noted, five technical names have been given to these five courts, *antar-maṇḍala* (innermost court), *antanihāra* (the second court), *madhya-nihāra* (the middle court), *prākāra* (the fourth court) after which the chapter has been named and which is stated to be first introduced in the *Mānasāra*, though as many as seven courts are described in the *Mṛichchhakaṭika*. The fifth one is called *mahā-maryādā* or extreme boundary. Thus in the *Mānasāra* the courts receive their names from their situation, and not from their forms. Forms are discussed in the *Mānasāra* also. In fact the treatment of this subject, like all others, is by far the more exhaustive in the *Mānasāra*. Even the five gate-houses of the five courts have been treated at great length in a separate chapter (XXXIII) and given five technical names, *dvāra-śobhā* (beauty of the gate) belonging to the *antar-maṇḍala* or first court, *dvāra-śālā* (lit., 'gate house', of the second court), *dvāra-prāsāda* (lit., edifice of the gate), *dvāra-harmya* (lit, palace of the gate), and *mahā-gopura* (lit., great gate-house).[1]

Within these courts, buildings of different requirements have been similarly distributed by the two authorities. For instance, in the *Mānasāra*, chapter XXXVI is called *Gṛiha-māna-sthāna-vinyāsa*, literally meaning, 'location and measurement of house', and chapter XXXII is called *Parivāra-vidhāna*, meaning, 'the

---

[1] For references see pages 51, 52.

buildings for the members of the family' (of gods). The corresponding chapters (Book VII, chapters, I, II, IX) are named by Vitruvius 'situation of buildings according to the nature of different places,' 'proportions of private buildings to suit the nature of the sites,' and 'proportions of houses in the country.' Detached buildings, situated both within the compound and outside, have been described in the *Mānasāra* in two very long chapters XXXIV, XXXV) called *Maṇḍapa* and *Śālā*. The term *Maṇḍapa* is used to imply, first, a house or pavilion set up in a village or on the bank of a sea, river, tank or lake; secondly, all the detached buildings within a compound which is divided into five courts; lastly, it implies various sorts of rooms in a temple or residential building. *Śālā* also implies almost the same kinds of buildings; but they are more commodious, and their forms and twelve storeys are taken into special consideration. Chapter VI (Book I) called by Vitruvius 'distribution and situation of buildings within the walls' may be compared with '*Maṇḍapa*' and '*Śālā*' with respect to general principles and methods. But Vitruvius's treatment of the subject is comparatively brief. The brevity of his account of individual buildings also becomes obvious when the 'arrangement and parts of Grecian houses' and 'interior of the cell and the arrangement of Pronaos', described in two small chapters (Book VI, chapter X, Book IV, chapter IV), are compared with the exhaustive description of similar subjects detailed in some thirteen chapters (XVIII—XXX) in the *Mānasāra*.

Doors are separately described by both the authorities. Vitruvius calls the chapter 'Proportions of the doors of temples' (Book IV, chapter VI) In the *Mānasāra* the subject is treated under two chapters (XXXVIII, XXXIX), called *Dvāra-sthāna* (location of doors) and *Dvāra-māna* (measurement or proportions of doors). Both the authorities classify doors under three species. Vitruvius calls them Doric, Ionic, and Attic; and in the *Mānasāra* they are called *Chhanda*, *Vikalpa*, and *Ābhāsa*. Here is a striking point of similarity with respect to an important omission. In the *Mānasāra* the *Jāti* class always goes with the other three classes mentioned here. Vitruvius has also omitted Corinthian and Tuscan which generally go with Doric and Ionic. In the *Mānasāra* the height of the door is stated to be, as a general rule, twice its breadth. "Their width," says Vitruvius, "is found by dividing the height into two parts and a half, and taking one and a half for the width below." Single folded as well as double folded doors are mentioned in the *Mānasāra*. Vitruvius has referred also to four-fold doors. Indian doors are decorated with foliated and floral ornaments, as well as with the images of deities. "These doors," says Vitruvius, "are not to be inlaid cerestrota), nor in two folds, but single folded, and to open outwards." According to Vitruvius doors are generally constructed in the middle of the front wall. But according to the *Mānasāra* doors may also be constructed sometimes not in the centre of the frontage, but on either side of the middle.

Windows are not separately described by Vitruvius. But in the *Mānasāra* a long account of them has been given at the end of chapter XXXIII; similarly an account of stair-cases, omitted by Vitruvius, is found in the *Mānasāra* at the end of chapter XXX. No separate mention has also been made by Vitruvius of arches, to which subject an entire chapter (XLVI) has been devoted in the *Mānasāra*. Vitruvius has left out the accounts, given in the *Mānasāra*, of cars and chariots (chapter XLIII), couches (XLIV), thrones (XLV), crowns (XLIX), ornaments of the body and articles of house furniture (M. L), as well as the ornamental tree (XLVIII).

In the *Mānasāra*, on the other hand, a very brief reference is made to an object resembling a theatre, to which Vitruvius has devoted several chapters (Book V, chapters III—IX). Vitruvius has not treated separately the royal palaces found in the *Mānasāra* (chapters XL—XLII), nor does the *Mānasāra* contain any account of his special buildings, such as 'Forum and Basilica,' 'Treasury, Prison, and Curia,' 'Harbours and other buildings in water' (Book V, chapters I, II, XII). Building materials, though frequently mentioned, are not described in the *Mānasāra* under separate chapters. Vitruvius has devoted some eight chapters (Book II, chapters III—X) to the subject of building-materials, namely, bricks (compare the *Mānasāra*, chapter XII, last part), sand (M. XII), lime (M. LI), Pozzolona, stone quarries (M. XV), timber (M. XV) and firs, called Supernas and Infernas, and the Apennines

Vitruvius deals with painting and preparations of colours in the larger part of a book (VII) of fourteen chapters. This subject, as well as Vitruvius's books (VIII—X) on Instruments. Machines and Engines, have no place in the *Mānasāra*. In place of these matters, some twenty chapters (LI—LXX) of the *Mānasāra* have been devoted to sculptural matters to which only the following brief and casual reference has been made by Vitruvius (Book III, chapter I):

"In truth they (symmetry and proportion) are as necessary to the beauty of a building as to that of a well formed human figure, which nature has so fashioned, that the face, from the chin to the top of the forehead, or to the roots of the hair, is a tenth part of the height of the whole body. From the chin to the crown of the head is an eighth part of the whole height, and from the nape of the neck to the crown of the head the same. From the upper part of the breast to the roots of the hair a sixth, to the crown of the head a fourth. A third part of the height of the face is equal to that from the chin to the under side of the nostrils, and thence to the middle of the eyebrows the same; from the last to the roots of the hair, where the forehead ends, the remaining third part. The length of the foot is a sixth part of the height of the body. The fore-arm a fourth part. The width of the breast a fourth part. Similarly have the other members their due proportions by attention to which the ancient painters and sculptors obtained so much reputation. . . . . ."

"The navel is naturally placed in the centre of the human body, and if, in a man lying with his face upward, and his hands and feet extended, from his navel as the centre, a circle be described, it will touch his fingers and toes. It is not alone by a circle that the human body is thus circumscribed, as may be seen by placing it within a square. For measuring from the feet to the crown of the head, and then across the arms fully extended, we find the latter measure equal to the former; so that the lines at right angles to each other, enclosing the figure, will form a square."

"If nature, therefore, has made the human body so that the different members of it are measures of the whole, so the ancients have, with great propriety, determined that in all perfect works, each part should be some aliquot part of the whole; and since they direct that this be observed in all works, it must be most strictly attended to in temples of the gods, wherein the faults as well as the beauties remain to the end of the time." This is all about the defects, to which in the *Mānasāra* practically a whole chapter (LXIX), one of the two concluding chapters of the work, is devoted. It is called *Aṅga-dūshaṇa*, literally, 'defects of the limbs.' In both the authorities the subject is discussed in connection with sculptural objects, but curiously enough, defects and consequent penalties concerning images and idols have been entirely left out both by Vitruvius and the *Mānasāra*. Both the authorities have referred to the subject as concerning buildings only. This sort of similarity can hardly be due to more coincidence.

"It is worthy of remark," says Vitruvius, "that the measures necessarily used in all buildings and other works, are derived from the members of the human body, as the digit, the palm, the foot, the cubit, and that these form a perfect number, called by the Greeks *Téleios*." Phonetically this sounds like what the Indians call *Tālas*; and there is a similarity in meaning also[1]. In the above quotation Vitruvius has briefly referred to only the eighth variety with which the male human figure is measured also by the Indian authorities. Details of the *tāla* measures given in the writer's Dictionary need not be repeated here. It should also be noted that in both the authorities the face from the chin to the top of the forehead is taken as the standard of all the *tāla* measures which number ten in the *Mānasāra*.[2]

---

[1] Téleios is an adjective from telo-s, meaning end, and tāla is derived from tala and implies the distance between the ends of two fingers (see page 123).

[2] See page 123 above.

The last point of comparison between Vitruvius and the *Mānasāra* is in respect of the linguistic style. We have already pointed out that *Śilpa-śāstras* or architectural treatises in India were written in a very peculiar style. Sanskritists like Dr. G. Bühler and Sir R. G. Bhandarkar have truly branded it as the 'most barbarous Sanskrit.' This remark really means that all possible sorts of violation of the rules of grammar and rhetoric have been committed in the language of the *Śilpa-śāstras*. The matter has been discussed elsewhere in great detail, which need not be repeated here. One of the theses presented by the writer before the Leiden University and passed in his favour by that learned assembly after long discussion was this :

"The ungrammatical style of Sanskrit revealed in the branch of literature of which the *Mānasāra* is a representative, is due to the want of literary proficiency on the part of the professional architects who seem to have been the authors of it." With this the following apology, for ungrammatical style, of Vitruvius may very fruitfully be compared.

"I beseech you, O Cæsar," says Vitruvius, "and those who read this my work, to pardon and overlook grammatical errors; for I write neither as an accomplished philosopher, an eloquent rhetorician, nor an expert grammarian, but as an architect : in respect, however, of my art and its principles, I will lay down rules which may serve as an authority to those who build, as well as to those who are already somewhat acquainted with the science." (Book I, chapter I).

I cannot help thinking that if the writers of the *Śilpa-śāstras* generally, and the author of the *Mānasāra* in particular, were conscious of the nature of their style they would certainly have added to their treatises an apology like that of Vitruvius.

There is yet another curious similarity between Vitruvius and the *Mānasāra*. It is regarding the titles of both the works. Both are hidden in a mystery. Vitruvius's work bears practically no title. It is called by his translators 'The architecture of Marcus Vitruvius Pollio.' It has been pointed out in the Preface that the term 'Mānasāra' also admits of various interpretations. For a sage, *Mānasāra* is a very unfamiliar name. No such sage is mentioned in the various branches of Sanskrit literature except in this newly discovered Vāstu-śāstra. A king of Malwa, however, bore this name. As a derivative name, *Mānasāra*, meaning essence of measurement, and suitable for the title of a work like this, has some philological resemblance with *mensuration*. The derivative meaning of the term 'Vitruvius' is uncertain. The point, however, to which attention is invited, is the curious similarity between the treatise of Vitruvius and the *Mānasāra* in respect of the uncertain signification of their titles.

There is also an uncertainty lurking over the ages in which the architecture of Vitruvius and the *Mānasāra* were composed. "It is *likely* that" the former "was composed twenty-five years before the Christian era." This conjecture is based mainly on Vitruvius's mention of his patron, Julius Cæsar. But there is no mention of anybody under whose patronage the *Mānasāra* might have been composed.

The similarities so briefly outlined will be more convincing to those who have carefully studied both Vitruvius and the *Mānasāra*.

Those who are, however, inclined to think like myself and refuse to attribute all these affinities to mere chance, will be anxious to find out the connecting link between the two authorities. The question was put before the Oriental Conference held in Calcutta in January, 1922, to point out the link, about the existence of which there seems no reasonable doubt. A learned discussion was held on the paper but no suggestion was received on this point.

There is the expedition of Alexander the Great to explain the Grecian influence on the Gāndhāra sculpture. The 'Questions of Menander' may perhaps stand for the title *Milanda-paṅha*. There is again the *Romaka-siddhānta* to indicate the influence of the Roman astronomy upon the Indian *Jyotisha-śāstra* which had, however, already established itself as one of the six essential limbs of the Veda, the most ancient extant lore of human learning. Similarly the art of building, which is intimately connected with all living beings, was developed by the ancient Hindus at the early Vedic period. But the *Śilpa-śāstra*, which is but an analysis and commentary of the art, was necessarily evolved much later. There are reasons to think that the *Mānasāra* is not the first work in which the 'essence of measurement and the system of proportions' were codified in the form of *Śāstra*, though this may be the standard treatise.

Until the missing link is found out, it is, however, possible to think that there was some work or works, or some floating traditions, which influenced both treatises. It will, therefore, serve no useful purpose in trying to further develop the nature of the various similarities between Vitruvius and the *Mānasāra*. I would not, therefore, hazard an opinion at present as to the precise nature of the connection between these two treatises There are arguments which might support a claim of priority on behalf of either work. I shall be content, for the present, if the learned world be convinced that there are undeniable similarities between the two standard works and that these affinities do not seem to be accidental.

V

AGE OF THE MĀNASĀRA

In trying to establish, in the preceding section, a relation of influence between Vitruvius and the *Mānasāra*, one of my objects was to find out a land-mark for the latter, as the date of the former is known approximately.

"From the fragments of inscriptions relative to the Vitruvia family found in the neighbourhood of Farmiae (the present Mola di Gaeta), it has been presumed without a great stretch of probability, that it was in this territory Vitruvius was born. The age in which he lived was doubtless between the time of the death of Julius Cæsar and the battle of Actium, though some have assigned it to the reign of Titus. But his omission of the mention of a great number of magnificent buildings, erected after the time of Augustus, and his especial mention of the theatre of Pompey as the only one of stone, sufficiently prove that such a conjecture is not warranted by circumstances. The dedication, moreover, points to Augustus as the patron of Vitruvius, and the incident of C. Julius, the son of Masanissa, who was born in the army of Julius Cæsar, having lodged with him, as related in the third chapter of his eighth book, seems clearly to indicate the time of his existence. It is likely that the following treatise (of Vitruvius) was composed when he was advanced in life, and that it was presented to his patron after he had assumed the title of Augustus, that is, twenty-five years before the Christian era, inasmuch as he speaks of a temple erected to Augustus, in his Basilica at Fano."[1]

The other land-mark may perhaps be supplied by the following thesis admitted by Leiden University. "There seems to have been a relation of indebtedness between the *Mānasāra*, on the one hand, and on the other hand, the architectural portions of the *Agni-purāṇa*, the *Garuḍa-purāṇa*, the *Matsya-purāṇa* and the *Bhavishya-purāṇa*, the *Kāmikāgama*, the *Suprabhedāgama*, and the *Bṛihat-saṁhitā*." The reasons for and the arguments in favour of such a belief have been discussed in great detail elsewhere,[2] and need not be repeated here. For further scrutiny and more minute comparison, the *Bṛihat-saṁhitā* of Varāhamihira, one

[1] Prof. Gwilt, Preface, xii.

[2] See pages 110–131.

of the nine gems[1] at the court of a mythical Vikramāditya, is selected. Professor Kern has given a probable date, 550 A. D., to the *Bṛihat-saṁhitā*. The ages of the *Purāṇas* and the *Āgamas* mentioned in the thesis are more conjectural.

Although primarily not a treatise on architecture the *Bṛihat-saṁhitā* has devoted five chapters[2] (LIII, LVI, LVII, LVIII and LXXIX) to this art. Three of these, called *Vāstu-vidyā* or the science of architecture, *Prāsāda-lakshaṇa* or the description of temples under twenty types, and *Śayyāsana-lakshaṇa* or the description of bedsteads and couches, deal with architecture proper; and the other two, called *Vajralepa* or the first casting of image and *Pratimā-lakshaṇa* or the description of images, briefly refer to sculpture. The following similarities between the *Mānasāra* and *Bṛihat-saṁhitā* may be noticed:

	Mānasāra	*Bṛihat-saṁhitā*
Origin and development of the science of architecture	I, 1	LIII, 1.
Objects of architecture ...	III.	LIII, 2—3 (details differ).
Testing of soil ...	IV—V.	LIII, 95—97, 85—92, 115—117.
Ground plan	VII.	LIII, 42—69, 83—84.
Offerings to deities ...	VIII.	LIII, 99—100.
Dimension of storeys ...	XI	LIII, 4—26, LVI, 29—30.
Columns	XV.	LIII, 27—30, 112—113, 121—123.
Temple-buildings ...	XVIII	LVI, 3—8 (site), 9 (ground), 10—16 (general), 17—19 (twenty types).
One-storeyed buildings ...	XIX	LVI, 23, 26.
Five-storeyed buildings ...	XXIII.	LVI, 27.
Six-storeyed buildings ...	XXIV.	LVI, 22.
Seven-storeyed buildings...	XXV.	LVI, 24.
Eight-storeyed buildings	XXVI.	LVI, 21.
Ten-storeyed buildings ...	XXVIII.	LVI, 20.
Halls and pavilions ...	XXXIII XXXIV.	LIII, 118.
Situation and measurement of houses	XXXVI.	LIII, 70.

[1] धन्वन्तरिः क्षपणकोमरसिंहशङ्कुवेतालभट्टघटकर्परकालिदासाः ।
ख्यातो वराहमिहिरो नृपतेः सभायां रत्नानि वै वररुचिर्नव विक्रमस्य ॥
(ज्योतिर्विदाभरण, Kern. B. S. 17).

The existence of these gems as contemporaries has been held to be untenable.

[2] This refers to Kern's edition published by A. S. Great Britain and Ireland. In some other editions, for instance, in that of Sudhākara Dvivedi, Benares, Vikrama era 1658, these chapters have got a different numbering. Our references to the Bṛihat-saṁhitā are mostly to Kern's edition.

	Mānasāra	*Bṛihat-saṁhitā*
Ceremonial entry into a newly-built house ...	XXXVII	LIII, 125.
Situation and measurement of doors	XXXVIII XXXIX.	LIII, 26—27, 70—82; LVI, 10, 12—16.
Phalli	LII.	LVIII, 53—55.
Images of female deities...	LIV.	LVIII, 56.
Images in general ...	LXIV.	LVIII, 31—52, 57—58 (ends abruptly)
Largest type of ten *tāla* measures	LXV.	LVIII, 4—30.
First casting of images ...	LXVIII.	LVIII, 1—3.

An elaborate discussion has already been introduced regarding the types of buildings[1] and the five orders.[2] Two other points of special interest and general importance may be elaborated here.

The ground plans are treated under twenty-four schemes in the *Mānasāra*. Of these, descriptions in detail are given of the eighth and the ninth schemes which consist respectively of sixty-four and eighty-one squares. In the *Mānasāra* it is stated, by way of explanation, that these two plans were much in use. Varāhamihira also has described only these two plans. In the *Bṛihat-saṁhitā* there is not the slightest reference to the other twenty-two schemes. As is usual with him, Varāhamihira has changed the names or location of the squares here and there. Another striking point of similarity is that only the square plans are described in both the treatises, although in the *Mānasāra* five shapes or forms are given to the buildings. Varāhamihira also has referred to the round type of buildings. Corresponding to these shapes there should be the ground plans also. But these are unexpectedly missing in the *Mānasāra* and also in the *Bṛihat-saṁhitā*. But the details of round or circular plans and also of triangular plans, both consisting of eighty-one squares, have been quoted from a mythical Bharata-muni by Bhaṭṭotpala, a commentator of the *Bṛihat-saṁhitā*. So in matter of such a striking omission also Varāhamihira seems to have faithfully followed the *Mānasāra*, *Garga*, or whatever else his sources might have been.

The other point proposed to be discussed here is that concerning the sources of the *Bṛihat-saṁhitā* in architectural matters. Varāhamihira says that the science of architecture has come down to him from Brahmā (Kamalabhū) through several generations of sages. He further admits that all matters relating to

[1] See pages 111—119. [2] See pages 125—128, 140—159.

architecture are taken from Garga, and small portions of the architectural treatises of Manu and others have been put in from memory.[1]

The names of the sages passed over here may be gathered together from casual references. Mention is made of Vasishṭha, Maya, Viśvakarman, Bhāskara and Nagnajit.[2] The Purāṇas are not mentioned by Varāhamihira. But some of the Purāṇas are no doubt earlier than the *Bṛihat-saṁhitā*.[3]

It has been shewn that with regard to the technical names and other details of the twenty types, under which temple-buildings are described, the *Matsya-purāṇa* (chapter 269, verses 28—53), the *Bhavishya-purāṇa* (chapter 130, verses 27—35), and the *Bṛihat-saṁhitā* (chapter 56, verses 20—28) are identical.[4] The *Bhavishya-purāṇa* (chapter 130, verses 15—26, 36—37, 27—35) can be read, letter for letter, in the *Bṛihat-saṁhitā* (LVI. 8—19, 30, 20—28). When verses 22 and 36—37 of the former are compared with the identical verses 15 and 29—30 of the latter, it seems as if Varāhamihira were the debtor.[5] It should be noted that the linguistic defects of the *Bhavishya-purāṇa* are removed in the *Bṛihat-saṁhitā*.

---

[1] प्रासादलक्षणमिदं कथितं समासाद् ।
गर्गेण यद्विरचितं तदिहास्ति सर्वम् ॥
मन्वादिभिर्विरचितानि पृथूनि यानि ।
तत्संस्मृतिं प्रति मयात्र कृतोधिकारः ॥ (Bṛihat-saṁhitā, LVI, 30-31).

[2] चतुरश्रं वसिष्ठः कथयति नैत्रान्तकर्णयोर्विवरम् । LVIII, 8.
मयकथितो योगोयं विज्ञेयो वज्रसङ्घातः । LVII, 8.
भूमिकाङ्गुलमानेन मयस्याष्टोत्तरं शतम् ।
सार्धहस्तत्रयं चैव कथितं विश्वकर्मणा ॥ LVI, 29.
सर्वप्रतिमास्वेवं शुभाशुभं भास्करोक्तसमम् । LVIII, 52.
आस्यं सकेशनिचयं षोडशदैर्घ्येण नग्नजित् प्रोक्तम् । LVIII, 15.
नग्नजिता तु चतुर्दशदैर्घ्येण द्राविडं कथितम् । LVIII, 4.

[3] See page 194.

[4] See pages 114—118.

[5] शैलमङ्गल्यविहगः श्रीवृक्षः स्वतिकैर्घटैः ।
मानाष्टमेन भागेन प्रतिमा स्यात्सपिण्डिका ॥ 22.
सहस्रत्रितयं चैव कथितं विश्वकर्मणा ॥ 36.
प्राहुः स्थपतयश्चात्र मतमेकं विपश्चित ।
कपोतपालिनीयुक्तमतो गच्छति तुल्यताम् ॥ 37.

Similar illustrations can be drawn from the *Matsya-purāṇa* and the *Bṛihat-saṁhitā* also. For instance[1] of the former verses 2 (chapter 255), 19 and 20 (chapter 270) can be compared with the latter in respect of LIII, 28 and LVI, 12, 13. Varāhamihira's is apparently the improved version in the revised edition. On this ground one is tempted to place these *Purāṇas* before the *Bṛihat-saṁhitā*. But Varāhamihira himself has not admitted his debt to these authorities. In these circumstances priority might be claimed for him.

There is one other point, which deserves special notice. In the *Matsya-purāṇa* eighteen professors[2] of the science of architecture are mentioned, namely, Bhṛigu, Atri, Vasishṭha, Viśvakarman, Maya, Nārada, Nagnajit, Viśālāksha, Purandara, Brahman, Kumāra, Nandīśa (Śiva), Śaunaka, Garga, Vāsudeva, Aniruddha, Śukra and Vṛihaspati. Of these eighteen professors, Garga, Maya, Viśvakarman, Vasishṭha

---

and शेषं मङ्गल्यविहगैः श्रीवृक्षैः स्वस्तिकैर्घटैः ।
मिथुनैः पत्रपङ्क्तिभिः प्रमथैश्चोपशोभयेत् ॥ 15.
सार्धं हस्तत्रयं चैव कथितं विश्वकर्मणा ॥ 29.
प्राहुः स्थपतयश्चात्र मतमेकं विपश्चितः ।
कपोतपालिसंयुक्ता न्यूना गच्छन्ति तुल्यताम् ॥ 30.

[1] रुचकश्चतुरःस्यादष्टास्रो वज्रोच्यते । 255, 2.
and समचतुरस्रो रुचको वज्रोऽष्टास्रिर्द्विवज्रको द्विगुणः । LIII. 28.
विस्ताराधों भवेद्गर्भो भित्तयोऽन्याः समन्ततः ।
गर्भपादेन विस्तीर्णं द्वारं त्रिगुणायतम् ॥ 270, 19.
and विस्ताराधों भवेद्गर्भो भित्तयोऽन्याः समन्ततः ।
गर्भपादेन विस्तीर्णं द्वारं द्विगुणमुच्छ्रितम् ॥ LVI. 12.
again तथा द्विगुणविस्तीर्णमुखस्तद्वदुदम्बरः ।
विस्तारपादप्रतिमं बाहुल्यं शाखयोः स्मृतम् ॥ 270, 20.
and उच्छ्रायात्पादविस्तीर्णा शाखा तद्वदुदम्बरः ।
विस्तारपादप्रतिमं बाहुल्यं शाखयोः स्मृतम् ॥ LVI. 13.

[2] Matsya-purāṇa, chap, 255, 2—4.

Compare:

इति प्रोक्तं वास्तुशास्त्रं पूर्वं गर्गाय धीमते ।
गर्गात्पराशरः प्राप्तस्तस्मात्प्राप्तो बृहद्रथः ॥
बृहद्रथाद्विश्वकर्मा प्राप्तवान् वास्तुशास्त्रकम् ।
स एव विश्वकर्मा जगतो हितायाकथयत्पुनः ॥
वासुदेवादिषु पुनर्भूलोके भक्तितोऽब्रवीत् ॥

(Viśva-karma-prakāśa, Benares, 1888. XIII, 25—27).

and Nagnajit have also been mentioned in the *Bṛihat-saṁhitā*. Varāhamihira, the author of the *Bṛihat-saṁhitā*, has included Bhāskara and Manu, who are not met with in the *Matsya-purāṇa*. The identity of these mythical sages is a vexatious matter in Sanskrit literature. One Bhāskara or Bhāskarāchārya was the author of the Lilāvatī and the Siddhānta-śiromaṇi. Of Manu, we shall presently speak more. But the *Matsya-purāṇa* does not include these names in its lists, nor does it mention Varāhamihira.

In the *Mānasāra* there is a list of thirty-two authorities, namely, Viśvakarman, Viśveśa, Viśva-sāra, Prabodhaka, Vṛita, Maya, Tvashṭar, Manu, Nala, Māna-vid, Māna-kalpa, Māna-sāra, Māna-bodha, Prashṭar, Viśva-bodha, Naya, Ādisāra, Viśāla, Viśva-kāśyapa, Vāstu-bodha, Mahātantra, Vāstu-vidyāpati, Pārāśarīyaka, Kāla-yūpa, Chaitya, Chitraka, Āvarya, Sādhakasāra-saṁhitā, Bhānu, Indra, Lokajña, and Saura. In the opening verse it is stated that the science of architecture has come down to the sage Mānasāra from Śiva, Brahmā and Vishṇu, through Indra, Bṛihaspati, Nārada and all other sages. In a mythical genealogy of the artists it is further stated that from the four faces of Brahmā originated the four heavenly architects, namely, Viśvakarman, Maya, Tvashṭar, and Manu. Their four sons, called respectively, Sthapati or the chief architect, Sūtra-grāhin or the designer, Vardhaki or the painter, and Takshaka or the carpenter, represent the guild of the modern architects.[1]

It should be noted that Viśvakarman, Maya, Manu and Tvashṭar are mentioned twice, once to represent the heavenly architects, and again as modern architects. In the same sense Indra is also mentioned twice.

Viśva-karman and Maya, to whom many extant architectural treatises are ascribed, are common in the *Mānasāra*, the *Matsya-purāṇa*, and the *Bṛihat-saṁhitā*. The *Mānasāra* and the *Matsya-purāṇa* have, therefore, in common five authorities, namely, Bṛihaspati, Indra under the name Purandara in the *Purāṇa*, Viśālāksha *alias* Viśāla in the *Mānasāra*, Viśva-karman, and Maya. The *Mānasāra* and the *Bṛihat-saṁhitā* have in common Viśva-karman, Maya and Manu.

प्रोक्तानि पंचरात्राणि सप्तरात्राणि वै मया ॥
व्यस्तानि मुनिभिर्लोके पंचविंशति संख्यया ।
हयशीर्षं तन्त्रमाद्यं तन्त्रं त्रैलोक्यमोहनम् ॥
वैभवं पौष्करं तन्त्रं प्रह्लादं गार्ग्यगालवम् ।
नारदीयं च संप्रश्नं शाण्डिल्यं वैश्वकं तथा ॥
सत्योक्तं शौनकं तन्त्रं वासिष्ठं ज्ञानसागरम् ।
स्वायंभुवं कपिलं च तार्क्ष्यं नारायणीयकम् ॥
आत्रेयं नारसिंहाख्यमानन्दाख्यं तथारुणकम् ।
बौधायनं तथार्षं तु विश्वोक्तं तस्य सारतः ॥
(Agni-Purāṇa, chap. 39, v. 1—5.)

[1] Chapters, LXVIII, I, II; see pages 66, 34, 35.

Viśva-karman, etymologically implying the Creator of the universe, is more or less a professiónal name for an architect. Manu is less so. This is a generic name. Mention is made of fourteen Manus,[1] namely, Svāyambhuva, Svārochisha, Auttami, Tāmasa, Raivata, Chākshusha, Vaivasvata, Sāvarṇi, Daksha-sāvarṇi, Brahma-sāvarṇi, Dharma-sāvarṇi, Rudra-sāvarṇi, Rauchya-daiva-sāvarṇi, and Indra-sāvarṇi. Manu is a sort of second Creator, the Indian Adam, representative of man and father of human race. It seems, however, clear that there must have been an architect Manu also in the ordinary sense of the term, because with him several architectural works are associated. He is stated in the Rāmāyaṇa[2] to have built the ancient city of Ayodhyā, the capital of king Rāma.

Maya is a more historical person. Several existing architectural treatises are ascribed to him.[3] He may not be as old as the Zend Āvesta. Ahura-Mazda and Maya-Asura are perhaps not one and the same person. But he is mentioned in unmistakable terms as the architect of a wonderful council hall, of which it is stated there could not be any parallel in the world of the mortals, and whereon all heavenly ideas were depicted in bricks and stones. He declares himself as a great poet of architecture (*mahākavi*), a Ruskin, among the rivals of gods, and he is their Viśvakarman who was the heavenly architect among the gods.[4]

[1] Manusaṁhitā I, 63.

[2] अयोध्या नाम नगरी तत्रासील्लोकविश्रुता ।
मनुना मानवेन्द्रेण या पुरी निर्मिता स्वयम् ॥

(Rāmāyaṇa, Ādikāṇḍa, verse 6).

[3] See the writer's Dictionary, Appendix I, where a note on the latest discoveries of the Maya civilisation in America is also given.

[4] अहं हि विश्वकर्मा वै दानवानां महाकविः ।
सोऽहं वै त्वत्कृते किञ्चित्कर्तुमिच्छामि पाण्डवाः ॥ 5
ततो विचिन्त्य मनसा लोकनाथः प्रजापतिः ।
चोदयामास तं कृष्णः सभा वै क्रियतामिति ॥ 9
यदि त्वं कर्तुकामोऽसि प्रियं शिल्पवतां वर ।
धर्मराजस्य दैतेय यादृशीमिह मन्यसे ॥ 10
यां कृतां नानुकुर्वन्ति मानवाः प्रेक्ष्याधिष्ठिताः ।
मनुष्यलोके सकले तादृशीं कुरु वै सभाम् ॥ 11
यत्र दिव्यानभिप्रायान् पश्येम हि कृतांस्त्वया ।
आसुरान्मानुषांश्चैव सभां तां कुरु वै मय ॥ 12

(Mahābhārata, Sabhā-parvan, chapter I, 5, 9—12).

The famous commentator Nīlakaṇṭha adds the following note :—

Like Manu, Maya is also a generic name. He is also known by some other personal names.[1] So the Maya of the *Mānasāra*, of the *Matsya-purāṇa* and of the *Bṛihat-saṁhitā* may not be one and the same person. It is just possible that there might have been a Maya, who borrowed from or based his treatise in any case upon the *Mānasāra*.[2] In fact it is perfectly clear from the list of authorities quoted from the *Mānāsara* that there must have been at least one more Mānasāra, from whom or from which our *Mānasara* has borrowed. It has also been pointed out[3] that the term *Mānasāra* has been used to imply both a person and a treatise. The uncertain identities and the confusing chronology are indeed stumbling-blocks in the field of Sanskrit researches.

In all items of comparison between the *Mānasāra* and the cognate works, we have seen[4] that the *Mānasāra* contains fuller lists. In the present instance also there are more than thirty-two authorities mentioned in the *Mānasāra*, while the *Matsya-purāṇa* is content with a list of eighteen, and the *Bṛihat-saṁhitā* has specified only seven. But none of these three treatises has admitted the authority of either of the other two. From this it would appear as if they were quite ignorant of the existence of one another, being separated by an insuperable gap in time or space. But such a relation is untenable, I should say improbable, between the *Matsya-purāṇa*, the *Bhavishya-purāṇa* and the *Bṛihat-saṁhitā* in any case, unless however we choose to suppose that there might have been an unknown authority or some floating tradition, by which these treatises have been influenced in the same way even to the extent of chapter and verse, but without any knowledge of one another. But I have failed to satisfy myself with such a hypothesis. For we have seen identical passages in these works.[5] All these three contain the same list of twenty types of buildings bearing the same technical names, and identical in other details.[6] Buildings are described under certain types in all the architectural works. Their technical names have no signification. Unless one list is copied from the other, these names need not be identical. In fact such is the case with regard to the fuller list in the *Mānasāra*. Therein we have seen ninety-eight types of buildings described under more architectural divisions and with fuller architectural details

---

विश्वं कर्मकृति साध्यं यस्य स विश्वकर्मा। महाकविः शिल्पविशतः। आसुरान् मानुषान् इत्युपलक्षणं देवगन्धर्वादीनामपि अभिप्रायान् लेपचित्रे लेख्यचित्रे च चतुर्दशभुवनान्तरस्थ तत्तज्जातीयस्वाभाविकनानाविधलीलाप्रदर्शनेन मनोवृत्तोः पश्येम यद्दर्शनेन ब्रह्माण्डान्तर-वर्ति सर्वं वस्तुजातं दृष्टप्रायं भवतीत्यर्थः।

1 See pages, 89, 91
2 See page 91.
3 See Preface, pages 2-3
4 See pages 110—131.
5 See pages 163, 164.
6 See pages 114—118.

than in these non-architectural works.[1] But except in one or two solitary instances like Kailāśa, the names of these types of buildings are not identical. But there are certain similarities all the same. For instance, the Merukānta of the *Mānasāra* is read simply as Meru in the *Purāṇas* and the *Bṛihat-saṁhitā*. This is certainly an improved reading, first, because Meru as the name of a mountain or as a geographical term is well known in Sanskrit literature[2], and secondly, '*kānta*' in the expression '*merukānta*' is meaningless. Similarly the reading Vṛitta of the *Purāṇas* and the *Bṛihat-saṁhitā* is an improved version, a good emended form of *vivṛita* of the *Mānasāra*. Almost similar is the case with regard to another architecturally very important object, namely, the column or order, for the columns are stated by the authorities to be the regulator of the whole composition. In this case also the *Mānasāra* contains a fuller list. It has two sets of five technical names for the orders, while the *Matsya-purāṇa* and the *Bṛihat-saṁhitā* contain only one set of the five orders. The names of these orders in the *Mānasāra* are different from those in the *Purāṇa* and the *Saṁhitā*, but Varāhamihira has given the very same five names to the orders as the *Matsya-purāṇa*, and they have also the very same eight names for the mouldings or the component parts of a column. The *Mānasāra*, as in all other cases, has a fuller list of mouldings also. It contains more than forty-seven mouldings for the pedestal, base, shaft, and entablature; the shaft being given five special mouldings. And as in the case of the types of buildings, there are some names of mouldings, for instance, *ghaṭa* and *hāra*, common in the *Mānasāra*, the *Matsya-purāṇa*, and the *Bṛihat-saṁhitā*.

So in three important architectural matters, namely, the preceding authorities, the types of buildings, and the orders and their component parts, the *Mānasāra* has fuller lists than those in the *Matsya purana* and the *Bṛihat-saṁhita* which are exactly identical in these matters. In these circumstances one is ordinarily likely to think that a later work only can make a thing more complete. But there is another essential point to consider, namely, that the *Mānasāra* is avowedly an architectural treatise, while the *Matsya-purāṇa* and the *Bṛihat-saṁhita* are not, their treatment of architectural matters is but casual, and in fact they have entirely left out purely architectural description. It is clear beyond doubt that the *Purāṇa* and the *Saṁhitā* must have consulted an architectural treatise for their information and guidance in architectural matters, just as they have certainly, based their references, for instance, on medicine, to a standard medical treatise.

[1] See pages 110–118.

[2] For instance, Naishadhacharita, 16; Bhartṛihari, Vairāgya-śataka, 150, etc. Compare the terms like Sumeru, Uttarameru, etc.

[3] See pages 125—128

If the *Mānasāra* had an opportunity of consulting Varāhamihira or the *Matsya-purāṇa*, the reading like *Vivṛita* for *Vṛitta*, or *Meru-kānta* for *Meru* could not have remained unamended in it. Besides, if the *Mānasāra* had been composed after the works like the *Matsya-purāṇa* and the *Bṛihat-saṁhitā*, why should it not have added these two to its long list of authorities? It would be no argument to say that the author of the *Mānasāra* might not have consulted these authorities or might have been quite ignorant of their existence. For, though not primarily works on architecture, the *Matsya-purāṇa* and the *Bṛihat-saṁhitā* have been well known to subsequent literature, and we shall presently show that the author of the *Mānasāra* had an extensive knowledge of things from a wide study and observation.

In these circumstances, though ready to readjust my views in the light of new facts, my present impression is that there must have been a direct influence between the *Matsya-purāṇa*, the *Bṛihat-saṁhitā*, and the *Bhavishya-purāṇa* while the connection between these treatises and the *Mānasāra* might have been indirect. The age of the *Mānasāra*, however, is indicated by other things also; and these will be discussed presently.

There are only a few treatises wherein the term *Mānasāra* is mentioned. The *Agni-purāṇa*, as already pointed out,[1] has some passages of uncertain meanings, wherein the term occurs. For instance, it is stated, that above the *Śuka-nāsa* (literally, parrot's nose) or gargoyles, that is the water-spout in a building, there should be a *vedi* or platform furnished with a neck. And this should be as prescribed in the *Mānasāra* (*mānasāraka*), or, the object of it is to make a passage for refuse (*malasāraka*).[2] This latter interpretation seems untenable; for the adjective is used in the neuter singular, and ordinarily would not qualify a feminine singular noun. If the first rendering be acceptable, the expression would form a separate clause, *iti mānasārakam*, meaning, this is in accordance with the rules of the *Mānasāra*.

There are reasons to think that a relation of direct influence exists between the *Agni-purāṇa* and the *Garuḍa-purāṇa*.[3] And through the latter the former may be connected with the *Matsya-purāṇa*, the *Bhavishya-purāṇa* and the *Bṛihat-saṁhitā*.[4]

The *Śukra-nīti* is another important work, which, though not an architectural tre-tise, deals largely with subjects relating to arthitecture and sculpture.[5] It

[1] See Preface. Compare also note 2, page 164—165.

[2] तदूर्ध्वं तु भवेद्वेदी सकण्ठा मनसारकम् (? मानसारकम् or मलसारकम्) ।
(Agni-purāṇa, XLII, 17)

[3] See pages 113-114.

[4] See pages 114—118 and the writer's Dictionary under *Prāsāda*.

[5] chapter IV. Section 4. (1) देव मन्दिरादिनिर्माणव्यवस्था, (2) प्रतिमानिर्माणव्यवस्था etc. (see details in appendix I, in the writer's Dictionary).

is a work on royal polity ascribed to an author, Śukrāchārya, whose age has not been clearly established. It appears to be anterior to the *Matsya-purāṇa* for the reason that the latter has included Śukra as one of its eighteen authorities.[1] The question of the identity of Śukrāchārya with this Śukra must necessarily come in. But there is hardly a satisfactory answer to give.

In the *Śukra-nīti* we notice also a large number of passages common to it with another work called the *Kāmandakīya-nīti* which has been assigned by Dr. R. L. Mitra to the fourth century of the Christian era on the ground of its dedication to Chandra Gupta, existence of Hindu temples and absence of any trace of Buddhism in the fifth century A. D. when the Chinese traveller Fahien visited Java, where in an island called Bali the work has been discovered.[2]

This *Kāmandakīya-nīti*, which has apparently borrowed from the *Artha-śāstra* of Vishṇu Gupta,[3] seems in its turn to have been freely drawn upon by the *Agni-Purāṇa*.[4] This *Purāṇa*, we have shewn, may have borrowed from the *Mānasāra* also.[5]

This introduction of the *Śukranīti*, the *Kāmandakīya-nīti* and the *Artha-Śāstra*, together with the *Matsya-purāṇa*, the *Agni-purāṇa* and the *Mānasāra*, may appear as an episode. But a time may come when the inter-relation of all these treatises will be more satisfactorily established.

The next external references to the name of Mānasāra are met with in a famous prose romance, the *Daśa-Kumāra-Charita*[6], by a very eminent author, Daṇḍin,

---

[1] Page 164.

[2] यस्य प्रभावाद्भुवनं शाश्वते पथि तिष्ठति ।
प्राजहार नृचन्द्राय चन्द्रगुप्ताय मेदिनीम् ॥ (Kāmandakīya-nīti, 1—5).

Here, it is argued, Chandra Gupta refers to I, or II Chandra Gupta of the Imperial Gupta Dynasty who are assigned respectively to 320—326 A.D., and 375—413 A.D.

[3] नीतिशास्त्रामृतं धीमानर्थशास्त्रमहोदधेः ।
समुद्दध्रे नमस्तस्मै विष्णुगुप्ताय वेधसे ॥
(Kāmandakīya, I. 6).

Dr. Jacob places the Artha Śāstra in the fourth century B. C., (Berlin Academy Seitzungaberichte, 1911, pages 954—978; 1912, pages 832—849). Prof. Keith tends to bring it down to the second or first century B. C. (J. R. A. S. 1915).

[4] Dr. R. L. Mitra, Kāmandakīya, Bibl. Ind. page 4.

[5] See pages 110—118.

[6] Edited by Kale, Bombay, 1917; see page 4; repetition below is felt unavoidably necessary :—

(i) Page 4, paragraph 2, line 3— मगधनायको मालवेश्वरं प्रत्यग्रसंग्रामघस्मरं समुत्कटमानसारं मानसारं प्रति............संग्रामाभिलाषेण रोषेण महाविष्टो निर्ययौ ।

(ii) P. 6, para 1. line 8— मालवनाथो जयलक्ष्मीसनाथो मगधराज्यं प्राज्यं समाक्रम्य पुष्पपुरमध्यतिष्ठत् ।

who "probably dates from the sixth century A. D." Therein Mānasāra is repeatedly mentioned in unmistakable terms as the king of Mālava, (modern Mālwa) with whom was engaged in war king Rājahaṁsa of Magadha or Pāṭalī-putra, the mordern Patna. The latter was the father of Rājavāhana, the chief of the ten princes or *Daśa-Kumāra* after whom the work is named.

Here is a possibility of the *Mānasāra* being connected with the king of Mālwa bearing the name Mānasāra. There are several works in the Sanskrit literature, which seem to have been named after their patron, for instance, the *Skanda-purāṇa* is supposed by some scholars to have been associated with the name of Skanda-Gupta of the Imperial Gupta Dynasty. The *Harsha-charita* has undoubtedly been named after king Harsha. But nothing more is known about king Mānasāra of Mālwa; nor is anything stated, directly or indirectly, about him in the *Mānasāra* itself. On the other hand, the internal references to the expression *Mānasāra*, which have been already introduced elsewhere,[1] prove that the term has been used in three different senses, namely, a treatise, an architect, and a class of sages or professors of architecture bearing the surname, like, Manu or Maya, or the professional epithet, *Mānasāra*. In none of these senses, however, would the king of Mālwa fit in. If he were a real personage and had any connection with this standard treatise on architecture, and preferred to remain incognito, the author of the *Mānasāra* would have added a fourth ambiguity referring to his anonymous patron. In the body of the *Mānasāra* there are several passages, which will be presently discussed, evincing on the part of its author not only a clear knowledge of man and things of the then Magadha and Mālwa but also of all other chief cities and the broadest divisions of India of his time.

The third external reference to (the architect) Mānasāra is found in two epigraphical records of uncertain reading. In these unpublished documents the epigraphist reads the expression, which is used in two inscriptions to imply the name of an architect, as *Māna-sarpa* and not *Mānasāra*. In the light of information presented for the first time in our volumes, the epigraphist may perhaps be ready to revise his reading of the expression when the inscriptions are properly edited and finally published.[2]

(iii) P. 12-1-3—राजहंसो मुनिमभाषत, भगवन्, मानसारः प्रबलेन दैवबलेन मां निर्जित्य मद्भोग्यं राज्यमनुभवति ।

(iv) P. 48-1.4—अवन्तिसुन्दरी नाम मानसारनन्दिनी...............नगरोपान्तरम्योद्याने विहारो- त्कण्ठया मनोभवमर्चयन्ती रेमे ।

[1] See Preface, pp. 2, 3.

[2] Epigraphist's Report, Madras, 1901, nos. 207, 209 See pages 4, note 2; 180, note 5; 176. nn

In an architectural compilation, *Śilpa-saṁgraha*, of apparenly a very late date, we have shewn already[1], that the *Mānasāra* is quoted in its true form. About the worth of considering this reference I am rather doubtful. Not that I am unwilling to bring down the *Mānasāra*, but because there are several facts, which cannot fit in to a very late date, like 1830 A. D. when a manuscript[2] of the *Mānasāra* was copied. The compilation could have easily consulted the *Mānasāra* even if the latter were placed side by side with Vitruvius, or before Maya-Asura of the *Mahābhārata* or Ahura-Mazda of the *Zend-Āvesta*.

Of the internal evidences from the *Mānasāra* the following points may be considered.

For the orientation of buildings it was necessary for the Indian architects to ascertain the right cardinal points. For this purpose the *Mānasāra* in agreement with all complete works on architecture including Vitruvius, makes use of a gnomon,[3] obviously because the mechanism of the compass was not known to the ancient architects. For similar purpose the astronomical treatises[4] also like the *Sūrya-siddhānta*, and the *Līlāvatī* and the *Siddhānta-śiromaṇi* of Bhāskarāchārya use the gnomon. The calculation of the shadow is the main object in this matter, and the gnomon is used simply to ascertain the shadow The sun's rays falling on an object like the gnomon causes the shadow. So at first the obstructed light which gives rise to the shadow, must naturally be taken from the sun. But the sun's light is uncertain and cannot be adjusted according to the requirements of the scientific and advanced study. It is, therefore, not difficult to believe that the later astronomers easily found out some artificia and adjustable light to replace the natural and unadjustable light from the sun. In the *Mānsāra* only the sun's light is made use of, while in the *Sūrya-siddhānta* and other astronomical works lamp light was used in order to measure the shadow. These latter works also followed an improved method in ascertaining the level whereupon the gnomon was erected in order to

---

[1] See page 106.

[2] Called 'C' in the description of manuscripts attached to our edition of the Mānasāra. 'B' is dated 1677 of the Śālivāhana era (1823); 'D' is dated 1656 of the Śaka era (1734). The remaining eight copies, A. E. F. G. H. I. J. K. are not dated.

[3] For full description see the writer's Dictionary under *Śaṅku*.

[4] Sūrya-siddhānta, III, 1—4; Līlāvatī, part 2, section 4, chapter 2; Siddhānta-śiromaṇi, last part, chapter VII, 36—49. Cf. Vitruvius Book I, chapter VI, Book IX, chapter IV, VIII. The actual process of working the gnomon for ascertaining the cardinal points and dialling is described in full details from all these authorities in the writer's Dictionary under *Śaṅku*.

calculate the movement of the shadow accurately. The methods followed in the *Mānasāra* are antiquated. It seems, therefore, that the *Sūrya-siddhānta* and other astronomical works must come after the *Mānasāra*.

The next internal evidence presented here for consideration is that concerning the knowledge evinced in the *Mānasāra* of the most prosperous countries throughout India. We have seen that ninety-eight types of buildings are described in the *Mānsāra* under twelve divisions, namely, of one to twelve storeys. Although sixteen-storyed or even seventeen-storeyed gate-houses (*gopuras*) are mentioned, religious or residential buildings are not erected beyond twelve storeys.[1] The technical names of buildings of one to eleven storeys are more or less poetical. But the buildings of twelve storeys, largest and most gorgeous of all edifices, bear more significant names:

They are called Māgadha, Janaka, Madhya-kānta, Vaṁśaka, Virāṭa, Pāñchāla, Sphū(Gū)rjaka, Kerala, Drāviḍa, and Kāliṅga. These are the names of ten countries which cover the length and breadth of India. At one time or another they seem to have been very prosperous, possessing as they did distinctive types of the largest and most magnificent edifices.

Magadha[2] is the country of South Bihar, where the Pāli language was spoken. Janaka or the country of some twenty one generations of Janaka kings, otherwise called Videha with capital city Mithilā, is North Bihar, which corresponds to the modern Tirhut and Purniyā divisions between the Gaṇḍakī and Kośī rivers. Madhya-kānta stands for the Madhya-deśa, the middle country or the tract situated between the Himālayas and the Vindhya range to the east of Vinaśana and to the west of Prayāga or Allahabad.[3] Some authorities make it the Doab. Vaṁśaka is the country of the Vatsa kings, of which Kauśāmbī was the capital city. It apparently bordered on Madhya-deśa. Virāṭa[4] is the country in the vicinity of the modern Jaipur wherefrom the Pāñchāla country

---

[1] See pages 52, 47—51, 111—113.

[2] Magadha is also mentioned in the Daśakumāra-charita: अस्ति मगधेषु पुष्पपुरी नाम नगरी, which was conquered by king Mānasāra of Mālava (see Preface p. 4, note). But Mālwa is not honoured with a separate type of twelv-estoreyed buildings; and it would appear strange and unusual if this king Mān sāra were the patron of the *Mānasāra*, the standard work on architecture.

[3] हिमवद्विन्ध्ययोर्मध्यं यत्प्राग्विनशनादपि ।
प्रत्यगेव प्रयागाच्च मध्यदेशः स कीर्तितः ॥ (Manu, II, 21).

[4] It was at the court of the king of Virāṭa that the Pāṇḍava princes and Draupadī passed the thirtee th year of their exile incognito. The Virāṭa princess Uttarā was married to Arjuna's son Abhimanyu who at the age of sixteen only gallantly challenged simultaneously seven most famous generals of the Kaurava army at the battle of Kurukshetra.

begins. The present town of Bairat is one hundred and fifty miles south of Delhi. Pāñchāla is the Punjab, "with a little territory in the more immediate neighbourhood of Hastināpura," extending north and west from Delhi from the foot of the Himalayas to the Chambal, Ahi-chhatra being the capital city of north Pāñchāla or Rohilkhand, and Kāmpilya of south Pāñchāla or the Gangetic Doab.[1] The reading of the name of the country mentioned next is uncertain. I would read it Gūrjaka for Gūrjaraka instead of Sphūrjaka[2] and identify it with the country of Gujarat. Kerala is the country of Malabar proper on the western coast extending farther down from Gujarat. Then comes Drāviḍa[3] or the country, where the Tamil language is spoken, extending from Madras to Cape Comorin. This tract is roughly bounded by the Vindhya range on the north where Madhyadeśa ends, Kerala or Malabar coast on the west, and Kaliṅga or Coromandal coast on the east. Kāliṅga implies the twelve-storeyed buildings of Kaliṅga[4], the country along the Coromandal coast, north of Madras, wherefrom the Drāvida country begins. It is clear, therefore, that India comprising these ten countries extends from the Himalayas on the north to the Cape Comorin on the south, from Bihar including perhaps north Bengal on the east to the Punjab and Gujarat on the west.

According to the Mahābhārata king Virāṭa's capital was called Matsya which Cunningham finds in the neighbourhood of Jaypur. Wilson says: "Dinajpoor, Rungpoor, and Cooch Behar." Apparently there was more than one country of this name and one would appear in Northern India. Manu (II. 19) places Matsya in Brahmarshi-deśa.

[1] According to the Mahābhārata (Smith's History, page 348), it would seem to have occupied the Lower Doab. Manu (II. 19) places it near Kanauj. Wilson will have it extending north and west from Delhi from the foot of the Himālaya to the Chambal and separated by the Ganges into Northern and Southern Pāñchāla. Cunningham considers North Pāñchāla to be Rohilkhand with the capital city Ahi-chhatra represented by the ruins near Rāmnagar, and the South Pāñchāla to be the Gangetic Doab with the capital city Kāmpilya between Budāun and Farrukhābad.

[2] This term seems to mean literally something belonging to the first union of lovers characterised by joy in the beginning and some expectation of fear in the end. Of the ten names, it should be noted, this is the only one which as the name of a country can be doubted if the amended reading be not acceptable.

[3] As applied to the classification of Brahmins (Pañcha-Drāviḍa, namely, Drāviḍa, Karṇāṭa, Gurjara, Mahārāshṭra, and Tailaṅga), it has a much wider application embracing Gujarat, Mahārāshṭra, and all the southern countries.

[4] The Calingæ proximi mari of Pliny.

जगन्नाथात्समारभ्य कृष्णातीरान्तगः प्रिये ।
कलिङ्गदेशः संप्रोक्तो वाममार्गपरायणः ॥ (Tantras, see Apte's Dictionary)
उत्कलादर्शितपथः कलिङ्गाभिमुखो ययौ । (Rāmāyana, IV. 38).

A number of questions may now arise. Did these ten countries exist in a prosperous condition at any one time in the history of India? Did they ever possess gorgeous edifices of twelve storeys admitting of ten different types? How could the author of the *Mānasāra* come to know of them? Was the description of these buildings based on the details of the existing edifices, or was it meant to be an injunction to be followed in erecting edifices in these countries? Is there any reason to think that the *Mānasāra* is a technical treatise on architecture, and not a work on poly-technics like the *Bṛihat-saṁhitā* dealing casually with architecture and sculpture, nor an encyclopædic work like the *Purāṇas* of northern India and the *Āgamas* of southern India, which too have incorporated within them architectural and sculptural as well as literary, religious, and scientific subjects?

That the *Mānasāra* is an avowedly architectural treatise meant for professional students of architecture and written by an architect, there need be no doubt. This will be clear beyond doubt even to a casual reader of this volume, not to speak of those who care to look up the writer's Dictionary, and Text or Translation of the *Mānasāra*. To me it is, further, clear that the *Mānasāra* was largely based on details gathered together from the existing buildings and partly on details from the existing literature on the subject. It was, of course, meant to be a guide book; but it never aimed at being the sort of poem which is read for the beauty of its language or the general interest of its theme. It is very likely that the author of the *Mānasāra* was aware of the condition of buildings existing in the then India comprising the ten countries mentioned above. There might not have existed simultaneously buildings of twelve storeys in all the ten countries. What seems to be really meant is the distinctive types of magnificent buildings belonging to each of these countries.[1] For the *Mānasāra* is not an history of buildings of any country; it is a guide book, and as such it must give illustrations and generalise its findings. It matters not, therefore, if these countries were not equally prosperous at any one time. It is sufficient that these countries had flourished, and that they were well known in the history of India, and also that every one of these could at some time or other claim prosperity, and magnificence. Of these, Pāñchāla and Drāviḍa are stated to be of the smallest types; next higher in size and importance are Madhyadesa, Kaliṅga, Virāṭa. Kerala and Vaṁśaka; the largest and most important are Magadha and Janaka. Sphū(Gū)-rjaka is not specified (*Mānasāra*, XXX. 10-:36).

---

[1] About the existence of these types there need not be much doubt; because, for instance, Māgadha, Pāñchāla, Drāviḍa and others are used to imply types other than of buildings also. For instance Māgadha stands for a Prākṛit language, a tribe of people born of a Vaiśya mother and Kshatriya father; Pāñchāla stands for one of the four styles of composition; and Drāviḍa for a language, a class of Bramhins, etc. The point is sufficiently elaborated later on.

The last question to answer is how the author of the *Mānasāra* came to know of these countries or divisions of India. If these countries were autonomous and independent of each other, the knowledge of them must have been received through literature, should a tour all over India for a purpose like this be thought an improbability in days before the establishment of the British Government. If on the other hand the internal affairs of all these countries were settled by a common and central authority, who alone could decide upon a policy for common good and under whom alone guide books like the *Mānasāra* discussing general methods and principles of building for all countries could flourish, there must have been an empire comprising all or most of these countries. The probability of the latter view is strengthened by the consideration of the styles of architecture, apart from the types of buildings discussed above. These styles are also designated by geographical names, which imply much broader divisions, namely, Northern, Southern and Eastern. They are called Nāgara, Drāviḍa and Vesara In case of some architectural objects Vesara admits of two other branches, namely, Andhra and Kaliṅga, the three together constituting Tri-kaliṅga or three Kaliṅgas.

The Nāgara style is distinguished by its quadrangular shape, the Drāviḍa by its octagonal or hexagonal shape, and the Vesara by its round shape[1].

---

[1] वेदाश्रं नागरं प्रोक्तं वस्वश्रं द्राविडं भवेत् ।
सुवृत्तं वेसरं प्रोक्तमन्श्रं स्यात्तु षडश्रकम् ॥ (Mānasāra, XLIII,124-5).

This is applied to cars and chariots. The rules referring to buildings proper are given in XVIII, 92–104; XXVI; 76; XXI, 72–73, etc. etc.; referring to sculpture proper, see for instance, LII,78 100; LIII. 46 47 53-54, etc.

द्वारभेदमिदं प्रोक्तं जातिभेदं ततः शृणु ।
नागरं द्राविडं चैव वेसरं च त्रिधा मतम् ।
कण्ठादारभ्य वृत्तं यद्वेसरमिति स्मृतम् ॥
ग्रीवमारभ्य चाष्टाश्रं विमानं द्राविडाख्यकम् ।
सर्वं वै चतुरश्रं यत्प्रासादं नागरंत्विदम् ॥ (Suprabhedāgama, XXXI, 87—89).

These also refer to buildings. For rules referring to sculpture see the Kāmikāgama, LXV. 6—7, 12-18; and the Bṛihat-saṁhitā, LVIII. 4 (Kern's edition).

"An interesting record from Holal is the label cut out on the capital of a finely carved pillar in the Amṛiteśvara temple. It is called in the inscription a Sūkāra pillar. Speaking of the sculptor who made it, the record says that he Bammaja, the pupil of Pādoja of Sogo, was a Viśvakarman, i.e., the architect of the gods in this Kali age; the master of the sixty-four arts and sciences, the clever builder of the sixty-four varieties of mansions, and the architect who had invented [? discovered] the four types [styles] of buildings viz., Nāgara, Kaliṅga, Drāvida and Veśara."

(Progress report of the Assistant Archæological Superintendent for Epigraphy. Southern Circle, 1914-20, page 90).

In another inscription (Ep. Carnat, volume VIII, part 1, Sorab Taluq, Inscription, no. 275, Roman text, page 92, translation page 46, note 1) these styles are called "Drāvida, Bhūmija, and Nāgara," of which Bhūmija, which literally means 'grown up on the spot', may refer to the Vesara style with Kaliṅga and Andhra as its two branches.

These and many other quotations will be found in the writer's Dictionary under *Nāgara*.

"So far as is yet known, we cannot point to any buildings......of very early date, or before the sixth or seventh century, if indeed quite so early." This is the statement made by authorities like Fergusson, Burgess, Smith and others. This may be referred to all parts and all styles of India. Cunningham has gathered together fragments of what he calls the Gupta style, of which, however, no single example in its entirety can be cited.

The Dravidian "temples generally consist of a square base ornamented externally by thin tall pilasters, and containing the cell in which the image is kept. In front of this may be added a *maṇṭapam* or hall, or even two such, but they are not characteristic of the style. Over the shrine rises the *śikhara*, of pyramidal form, but always divided into storeys and crowned by a small dome, either circular or polygonal in shape. Another special feature of these temples is the *gopurams* or great gateways, placed in front of them at the entrances to the surrounding courts, and often on all the four sides. In general design they are like the *vimānas* or shrines, but about twice as wide as deep, and very frequently far more important than the temples themselves. Another feature is the cornices of double curve; in other Indian styles the cornices are mostly straight and sloping downwards. As the contemporary northern styles are characterized by the prevalence of vertical lines, the Dravidian is marked by the prevalence of horizontal mouldings and shadows, and the towers and *gopurams* are storeyed. Then the more important temples are surrounded by courts enclosing great corridors or *prākāras*, and pillared halls."

"The square rathas were evidently models of Buddhist *vihāras*, and became the designs from which the temples proper or *vimānas* of Southern India were for long copied; and further, the oblong raths, like Arjuna's temple, appeared to have given the first form to the great gate-ways or *gopurams*."[1] Pierced stone windows are found at Ellora and other places.

Regarding the Chālukyan style, which covers the Hyderabad territory, the Central Provinces, Berar, and the Marathi-speaking, and a part of the Kanarese-speaking districts of the Bombay presidency, it is stated that "the earliest temples within this area, however, are not very clearly marked off from the Drāvidian and the more northern style—some of them have distinctly northern spires, and others are closely allied to the southern style." For instance, "the old temple of Pāpanāth at Pattadakal presents a curious combination of styles. The

[1] Burgess cites (Imp. Gazetteer, II, pages 172, 171) as example temples at Maḍura, Rāmeśwaram, Tinnevelly, Śrīrangam, Kanchipuram; Pattadakal (Virupāksha temple), Ellora (rock-cut Kailāsa temple).

body of the temple is Dravidian but the *Śikhara* is a curious approximation to the form of the early northern Hindu or Indo-Aryan order, while in details the temple shows a strong leaning to the Dravidian." "Still in Mysore, Dharwar, and Belgaum, as well as in Berār and Maharatha districts, sufficient remains still exist to illustrate the various development of the (Chālukyan) style."[1]

"In the Chālukyan temples the corners are often made prominent by increments placed over them, or the whole plan is star-shaped, the projecting angles having equal adjacent faces lying in a circle as in the temple of Belur in Mysore (built about 1120 A. D.)." There are other examples, where "the *Śikhara* did not preserve the southern storeyed form but was rather stepped, forming square pyramid with breaks corresponding to the angles in the wall, and with a broad band answering to the larger face in the middle of each exposed side of the shrine." "The pillars are markedly different from the earlier Dravidian forms; they are massive, richly carved, often circular and highly polished. Their capitals are usually spread out while middle section of the shaft is richly carved with mouldings in the round. They are almost always in pairs of the same design." The richly carved and richly ornamented pierced windows belong specially to this (Chālukyan) style as we see it at Ajanta and elsewhere, just like the pierced stone windows employed in Dravidian temples at Ellora and other places. "The buildings were erected without mortar, and the joints were carefully fitted. The whole was covered with sculpture, often of geometric and floral patterns, intermixed with numerous mythological figures; and in the later examples, the courses of the base were carved with the succession of animal patterns prescribed for them in the *Śilpa-Śāstras*. This is very fully exemplified in the great temple of Hoysaleśvara at Halebīd."[2]

These peculiarities of the Dravidian and the Chālukyan styles are taken from existing examples. Most of these details are also found under the Drāviḍa style of the *Mānasāra* which, however, does not refer to the Chālukyan style as a separate order.

The Northern or Indo-Aryan style of architecture covers the whole area once occupied by the Aryans "usually designated as Hindustan" to the north of the Tāpti and Mahanadi rivers. "What is known as the Jain style of architecture in Western India is a development or variety of this Indo-Aryan order, and was used by the Hindus and Jains alike all over Rājputanā, Mālwa and Gujarāt. It was employed in its most ornate form by the Jains in their famous marble temples on Mount Abu, and by both the Jains and Hindus at Nāgdā near Udaipur. At Girnār also and Śatrunjaya in Gujarāt as well as Khajurāho in Bundelkhand are clusters of temple of this order."[3]

---

[1] Burgess, ibid. p. 175. [2] Ibid, pages 176, 177. [3] Ibid. page 177, 179.

"Under this style are classified monuments of very various orders which may be separated into two or more distinct types." The Vesara of the *Mānasāra* is apparently one of these orders.

"The shrines and *maṇḍapas* are *square*, and only slightly modified by additions to the walls of parallel projections, which in the earlier examples, were thin; the walls were raised on a moulded plinth (*pīṭha*) of some height, over which was a deep base [*adhishṭhāna*], the two together rising, roughly, to about half the height of the walls; over this is the paralleled face of the wall, usually of less proportionate height than in the Chālukyan style, and though devoted to figure sculptures in compartments, the tall thin pilasters of the southern style have disappeared, over this is the many-membered architrave, and cornice, above which rise the spire and roof. The spires follow the vertical lines of the wall, and present no trace of division into storeys, but vary in details with the age. In the earlier examples the summit was crowned by a large fluted, circular block called *amala* (pure, shining)-*Śilā*, probably mistaken for *Amalaka* (Phyllanthus Emblica). The finial over this is of the shape of a vase, known as the *Kalaśa or Karaka*." "One of the most striking features of the style is the richly carved domes over their *maṇḍapas* or porches. (Nothing can exceed the elaboration and delicacy of details in the sculptured vaults of the temples at Abu and Nāgdā). These, with the diversified arrangement of variously placed and highly ornamented pillars supporting them, produce a most pleasing impression of symmetry and beauty."[1]

"The earlier examples were apparently astylar, then—like the southern forms—with columns arranged in the *maṇḍapas* in groups of four, and later, especially in Western India, the larger domes or twelve pillars formed the central area of the halls. These *maṇḍapas* in early examples were roofed with long, sloping slabs; but, to provide for carved conical roofs inside, their outer forms represented courses of masonry, which were carved as in temples of Kanarak, Bhuvaneśvara (older; Ambaranāth, Baroli, Khajurāho, Abu and Chitor (mediaeval); Nāsik, Benares, Udaipur, Śatrunjaya, etc. (recent)."[2]

The peculiarities of the Nāgara style, except in one or two rather unessential points, would correspond to these details of "Northern or Indo-Aryan style." The *Amala* or *Amalaka śilā* is not mentioned in the *Mānasāra* under this appellation; but the *murdhni-ishṭaka* (brick at the top) seems to serve the same purpose as the *Amala-śilā*. The *kalaśa* or dome, *śikhā* and *śikhara*, are the distinguishing features of the style found also in the *Mānasāra* in addition to the *square* shape.

"The temples at Bhuvaneśvara . . . differ very markedly from those in the west in being almost entirely astylar—pillars having been introduced in later

[1] Ibid pages 178, 179. [2] Ibid. pages 181, 180.

additions. They have the early form of *śikhara*—nearly perpendicular below, but curving near the summit; and the crowning member has no resemblance to any thing like the small domes on Chālukyan spires."

Burgess, following the classification of Fergusson, has included the style found at Puri, Bhuvaneśvara, and Kanarak under the Indo-Aryan or Northern style. But he has admitted that it "may be separated into a distinct order." What is called the Vesara in the *Mānasāra* seems to be identical with this style. The main characteristic feature of this style is, according to the *Mānasāra*, its round shape, and this is clearly exhibited by temples and images in the Orissan countries.

The identification of Nāgara with Northern India needs, however, an explanation. It seems to have been never before used exclusively in that sense. Moreover, it is the name of an extensive division in Mysore, a part in Tanjore and a number of ancient villages in the Deccan [1]. But it is found used more frequently as the name of villages, towns and rivers in Bengal, Bihar, the United Provinces of Agra and Oudh, Rajputana, the Punjab, and Gujarat [2]. Nāgara is also the name of a portion of the *Skanda-Purāṇa*, of a sect of northern Brahmins, and of a script. The *Skanda-Purāṇa*, which to some scholars seems to have been named after Skanda-Gupta (455—480 A. D.), the seventh emperor of the early Gupta dynasty, contains a part called Nāgara-khaṇḍa. In this part of the *Skanda-Purāṇa* it is claimed that the Nāgara Brahmins are superior to all other Brahmins. It is held that they came over from the north and settled down in Gujarat at a place known as Nāgarānandana-pura. From these Nāgara Brahmins, it is said, came the use of the Nāgarī alphabet, which belongs exclusively to Northern India. Indeed it is very famous as the name of a script particularly of Northern India extending from Bihar on the east to the Punjab and Gujarat on the west, and from the foot of the Himalayas on the north to the Vindhya range on the south. This is the very tract which seems to have been covered by the Nāgara style about the time of the *Mānasāra*.

The southern and eastern tracts represented by the Drāviḍa and the Vesara styles can also be associated respectively with the Tāmil, and the Telugu including the Orissan scripts. As based on scripts and languages, these divisions Nāgara, Drāviḍa and Vesara, have existed apart from the architectural styles.

The expression Nāgara is certainly not coined in the *Mānasāra*. Nagara is a common name for the town, and Nāgara is an adjective therefrom and implies something connected with a city. Madurā of Southern India is apparently an identical

---

[1] See the writer's Dictionary under *Nāgara*.

[2] J. A. S. B., 1896, volume LXV, part I, pages 116—117. Basu's collection of references in this Journal and many other quotations will be found under *Nāgara* in the writer's Dictionary of Hindu architecture.

name to Mathurā of Northern India. In the same way, the Nāgara-khaṇḍa of Mysore, the port Nāgore of Tanjore, and the village Nāgara of the Deccan can be accounted for. There are several things to prove conclusively that the Aryan influence and civilization were spread, from Aryāvarta or Northern India, all over the Dākshiṇātya or Southern India. It is true that the borrowed names sometimes become more prominent than those of which they are but imitations. New York of America, for instance, is much more prominent than old York of old England. Similarly the name Nāgara, though originated in and indicating Northern India, might have become more prominent in Southern India.

All these divisions are indicated by terms which were already in use as class names. The architecture of the country is divided into three broad styles and ten types, corresponding to the geographical divisions and the political entities. And there seems to have been a bond of union between these entities, however autonomous and independent they may have been in their mutual relation. In the total absence or rather non-existence of a unifying authority, the growth of a record of generalization, a guide book for the whole country, would be highly exceptional if not improbable. In other words, the presence of a standard work on architecture like the *Mānasāra* seems to presuppose an empire comprising countries having their own styles, methods, and principles, which are recorded and illustrated under so many divisions. Whether or not such books of generalization could have been written in those ancient days of India even without the patronage, active or passive, direct or indirect, of an imperial authority, it will be a useless, at any rate an unnecessary, discussion for our purpose. It is sufficient for me that the existence of such an empire may be taken to be conducive to the growth of such a treatise as the *Mānasāra*.

Existence of an empire at the time of compilation of the *Mānasāra* seems to be indicated also by the following facts.

In connection with construction and disposition, according to ranks, of royal palaces, thrones and crowns, royalty is divided into nine classes.[1] They are called, in descending order, *Chakravartin*, *Mahārāja* or *Adhirāja*, *Mahendra* or *Narendra*, *Pārshṇika*, *Paṭṭadhara*, *Maṇḍaleśa*, *Paṭṭabhāj*, *Prāhāraka* and *Astragrāhin*. The number of storeys and halls in a palace, the divisions of the whole compound into different courts, the quarters for royal personages and officials, and other buildings, which are necessary adjuncts of an Indian palace, are described. The royal qualities, courts, army, and rate of revenue in accordance with the class to which a king belongs, are also incidentally mentioned. A consideration of these matters might have helped us in arriving at a time in the history of ancient India, if the historical materials and especially chronological data were available.

---

[1] Mānasāra, chapters XL, XLI, XI; see pages 75—60, 42 of this volume.

What, however, concerns us most here is to ascertain the relation existing between these nine classes of kings. They are mentioned by their common names, and not by proper and personal names.

An empire in any case has been expressly recognised in the *Mānasāra*. It is clearly declared that the *empire* of the *Chakravartin* or universal monarch reaches as far as the four oceans.[1] So it must include the whole of India, divided into three divisions, Northern, Southern and Eastern, otherwise apparently known as Nāgara, Drāviḍa and Vesara. According to another classification, we have seen, this empire seems to have comprised ten kingdoms. But here the empire is stated to have nine kinds of rulers.

The *Chakravartin* is the suzerain of all the subordinate kings who send up tributes and taxes to him.[2] The next king, called both *Mahārāja* and *Adhirāja*, is the lord of seven kingdoms.[3] *Mahendra* or *Narendra* is the master of three kingdoms, and more honourable than the *Pārshṇika*, *Paṭṭadhara*, *Maṇḍaleśa*, and *Paṭṭabhāj* classes of kings.[4] The *Pārshṇika* is responsible for the administration of one kingdom, and the *Paṭṭadhara* governs only half a kingdom.[5] The rest seem to be chiefs rather than kings though they possess their own army and courts. The *Maṇḍaleśa* is stated to be content with a *maṇḍala* or province, while half a *maṇḍala* or province is left to the charge of the *Paṭṭabhāj*[6]. The *Prāhāraka* is the king of several *jana-pada* or divisions; and the *Astragrāhin* looks after several districts and is the ruler in a large city.[7]

About the *Adhirāja* it is stated that he must belong to the solar or the lunar race.[8] The kings of these races are Kshatriya by caste. Nothing is specified regarding the caste or castes of the other classes of kings. But the *Prāhāraka* is expressly stated to be born in a Brahmin, Kshatriya, Vaiśya, or Śūdra family[9] This state of things points to a time when the Śūdras were also recognised as kings.

---

[1] चतुःसागरपर्यन्तां महीं स्वीकृत्य बलवान् ।
जित्वा द्वारस्य पुरतो घंटामाबध्य संस्थितः । (M. XLII, 6—7).

[2] सर्वावनीन्द्रवन्द्योसौ चक्रवर्तीति कीर्तितः । (M. XLII, 10).
एवं क्षुद्राश्च भूपालाः स्वे स्वे जनपदे करान् ।
स्वीकृत्य चक्रवर्त्यादिराजानो च कुर्वन्त्यपि॥ (M. XLII, 75—76).

[3] M. XLII, 11—13.

[4] M. XLII, 14—15.

[5] M. XLII, 18, 21—22?

[6] M. XLII, 23—28.

[7] M. XLII, 29—35.

[8] M. XLII, 12—13.

[9] ब्राह्मणक्षत्रियवैश्यशूद्राणामेककुलोद्भवः । (M. XLII, 20).

There does not seem to be much doubt that the recognition of these divisions presupposes the existence of an empire, the extent and the boundaries of which are made clear by the geographical classification of the ten types of gorgeous buildings and the three styles of the architectural and sculptural objects. These various divisions seem to represent the different schools of one system, the different branches of one united civilization and culture. For such an empire, it is not absolutely necessary to find out a political head who can keep together the apparently separate and exclusive entities under his direct military control.

When was there such an empire existing in India embracing the Nāgara, the Drāviḍa, and the Vesara portions all within itself? It is true perhaps that even in the time of Manu tracts of the country south of Vindhyas were known to the Aryans, and truer still that in the time of king Aśoka, who partially conquered a portion of what we are now describing as Vesara and Drāviḍa, there was a friendly intercourse subsisting between the north and the south. But the south was south still, and did not come to be considered as forming, along with the north, part of one and the same whole. The idea of such an empire as would include whole India from the Himalayas to the cape Comorin, from Gujarat to Bengal, had not yet grown up. It was still to come, and arrived much later when all the different parts came to be united under one hand. This leads us to consider next the course of development of such an empire, the story of which as a matter of fact is the story of the gradual spread of the Aryan influence and power from Aryāvarta or Northern India southwards.

Dr. Bühler seems inclined to think that the Aryan conquest of South India took place " a considerable time before the Vedic period came to an end, and it certainly was an accomplished fact, long before the authentic history of India begins at the end of the fourth century B. C." [1] According to Rhys Davids, till about the time of Buddha, Kaliṅga and part of the Deccan below the banks of the Godāvarī were outside the area of Hindu settlement.[2]

King Aśoka conquered Kaliṅga and annexed it to his empire. The same monarch in his edict (XIII) refers to the Cholas, Pāṇḍyas, and Keralaputras as his *pāchantas* or neighbours. It is evident from this edict of king Aśoka that the three South Indian powers—the Cholas, Pāṇḍyas and Keralaputras—were, till the third century B. C., quite independent of Magadha. But presumably the friendly relation, which had existed between king Aśoka and those three powers, opened for

---

[1] Āpastamba, S. B E., II, page XXXVI—XXXVII.

[2] Sütta-Nipâta, 1011 ; see also Aṅguttara Nikaya, I. 213 ; IV, 252, 256, 260 ; Vinaya texts, II. 146.

The account of Rāma's advance up to Ceylon as given in the Rāmāyaṇa reflects a travel rather than a conquest.

the first time the road of an exchange or amalgamation of two distinct civilizations, namely, the Aryan and the Dravidian. It is also not inconceivable that in or before the third century B.C., Andhra or Telugu country was in part Aryanised.

And lastly it is clear from the Allahabad pillar inscription of Samudragupta that this Indian Napoleon directed his campaigns against eleven kings of the south, nine named kings of Āryāvarta, besides many others not specified, the chiefs of the wild forest tribes, and the rulers of the frontier kingdoms and republics. He had also diplomatic relation with very remote foreign powers. "Although it is at present impossible to identify every one of the countries, kings and peoples enumerated in the inscription, enough is known to enable the historian to form a clear idea of the extent of the dominions and the range of the alliances of the most brilliant of the Gupta emperors."

He conquered south Kośala in the valley of the Mahānadi, subdued all the chiefs of the forest countries, which constitute the tributary states of Orissa; and the more backward parts of the central provinces, Pishṭapura, the ancient capital of Kaliṅga; the hill-forts of Mahendragiri and Kottur in Ganjam; the kingdom of Manṭaraja on the banks of the Kolleru lake; Vengi between the Krishṇā and the Godāvarī; Kāñchī to the south of Madras; Pālakka in the Nellore district; Devarāshṭra or the modern Mahratta country; and Erandapalla or Khāndesh. This would imply the whole of the Drāviḍa country bounded by the Coromandal and the Malabar Coasts. The only place left by Samudragupta for his son Chandragupta to conquer and to annex to the empire was Kathiawar in Gujarat.

"The dominions under the direct government of Samudragupta thus comprised all the countries of Northern India. It extended from the Hooghly on the east to the Jamunā and Chambal on the west; and from the foot of the Himalayas on the north to the Narmadā on the south. Beyond these wide limits, the frontier kingdoms of Assam and the Gangetic delta, as well as those on the southern slopes of the Himalayas, and the free tribes of Rajputana and Malwa, were attached to the empire by bonds of subordinate alliance, while almost all the kingdoms of the south had been overrun by the emperor's armies and compelled to acknowledge his irresistible might. The empire thus defined was by far the greatest that had been seen in India since the days of Aśoka. He maintained diplomatic relations with the Kushan kings of Gandhara and Kabul, and the greater sovereign of the same race, who ruled on the banks of the Oxus, as well as with Ceylon and other distant islands."[1]

We now see that it was not until the time of the Imperial Gupta dynasty that the kind of empire implied in such a work as the *Mānasāra* came into existence. It is not our intention to say indeed that before or after

[1] V. A. Smith, History of India (1908), pages 271-72.

this there had been nothing in the shape of an empire. It cannot certainly be gainsaid that there was a flourishing empire under king Aśoka. It cannot be denied either that there was an empire flourishing in the south independent of the Aryans, that of the Andhras, so far back as about the beginning of the Christian era. The Chālukyas also built up an empire after the fall of the early Guptas and remained powerful till about the middle of the eighth century, when the Government of the country passed into the hands of the Rāshṭrakūtas for more than two hundred years. Harshavardhana of Kanauj also built an empire which, however, did not include within itself the Dravidian countries. What appears clear to us is that not till the reign of Samudragupta (326—375) or until Chandragupta II (375—413) was there any one empire which comprised the whole land, including the Telugu and the Tamil speaking places. It is further clear from the Allahabad inscription of Samudragupta that some of his subordinated kings belonged to the Śūdra caste.

The next internal evidence to be considered is one regarding religion. This is illustrated in the *Mānasāra* by the indifferent treatment accorded to the Buddhists and the Jains, and also by the unusually dignified manner of addressing the Brahmins as the gods on earth (*bhū-sura*), and lastly by the predilection for Vaishṇavism.

Two separate chapters are, however, devoted to the description of the Jain and the Buddhist images.[1]

The description of the Jain deities, ostensibly the main object of a chapter, is submerged in a lengthy discussion of the various measurements used both in architecture and sculpture. The twenty-four Tīrthaṅkaras or Jain apostles are referred to, but not specified. The whole description of the Jain images is disposed of in a few lines at the fag end of the chapter. The Buddhist images are also described in a very small chapter of eighteen lines only. The account of these images too is very meagre. Evidently the author had in mind solely the effigies of Buddha, not of other Buddhist deities. This slight seems to have struck the author himself. So he adds in conclusion that the rest should be in accordance with the directions given in treatises specially dealing with these images.[2]

The Buddhists and the Jains have been mentioned, it is true, in connection with all matters referring to people of different sects. But the indifferent treatment accorded to the followers of Buddhism and Jainism is clear beyond doubt. For instance, in connection with the village scheme described in a chapter of five hundred and forty lines, only two lines are devoted to them. The slight is all the more prominent from the fact that rather unwelcome quarters are reserved for the

[1] Chapters LV, LVI, see pages 76-79 of this volume.

[2] शेषं प्रागुक्तवत्कुर्यात्तत्तदागमवद्बुधः । (M. LVI. 18, the last line).

Buddhists and the Jains, and that the temples of their deities are built outside villages and towns.[1]

Similarly in connection with buildings of different storeys they are treated with indifference, and nothing is specified about them.[2]

The same treatment is also apparent in connection with the temples of attendant deities. The Buddhist and the Jain temples are passed over with the remark that they should be built according to the rules of their own Śastras. It is true, however, that Buddha is recognised as one of the ten incarnations of Vishnu, whose family consists of the three groups of eight, sixteen including Buddha, and thirty-two deities.

Again, in the chapter on pavilions (*maṇḍapa*) which consists of five hundred and seventy-six lines, only one is given to the Buddhists and the Jains.[3]

In connection with the description of cars and chariots, it is stated in only one line that there should be one to seven platforms in the cars of the Budddist and the Jain deities.[4] Thrones and seats for the Buddhists and the Jains are left undescribed with the remark that they are 'thus stated.'[5]

---

[1] बौद्धं वायुपदे चैव नैरृत्ये तु जिनालयम् । (IX, 387)
दुर्गां गणपतिं चैव बौद्धं जैनं गतालयम् ।
अन्येषां षण्मुखादीनां स्थापयेन्नगराद्बहिः ॥ (IX 405—6)

[2] एवं तु चोक्तवत्कृत्वा बौद्धादिजिनकालयम् ।
तत्तद्विमानस्योर्ध्वे तु तत्तद्देवान्न्यसेत्क्रमात् ॥
(XIX, 252—3; two lines out of 268 lines).

देवता दिशि चाष्टतो न्यसेद्विष्णोरीश्वरजिनादेरालये ।
(XXI. 73—74, last two lines).

क्षुद्रमन्यमथ मुख्यं भौमके रुद्रविष्णुजिनकादिहर्म्यके । (XXII, 98—99)

[3] See the summary, chapter XXXIV, pages 53—54.
and compare the following :—

नैरृत्ये तु बौद्धं स्यान्नयन्ते पैत्रिकालयम् ।
बौद्धं च जिनकं चैव तत्तच्छास्त्रोक्तमार्गवत् ।
बौद्धस्यालये तज्जिनालयेऽपि क्षुद्रालये सर्वशः ।
शास्त्रस्यालयतोरणे कथितं तत्परिवारकं कुर्वीत ॥ (XXXII, 149, 157, 165—6).

[4] विष्णोस्त्र्यम्बकस्यापि चैकाद्ये(दि)नववेदिकाः ।
बौद्धादिजिनकान्तानां सप्तान्तं चैकादितः ॥
(XLIII. 144—5).

[5] विष्णुरुद्रजिनकेन्द्रमुख्यकानां सर्वदेवगणचक्रवर्तिनाम् ।
आसनानि कथितानि तानि वै चोत्सवानि कथितानि सूरिभिः ॥
(XLV. 211—212, last two lines).

Lastly in connection with the general description of images, the Buddhists and the Jains are left unspecified with a similar remark as before.[1]

These are all the instances where the Buddhists and the Jains are at all mentioned. A significant point of omission also may be considered. Monasteries and such other architectural objects as are intimately associated with Buddhism and Jainism, have not been referred to, while the minute details of Brahmanical Hindu temples have been rather elaborately described. From all this, two points seem to me to be clear. First, the Buddhists and the Jains, at the time of the *Māna-sāra*, were not in a flourishing condition, secondly, they were not persecuted either. It was apparently a time of toleration for them.

The next point to be clear about, is, which religion had the preference? It was Vaishnavism. The following references will, I hope, confirm this view.

In support of the indifferent treatment accorded to the Buddhists and the Jains, the passages quoted above contain references to Śaivism and Vaishṇavism also. Vishṇu, Iśvara; Vishṇu, Rudra; Vishṇu, Trambaka; and Brahmā, Vishṇu, Rudra are mentioned alongside Buddha and Jina[2]. From this it must not be concluded, however, that Brahmā, Vishṇu, and Śiva are treated in the same way as Buddha and Jina. In these passages it is directed how the latter should be treated, the former having been elaborately described. But in the treatment of Brahmā, Vishṇu, and Śiva themselves a clear distinction and predilection have been shewn. It is true that the opening verse is an invocation to Brahmā, not to Vishṇu or Śiva, and that in the next verse the ultimate sources of the Śilpa-Śāstras, like many other Śāstras, have been ascribed to Śiva, Brahmā, and Vishṇu.[3] These deities are described in the usual order of Brahmā, Vishṇu, and Śiva in the chapter dealing with the images of the Hindu triad.[4]

In describing the riding-animals (*vāhana*) of the Triad, the same order has been followed, the goose, the garuḍa bird, and the bull being treated in turn[5].

---

[1] ब्रह्माविष्णुरुद्राणां बुद्धस्य जिनकस्य च ।
अन्येषां च प्रतिमानामेवं मानं तु संग्रहम् ॥ (XLXIV. 91—92)

[2] See notes 4, 5, page 186.

[3] Mānasāra, I. 1. 2;

गङ्गाशिरः कमलभूः कमलेक्षण, this is the order; but in Sanskrit, the order may be changed; here, however, the terms form component parts of a *dvanda* compound where the order of terms has some significance

[4] Chapter LI, see page 70

[5] Chapters LX, LXI, LXII, see pages 81—82.

It is also true that the phallus of Śiva and his pedestal (*pīṭha*) have been elaborately treated in two separate chapters.[1] This, however, does not seem to have been due to the author's or his patron's predilection for Śaivism. For the phallus of Śiva is a very famous object of the Hindu sculpture ; and it would have been given the prominence all the same even if the artist had belonged to an entirely different sect, because without this his treatise would have been incomplete. Similarly the extollation of the phallus worship added in conclusion may be explained[2].

Preference for Vaishṇavism seems clear also from the following points:—

The whole compound of a large building is divided into five courts[3] around which the temples of attendant deities are built. Brahmā, Vishṇu and Śiva may individually possess attendant deities. There are, therefore, no reasons why the attendant deities of any one of the Triad should be specially treated, unless the author were closely in touch with the temples of any one group of the attendant deities, wherefrom his ideas and illustrations originated. In this connection the groups of eight, sixteen and thirty-two deities of the Vishṇu family alone are illustrated. The ten incarnations of Vishṇu are also dealt with. But no mention is made of the attendant duties of Brahmā or Śiva.[4] This omission is significant, all the more because the *Mānasāra* is avowedly a treatise on architecture. If the work had been compiled in a place where Śaivism or Brahmā worship was favoured, the temples of their attendant deities could not but have been described in this connection.

A similarly striking omission in connection with the Śiva temples is also noticed in another important matter, namely, the foundations. Foundations of buildings are divided into two classes—according as they belong to temples and to human dwellings. Of the residential buildings, there are four classes of foundations according to the four castes, Brahmin, Kshatriya, Vaiśya and Śūdra[5]. Of temples, those of Vishṇu and Brahmā are illustrated. Śiva is not mentioned at all in this connection beyond the author's usual method of passing on with the remark that the others should be similarly done. Very little is authoritatively known about the places in India where Brahmā worship was ever so much favoured as Vaishṇavism in Northern India, and Śaivism in Southern India. The author's predilection for Vaishṇavism seems to be indicated by this point also.

[1] Chapters LII, LIII, see pages 72—74.

[2] Chapter LII, see page 74.

[3] Chapters XXXI, XXXIII, see pages 51, 52-53.

[4] Chapter XXXII, see pages 51-52.

[5] Chapter XII, see pages 42-43.

In the laying out of villages and towns also the Vishṇu temples have been given preference. It is stated that the Vishṇu temples may be built any where in the village under the innumerable epithets of Vishṇu, such as, Śrīdhara in the east, Vāmana in the south, Vāsudeva, Ādi-Vishṇu or Janārdana in the west, Keśava or Nārāyaṇa in the north; Nṛisiṁha, Gopāla, Rāma (?) and others at the four corners. No such details are given regarding the Śiva temples. It is simply stated that the Īśa (Rudra) temples may similarly be built in the quarters known as Rudra-jaya, Āpa-vatsya, Jayanta, Parjanya and such other quarters, which are by no means prominent places in the village[1].

In the case of towns, the Vishṇu temples alone have been taken into consideration. In the capital cities, it is distinctly stated that the Vishṇu temples should be built at the main entrance[2].

---

[1] Mānasāra IX. 255 f., and 383; for instance:

आर्यादिषु चतुर्दिक्षु ग्रामस्यापि चतुर्दिशि । 255
एवं यथेष्टदिग्देशे विष्णुधिष्ण्यं प्रकल्पयेत् ॥
अथवा बहिरङ्गे तु चेष्टदिग्विष्णोरालयम् ।
इन्द्रादिषु चतुर्दिक्षु विष्णुस्थानं तु राक्षसे ॥
पूर्वके श्रीधरं प्रोक्तं दक्षिणे वामनं तथा ।
पश्चिमे वासुदेवं वा चादिविष्णुं जनार्दनम् ॥
उत्तरे केशवं प्रोक्तं नारायणमथापि वा ।
अन्तः प्रागुत्तरदेशे विष्णुमूर्तिं यथेष्टकम् ॥
पितृदेवेशकोणे वा यथा नृसिंहालयं भवेत् ।
अग्निकोणे यथा रामं गोपालालयमेव च ॥
मित्रे च त्रितलं कुर्यात्स्थानकं चादिभूमिके ।
द्वितीये चासनं प्रोक्तं तृतीये शयनं भवेत् ॥
अथवा स्थानकं चोर्ध्वे शयनं मूलकस्थले ।
इष्टदिग्विष्णुहर्म्याणां द्वारं कुर्याद्विचक्षणः ॥
ग्रामस्याभिमुखं विष्णुं नरसिंहं पराङ्मुखम् ।

But in the case of Śiva it is simply stated:

ईशे वाथ जयन्ते वा पर्जन्यस्य पदेऽपि वा । 273
एवमीशालयं कुर्याद्ग्रामस्य तु पराङ्मुखम् ॥

[2] See also 383, etc.

सर्वेषां नगरादीनां भेदं लक्षणमुच्यते ।
नगरं राजधानीयं केवलं नगरं तथा ॥
पुरं च नगरी चैव खेटं खर्वटमेव च ।
कुब्जकं पत्तनं चैव शिबिरं वाहिनीमुखम् ॥

Similar illustrations from the body of the *Mānasāra* can be multiplied. But the point seems to be clear. Vaishṇavism appears to have been the leading religion of the place where the *Mānasāra* was compiled. The author himself may have had a personal preference for Śaivism or even for Brahmā-worship: but his patron or the influence under which the author was working apparently had a leaning towards Vaishṇavism in all its various phases and aspects, including even Buddha as one of the ten incarnations of Vishṇu. Buddhism and Jainism, though by no means favoured religions, were allowed to continue. The influence seems to be one of non-interference, a universal toleration, with special preference for Vaishṇavism.

In which period of the history of ancient India, then, could Buddhism and Jainism have got on alongside Brahmanical Hinduism? The state of things that is reflected in the generous treatment of the followers of different religions, was possible only in the period from the fourth to the eighth or ninth centuries of the Christian era. For during the reign of Aśoka in the third century B. C., and some time after, Buddhism was in a very flourishing condition, while after the eighth or the ninth century both Jainism and Buddhism were declining.

During this period kings of three distinguished dynasties reigned in the country. The Gupta empire in its entirety dates from the reign of Samudragupta (326—375), more accurately from the reign of Chandragupta II (375—413). The seventh or last emperor of the Gupta dynasty is Skandagupta. The imperial authority of the Guptas perished with Skandagupta (455—480), and the empire broke up, although the dynasty continued till about the middle of the seventh century or perhaps a little later. The Chālukyas came into power in the south at the beginning of the sixth century after the fall of the Guptas, and remained powerful till about the middle of the eighth century, when the government of the Chālukya dominions passed into the hands of the Rāshṭrakuṭas for more than two hundred

---

स्थानीयं द्रोणकं चैव संविद्धं कोलकं ततः ।
निगमं स्कन्धवारं च दुर्गं चाष्टविधं भवेत् ॥
नगरादीनि संग्रामं प्रोक्तदुर्गं च सप्तमम् ।
राष्ट्रमध्ये नदीतीरे बहुपुष्पजनावृतम् ॥
मध्ये राजयुतं चैव नगरं कृतमिष्यते ।
तत्रागते नगर्यन्तं यदि विष्णुालयं भवेत् ।
राजधानीति तन्नाम विद्वद्भिर्वक्ष्यते सदा ।

(Mānasāra, X. 35—47).

years. After their fall the Chālukyas again came into power.[1] Harshavardhana (606—648) also built up an empire in Northern India about the time when the Chālukyas were powerful in Southern India. None of these empires, however, comprised whole India. Buddhism and Jainism could not have flourished alongside Brahmanical Hinduism under the Rāshtrakutas. Some of the Rāshtrakuta Kings may have been in favour of Jainism but none seems to have favoured Buddhism. "Under them," says Sir R. G. Bhandarkar, "the worship of the Purāṇic gods rose to much greater importance than before. The days when kings and princes got temples and monasteries cut out of the solid rock for the use of the followers of Gautama Buddha had gone by, never to return"[2].

"During the two centuries of the rule of the early Chālukya dynasty of Vātapi," says Vincent Smith,[3] "great changes in the religious state of the country were in progress. Buddhism, although still influential, and supported by a large section of the population, was slowly declining, and suffering gradual supersession by its rivals, Jainism and Brahmanical Hinduism. The sacrificial form of the Hindu religion received special attention, and was made the subject of a multitude of formal treatises. The Purāṇic forms of Hinduism also grew in popularity; and everywhere elaborate temples dedicated to Vishṇu, Śiva, or other members of the Purāṇic pantheon, were erected. The orthodox Hindus borrowed from their Buddhist and Jain rivals the practice of excavating cave-temples.[4] Jainism was specially popular in the southern Marātha country."

On the other hand, the history of the early Gupta dynasty has all the necessary features. The empire of the Guptas comprised all the countries and divisions indicated in the *Mānasāra*. Brahmanical Hinduism was the leading religion, but Buddhism and Jainism were tolerated. King Meghavarṇa of Ceylon

---

[1] The early Gupta kings, about 300—530, the later Guptas 535—720 A D,
The Chālukyas of Bādāmi, 550—753 A.D.
The Rāshṭrakutas of Mānyakheta, 753—973 A.D.
The Chālukyas of Kalyāṇī, 973—1190 A.D.

[2] The History of Dekkan, p. 208.

[3] V. Smith, ibid. p. 386.
See also Bhandarkar, ibid p 191.

[4] There is no reference in the Mānasāra either to cave-temples or rock-cut pillars. Nor have free pillars like those of Aśoka been specially described in the Mānasāra. There is no reason to think that an author who gives particulars of all sorts of buildings found all over the country should have remained entirely ignorant of these wonderful architectural objects. Their omission seems to have been due to this: the Mānasāra is not an history of architecture. It is a guide book and was intended to help professional architects. Architectural objects like the cave-temples, rock-cut pillars and free pillars had no more use for architects, presumably because they had become out of date at the time of the Mānasāra

was allowed to despatch a mission with valuable presents to king Samudragupta for permission to build a monastery near the sacred Bo-tree at Gaya. The reign of Chandragupta II, the son and successor of Samudragupta, is noted for the visit of the Chinese pilgrim Fa-hien who, being a Buddhist pilgrim, necessarily saw everything through Buddhist spectacles. In his account mention is made of a number of monasteries along his journey from the Indus to Mathura in which neighbourhood he found twenty of these buildings. "It is evident that, with a Brahminical supreme Government, Hinduism of the orthodox kind must have been far more prominent than his account would lead the reader to suppose."[1] Fa-hien was never "stripped by brigands, a misfortune which befell his successor Hiuen Tsang. Probably India has never been governed better. The Government did not attempt to do too much but let the people alone, and was accordingly popular." Though "the sovereign was a Brahminical Hindu, the tendency to the harassing kind of persecution, which a Buddhist or Jain government is apt to display, was kept in check, and liberty of conscience was assured."[2]

During the long and rather obscure reign of the next emperor Kumāragupta (413—455) also Brahmanical Hinduism was the popular religion. This is clear from the fact that Kumāra, like his grandfather, celebrated the horse sacrifice, a ritual repugnant equally to Buddhism and Jainism. Both Skandagupta (455—480) and Narasiṁhagupta Bālāditya (485—535) "continued to pay their devotions to the Hindu gods, while exhibiting, like Harsha in the seventh century, a strong personal predilection for Buddhist doctrine."[3]

"Whatever may have been the causes, the fact is abundantly established that the restoration of the Brahmanical religion to popular favour, and the associated revival of the Sanskrit language, first became noticeable in the second century, were fostered by the western Satraps during the third, and made a success by the Gupta emperors in the fourth century. These princes, although perfectly tolerant of both Buddhism and Jainism, and in two cases personally interested in the former.

[1] & [2] V. Smith, ibid. pp. 292, 293.

[3] Paramārtha, a Buddhist of the sixth century, who wrote the life of Vasubandhu states that "Vikramāditya of Ajodhya, who at first was a liberal patron of the Sāṁkhya philosophy, which is considered to have a strong affinity to both Buddhist and Jain doctrines, was induced by the eloquence of the celebrated Vasubandhu of Peshāwar to turn a favourable ear to the teachings of Buddhism and to patronize its professors with equal liberality. The Queen and Prince Bālāditya, who afterwards, about 485 A. D., succeeded to the throne as Narasiṁhagupta, both became disciples of Vasubandhu, and Bālāditya after his accession continued his favours to the Buddhist sage. The coinage and official inscriptions of the Gupta Kings are so distinctly Brahmanical that these statements might cause surprise." But "it is fully confirmed by Hiuen Tsang, who describes Bālāditya as a zealous Buddhist.'

V. Smith, ibid. p. 292; Takakusu, J. R. A. S. 1905. page 44; Watters, I, 288).

were themselves beyond question orthodox Hindus, guided by Brahmin advisers, and skilled in Sanskrit. An early stage in the reaction against Buddhist condemnation of sacrifice had been marked by Pushyamitra's celebration of the horse-sacrifice towards the close of the second century. In the fourth, Samudragupta revived the same ancient rite with added splendour; and in the fifth, his grandson repeated the solemnity. Without going further into detail the matter may be summed up in the remark that coins, inscriptions, and monuments agree in furnishing abundant evidence of the recrudescence during the Gupta period of Brahmanical Hinduism at the expense of Buddhism, and of the favour shown by the ruling powers to classical Sanskrit at the expense of the more popular literary dialects, which had enjoyed the patronage of the Andhra kings."[1]

It is, further, clear from coins, inscriptions, and monuments that Vaishnavism was the predominating religion during the Gupta period. And this is the state of religious affairs evinced in the *Mānasāra*, namely, a Brahmanical Hinduism with preference for Vaishnavism and tolerant of both Buddhism and Jainism.

The appearance of treatises like the *Mānasāra* during the period of the early Guptas seems to be indicated by other reasons also. Following the spread and consolidation of the Gupta empire under Samudragupta there came a time of peace and quiet, especially during the reign of Chandragupta II, favourable to the cultivation of art and literature, and an intercourse of ideas and thoughts between the different parts forming members of one empire. It was in this Gupta period that a general literary impulse was extended to every department. In this classical period of Indian history an all-sided improvement in arts, literature and science came to be achieved. It was, again, during this period that the *Sūtra* style of literature began to give place to the classic style. It has been shown elsewhere that the language of the *Śilpa-Śāstras* represented by the *Mānasāra* seems to be the meeting place of the two.[2] Sanskrit was gradually raised to the position, which it long retained, as the sole literary language of Northern India.

"The literary revolution," says Vincent Smith, "necessarily was accompanied by corresponding changes in the art of architecture. The forms of buildings, specially adapted for the purposes of Buddhist ritual dropped out of use, and remarkable developments in the design of the Hindu temple were elaborated, which ultimately culminated in the marvellously ornate styles of the mediæval period, extending from the ninth to the end of the twelfth century."[3]

[1] Smith, ibid. page 287.
[2] See Appendix, and pages 211–214.
[3] Smith, ibid, page 288; also refers to the seven characteristics of the Gupta style of architecture (see pages 195–196 of this volume).
Cunningham, Arch. Reports, IX. 42, I, V, X, XI, XIV, XVI, XX and XXI.

The external evidences, mainly based on a comparison between the *Purāṇas* and the *Śilpa-Śāstras* also point to the same conclusions. The reasons have been elaborated for the belief that there is a relation of indebtedness between the *Mānasāra* on the one hand and on the other the *Matsya-Purāṇa*, the *Bhavishya-Purāṇa*, the *Agni-Purāṇa*, and the *Bṛihat-saṁhitā*. "To the same age probably (Gupta period)", says Vincent Smith, "should be assigned the principal *Purāṇas* in their present form."

Bāṇa, the author of the *Harsha-charita* who wrote about 620 A.D., "carries back the proof of the antiquity of the Agni, Bhāgavata, Mārkaṇḍeya and Vāyu *Purāṇas* four centuries further back than Alberuni, who in 1030 gives the list of the eighteen *Purāṇas* as given in the Vishṇu *Purāṇa*, having seen three of them himself."

The discovery of the Bengal manuscript written in Gupta hand has assigned the *Skanda-Purāṇa* to the middle of the seventh century on palæographical grounds.[1] Many other early quotations from, or references to, the *Purāṇas* have been collected by Bühler, who points out that the account of the future kings in the *Vāyu*, *Vishṇu*, *Brahmāṇḍa* and *Matsya Purāṇas* seems to stop with the imperial Guptas and their contemporaries.[2]

"This last observation," adds Vincent Smith, "indicates that the date of the redaction of the four works named (including *Matsya-Purāṇa*, which seems to be intimately connected with the *Mānasāra*) cannot be very far removed from 500 A. D., the imperial Gupta dynasty having ended about 480 A. D. Bühler speaks of 'future kings', because all the historical statements of the *Purāṇas* are given in the form of prophecy, in order to maintain the appearance of great antiquity in the books, which in their oldest forms were undoubtedly very ancient."[3]

The *Mānasāra* seems, therefore, to point to the Gupta period in view of the accumulation of external and internal evidences, both political, religious and social, namely, the date of the *Purāṇas*; the existence of an empire comprising the whole of India; the division of royalty into nine classes including the Śūdras also; the popularity of the Brahmanical religion with predilection for the Vishṇu cult and non-interference and toleration of Buddhism and Jainism; a general

---

[1] J. R. A. S., 1903, page 193.

[2] Ind. Ant. XXV, page 323.

[3] Ibid. pages 19, 20 compare also :

"The Vāyu Purāṇa in its present shape seems to be referred to the fourth century A. D. by the well-known passage describing the extent of the Gupta dominions, which is applicable only to the reign of Chandragupta I in 320—326 A. D."

The Purāṇas seem also to have been known to the author of the 'Questions of Milinda (Milindapañha)' who composed a part of the work where the first references occur, almost certainly earlier than 300 A. D.

(S. B. E., volume XXXV, pages 6, 247).

impulse to arts and literature; the appearance of the peculiar Sanskrit of the *Śilpa-Śāstras* and characteristics of architecture and sculpture consisting mainly of the three styles and ten types of buildings.

At the time of the composition of the *Mānasāra* the memory of the first seven Gupta princes seems to have been fresh in the minds of the people. An expression *gupta-viṁśa* has been used in the *Mānasāra* [1] to imply *sapta-viṁśa* or seven and twenty. *Gupta* in the sense of *seven* seems to have been coined in the *Mānasāra.* Perhaps it was due to the great fame and some patronage to the *Mānasāra* of the early Gupta princes consisting principally of seven kings. For after the death of Skandagupta in 480A.D, the seventh king of the dynasty, the empire broke up: the next princes, Puragupta Prakāśāditya and Narasiṁhagupta Bālāditya being but chiefs.

These conclusions are, however, in an apparent conflict with certain other matters. Cunningham has gathered together fragments of the Gupta buildings, wherefrom he draws the following peculiarities of what he calls the Gupta style:

"The chief characteristic features of the Gupta temples are:—

(1) Flat roofs, without spires of any kind, as in the cave temples.

(2) Prolongation of the head of the door-way beyond the jambs, as in the Egyptian temples.

(3) Statues of the rivers, the Ganges and the Jumna, guarding the entrance door.

(4) Pillars, with massive square capitals ornamented with two lions back to back, with a tree between them.

---

[1] तद्दक्षोऽष्टकवृद्धिःस्याद्गुप्तविंशक्षयो भवेत् ।
वारं षड्गेण वृद्धिः स्यात्सप्तमिक्षयो भवेत् ॥ (Mānasāra, LXI, 32—33).

This refers to the following Shaḍvarga, a set of six formulas, with which any particular measurement must conform before it can be accepted—

आय	..	..	..	..	remainder of $\frac{\text{length} \times 8}{12}$
व्यय	..	..	..	..	,, $\frac{\text{breadth} \times 9}{10}$
ऋक्ष	..	..	..	..	,, $\frac{\text{length} \times 8}{27}$
योनि	..	..	..	..	,, $\frac{\text{breadth} \times 3}{8}$
वार	..	..	..	..	,, $\frac{\text{Circumference, thickness or height} \times 9}{7}$
तिथि or अंश		..	..	..	,, $\frac{C \times 9}{30}$
		..	..	..	,, $\frac{C \times 4}{9}$

More details will be found in the writer's Dictionary under *Shadvarga*.

(5) Bosses on the capitals and friezes of a very peculiar form like the Buddhist Stūpas or beehives, with projecting horns.

(6) Continuation of the architrave of the portico as a moulding all round the building.

(7) Deviation in plan from the cardinal points."

None of these characteristics seems to be applicable in its entirety to the buildings described in the *Mānasāra*. Spires or *śikhara* and *śikhā* as well as the *kalaśa* or domes are the chief characteristic features of the buildings described in it. These seven characteristics would point to the antiquated period of structural architecture. And Cunningham himself admits the fact :

"The style is similar to that of the cave temples of Udayagiri, and of the structural temples at Eran." "The use of flat roofs would seem to show that these buildings must belong to the very earliest period of structural architecture. When the architect, whose work has hitherto been confined to the erection of porticoes in front of caves, was first called upon to build the temple itself as well as the porticoes, he naturally copied this only prototype, and thus produced in a structural form the exact facsimile of a rock-hewn cave."[1]

This seems to explain away the main objection. What is designated as the *Gupta style* points really to buildings of much earlier periods. By the time the Gupta dynasty was consolidated the methods and principles of architecture seemed to have considerably improved : the architect invented the use of domes and other ornaments over the 'flat roofs' copied in the earlier periods from the rock-hewn caves. In the Gupta period proper, as truly held by later scholars like Vincent Smith, "remarkable developments in the design of the Hindu temple were elaborated, which ultimately culminated in the marvellously ornate styles of the mediæval period, extending from the ninth to the end of the twelfth century." So the characteristics of the real Gupta buildings notably those which existed under the Guptas and are discussed in the *Śilpa-Śāstrās*, would be different from those given by Cunningham. The buildings described in the *Mānasāra* would conform, we have seen, to the characteristics of the Indo-Aryan and Chālukya-Dravidian styles recorded from the existing examples by both Fergusson and Burgess. But none of these extant examples belonged to a period earlier than the sixth or seventh century A.D. These were, however, not the first of their class : buildings of this class must have existed long before the sixth or seventh century, because the extant examples themselves clearly show that they have passed through different stages in their development.

[1] Cunningham, Archæological Survey Report, volume IX, page 43. Some drawings are given in this volume as well as in I, V, X, XI, XIV, XVI, XX etc.

The next objection may be one concerning the *Gopuras*, *Prākāras* and such other objects which have been exhaustively described in the *Mānasāra*. These are undeniably the peculiarities of southern architecture. This objection may be easily disposed of. There seem to be sufficient reasons to hold that the account of architecture in the *Mānasāra* has reference to buildings of all parts of India, comprising the northern, southern and eastern styles. The southern style might be as elaborately described as the northern or eastern, even when the *Mānasāra* was compiled under the patronage of a northern emperor.

The mixture of styles or the preferential treatment of one style over the other may similarly be accounted for. The "sporadic appearance of temples of a style removed from their proper area may be accounted for in various ways; great temples were constantly being visited by pilgrims on their way from one shrine to another, and the repute of any new fane was soon spread over all India; and thus, when a prince undertook to build a new temple, an architect (*sthapati*) of acknowledged ability might occasionally be sent for from the most distant province, and engaged to design the work, which of course, would be in his own style."[1] In the very same way the author of the *Mānasāra* might have been sent for from southern India to compose the standard work on Indian architecture.

The last point to be considered is the mention of Mānasāra in the *Daśa-kumāra-charita* as a king of Malwa. This king Mānasāra is the hero of a fiction. There are no doubt historical facts concealed in a fictitious work. But it is not easy to sift facts from fictions. Those who are, however, inclined to connect the *Mānasāra* with this king of Malwa would assign the treatise to the seventh century, because the author of the fiction, Daṇḍin, would be 'contemporary of Bhāravi' who is mentioned in an inscription of 634 A.D.[2] and also of Harsha who reigned from 606—648 A.D.

Historical facts, as stated above, cannot generally be extricated adequately from the complexities of the fiction. Moreover although some vague conclusion has been inferred from the circumstantial evidence about the period in which Daṇḍin, the undeniable author of the *Daśa-kumāra-charita* lived, no such vague idea even is available about the period or periods in which the semi-historical incidents described in the *Daśa-kumāra-charita* might have taken place. Besides King Mānasāra of the *Daśa-kumāra-charita*, it may be incidentally pointed out, was not the hero or even one of the chief characters of the fiction. He is stated, as pointed out above, to be the King of Malwa and a contemporary of King Rājahaṁsa of Magadha who was the father of Rājavāhana, the chief of the ten princes (daśa-kumāra). In the *Daśa-kumāra-charita* itself King

[1] Burgess, ibid, p. 178.
[2] Macdonell, History of Sanskrit Literature, pages 329, 332.

Mānasāra is stated to have been engaged in a war with King Rāja-hamsa, that is all. There is in the fiction practically no direct or indirect reference made as to the nature of interest which King Mānasāra might have been in the habit of taking in literary or artistic matters; it must, however, be admitted that there were no real occasions for such a reference[1]. In this connection another incident too may be advantageously taken into consideration: neither in the three styles mentioned in the treatise *Mānasāra* under three geographical names (Nāgara, Vesara and Drâvida) nor in the ten types of buildings bearing again geographical names and provincial divisions (Pāñchāla, Drāvida, Madhyakānta, Kalinga, Virāta, Kerala, Vaṁśaka, Magadha, Janaka, and Gurjaka) is included Mālava which was presumably the capital city and provincial kingdom of king Mānasāra of the *Daśa-kumāra-charita*. In the circumstances it would be really doubly unwarranted to take any decision about the possibility or otherwise of King Mānasāra's patronage or instrumentality in the production of the standard treatise on architecture which, as its title would seemingly indicate, might have been named after him.

In view of these facts we venture to expect that the reader may be inclined to consider more seriously the other evidences which are undoubtedly more authenticated and substantial, including those regarding the connection of the *Mānasāra* with *Matsya-Purāṇa* (450 A. D.) on the one hand and the *Brihat-saṁhitā* (550 A. D.) on the other. On this assumption we shall perhaps be justified in placing the *Mānasāra* before the *Bṛihat-saṁhitā* and somewhere close to the *Matsya-Purāṇa*. In any event, we venture to hold that the evidences submitted above would warrant the extension of the period of the *Mānasāra* from 500 to 700 A. D[2].

---

[1] In this two recently discovered works called the *Avanti-Sundarī-Kathā* in prose and the *Avanti-Sundarī-Kathāsāra* in verse Daṇḍin, the author of the *Daśa-kumāra-charita*, is held to be "well learned in architecture of royal and divine structures."

(Proceedings of the second Oriental Conference, 1922, pages 194, 196; see also page 171 of this volume.)

[2] Until, however, the identity of the real author of the *Mānasāra* is established, and the missing link connecting the *Mānasāra* with Vitruvius is discovered and definitely ascertained, it would not be quite possible to be more precise about the date of the *Mānasāra*.

APPENDIX

The Language of the Śilpa-Śāstra

The following instances taken exclusively from the *Mānasāra* will, it may be hoped, illustrate the style of Sanskrit used in it. Similar illustrations have also been added from a number of inscriptions. They might also be taken from other Śilpa-śāstras; but they are left out for the present in view of the fact that these Śilpa-śāstras are still in manuscript form, and that until their publication, reference to chapter and verse will be practically useless. When a sufficient number of Śilpa-śāstras have been critically edited, and when lists of irregularities like the one we are presenting here have been made from different treatises, a useful attempt may be made to treat the subject in a more systematic manner.

Case irregularities

अमरात् *for* अमरस्य VII, 247.

अक्षौ *for* अक्षिभिः III, 17.

आदि *for* आदौ VI, 37, 38.

आलयादिभिः *for* आलयादिषु XII, 150.

आसनार्थात् *for* आसनार्थाय (or आसनार्थम्) VII, 55 note.

इन्द्रराजके *for* इन्द्रराजकाय VIII, 47

इन्द्रे चाग्निः *for* इन्द्राग्निभिः IX, 146.

इन्द्रैः *for* इन्द्राय VIII, 47.

ईश्वरे *for* ईश्वरः VII, 91.

ऋषि *for* ऋषिका IX, 72.

एतेषु *for* एतानि XI, 115.

कर्त्ता *for* कर्त्तुः XI, 115.

करैः *for* करेण XI, 87.

करौ *for* कराभ्याम् VII, 158.

कुम्भौ *for* कुम्भयोः VI, 84.

कोणैः *for* कोणेषु IV, 30.

क्रमात् *for* क्रमम् VIII, 13.

गन्धैः *for* गन्धान् III, 15.

जिनादि *for* जिनादेः XXI, 74.

तरोः *for* तरुणा III, 19, IV, 24.

धरादिभिः (3rd plural) for धरादि (neuter singular), apparently for the sake of metre, III, 313.

नाम *for* नाम्ना II, 23.
II, 31.

पङ्क्तिः *for* पङ्क्तेः VI, 65.

पञ्चात् *for* पञ्चभ्यः XLIII, 142.

परमाणुः *for* परमाणुम् II 40.

CASE IRREGULARITIES—(*concluded*)

पार्श्वात् *for* पार्श्वेन II, 72.
पुंल्लिके *for* पुल्लिङ्काय VIII, 30.
पुष्पदन्तं *for* पुष्पदन्ताय VIII, 37.
भानुः *for* भानुना or भानुभिः IX, 68.
भानुषु *for* भानुम् IX, 200.
भास्करः *for* भास्कराय VIII, 27.
भित्तिं सह *for* भित्त्या सह XXXIX, 152.
मधुगन्धो *for* मधुगन्धे VIII, 27.
महेन्द्रके *for* महेन्द्राय VIII, 26.
माला *for* मालाम् VII, 158.
मासौ *for* मासयोः VI, 31.
मोनयोः *for* मीनेषु VI, 33.
मुख्यके *for* मुख्यकस्य VIII, 41.
मृगात् *for* मृगस्य VII, 153.
मृगे *for* मृगाय VIII, 43.
शयने Loc. *for* शयनम् Acc II, 54.
रोगं *for* रोगः VII, 91.
वितये *for* वितथाय VIII, 31.
विवस्वान् *for* विवस्वतः VII, 113.
विशेषतः *for* विशेषेण II, 47.
विस्तारे *for* विस्तारस्य III, 24
विष्ण्वालयम् *for* विष्णोरालयम् or विष्ण्वालयम् IX, 257.
शालानां *for* शालाभिः XXIV, 38; see also XXV, 34.
शास्त्रे *for* शास्त्रात् IV, 1.
शूद्रैः *for* शूद्राणाम् III, 34.
शोषे *for* शोषस्य VIII, 39.
संग्रहणं पश्चात् *for* संग्रहणात् पश्चात् II, 54.
सुग्रीवे *for* सुग्रीवस्य VIII. 37.
सूत्रम् *for* सूत्रेण VII, 51.
हिक्कात् *for* हिक्कायाः LXV, 169, 170, note.
हिक्कात् *for* हिक्काय LXVI, 9.

DISAGREEMENT IN GENDER, NUMBER OR CASE BETWEEN NOUN AND ADJECTIVE

अष्टकं वीथिका IX, 325.
आवरणाः सर्वम् *for* आवरणम् सर्वम् IX, 253.
उत्तरस्य मुखे *for* उत्तरस्मिन् मुखे II, 12.
उत्तरे दिशि *for* उत्तरस्यां दिशि XXXV, 86.
गुलितं धूलिः स्मृतम् II, 41.
तस्य (*for* तस्मात्) देवालयात् IX, 411.
तस्य (*for* तस्मात्) पकुष्ठात् LXV, 141.
दारु (n. or m.) प्रकीर्तिता VI, 11.
देवताः सर्वे *for* देवताः सर्वाः VIII, 57.
देवान् उदितं *for* उदितान् XXXII, 1 0.
मञ्जरीणां (feminine) सर्वेषाम् (masculine) X, 110, note.
निम्नानि मौक्तिकोपेतं *for* मौक्तिकोपेतानि XLV, 123.
पूर्वामं शिला सर्वे (feminine plural noun, masculine plural pronominal adjective and neuter singular adjective), LII. 193, cf. 211, 212.
प्रतिमां कोहजं प्रोक्तम् LXX, 100.
प्रोक्तां *for* प्रोक्ता III, 2.
मही (feminine singular noun and the qualifying adjective neuter singular), III, 18—20, 21, 22, 23 25, 26—27, 29, 31.
मुष्टिः स्मृतम् (*for* स्मृता) II, 51.
मूर्तिः प्रोक्तम् (*for* प्रोक्ता) II, 68.

DISAGREEMENT IN GENDER, NUMBER OR CASE BETWEEN NOUN AND ADJECTIVE—(*concluded*)

यस्मिन् हर्म्येषु *for* येषु हर्म्येषु XXX, 66.
युक्तं *for* युक्तः II, 81.
युक्तं लिक्षा परिकीर्त्तितम् II, 43.
रज्जुः (masculine or feminine noun in the first case neuter) वर्जिताम् (acc. feminine adjective) II, 74.
वस्त्वादयः कृतानि *for* वस्त्वादीनि कृतानि LXX, 5.
विशालता प्रोक्तं *for* विशालता प्रोक्ता XLVIII, 34.
शिल्पिभिः प्राज्ञाः कुर्यात् LXX, 28.
सर्वेषाम् *for* सर्वासाम् XII, 150; XXXIV, 281.
सर्वेषां देवदेवीनाम् *for* सर्वासां देवदेवीनाम् LXVII, 77-95.
सर्वेषां वीथीनाम् *for* सर्वासां वीथीनाम् IX, 197.
सर्वेषां शक्तीनाम् *for* सर्वासां शक्तीनाम् XLIX, 52.
सर्वेषां शालानाम् *for* सर्वासां शालानाम् XXXV, 60, 115.
सर्वेषु (plural) गोपुरे (singular) XXXIII, 61.
सर्वेषु दिक्षु *for* सर्वासु दिक्षु XXXV, 51.

IRREGULARITIES IN GENDER

द्रव्याणि (masculine) *for* द्रव्याणि (neuter) VIII, 7, 9.
प्रादेशोमं (neuter) *for* प्रादेशोमा (feminine) XI, 120.
धनुर्ग्रहं (neuter) *for* धनुर्ग्रहः (masculine) II, 52.
बलिं (neuter) *for* बलिः (masculine) VIII, 50.
मन्त्रं (neuter) *for* मन्त्रः (masculine) V, 30 ; VIII, 15, . but) मन्त्रः V, 7.
मित्रं *for* मित्रः (deity) VII, 170.
रोगं *for* रोगः VII, 91.
वर्धनं (neuter) qualifying धरा (feminine) IV, 7
वस्तु treated as feminine IV, 36, also note ; treated as masculine, III, 6 ; confused (वस्त्वादयः कृतानि) LXX, 5.
वितस्ति treated as neuter II, 49.
वृक्षं (neuter) *for* वृक्षः (masculine) VI, 12.
वृद्धिं (neuter *for* feminine) XXXIII, 24.
शङ्कु used in neuter instead of masculine VI, 16.
संयुक्तं (neuter) qualifying धरा (feminine) IV, 7.
सर्वेषाम् *for* सर्वासाम् (देवदेवीनां) XII, 150, XXXIV, 281.
हस्त (neuter) *for* masculine II, 52 ; but masculine II, 51.

DECLENSION MISTAKES

अदिते *for* अदितौ XII, 84.

उभय्ये: *for* उभयोः II, 68.

कर्मम् *for* कर्म VIII, 62.

कर्मस्य *for* कर्मणः I, 17.

कुक्षियोः *for* कुक्ष्योः XXXV, 200.

गुरौ *for* गुरु XLIX, 175.

चक्रवर्तिः *for* चक्रवर्ती XLII, 2; XLI, 48.

चक्रवर्तीनां *for* चक्रवर्तिनाम् XLV, 128.

जन्मम् *for* जन्म XLV, 143.

जात्यैः *for* जातिभिः XIII, 146.

जान्वयोः *for* जान्वोः LXVII, 36.

तपस्वीनां *for* तपस्विनाम् XXXII, 89

दण्डाद्यैः *for* दण्डादिभिः IX, 10.

दशाम् *for* दश XXXII, 153.

दारैं *for* दारौ XXXI, 70.

देवताम् *for* देवताः VII, 253.

देवभिः *for* देवैः XLVIII, 61.

द्रव्याण् *for* द्रव्याणि VIII, 79.

नगरस्याद् बहिः *for* नगराद् बहिः IX, 409.

नाभ्यात् *for* नाभ्याः LXV, 174.

नामम् *for* नाम II, 6, VII, 2, 11, 13, 20, 36, (not uniform, cf. 3, 4).

नामस्य *for* नाम्नः XXXIV, 541.

नाम्नैः and नामैः } *for* नामभिः XV, 304; VIII, 14.

नास्यैः *for* नासिभिः XXIV, 40.

पश्चात् *for* पश्चाभ्यः XLIII 142.

परिखैः *for* परिखाभिः X, 106.

परिखैः *for* परिखाभिः X, 100, note.

पार्श्वयोः *for* पार्श्वयोः LXVII, 37, 82

पूषस्य *for* पूष्णः VII, 137.

भ्रुवयोः *for* भ्रुवोः LXVII, 33.

मन *for* मनस् LIV, 3.

मात्रं *for* either मातरः or मातृः XXX, 79.

मित्रस्यम् (an impossible form) VII, 114.

रथ्येषु *for* रथ्यासु IX, 323.

रेखैः *for* रेखाभिः L, 206.

वारुणे *for* वारुणाय XIII, 39.

विधातस्य *for* विधातुः VII, 138, 139.

विवस्वते *for* विवस्वति XII, 86.

वृक्षरेन *for* वृक्षराः XXXIII, 67.

वेदिकाद्यैः *for* वेदिकादिभिः XXXV, 93.

वेद्यैः *for* वेदिभिः XXI, 65.

शङ्कुः *for* शङ्कून् VI, 120.

शालैः *for* शालाभिः XXII, 95.

शिरस्य *for* शिरसः XLIX, 130. LIV, 121.

शिल्पीनाम् *for* शिल्पिनाम् II, 1, 39, see note.

श्रोवयात् *for* श्रोवयाः LXVI, 35; LXVII, 62, 137.

संख्येन *for* संख्यया XI, 105.

संध्ययोः *for* संध्योः XXXV, 242.

सप्तमात्रं *for* सप्तमातरं XXX, 11.

सर्वे *for* सर्वस्मिन् VII, 117, also note; XXIV, 17, XXXIII, 108.

सवित्रे *for* सवित्राय VIII, 46

हिकात् *for* हिकायाः LXV, 169, 170, note.

DECLENSION MISTAKES—(*concluded*)

हिक्कात् *for* हिक्कायाः LXVI, 9.
हेमम् *for* हेम XLIX 74, 83.
Nouns ending in न् *and* स् *treated as* स्वरान्त (अकारान्त *or* इकारान्त) :
कर्मस्य *for* कर्मणः I, 17.
कर्मम् *for* कर्म VIII, 62.
चक्रवर्तिः *for* चक्रवर्ती XLII, 2 ; XLI, 43.
जन्मम् *for* जन्म XLV, 143.
जन्मन् used as जन्म XIII, 119, 144, 241, 260,
not as a rule, cf. XIII, 271 ; XV, 213 ; XXVI, 6.
दाम *for* दामन् LIV, 10, 95.
नामं वक्ष्ये (*for* नाम) II, 6.
नामस्य *for* नाम्नः XXXIV, 541.
नाम *for* नामन् XXVII, 18 ; XXVI, 6.
नाम्नैः *for* नामभिः XV, 304.
नाम्नैः „ „ VIII, 14.
नामम् *for* नाम VII, 2, 11, 13, 20, 36, not uniform, cf. 43.
नाम *for* नाम्ना II, 23, 31.
पूषस्य *for* पूषणः VII, 137.
मन *for* मनस् LIV, 3.
शिरस्य *for* शिरसः LIV, 121 ; XLIX, 130.
शिर *for* शिरः XXII, 9, 41 ; XXI, 48.
सद्मन् used as सद्म XVI, 9.
हेम *for* हेमन् LIV, 55.
हेमम् *for* हेम XLIX, 74, 83.
हेमन् used as हेम XII, 144, 160, 161 ; XV, 417.

OMISSION OF CASE-ENDINGS

कनिष्ठ *for* either कनिष्ठे or कनिष्ठः II, 48.
कर्मन् *for* कर्म XII, 212 ; XVII, 2.
जन्मन् *for* जन्म XIII, 119, 144, 241, 260.
नाश *for* नाशः VII, 91.
पैशाच *for* पैशाचम् VII, 57, 58.
मानोपकरणोच्यते *for* मानोपकरणमुच्यते II, 39.
लोष्ठ *for* लोष्ठेन VI, 115.
वर्ण *for* वर्णः or वर्णम् II, 30.
वर्धकीर्ति *for* वर्धकिरिति II, 19, 23, 25, 33.
विष्णु *for* विष्णोः XXI, 74.

WRONG COMPOUNDS

त्र्यङ्गुल, त्रियङ्गुल } *for* अङ्गुलत्रय or त्र्यङ्गुल VI, 20 and note.
त्रिदश *for* त्रयोदश XI, 25, cf. 41, 45, 49.
प्रथमारथ्ये *for* प्रथमायां रथ्यायां or प्रथमरथ्यायां IX, 222.

WRONG COMPOUNDS—(*concluded*)

पदाभिके *for* पदे or पदः अभिके VII, 127.

विष्णुरालयम् *for* विष्णवालयम् or विष्णोरालयम् IX, 257.

शिलावेष्टकयेा *for* शिलेष्टकयेाः XL, 68.

समविस्तार *for* विस्तारसम IX, 165.

WRONG SANDHI

अधोप्रवेश *for* अधःप्रवेश XXXIII, 81.

आदित्यो तत *for* आदित्यस्तत् XXXV, 191.

चतुःपश्च *for* चतुष्पश्च (compulsory *sandhi* ignored) IX, 199; XII, 199.

अम्भनेापरि *for* अम्भन उपरि XLV, 179, etc.

इयैक *for* इयेक XXXIV, 310.

देव ऋषेः *for* देवर्षेः II, 19, cf. I, 8, 43.

वयाकुल *for* वयकुल VI, 62.

वंशक *for* व्रणंशक XXVIII, 24, (correct forms XXVIII, 28).

पुरतेाक्त *for* पुरत उक्त XXXIV, 486.

बन्धांश *for* बन्धवंश XXXIII, 231; XXXVIII, 47.

बन्धांश *for* बन्धवंश (contd.) XLVI, 27; LVII, 36 (correct form XXXIII, 242).

मुक्तेशः *for* मुक्त ईशः XXXII, 34.

मानसार ऋषिकृत (compulsory *sandhi* ignored) I, 43.

मानसार ऋषिणा I, 8.

शिरेातार *for* शिरस्तार XXXIII, 539.

शिरेार्ध्वे *for* शिर ऊर्ध्वे LX, 33.

श्रेणितेात्तर *for* श्रेणित उत्तर IX, 241.

सहस्रेक *for* सहस्रैक IX, 43.

सेाम ईशानयेार्मध्ये *for* सेामेशान etc. XXXII, 17 (compulsory *sandhi* ignored) 271.

CONFUSION BETWEEN WORDS

यदा *for* यथा IV, 27 note.

वाम् *for* वा IX, 309 note.

शशिं *for* शिवम् LIV, 117.

UNGRAMMATICAL FORMS AND IMPOSSIBLE WORDS

उद्वीक्ष्यं *for* उद्वीक्ष्य II, 40.

उन्नत *for* उन्नति (adjective for abstract noun) XXI, 7.

उपरिः *for* उपरि XLV, 103.

चार *for* द्वार XXXIV, 418.

वार *for* द्वार XXXIX, 138, note.

दीर्घ *for* दैर्घ्य (adjective for abstract noun) XXI, 27; XL, 26; LIX, 92, etc.

देवत्वम् *for* दैवतम् or दैवम् VII, 58.

दैवत्य *for* दैवत L, 207, 208, 209.

द्वारक *for* द्वार XXXIV, 496.

Disagreement between noun and verb in number, etc.

कुर्यात् विचक्षणैः (active verb, passive nominative) IX, 78.

कुर्यात् शिल्पिभिः (active verb, passive nominative) XXXII, 9;
LIII, 56.

त्यजेत् बुधैः (active verb, passive nominative) LXIV, 18,

विद्वद्भिः कुरु (passive plural nom. and active, singular, imperative verb) LXIX, 68.

शिल्पिभिः प्रक्षालनं कुरु LXX, 46.

शिल्पिभिः प्राकारः कुर्यात् LXX, 28.

स्थापकेन बलिं ददेत् XXXVII, 17.

Wrong conjugations

ददेत् *for* दद्यात् LXX, 51, 54, 65, 80, 88, 94.
XV, 408.

दधेत् *for* दध्यात् XV, 428.

परिग्रहेत् *for* परिगृह्णीयात् XLII, 60, 63 note, 64, 65.

परीक्षेयं *for* परीक्षेत V, 31, note.

पश्यते *for* दृश्यते or पश्यति XXXII, 170.

प्रयुञ्जीयात् *for* प्रयुञ्जीत XXXIII, 83.

बन्धयेत् *for* बध्नीयेत् V, 77.

विनश्यति *for* विनश्यते (passive) VIII, 63.

वृध्यगात् *for* वर्धयेत् XXXI, 101.

Irregularities in use and forms of verbs

धीयते *for* अभिधीयते II, 31.

परीक्ष्य (infinitive absolute without finite verb) III, 16.

संज्ञात्वा *for* संज्ञाय or ज्ञात्वा VII, 38.

स्थाप्य *for* स्थापयित्वा XXXII, 10, 13, 33, 37, 43, 50, 58; LIV, 5.

Elimination of द् *before* व्—

वार *for* द्वार IX, 300, 519;
XXXIII, 383 note;
XXXIV, 119, 190, 200,

वार *for* द्वार (contd.) 394, 408, 514, 521, 526, 529;
XXXV, 100, 120 note, 123 note, 238, 243, 265 note,
XXXIX, 128 note.

वि वि *for* द्वि द्वि XXVI, 14.

वितयोः *for* द्वितयोः IX, 188.

विधा *for* द्विधा XXX, 90.

विभाग *for* द्विभाग XXVI, 9,
XXVI, 7, 30 note.

Wrong numerals

चतुर *for* चतुः XXX, 17.

चतुर्थ *for* चत्वारः (ordinal for cardinal) XXXIX, 117.

चतुर्विंशत *for* चतुर्विंशति XXXV, 6, 8, 12.

त्रयोविंशत *for* त्रयोविंशति XXXV, 6, 8, 12

त्रिदश *for* त्रयोदश XI, 25, cf. 41, 45, 49.

त्रिय *for* त्रय V, 82.

त्रिंश, त्रिंशत्, त्रिंशति (indiscriminately used) XI, 81, 85, 86, etc.

त्रिंशत् *for* त्रिंशता IX, 78.

द्वय *for* द्वि (ordinal for cardinal) XXI, 7; XXII, 19.

पञ्चादश *for* पञ्चदश XI, 28; XIII, 10, 23; XXXI, 33.

विंशत्, विंश, विंशति XI, 50, 51, 79.

षष्ठमं *for* षष्ठं XX, 33.

सप्तादश *for* सप्तदश XXXIII, 19, 27 note, 106; XXXIX, 9.

Wrong spelling

अङ्गुल्यं *for* अङ्गुलम् LIX, 93, 94, etc. [Sometimes it is noticed that अङ्गुल्य is used to imply the finger or toe, while अङ्गुल to imply the finger-measure.]

अत्यर्धं *for* अध्यर्धं XXV, 12.

अलिन्द्रक *for* अलिन्दक LXIX, 8, 49.

कुड्मल, कुट्मल and कुड्मल indiscriminately used XVIII, 102, 111, 119, 124, 131, 244, 249.

गौलि *for* गौरी IV, 35.

चमेति *for* चेति XXVII, 14.

चयेष्टे *for* चेष्टम् IX, 309 note.

चर *for* द्वार XXXIV, 418.

चरगिये *for* चरग्यै (क्यै) VIII, 54.

चार *for* द्वार XXXIX, 138 note.

त्रिखेत्रम् *for* त्रिनेत्रम् VII, 198, 211, XII, 120.

तैतल *for* तैतिल III, 1; XXX, 107; XXXIII, 1, 3, 4.

त्रितीय *for* तृतीय XXXI, 11 note, (correct forms 17, 23, etc).

त्रियंश *for* त्र्यंश XI, 15, 18; XXIV, 6; XXVII, 32; XXXIV, 302.

(correct forms XXVIII, 21).

त्रिंशक *for* त्र्यंशक XXXIII, 274.

देष *for* देश LIX, 85.

दैविक *for* दैवक IX, 171, 175, 179.

द्विंश *for* द्व्यंश XIV, 9, 26, 45, 60, 78, 148, 162, 176, 180, 184, 185, 217, 241, 260, 268, 270, 276, 279, 305, 306, 316;

XV, 103, 186, 215.

WRONG SPELLING—(*continued*)

द्विशं *for* द्वंश XVIII, 188, 197, 267; (contd.)

XXII, 39, 50, 51 note, 54, 64, 76 note, 79, 80;

XXV, 4, 11;

XXVI, 56 note;

XXVII, 13, 34 note, 37 note;

XXX, 19 note, 21;

XXXI, 94;

XXXIII, 58, 131, 270 note, 272, 480 note;

XXXIV, 129, 135, 137, 197, 268, 289, 327, 377, 392, 428;

XXXV, 107, 132, 141, 212, 213, 226, 228, 229 note, 244.

Correct forms XVI; 62, 63, 75, 88; XXII, 61.

द्विकुल *for* द्वयकुल XXXI, 94.

द्विलोत्र *for* द्विनेत्र IX, 92 note.

द्विरष्ट *for* द्व्यष्ट XLV, 143

द्विंशोक *for* द्वयंशैक XVIII, 188, 197.

द्विंशाक *for* द्व्यंशाक XXVII, 6.

त्रिंशत् *for* त्रिंशता IX, 73.

धनुग्रह *for* धनुर्ग्रह II, 52, see note.

धनू *for* धनुः VI, 67.

नासि and मासी XXXIII, 543, 547, 549, 550, etc.

निभिः *for* निभा IV, 35.

नैऋत्य *for* नैर्ऋत्य XXXII, 39 (but generally correctly spelt, cf. 82).

नैऋत *for* नैर्ऋत XII, 190.

पट्टमाक् चालयं *for* पट्टभागालयं XL, 84.

पदैः *for* पदं VII, 38.

पञ्चादश *for* पञ्चदश XI, 28; XIII, 10, 23; XXXI, 33.

पुन्नाग *for* पुंन्नाग XVII, 24, 25.

प्रणव *for* प्रवण IX, 510 note.

परिघा *for* परिखा IX, 450 note; IX, 62 note, 106, 142.

बन्ध *for* बन्धु XIX, 99; XXII, 27, 37, 52; XXIV, 48; XXV, 6; XXIX, 24, 39; XXXIX, 65, 66.

बन्धांश *for* बन्ध्वंश XIII, 111, 179, 284; XVI, 24, 105; XXIII, 4; XXXIII, 231; XXXVIII, 47; XLVI, 27; LVII, 36, (correct form XXXIII, 242).

बिन्धो *for* बिन्धोः VI, 85 note, 86.

भरेखया *for* भरखया VII, 203.

भारा *for* हारा XXIV, 30; XXVI, 23.

WRONG SPELLING—(concluded)

मवदप *for* मण्डप IX, 138 note, XXXII, 8, etc. but मवडप 139, etc

मन *for* मनस् LIV, 3.

माधिक *for* अधिक VII, 41.

येाधक *for* येाधक IX, 225 note.

लिम्बक *for* अलिम्बक L, 280.

वक्रा *for* वर्जा IV, 16, see note.

वग्यंश *for* ग्रहगश XIII, 72.

विधि *for* बोधि IX, 203 note, 206, 333, 339, 340, 346, 348, 397, 463, 464, 520; X, 112 note, 113.

वृक्षेन *for* वर्धनेन XI, 62.

शाल *for* शाला indiscriminately (feminine used as masculine) XXVII, 7, 10, 11, 13, 31.

शालयम् *for* शाला XXXV, 74, 83.

शिर *for* शिरः XXI, 48; XXII, 9, 41; XXXIII, 188, 189.

शिल, सुध (feminine used as masculine) LI, 2, 3.

शिल्पिः *for* शिल्पी LII, 147.

शिल्पिवित् *for* शिल्पवित् VI, 26, etc.

शैत्य *for* चैत्य IV, 23 note.

षट्क (*for* श) तं XII, 25 note.

सम *for* समन XVI, 9.

समुह *for* समूह IX, 64 note.

सिह *for* सिंह VI, 32 note; VI, 58 note; VII, 246; XVIII, 292; (but सिंह XVIII, 316).

सुत्रभृत *for* सूत्रभृत् II, 24.

स्थूपि *for* स्तूप XVIII, 4, and see note.

स्मृत *for* सूत XIX, 116, 117, etc.

हेम *for* हेमन् XII, 144, 160, 161; XV, 417; LIV, 55.

WRONG METRES

अनुष्टुभ्—In this metre each verse should consist of eight syllables with only the following restrictions:

The fifth syllable of each पद् should be short, the sixth syllable long, and the seventh syllable long and short alternately in the four *pādas*.

In quite a large number of instances these restrictions are disregarded in the *Mānasāra*, for example:—

भूमिलम्बविधिं वक्ष्ये शास्त्रे संक्षेपतः क्रमात् ।
चतुरश्रमायताश्रं वर्तुलमायतं तदा ॥ XI, 1, 2.

Here the fifth and the sixth syllables of the third *pāda* are not short and long respectively as required, but they are the reverse – long and short.

पूर्वोक्तरथनामानि चाधुना प्रवक्ष्यते । XLIII, 111.

Here the fourth *pāda* has only seven syllables.

उक्तं हि भूमिलम्बं स्यादेकमेकान्तभूमिकम् ।

द्विकं त्रिकं चादौ द्वि द्वि करेण भूमिक्रमेण ॥ XI, 5, 6.

The fourth *pāda* of this verse is altogether irregular and unsuited in अनुष्टुभ verse. The number of syllables is ten instead of eight.

मानोपकरणं चादौ शिल्पिलक्षणपूर्वकम् ।

अथ वास्तुप्रकरणं भूपरीक्षाविधिं तथा ॥ I, 10.

In the third *pāda* here, the sixth and the seventh syllables are not long as required.

देवादीनां स्थापनाय पदविन्यासलक्षणम् ॥ I, 12.

Here the fifth syllable of the first *pāda* which ought to be short is made long, while the sixth which should be long is made short.

एवं हि द्व्यङ्गुलं न्यस्तं भूमिकाबाह्यमीनयोः ।

चतुरङ्गुलं प्रकर्तव्यं धनुः कुम्भौ षडङ्गुलम् ॥ VI, 83, 84.

Here the third *pāda* contains nine syllables instead of eight and the fifth syllable is long instead of short.

द्वितीयं चतुष्पदं चैव नाम पैशाचमेव च । VII, 3.

Here the first *pāda* contains nine syllables.

For the irregularities in metre the whole of chapter XI is an illustration.

False metre : XLIII, 111 ;

VI, 113 ;

VIII, 10.

A typical abuse of particles for the sake of metre, चापिमेव च LI, 64.

Unnecessary collection of particles for the sake of metre, सूचचैव चैवन्तु XII, 12

Too many particles, च, for the sake of metre :

IX, 285 ;
IX, 401 ;
IX, 358.

Repetition of the same term विस्तार, for the sake of metre, X, 20.

The use of a word (बहिः) for three times in the same line for the sake of metre, VII, 108.

Repetition of many verbs and particles in the same line for the sake of metre, VII, 262.

Untenable words for the sake of metre, XXXIII, 370.

Chapters end with verses of different metres, according to the rules of poetics, although the whole composition is nothing but versified prose, entirely lacking in poetry, see XLV, 191, etc.

Illustrations of barbarous Sanskrit, IV, 24, etc, etc.

That this kind of language is not limited to the *Mānasāra* nor even to the Śilpa-śāstra class of literature will be clear from the following illustrations picked up from inscriptions.

"Some peculiarities in spelling, the frequent use of single consonants for double ones, the use of short i and u for long ī and ū, and the occasional omission of the long ā (e.g. hemaṁtamase, no. v., Mahārajasya and masa, no. IXA), agree with the usage prevailing partly in all, partly some versions of Aśoka's edicts and of other ancient inscriptions. They make it difficult to decide, whether some of the curious forms, to be discussed below, are due to negligence in spelling or to grammatical irregularities." (Jaina inscriptions from Mathura, Ep. Ind. vol. I. p. 373, para 2).

"The language of these inscriptions shows the mixed dialect, consisting partly of Prākrit and partly of Sanskrit words and forms, as clearly as the formerly discovered documents. A fixed principle, according to which the mixture has been made, so far as I can see, is not discoverable." (Ibid. para 3, first two sentences).

"The omission of the case terminations in words, which qualify others standing in the same case, is common, as Professor von Roth has shown (Abhandlungen des VII ten Int. Or. Congresses, Arische, section, pp., 1 ff.) in the Ṛigveda. It occurs also not rarely in Pāṇini's Sūtras, is very frequent in the Northern Buddhist works, and is a fixed principle in the modern Indian Vernaculars as well as in other languages." (Ibid. p. 375, middle of first para).

"Thus in no. XVIII, there are only three words stāna for sthāna, pratishṭāpita for pratishṭhāpita, and perhaps chāndakā for chāndrakā, showing the influence of the Prākrit, though the great majority of the terminations are Prākritic.' (Ibid. p. 175, second para, second sentence).

"Moreover, it (no. CV) furnishes a good example of the Sanskrit, written by the Yatis of our days, and it may be useful for settling the controversy regarding the origin of the 'mixed' dialects found in older books and inscriptions as well as that regarding the advisability of bringing, by conjectural emendations, the language of somewhat older Jaina authors such as Merutuṁga, Rājaśēkhara and Jinamaṇḍana, into harmony with the rules of Sanskrit grammar."

(Jaina inscriptions from Śatruṁjaya, first para, Ep. Ind. vol. II, p. 34).

"Altogether the inscription has not been written carefully, and, though corrected in several places, it is by no means free from serious mistakes. The rules of saṁdhi are frequently disregarded, the verses of the genealogical portion are only partially numbered or have wrong numbers appended to them; single aksharas and whole words or groups of words are either given quite wrongly or left out ; and I hope to prove below that even one or more whole lines have been omitted by the writer."

(Samgamner Copper-plate inscription, Ep. Ind., vol. II, p. 218, last sentence of the 1st para).

"The language is very incorrect Sanskrit prose, greatly influenced by the Prākrit or vernacular of the author. In some places the case terminations are altogether omitted; in others we have wrong cases, false genders, and inappropriate or incorrect verbal derivatives. The influence of the Prākrit is shown by the substitution of single for conjunct consonants, the substitution of s, for ś and sh, and the omission of medial y and final consonants (e.g. *vidheānam* for *vidheyānām*, *kasyachi* for *kasyachit*)."

(India office plate of Vijayarājadeva, Ep. Ind., vol. III, p. 312, 1st para).

"In Ushavadātas cave [at Nāsik] we have one inscription (almost) entirely in Sanskrit, the rest are in Pāli or Prākrit, but we have an intermixture of Sanskrit words, and the conjuncts pra, tra, and ksha often appear. In these and the smaller inscriptions we have such words as *bāra* for *dvāra*, *bārasaka* for *vārshika*, *barisa* for *varsha*. *udisa* for *uddiśya*, while the Pāli forms of these words are *dvāra*, *vassika*, *vassa* and *uddessitvā*. Some of these inscriptions were engraved so late as the third century, when the Pāli could hardly have been the vernacular."

(Ind. Ant. vol. XII, p. 140, first column, middle).

It should be noted that *bāra* for *dvāra*, *yiś* for *iśa*, *yeka* for *eka*, *vu(bu)ttara* for *uttara*, etc., are frequently used in the *Mānasāra*.

"As regards the origin of this mixed dialect, as well as of all other mixed dialects, I agree with professor Kern (Jaartelling, p. 108 ff.) and Dr. R. G. Bhāndārkar (Indian Antiquary, vol. XII, p. 146) that it is the result of the efforts of half educated people to express themselves in Sanskrit, of which they possessed an insufficient knowledge and which they were not in the habit of using largely. All the Jaina inscriptions from Mathurā were no doubt composed by the monks who acted as the spiritual directors of the laymen, or by their pupils. Though no inscription has been found in which the author is named, the above inference is warranted by the fact that numerous later documents of the same character contain the names of Yatis who are said to have composed them or to have written them. The Yatis in the first and second centuries, no doubt, just as now, for their sermons and the exposition of their scriptures, used the vernacular of the day, and their scriptures were certainly written in Prakrit. It was a matter of course that their attempts to write in Sanskrit were not very successful. This theory receives the strongest support from the fact that the character and the number of the corruptions varies almost in every document, and from various single sentences,........., which latter reads exactly like a piece from a stupid school boy's exercise. It is also confirmed by numerous analogies, such as the language of the *janma patras* of the badly educated *Joshis* mentioned by Dr. Bhandarkar, the books of masons and carpenters, which have the rules for building houses in most barbarous Sanskrit, and many modern inscriptions, composed by clerks or *yatis*. A large number of specimens of the latter kind are contained in the collection of votive inscriptions from Pālitanā, lately copied by Mr. H. Cousens."

(Dr. G. Bühler, Jaina Inscriptions from Mathura, Ep. Ind. vol. I, p. 377.)

"As to the language of other inscriptions [in caves at Nāsik] which, like those of Gotamiputra and his son, were not composed by learned men, one can easily understand how ignorant persons not knowing Sanskrit or Pāli well, but still not ignorant enough to know nothing of both, would compound together Sanskrit, Pāli, and vernacular words. Even in our days we find this phenomenon in the *patrikās* or horoscopes written by our *Joshis* or astrologers, which are neither in pure Sanskrit nor in pure vernacular, but contain a mixture of both, and the Sanskrit words and forms in which are incorrectly written. And an explanation of this nature I have also to give of another variety of language that is found in the writings of the northern or Nepalese Buddhists. Unlike those of the Singalese and Burmese Buddhists these are written in Sanskrit, but in such works as the *Lalitavistāra*, or the life of the Buddha, we find along with prose passages in pure Sanskrit a number of verses which contain words or forms which are not Sanskrit. Thus, for instance we have—

Sarvaśubhakarmahetoḥ phalamidam śṛiṇutāsya karmasya ।
Pūjāraho bhavituṁ sarvajage anubandhita imamantayaśaṁ ॥

"You will here see that *karmasya*, *jage*, and *yaśam* are, as in the Pāli, treated like nouns in a. *Arha* is dissolved into *araha*,..............

"This language has, therefore, no fixed characteristics at all. We have seen that in such words as *karma*, *jaga*, and *yaśa* above, the final consonant is dropped, and these as in the Pāli and the Prākrits made nouns in a. But *yaśas* the original Sanskrit form, is also used as in *kīrtiyaśaścha* and these are instances in which other final consonants are preserved. Along with such a Pāli form as *suṇishyāti* noticed above, such a Sanskrit one as *śṛiṇvanti*, is found. It therefore appears to me that this is not an independent language; but that the writers of the *gāthās* knew the spoken language or Pāli, and that they were imperfectly acquainted with Sanskrit, knowing enough of it to see that the assimilation of consonants was a vulgarity, but not acquainted with its grammar. They intended to write in the more polished or literary language, but not knowing it well often used unconsciously the grammatical forms and the peculiar words of the vernacular. (At the time when the *gāthās* were written, the claims of the Pāli to be considered a separate language were probably not recognised, and it constituted the speech of the uninstructed.) Those who in this condition of things wished to write could not think of doing so in that form of speech, and therefore wrote in what they considered the language of educated men, but they knew it imperfectly, and hence produced such a heterogenous compound as we have seen."

(Sir R. G. Bhāndārkar, Indian Antiquary, vol. XII, pp. 140-141).

These weighty opinions on the origin of a peculiar style of Sanskrit will, it may be hoped, support the following thesis submitted by the present writer to Leiden University regarding the growth of the language of the Śilpa Śāstras

'The ungrammatical style of Sanskrit revealed in the branch of literature, of which the *Mānasāra* is a representative, is due to the want of literary proficiency on the part of professional architects who seem to have been the a hors of it.'

GENERAL INDEX

A

Ābhaṅga, slight flexion, a pose, 86.

Ābhāsa, a class of buildings, 41, 48, 110, 118, etc.; a type of door, 155; a kind of phallus, 72, etc; a building material, a sort of marble, three kinds—*chitra ardha-chitra* and *ābhāsa* proper, 70.

Abja, ambuja, padma or saroruha, names of a kind of moulding, partly corresponding to cyma, cymarecta or cymatium, 127

Abja-kānta, a class of ten-storeyed buildings, 50, 112, etc.

Abu, marble temples at Mount of, 178; further details, 179.

Āchāra-sāra, an illustration of the names of books ending in *sāra* meaning 'essence,' 2.

Actium, the battle of, referring to the age in which Vitruvius, the famous Roman architect, might have lived, 160.

Adam, the father of human race corresponding to Manu, 166.

Adbhuta, one of the five divisions of height of an architectural or sculptural object, determined in comparison with the width, the others being called *śāntika*, *paushṭika*, *pārshṇika* or *jayada*, and *sarvakāmika*, 41, 55, 124, etc.; name of a class of two-storeyed buildings also called *Prabhutaka*, 60, 111, 118, etc.

Ādhāra, a kind of support for a chariot, also called *Upādhāra*, 60; name of a moulding, 127, etc.

Adhirāja, one of the nine classes of kings, 59; for whose use different kinds of storeyed buildings, thrones, crowns, chariots, and ornaments, etc., are prescribed, 42, 60, 61, 67-68, etc.

Adhishṭhāna, the base, its sixty-four varieties divided under nineteen different types bearing technical names, 44; illustrations of its being dealt with in all purely architectural treatises, 89, 92, 106; comparison with Vitruvius's, 149 fol.

Adhivāsana, ceremony connected with the coronation of a king, 65.

Ādika, a kind of conveyance, first or fast conveyance, 36.

Ādimāna, primary measurement, 77; its nine varieties, 121, etc.

Ādisāra, an architectural treatise or author like *Mānasāra*, one of the thirty-two authorities on architecture, 165.

Ādi-Vishṇu, one of the epithets of Vishṇu, an illustration of the popularity of the Vishṇu cult at the time of the *Mānasāra*, 189,

Ādyeshṭaka-vidhi, laying the foundation stone, 28, etc.

Āgama, a traditional doctrine, a special class of works, belonging especially to Southern India like the Purāṇas of Northern India, and numbering twenty-eight, 23; deals extensively with architectural and sculptural matters, 24—28, (109), 118-119, 125, 126, 128, 130, 131, 132, 151. 160, 175.

Agastya, an authority on architecture, 97, 100, 101, 107.

Agastya-sakalādhikāra, a treatise on architecture, 100.

Aghana, hollow parts, 53; an architectural measurement taken by the interior of a structure, 124.

Agni-purāṇa, seems to be aware of *Mānasāra*, 4, 169; dilates on the subject of architecture at great length, 20; compared with various other treatises on architectural matters, 110, 160, 170; describes forty-five types of buildings under five classes which are identical with those given in *Garuḍa-purāṇa*, 113, 119; age of, 194.

Ahi-chhatra, the capital of north Pañchāla which is the name of a type of twelve-storeyed buildings, 174.

Ahura-Mazda, possible identity with Maya-Asura, 166, 172.

Airāvata, name of a class of five-storeyed buildings, 50, 112.

Aitareya-Brāhmaṇa, reference to the angula measure from, 122.

Ajanta, rock-cut cave temples of, 10; richly carved and ornamented pierced widows at, 178.

Akrakānta, a class of eleven-storeyed buildings, 50, 112.

Aksha, axle of cars and chariots, 60.

Akshi-mokshaṇa, chiselling the eyes of an image, 101, 107.

Alaka-(chūḍā), a kind of head-dress used by the queens of Prābhāraka and Astragrāha classes of kings, 65.

Ālambana-bāhu, balustrades, references from Buddhist literature to, 13.

Alaṅkāra-śāstra, illustrates the inductive method of treatment of the subject matter as in the *Śilpa-śāstras*, 133.

Alberuni, on the age of *Purāṇas*, 194.

Alexander, his expedition accounts for the Grecian influence on the Gāndhāra sculpture, 159.

Alinda, verandah, references from Buddhist literature to, 12.

Āliṅga, name of a moulding, 127.

Alpa, one of the twenty types of buildings mentioned in the *Kāmikāgama*, 118.

Amalaka, a large fluted circular block, being a characteristic feature over the summit of the earlier Indo-Aryan style of architecture, 179.

Āmalaka-vantika-pīṭham, chair with many legs, references from Buddhist literature to, 16.

Amara-kosha, the famous Sanskrit lexicon, refers to several architectural terms and illustrates the popularity of architecture in the dictionary class of literature, 33.

Ambaranāth, Indo-Aryan style of architecture of the mediaeval age at, 179.

Aṁśu, name of a moulding, 127.

Aṁśumad-bheda (of Kāśyapa), an architectural treatise of much reputation summarized, (91), 92; 99.

Aṁśumad-bhedāgama, references to architecture from, 28; reference to *Tāla* measure from, 123.

Andhra, one of the two branches of the Vesara style of architecture, 130, 131, 176; Aryanization of the country of, 184; patronage to popular literary dialects of the Andhra Kings, 193; empire of, 185.

Aṅghri, dwarf pillar, 63; name of a moulding, 127.

Āṅgīrasa, a treatise on architecture on which the Sanat-kumāra-vāstu-śāstra was based, 102.

Aṅgula, a finger, finger-breadth used as the standard measure, the smaller units of which it is made and its multiples, 35; the four kinds of, 77; similarly treated in all branches of Sanskrit literature, (121), 122.

Aṅgulīyaka, an ornament, finger-ring, 67.

Anila-bhadraka, one of the seven types of cars, 61.

Animals, for riding of gods, 81, 82, 83.

Aniruddha, one of the eighteen architectural authorities mentioned in the *Matsya-purāṇa*, 164.

Anta-nihāra, one of the five courts into which the compound of an edifice is divided, 51, 154.

Antarāla, anteroom, 49; a moulding, 127.

Antariksha-kānta, class of ten-storeyed buildings, 50, 112.

Antarita, otherwise called antara, antarāla and antarika, fillet, a moulding, 127.

Antar-maṇḍala, one of the five courts into which the compound of an edifice is divided, 51, 154.

Antika, a type of two-storeyed buildings, 111, also called Kāntika, 51.

Aṅukarma-vidhāna, minor works on sculpture, 90.

Apasaṁchita, a type of building, 24, 49, 111, 118.

Āpa-tattva, one of the several architectural treatises ascribed to Maṇḍana, 103.

Āpa-vatsya, name of a quarter, 139: compare ground-plan, 37-38.

Apelles, an eminent painter, 141.

Apollo, a deity, the temple of, 146.

Ārāma, rest-house, a garden house, elaborately described in Buddhist literature, 11.

Aranga, probably for Ranga, a class of buildings, 36.

Architecture, objects implied by, 1; one of the duties of the Buddhist order, 10; professors of, (86), 165.

Ardha-hāra, string of pearls worn round the neck, a chain of sixty-four strings, 68.

Ardha-nārīśvara, image of Śiva combined with his consort Pārvatī, 94, 100, 107.

Ardha-yoga, a type of Buddhist buildings, partly religious and partly residential, 10.

Argala, name of a moulding, 127.

Aristarchus, a grammarian, 141.

Aristoxenus, a famous musician, 141.

Arjuna, the temple of, 177.

Aræostylos, one of the five species of Vitruvius's temples, 147.

Ārsha, a class of phalli, 78.

Artha-śāstra, of Kauṭilīya, the architectual matters described in, 29; an example of Political works, 132; reference to party-walls, sewage system and windows, etc., from, 140; connection with *Purāṇas* and other works, 169-170.

Asaṁchita, a class of buildings, 24, 49, 111.

Āsana, a type of buildings in which the deity is carved in the sitting posture, 24, 49, 110; a class of three-storeyed buildings, 50, 111; one of the three postures, 86; seat, 97: name of a moulding, 127.

Āsandi, chairs, 16, 30.

Āsandako, rectangular chair, 16.

Ashṭaśra, a class of octagonal buildings, 116 (its description); 117, 118.

Ashṭa-tāla, a kind of measurement, 75, see Tāla (121, 173).

Aśoka, 183, 184, 185, 190.

Āśramāgāra, a class of seven-storeyed buildings, 50, 112.

Assembly-halls, of Indra, Yama, Varuṇa and Kubera as mentioned in *Mahābhārata*, 17.

Āsthāna-maṇḍapa, hall of public audience, 58.

Astragal, name of a moulding, 127, 152.

Astragrāhin, a class of kings, 59, 181, 182.

Asura, a deity, name of a plot in the ground-plan (*Pada-vinyāsa*) 88.

Aśva-māna-vidhi, name of a chapter in the *Viśvasāra* dealing with the measurement of horse's image, 108.

Atharva-veda, references to architectual matters from, 6.

Aśvatha tree, characteristic of Buddha, 78-79.

Atibhaṅga, excessive flexion, one of the poses in which an image is carved, 86.

Ātmārtha, (for one's own purpose), a class of phalli for personal worship as opposed to public worship, 73.

Atri, a sage, 6; one of the eighteen Professors of architecture mentioned in the *Matsya-purāṇa*, 164.

Aṭṭālikā, edifice, one of several architectural objects mentioned in Paṇini's grammar, 33.

Attic, one of the three species of doors mentioned by Vitruvius, 165.

Augustus, a Roman king, 160.

Auttami, one of the fourteen Manus, 166.

Avachchhāyā, light shadow, calculation of, in connection with the cardinal points for the orientation of buildings, 37.

Āvarya, one of the thirty-two architectural authorities mentioned in *Mānasāra*, 165.

Āyādi-shaḍ-varga, āya and other architectural formulas of measurement, 83, 24, 73, 74, 78, 103.

Ayodhyā, its town-plan, 17; builder of, 166; mentioned (as Ajoyya) in Buddhist literature, 9.

Āyudhālaya, arsenal, 58.

B

Babhru-(mushṭika), a type of building mentioned in the *Agni-purāṇa*, 114.

Bacchus, temple of, 146, 148.

Bādāmi, Chalukyas of, 191.

Bahir-bhūshaṇa, external ornaments, certain articles of furniture, 68.

Bahu-bhūmi-vidhāna, building of more than three storeys, the name of a chapter in the *Mayamata-Śilpa-Śāstra*, 90.

Bahu-liṅga, phalli in group, a class of phalli, 73.

Bāhulya, name of a moulding, 27, 152.

Bairat, town of, representing ancient Virāṭa, 174.

Ba(va)labhi, a rectangular type of building mentioned in the *Agni-purāṇa*, 113.

Bālāditya, a Gupta prince, 192.

Balance, architectual details of, 69.

Bāla-paryaṅka, small couch, 36.

Balaya (valaya), a round type of building mentioned in the *Agni-purāṇa*, 113.

Bali, an island, 170.

Bali-karma, offerings to gods in connection with constructing a building, 89.

Bāṇa, the author of the *Harsha-charita*, 194.

Bāṇa-śālā, castles, 30.

Bārāṇasi, the builder of, 9.

Baroli, type of temple at, 179.

Base, (adhishṭhāna), different varieties of, 44, 128.

Bauddhas, temples of 52; images of the deities of, 78.

Bedsteads, architectural details of, 61-62; references from the *Āgamas* to, 27.

Belur, type of temple at, 178.

Benares, type of temples at, 179.

Berāṅgula, a kind of measurement, 77, 84.

Bhadra, a type of pavilion used as a water-reservoir, store-house, etc., 154; balconies, 60; a type of square building mentioned in the *Agni-purāṇa*, 113; also in the *Kāmikāgama*, 118; a moulding, 127.

Bhadra-pīṭha, one of the four classes of pedestals, 74.

Bhadra-piṭham, state chair, 16.

Bhadrāsana, a type of throne for the Paṭṭabhāj class of kings, 63.

Bhāgavata-purāna, references to a class of devotees from, 80.

Bhairava, a class of phalli, 72.

Bhairavī, one of the seven mothers, image of, 75.

Bhānu, one of the thirty-two architectural authorities mentioned in *Mānasāra*, 165.

Bhāra (hāra), name of a moulding, 127.

Bharata, an architectural authority, 162

Bhārgava, one of several architectural authorities on which the Sanatkumāra's *Vāstu-śāstra* is stated to have been based, 102.

Bhāravi, contemporary and date of, 197.

Bhāskara, one of several authorities on which the architectural portion of the *Bṛihat-saṁhitā* appears to have been based, 163, 165.

Bhāskarāchārya, astronomical works of, 172.

Bhaṭṭotpala, a commentator of the *Bṛihat-saṁhitā*, 162.

Bhavabhūti, the great Sanskrit poet, architectural references from, 32.

Bhavana (bhuvana), a rectangular type of building mentioned in the *Agni-purāṇa* 113, and the *Garuḍa-purāṇa* 114.

Bhavana-kānta, a class of ten-storeyed buildings, 50, 112.

Bhavishya-purāṇa, architectural references from, 21; comparative study of, 23, 110, 119, 131, 160; twenty types of buildings from, 116-117; references to selection of site and examination of soil from 140; identical with the *Matsya-purāṇa* and the *Bṛihat-saṁhitā*, 163; age of, 194.

Bhikshāṭana-(mūrti-lakshaṇa), image of Śiva in the pose of a beggar, 94, 100.

Bhoga, a type of single storeyed building, 49; with round ears (wings), 111.

Bhojana-maṇḍapa, dining hall, a type of pavilion, 58.

Bhṛigu, one of the authorities on which Sanat-kumāra's *Vāstu-śāstra* is stated to have been based, 102; architectural references from, 107; further references from, 140; one of the eighteen professors of architecture mentioned in the *Matsya-purāṇa*, 164.

Bhṛiṅga-rāja, a deity, 88.

Bhū-devī, earth-goddess, image of, 71; see also Mahī, 74-75.

Bhūdhara, a round type of building mentioned in the *Agni-purāṇa*, 113.

Bhū-kānta, types of eight-and ten-storeyed buildings, 50, 112.

Bhū-lamba, dimensions of storeys, name of a chapter in the *Maya-mata*, 89; see Bhūmi-lamba.

Bhūmi-(lakshaṇa), soil, name of a chapter in the *Viśvakarma-Śilpa*, 96.

Bhūmi-lamba-vidhāna, dimensions of buildings of various storeys, 41, 25; definition and contents of the chapter so named, 147.

Bhūmi-phalam, fruit of soil, effect of soil upon the building, a chapter of the *Viśvakarma-Śilpa*, 96.

Bhūmi-saṁgraha, selection of site, details of, 36; comparative study of, 142.

Bhū-mukha, an oval type of building mentioned in the *Garuḍa-purāṇa*, 114.

Bhūpa-kānta, a class of eight-storeyed buildings, 50, 112.

Bhū-parigraha, selection of site, name of a chapter in the *Mayamata-Śilpa-śāstra*, 89.

Bhū-parīkshā, examination of soil, details of, 36, 89, 102; comparative study of, 142.

Bhūpati-Vallabha, perhaps identical with the *Śilpa-śastra* of Maṇḍana, 103.

Bhūshaṇa, a class of nine-storeyed buildings, 50, 112; an oval type of building mentioned in the *Agni-purāṇa*, 113.

Bhūshaṇālaya, house for keeping ornaments in, a store-room for jewellery, 58.

Bhūtas, goblins, images of, 61; compare Yaksha, etc., 80.

Bhūta-kānta, a class of five-storeyed buildings, 50, 112.

Bhuvaneśvara, type of temples at, 179; division of the style of architecture at, 180.

Bihar, country of Janakas, types of twelve-storeyed buildings at, 173.

Bimbamāna, references to sculptural matters from, 121, 122, 123.

Bimbisāra, a king, builder of Rāja-griha, 9.

Bodhika, name of a moulding, 126, 127, 151.

Boutique, a Buddhist building, 11.

Brahmā, image of, 71; name of a type of columns, 126, 151; according to Varāhamihira the science of architecture originated from, 162; in architectural matters the comparative treatment of, 187; the foundations of the temples of, 188; worship of, 190.

Brahma-bhāga, the name of the square stand of the phallus, 73.

Brahma-kānta, square pillar, 45, 125, 150; a pillar with four minor pillars, 45, 46; a class of three-storyed buildings, 50, 111; a class of five-storeyed buildings, 50, 112; a class of *gopuras* (gate-house), 52.

Brahma-mandira, a rectangular type of building mentioned in the *Agni-purāṇa* and the *Garuḍa-purāṇa*, 113, 114.

Brahman, one of the authorities on which Sanat-kumāra's *Vāstu-Śāstra* (science of architecture) is stated to have been based, 102; one of the eighteen professors of architecture mentioned in the *Matsya-purāṇa*, 164.

Brahmāṇḍa-purāṇa, references to temples and residential buildings from, 21; aṅgula-measures from, 122; tāla-measures from, 123; account of future kings ending with the Guptas in, 194

Brahmāṇī, one of the seven mothers, image of, 75.

Brahma-pīṭha, the royal chapel, 58.

Brahma-sāvarṇī, one of the fourteen Manus, 166.

Brahma-sthāna, the central plot in a village or town, where some public building is generally built, 56; the central place in a palace where the royal chapel is situated, 58.

Brahma-yāmala, an architectural treatise, 108.

Brāhmī, goddess, image of, 98.

Brahmor, in Chamba State, bronze Nandin from, 82.

Bṛihat-saṁhitā, by Varāhamihira, short description of, 22; method of treatment of architectural matters in, 28; definition of *hāra* from, 68; other works compared with, 109, 110, 116; twenty types of buildings from, 117, 118, 119; *aṅgula* and *tāla* measures from, 122, 123; the five orders from, 125, 150; eight kinds of mouldings from, 127, 151, 152; styles of architecture from, 130, 131; probably based on *Mānasāra*, 132; references to selection of sites and examination of soil from, 140; relation with other works, 160, 167, 168, 194, 198; detailed comparison with *Mānasāra*, 161, 164; mention of architectural authorities in, 165; as a polytechnical work, 175.

Bṛisha, a type of pavilion where Nandin is housed, 119.

Bṛihaspati, one of mythical authorities on which *Mānasāra* is stated to have been based, 34.

Buddha, his image described, 78-79; Hindu settlement at the time of, 183; effigies of, 185; as one of the ten incarnations of Vishṇu, 186, 190; temples and monasteries of the followers of, 191.

Buddha-charita, reference to monumental lamp pillars from, 68.

Buddha-ghosa, his explanations of the five kinds of Buddhist buildings, 10; his explanations of inner chambers, 12; of other architectural objects, 13, 14, 15, 16.

Buddhism, treatment of, 185; monasteries associated with, 187; included in Vaishṇavism and tolerted, 190; declining state during the early Chalukya dynasty of, 191; rise of Hinduism during the early Guptas at the expense of, 192, 193.

Buddhists, during *Mānasāra* indifferent treatment of, 185; further instances, 186, 187.

Buddhist images, description of, 78-79.

Buddhist literature, copious references to architectural objects in, 9—16.

Bull (Nandin), riding animal of Śiva, its description, 82.

Bundelkhand, styles of architecture of Khajuraho in, 178.

C

Callimachus, originator of the Corinthian order, 126.

Cape Comorin, southern boundary of an architectural division of India, 174.

Cars, description of, 60

Casting of images, process described, 86-87.

Cavetto, name of a moulding, 127, 152.

Cement, as mentioned in *Uttara-Râma charita*, 32, in *Bṛihat-saṁhitâ*, 22.

Ceres, temple of, 146.

Ceylon, ancient seven-storeyed and thousand-pillared buildings of, 14; Samudra Gupta's relation with, 184; King Meghavarṇa of, 191.

Chaityas, assembly houses of the Buddhists in Western India, 6; monumental Kāsmirian buildings, 30.

Chakora, perdix rufa, cage of, 70.

Chakra, discus of Vishṇu, 71; an octagonal type of buildings mentioned in the *Agni-purāṇa*, 113, and in the *Garuḍa-purāṇa*, 114.

Chakra-kânta, a class of eleven-storeyed buildings, 50, 112.

Chakra-vartin, emperor, palace of, 57; empire of, 59; one of the nine classes of kings, 181; his relation with other kings, 182.

Chākshusha, one of the fourteen Manus, 166.

Châlukya, a style of architecture, its territory and characteristic features, 177, 178, 179; its comparison with other styles, 196; temples of, 178; unique crowning members in the buildings of, 180; empire of, 185; period of, 190; of the Bâdâmi line, 191.

Châmuṇḍā, one of the seven mothers, the image of, 75.

Châmuṇḍī-dhyâna, characteristics of the demoness Châmuṇḍī, name of a chapter in the Brahma-yâmala, 109.

Chaṇḍeshânugraha, name of a chapter in *Aṁśumad-bheda* of Kâśyapa, 94; image of the deity described also in *Âgastya*, 100.

Chaṇḍita, name of a plot in a particular ground-plan, 38; a class of nine-storeyed buildings, 50, 112.

Chandra, one of the authorities on which Sanat-kumāra's *Vâstu-śâstra* is stated to have been based, 102.

Chandragupta II, date and empire of, 185, 190; incidents of the reign of, 192; progress of art and literature in the time of, 193.

Chandrakânta, a class of ten-storeyed buildings, 50, 112; name of one of the five Indian orders as given in the *Suprabhedâgama*, 125, 126, 150, 151.

Chandra-śālā, top-room, gable window, 115, 116.

Chandra-śekhara-mūrti-lakshaṇa, image of god Śiva, name of a chapter in the *Aṁśumad-bheda* of Kaśyapa, 94, and in the *Āgastya*, 100, 107.

Chāpākāra, shaped like the bow, the eye-brow to be shaped like, 84.

Charagī, one of the four evil deities, 88.

Chariots, description of, 60-61.

Chāru-bandha, name of a type of bases, 128.

Charuka, a square type of buildings mentioned in the *Agni* and *Garuḍa Purāṇas*, 113, 118.

Chātaka, cuculus melanoleucus, cage of, 70.

Chatur-asra, also called Chatush-koṇa, a class of four-cornered (square) buildings mentioned in *Matsya* and *Bhavishya Purāṇas*, and *Bṛihat-saṁhitā*, 116, 117, 118.

Chatur-mukha, a type of village, 39, 148; a class of four-storeyed buildings, 50, 112; a kind of halls (*śālās*), 55.

Chatush-koṇa, also called Chatur-aśra, a type of four-cornered (square) buildings, 117, 118.

Chhanda, a class of buildings, 41, 110, 118, 147; a type of phalli, 73; a kind of door, 57, 155.

Chhāndogya-Upanishad, aṅgula measure in, 122.

Chhidra, hole, of cars and chariots, architectural description of, 60.

Chīra, bark used as garment, of the image of Brahmā, 71.

Chitis, altars, particulars about their construction in *Taittirīya-saṁhitā*, *Baudhāyana*, and *Āpastamba*, 7-8.

Chiselling (the eyes of images), in *Kāmikāgama*, 27, and in *Mānasāra*, 88.

Chitor, Indo-Aryan or the Nāgara style of buildings at, 179.

Chitra, an octagonal type of building, 113.

Chitra-jñana, an authority on painting, 108.

Chitraka, one of the thirty-two authorities on architecture mentioned in *Mānasāra*, 165.

Chitra-kalpa, a class of ornaments, consisting of floral and foliated designs, to be used by the Chakravartin class of kings and gods, 67.

Chitra-karṇa, variegated ears, one of the five Indian orders of columns, 15, 125, 126, 150, 151.

Chitra-kumbha, a type of columns, 45.

Chitra-sāra, an authority on painting, 108.

Chitra-skambha, of variegated shaft, one of the five Indian orders, 125, 126, 150, 151.

Chitra-toraṇa, a type of ornamental arch, 63.

Chittātrāgāra, a picture gallery, as stated in Buddhist literature, 15.

Cholas, neighbours of King Aśoka, 188.

Chūḍā, a kind of head-dress, 65.

Chūḍā-maṇi, crest-jewel, 67.

Chullavagga, a Buddhist work, architectural references from, 10, 11, 12, 13, 15, 16.

Chunam, a kind of plaster, 15.

Columns, as mentioned in *Vedas*, 6; in *Purāṇas*, 19; in *Āgamas*, 25; in *Mānasāra*, 44—46; in *Mayamata*, 89; in *Kāśyapa*, 92; and in *Viśvakarma-śilpa* 96; details and comparative study of, 125—129, 149—153, 168.

Composite order, both Indian and European, 125, 150, 151, 152.

Construction, penalties for defects in, 87.

Corinth, country of, 151.

Corinthian, an order of columns, 125, 147, 148, 150, 152, 154.

Coromandal, Kaliṅga type of buildings in, 194.

Coronation, as stated in *Āgamas*, 27; description of, 64-65; four stages of, 65; ritual ceremonies of, 66.

Couches, description of, 61-62.

Courts (and enclosures), as described *Āgamas*, 26; and in *Mānasāra*, 51; compared with those of Vitruvius, 155.

Crowns, varieties and description of, 64—66.

Cyma, cymarecta or cymatium, name of a moulding, 127, 152, 153.

D

Dāgabas, topes, 15.

Daivika, a class of phalli, 78.

Daksha-Sāvarṇi, one of the fourteen Manus, 166.

Dakshiṇā-mūrti, image of the goddess Dakshiṇā, 94, 100, 106, 107.

Dākshiṇātya, Deccan, migration of culture from Āryāvarta or northern India to, 181.

Dala, a petal, name of a moulding, 127.

Dāman, garland worn round the shoulders, 68.

Daṇḍa, a class of buildings mentioned in the *Kāmikāgama*, 118; a moulding mentioned in the *Suprabhedāgama*, 126, 151.

Daṇḍaka, a class of villages, 39, 143; a type of pavilion (*maṇḍapa*) with two faces, 54; a type of hall (*śālā*), 55.

Daṇḍin, the author of *Daśa-kumāra-charita*, 170, 197.

Darpaṇa, mirror, 68; its architectural details, 69.

Dāru-chchhedana, cutting of wood, name of a chapter in the *Viśvakarma-Śilpa*, 97.

Dāru-saṁgraha, collection of wood, name of a chapter in *Āgastya*, 100.

Dārva, a type of pavilion (*maṇḍapa*) for an elephant's stable, 54.

Daśa-kumāra-charita, a prose romance, refers to Mānasāra as the King of Malwa, 170-171, 198; its age, 197.

Daśa-tala, ten-storeyed buildings, six types of, 50, 112.

Daśa-tāla, ten-tāla measures, its details, 84; three kinds of, 100.

Daśāvatāra, images of the ten incarnations of Vishṇu, 109; see also ten incarnations, 188.

Deha-labdhāṅgula, also called simply Dehāṅgula, a kind of measurement, 77, 84, 122.

Deva-durga, god's fort, 40, 143.

Deva-kānta, a class of eight-storeyed buildings, 50, 112.

Deva-maṇḍapa, a type of pavilion, 119.

Devarāshṭra, modern Mahratta country, included in the dominion of Samudra Gupta, 184.

Devāyatana, temples, as mentioned in the Epics, 17, 18.

Dhammilla, a kind of head-dress, reserved for use of a certain class of people, recognised as an architectural object, 65.

Dhanada, otherwise called Sarvakāmika, a kind of measurement, 55, 124.

Dhanur-graha-(hasta), a kind of measurement, a cubit of twenty-seven aṅgulas, 35.

Dhanur-mushṭi-(hasta), a kind of measurement, a cubit of twenty-six aṅgulas, 35.

Dhanus, measuring bow, a measurement of four cubits, 35.

Dhārā-(kumbha), a moulding, 127.

Dhāraṇa, a class of seven-storeyed buildings, 50, 112.

Dharma-Sāvarṇi, one of the fourteen Manus, 166.

Dhruva, an architectural authority on whose work Viśvakarma's treatise is stated to have been based, 97.

Dhruvādi-gṛiha-bheda, name of a chapter in Viśvakarma's treatise on architecture, 96.

Dhvajādhyāya, name of a chapter in Viśvakarma's treatise dealing with the making of flags, 96.

Dhyānas, description of the features of images, 88.

Dialling, 1; details given under gnomen, 87; principles of and comparison with Vitruvius's, 148.

Diana, temple of, 148.

Diastylos, a type of temples with columns wide apart, 147.

Dīgha-Nikāya, a kind of bath described with architectural details in, 14.

Dik-parichchheda, a chapter in the *Mayamata* dealing with cardinal points for the orientation of buildings, 89; 106.

Dik-pāla, quarter-masters, the images of, 98.

Dimensions (vistārāyāma-lakshaṇa) of building, 24, 41-43, 47, 49, 147.

Diṇḍima, hand-drum, an attribute of the image of Lakshmī (goddess of fortune), 75.

Dīpa-daṇḍa, lamp-post, an article of furniture, 68.

Dīpa-lakshaṇa, a chapter in the Maṇḍana's *Śilpa-śāstra* dealing with architectural details of lamps, 103.

Dīpta-tantra, a treatise on architecture, 109.

Dipteros, a type of building, 147.

Dīpti-sāra, a treatise on architecture, 109.

Displuviatum, a type of courts open at the top, 154.

Doab, probably identical with Madyakānta which represents a type of twelve-stroyed buildings, 173.

Dolā, swing, palanquin, an article of furniture, 68, 69, 97.

Doors, their detailed description in Buddhist literature, 12; location and measurement of, 56, 57.

Doria, city of, wherefrom Doric order has been originated, 126.

Draftsman (rekhāgña). qualifications of, 35.

Doric, an order of column, 125, 126, 147, 148, 150, 151, 152; a type of doors, 155.

Double-moat, reference from Buddhist literature to, 9.

Drāviḍa, a style of architecture, 24, 48, 110, 118, 119, 130, 131, 198; a type of twelve-storeyed buildings, 50, 118, 173, 174, 175; an octagonal type of cars, 61; a type of phalli, 73; distinguishing features of the buildings of, 176, 177, 178, 179; topography of, 180, 183.

Draviḍian, peculiarities of the style of, 178; civilization of, 184; country of, included in the empire of Samudra Gupta, 185.

Droṇaka, a class of forts, 40, 143.

Dundubhi, a round type of building mentioned in *Agni* and *Garuḍa Purāṇas*, 113, 114.

Durga, forts and fortified cities, 97.

Durgā, also called Gaurī and Pārvatī, consort of Śiva, detailed description of the image of, 75, 76.

Dvāra-harmya, gate-house of the fourth court, 52, 154.

Dvārakā, description of the city of, 17.

Dvāra-(lakshaṇa), doors, their description, 56, 57, 92.

Dvāra-māna, measures of the door, 57 77, 96.

Dvāra-prāsāda, gate-house of the third court, 52, 154.

Dvāra-śālā, gate-house of the second court, 52, 154.

Dvāra-śobhā, the beauty of the gate, gate-house belonging to the first court, 52, 154.

Dvāra-vidhāna, doors, their description, 90.

Dvi-bhūmi, two-storeyed buildings, 89, 106.

Dvi-chaturtha-tala-vidhāna, two to four-storeyed buildings, 93; various types of, 50, 111-112.

Dvi-kānta, a main pillar with two minor pillars, 46.

Dvi-vajra, an order of columns, 125, 126, 150, 151.

E

Earth-goddess, description of the image of, 76.

Eka-bhūmi, one storeyed-buildings, 48, 69; eight kinds of, 48-49, 111.

Eka-bhūmi-rodhana, one-storeyed buildings, 106.

Eka-kānta, a type of main pillar with one minor pillar, 46.

Eka-liṅga, a class of phalli, 73

Eka-tala-vidhāna, one-storeyed buildings, 93.

Elaka-padaka-pīṭham, a kind of chair raised on a pedastal, 16.

Ellora, pierced stone windows at, 177.

Entablature, comparative measures and varieties of, 46; noticed in various treatises, 128.

Eran, structural temples at, 196.

Eraṇḍapalla (Khaṇḍesh), limit of the Gupta empire upto, 184.

European styles (of architecture), use of the Græco-Roman orders in, 181.

Eustylos, name of a species of temple, 147.

Eutruria, Tuscan order originated from, 131.

Examination of soil (bhū-parīkshā), 35, 110.

F

Fahieu, visit to Java of, 170; condition of the Gupta empire at the time of the visit of, 192.

Fano, temple at, 160.

Fan-post (vyajana-daṇḍa), description of, 69.

Farmiae, inscriptions relative to the Vitruvia family found in the neighbourhood of, 160.

Fillet, (listel or annulet), name of a Græco-Roman moulding, 127.

Floating city, as mentioned in the *Mahābhārata*, 17.

Flora, a deity, Corinthian type appropriate to, 147.

Fort, noticed in Buddhist literature, 9; eight general varieties of, seven varieties according to situation, 40.

Foundation (garbha-nyāsa), noticed in *Āgamas*, 25; details of, 42; compared with those of Vitruvius, 149.

Foundation stone, laying of, 25, 26, 42, 149.

Frontinus, mention of Vitruvius by, and the treatise of, 134.

Furniture, articles of, as mentioned in great detail in Buddhist literature, 15-16, elsewhere, 66-70.

G

Gadā, the mace of Vishṇu, 71; an octagonal type of building mentioned in *Agni* and *Garuḍa Purāṇas*, 113, 114.

Gaja, an oval type of building mentioned in *Agni* and *Garuḍa Purāṇas*, 113, 114; a class of buildings resembling the elephant, noticed in *Matsya-purāṇa*, 115-116.

Gajaha-mūrti-lakshaṇa, image of Gaṇeśa, 94.

Gala, (grīva, kaṇṭha or kandhara), dado, a moulding, 127.

Gala-kōṭa, neck-peak, a distinguishing feature of a type of gate-houses, 52.

Gala-vidhāna, name of a chapter of the *Amśumadbheda* of Kāśyapa dealing with the neck-part of buildings, 92.

Gāṇava, a class of phalli, 73.

Gaṇḍakī, the river of, forming the boundary of the Janaka country which used to have a special type of twelve-storeyed buildings, 173.

Gandha-mādana, a type of pavilion (*maṇḍapa*), 54.

Gāndhāra, Kushan kings of, 184; sculpture of, 159.

Gandharvas, heavenly musicians, images of, 80.

Gangādhara-mūrti-lakshaṇa, image of Śiva conveying the Ganges on his head, 94.

Ganges, flight of stairs like the waves of, 32.

Ganjam, hill forts of, 184.

Gannamāchārya, stated to be the author of *Mayamata-śilpa-śāstra* 89, 91.

Gaṇya-māna, a comparative measure of heights of the component members of a structure, 124.

Garbha-bhājana, depth of the excavation, 42.

Garbha-gṛiha, shrine, 49; cella or sanctum 53, 73, 83.

Garbha-nyāsa, foundations, 28, 89, 93; different varieties of, 42, 43, 148.

Garga, the original main source of the architectural portions of Varāhamihira's *Bṛihat-saṁhitā*, 162-163; one of the eighteen professors of architecture mentioned in *Matsya-purāṇa*, 164.

Gārga-saṁhitā, an astronomical treatise, containing copious references to architectural matters and known more as a treatise on architecture, 31, 2, 140.

Gārgya, one of several authorities on which the *Vāstu-śāstra* of Sanat-Kumāra was based, 102.

Garuḍa, a mythical bird, genealogy of, 81; his image as the riding animal of Vishṇu, 81-82, 103; an oval type of building, mentioned in *Garuḍa-purāṇa*, 114; also in *Agni-purāṇa* as Garutman, 113; types of buildings as noticed in *Matsya-purāṇa* and *Bṛihat-saṁhitā*, 116, 117.

Garuḍa-Purāṇa, various architectural object described in, 20; compared with other treatises, 110; five classes and forty-five types of buildings noticed in, 113-114, 119; comparative study of, 160; closely connected with *Agni-purāṇa*, 169.

Garutman, an oval type of building noticed in *Agni-purāṇa*, 113; in *Garuḍa* and *Ma'sya Purāṇas* and *Bṛihat-saṁhitā* as Garuḍa, 114, 116, 117.

Gāthās, linguistic style of, 213, 214.

Gautama, one of several authorities on which Sanat-kumra's *Vāstu-śāstra* was based, 102; originator of Buddhism, 191.

Gavāksha, cow's eye, a window, the general plan and different varieties of, 53.

Gaya, Ceylonese monastery at, 192.

Geya, one of the twenty types of buildings described in *Kāmikāgama*, 118.

Ghana, solid parts of gate-houses, 53.

Ghana-māna, measurement by the exterior of an object, 124.

Ghaṭa, a class of buildings described in *Bhavishya-purāṇa* and *Bṛihat-saṁhitā*, 116, 117; a moulding resembling a pot, 126, 127; one of the five mouldings of the shaft, 151, 152, common in *Mānasāra*, *Masya-purāṇa*, and *Bṛihat-saṁhitā*, 168.

Ghṛita-vāri, a moulding of the pedestal of the phallus of Śiva, 74.

Giri-vṛaja, details of the hill fortress at, 9

Girnār, northern style of buildings at, 178.

Gnomon (Śaṅku), its measures and use, etc., 37.

Godhāra, details of the image of, 70.

Golden-hall, as mentioned in *Skanda-purāṇa*, 19-20.

Gomukha-(lakshaṇa), cow's face, apparently an architectural object, 106.

Goose (haṁsa), riding animal of Brahmā, details of its image, 81.

Gopāla, the child Kṛishṇa, temple of, 189.

Gopāna-(ka), name of a moulding, 127.

Gopura, gate-houses, 26, 27, 49, 90, 93, 106, 107, 108, 177; various classes, storeys and other details of, 52-53; reference to windows of, 57; sixteen or seventeen-storeys of, 173; belonging specially to South India, 197.

Gotamī-putra, peculiar style of Sanskrit in the inscriptions of, 213.

Græco-Roman orders, five varieties of, 125; geographical names of, 130, 151; four parts of the entablatures of, 150; eight mouldings of, 152; their striking similarities with the Indian orders, 150—153.

Grāha-kuṇḍala, ear-pendants, 75.

Graha-pratimā, images of planets, 98.

Grāma, villages with hundred enclosures or fortifications as mentioned in Vedic literature, 8; plans, as described in Budddist literature, 9; in *Āgamas*, 24, 28; in *Mānasāra*, 39-10, eight classes of, 39; in *Mayamata*, 89, 106; compared with Roman village as described by Vitruvius, 143-144.

Gṛiha, houses, the types at Vedic period, 6; five kinds in Buddhist period, 10; dimensions and various classes as described in *Mānasāra*, 41-42; foundations of, 42-43; general description of, 47-48; storeys of, 48—50; courts of, 51; compounds of, 52; location and measures of, 55-56; doors and windows of, of 57, 58; articles of furniture of, 15-16, 66-70.

Griha-kānta, a class of five-storeyed buildings, 50, 112.

Griha-kārikā, a treatise, selection of building-sites and examination of soil noticed in, 140.

Griha-mānādhikāra, measurement of houses, name of a chapter in *Mayamata*, 90.

Griha-praveśa, first entry into the house, ceremonies in connection therewith, 56, 90, 96, 97, 102.

Griha-rāja, king of houses, a rectangular type of building as noticed in *Agni*, *Garuḍa* and *Bhavishya Purāṇas*, 113, 114, 116.

Griha-saṁsthāpana, construction of houses, as described by Sanat-Kumāra, 102.

Ground-plan (pada-vinyāsa), as stated in *Kāmikāgama*, 24; thirty-two varieties and other details as given in *Mānasāra*, 37-38.

Guharāja, (see Griharāja), a class of buildings, as described in *Brihat-saṁhitā*, 117.

Guhās, undergronnd buildings, cave-temples, 10-11.

Gujarat, twelve storeyed buildings of, 174; northern type of buildings in, 178.

Guptas, connection of the *Skanda-purāṇa* with, 171, 180; fragments of the style of architecture of, 177; characteristic features of the temples of, 195—196, pointing to earlier style, 196; empire of, 184, 185, 190; dynasty and period of, 190—191; prevailing religion at the time of, 192-193; end of the reign of, 194.

Gupta-vaṁśa, an expression coined to imply the number twenty-seven, its signification, 195.

Gūrjaka (Sphūrjaka), twelve-storeyed buildings in, 51, 113, 174, 198.

Guvā-vriksha, a round type of building as noticed in *Garuḍa-purāṇa*, 114.

H

Halebīd, temple at, 178.

Halls (Śālā), different classes of, 54-55, 25

Haṁsa, goose, an oval type of building as noticed in *Agni*, *Garuḍa*, *Matsya*, and *Bhavishya Purāṇas*, 113, 114, 116; and in *Brihat-saṁhitā*, 117.

Hāra, string of pearls worn round the neck, a chain of 108 strings, 68; a moulding, bead, 127, 152, 168.

Harmya, a magnificent type of storeyed buildings, mentioned in Buddhist literature, 10-11; masonry house, 18; building, being one of the four classes of Vāstu (architecture), 36; royal palace, 57; one of the twenty types of buildings as noticed in *Kāmikāgama*, 113.

Harmya-garbha, large dining hall, as stated in Buddhist literature, 11-12.

Harmya-kānta, a class of seven-storeyed buildings, 50, 112.

Harsha, hero of the *Harsha-charita*, 171 ; period of the reign of, 197.

Harsha-charita, copious references to architectural objects from, 30 ; named after Harsha, 171 ; refers to some *Purāṇas*, 194.

Harsha Vardhana, ruler of Kanauj, 30 ; empire of, 185 ; period of the reign of, 191.

Haryardha-Hara, combined image of Śiva and Vishṇu, 94.

Hasta, cubit, used as a measurement, different kinds of, 35, 121.

Hastinā-pura, Pāñchāla is situated in the neighbourhood of, 174.

Hasti-prishṭha, a type of one-storeyed building, 49, 111.

Head-gears, different kinds of, 65, 98.

Hema-kūṭa, a type of pavilion, 54.

Hema-śilā, golden stone, image of Stone-god, 98.

Hercules, temples of, 146, 147.

Hetrurian Haruspices, his directions regarding the situations of temples, 146.

Hieun Tsang, the Chinese traveller, visited India during Harsha's reign, 30 ; condition of India at the time of his visit, 192.

Himaja, a type of pavilion, 53.

Hima-kānta, a class of seven-storeyed buildings, 50, 112.

Himālayas, the boundary of Madhya-Jesa, 173, 174.

Himavat, one of the ten types of buildings as noticed in *Suprabhedāgama*, 118.

Hinduism, its condition under the Rāshṭrakuṭas, 191 ; at the time of the Guptas, 192—193.

Hindus, stated to have borrowed the practice of excavating temples from Buddhists and Jains, 191.

Holal inscriptions, sixty-four kinds of buildings mentioned in, 4, 130, 171, 176.

Hot-air baths, as described in *Vinaya* texts, 14.

House-furniture, (Prasāda-bhūshaṇa), details of 25, 15-16, 67, 68—70.

Hyderabad, Chālukyan style of buildings in the territory of, 177.

Hypaethros, a type of temples, 147.

I

Idols, made of nine materials, 70 ; process of purification of, 27.

Ikshu-kānta, a class of six-storeyed buildings, 50, 112.

Images, two classes, *sthāvara* (stationary), and *jaṅgama* (movable), 71 ; of sages, 79 ; of devotees, 80 ; of demigods like Yakshas, 80 ; of riding animals and birds, 81—83 ; general description of, 83-84 ; of male and female deities, 84 ; first casting, etc. of, 86-87.

In Antis, one of the different forms of buildings, 147.

Indo Aryan style, otherwise called the Northern or Nāgara), territory, varieties and peculiarities of, 178—180.

Indra, science of architecture originated through, 34; image of, 98; as an authority on architecture called Purandara in the *Purāṇas*, 165.

Indraka (or Chandraka)-bhadraka, a class of cars, 61

Indra-kānta, a class of four-storeyed buildings, 50, 112; a class of gate-houses, 52.

Indra-prastha, description of houses in, 17, 18.

Indra-Sāvarṇi, one of the fourteen Manus, 166.

Indus, monasteries visited by Fahien along the route of, 192.

Ionians, associated with the Ionic order, 131.

Ionic, columns of the order of, 125, 150, 151; identified with an Indian order, 152; a type of doors, 155; pedestal of, 149.

Īśa, Śiva, his temples treated as inferior to those of Vishṇu, 189.

Īśa-kānta, a class of eleven storeyed buildings, 50, 112.

Ishṭaka, brick, mentioned by Pāṇini, 33; measures of, 43.

Isis, temple of, 146.

Īśvara, Śiva, mentioned along with Vishṇu, 187.

Īśvara-kānta, a class of four-storeyed buildings, 50 112.

Italy, Tuscan and Composite orders originated in, 126.

J

Jain, images of, their details, 76, 185, 186, 187; authors of, 211.

Jainism, inferior treatment of, 187; the time of toleration of, 190, 191, 192, 194.

Jaipur, the territory of the Virāṭa type of twelve-storeyed buildings in the vicinity of, 173.

Jala-dhārā, water-passage, drain, a part of the pedestal of the phallus of Śiva, 74.

Jala-durga, water-fort, 40, 143.

Jala-dvāra, water-passage, drainage, drain, 39,57.

Jālaka, a screen, perforated window, 53, 92.

Janaka, a type of twelve-storeyed buildings, 51, 113, 175, 198; its territory, 178.

Jana-kānta, a class of eight-storeyed buildings, of twelve-storeyed buildings, 50, 51, 112, 113.

Janman, plinth, name of a moulding, part of a pedestal, 44, 127.

Jaṭā, a kind of head-dress, details thereof, 65.

Jātakas, references to architectural matters from, 10.

Jāti, a classification of buildings, its characteristic features, 41-42, 48-49, 57, 110, 118, 119, 147; a class of phalli, 73.

Java, Fahien's visit to, 170.

Jaya-bhadra, a type of pavilion (*maṇḍapa*), 119.

Jayada, a formula of height, 55, 124.

Jayāla, a pavilion (*maṇḍapa*) for a summer residence, 54.

Jayanta, name of a quarter in a ground-plan, 189.

Jayanti, a moulding, 126, 151.

Jayantika, a type of one-storeyed buildings, 49; also called Vaijayantika, 111.

Jinaka, thrones of, 63.

Jina-maṇḍana, a Jain author, 211.

Jina-pratishṭhā, consecration of Jain images, 104.

Jīrṇoddhāra, repairs of temples, 98, 104, 108.

Julius Cæsar, patron of Vitruvius, 19, 160.

Juno, temple of, 146, 148.

Jupiter, temple of, 146.

Jyotish-kānta, a class of six-storeyed buildings, 50, 112.

Jyotisha-lakshaṇa, astrology, name of a chapter in the *Śilpa-śāstra* of Maṇḍana, 104.

Jyotis-sāra, an example of works ending in *sāra*, 2.

K

Kailāśa, a class of three-storeyed buildings, 50, 111; a round type of buildings having different varieties, as noticed in *Agni* and *Garuḍa Purāṇas*, 13, 114; a type of nine-storyed buildings as noticed in *Matsya-purāṇa*, 115; a type of eight-storeyed buildings as noticed in *Bhavishya-purāṇa* and *Bṛihat-saṁhitā*, 116, 117; another type noticed in *Suprabhedāgama*, 118; identical in several works, 168.

Kākāshṭa, a kind of couch (*paryaṅka*), 76.

Kāla-dahana, image of Śiva, 101, 107.

Kālaha-mūrti-lakshaṇa, image of Kālaha, 94.

Kāla-kūṭa, deadly poison, a peculiar mark on the image of Śiva, 72

Kāla-mukha, a class of phalli, 72.

Kalaśa, a round type of building as noticed in *Agni* and *Garuḍa Purāṇas*, 113, 114.

Kāla-yūpa, one of the authorities on which *Mānasāra* was based, 165.

Kalhaṇa, his history of Kashmir wherein many details of architecture are met with, 31, 78.

Kālidāsa, the famous Sanskrit poet in whose works many architectural details are mentioned, 22, 32.

Kāliṅga-(kānta), an oval type of cars and chariots, 61; a distinct style of architecture, 130; one of the two branches of the Vesara style 131, 176; a class of twelve-storeyed buildings, 50, 113, 173, 174, 198; topography of, 174; comparative size of, 175; conquered by Aśoka, 183.

Kalka-saṁskāra, preparation of mixtures, cement, 94.

Kalpa-Sūtras, of which the Śulva-sūtras deal with the details of altars or *vedis*, 7.

Kalpa-vṛiksha, the desire-fulfilling tree, ornamental tree, a decorative device for a throne and other architectural objects, 64, 78.

Kalyāṇa-sundara, image of, 94, 100, 107.

Kalyāṇī, Chalukyas of, 191.

Kamala, a class of six-storeyed buildings, 50, 112.

Kamalāṅga, a class of three-storeyed buildings, 50, 111.

Kāmandakīya-(nīti-śāstra), its similarities with the *Śukra-nīti*, 170; a politechnical treatise, 132.

Kāmikāgama, a large variety of architectural subjects systematically treated in, 23, 24—26, 128; dimensions of storeys defined in, 41, 42, 147; comparative study of, 110, 119, 160, various classifications and types of buildings described in, 118; references to *tāla-māna* from, 123; three styles of architecture noticed in, 131.

Kampa, fillet, a moulding, 74, 127.

Kampa-bandha, a class of bases, 128.

Kampa-dvāra, a kind of moving door, 92.

Kampa-karṇa, a moulding, 128.

Kampana, fillet, name of a moulding, 127.

Kampilla, city of, 9.

Kāmpilya, capital of South Pāñchāla, 174.

Kāmya, one of the five classes of *prā-kāra* (court), 51.

Kanarak, the style of temples at, 179.

Kanauj, capital of Harsha-vardhana, 185.

Kāñchī, conquered by Samudra Gupta 184.

Kandhara, the neck, a moulding of th pedestal, 74.

Kaṅgu, panicum italicum, one of the ten kinds of cereals used for the foundations of buildings, 43.

Kaṅkāla-mūrti, image of a skeleton, 94.

Kaṅkaṇa, bracelet, an ornament, 67.

Kāntāra, a class of six-storeyed buildings, 50, 112.

Kaṇṭha, neck, a moulding, 126, 151.

Kāntika, (also called Antika), name of a class of two-storeyed buildings, 50, 111.

Kapiñjala-saṁhitā, a treatise, architectural details from, 108.

Kapota, a pigeon, a moulding, 127.

Kārāgāra, the jail, details of, 58.

Ka (kā)raṇāgama, references to architectural objects from, 26; process of casting an image described in, 87; references to *tāla-māna* from, 123.

Karaṇādhikāra-(lakshaṇa), name of a chapter in Karaṇāgama, dealing with objects like columns, couches, chairs, head-gear, etc., 28.

Karaṇḍa, a kind of head-dress, used by female deities, kings, and semi-divine beings, 65, 80.

Kārmuka, a class of villages, 39, 143.

Karṇa, ear, name of a moulding 127.

Karṇa-padma, name of a moulding, 128.

Karshaṇa, ploughing of the site selected for a building, 92.

Kāśmīrian architecture, details of, 31.

Kāśyapa, author of the *Aṁśumad-bheda*, 28, 99; father of Garuḍa, 81; references to architectural objects from, 106, 140.

Kaṭaka, an armlet, 67.

Kaṭi-sūtra, an ornament, a chain worn round the loins, 68.

Kaumārī, one of the seven mothers, image of, 75.

Kaumudī, a treatise, references to architectural objects from, 108.

Kauśāmbī, capital of Vaṁśaka or the country of Vatsa kings, 173; noticed in Buddhist literature, (see Kośāmbi), 9.

Kauśika, a pavilion used as a horse-stable, 54.

Kauṭilīya-Artha-śāstra, ambiguous meaning of the title of, 2; references to architectural measurement from 122; a polytechnical treatise, 132.

Kautuka-bandhana, experimental yoking for the purpose of ploughing the building-site, 27.

Kendra, centre (of a circle), name of a moulding, 127.

Kerala, a class of twelve-storeyed buildings, 50, 113, 173, 175, 198; topography of, 174.

Kerala-putras, independent of Magadha at the time of Asoka, 183.

Keśa-bandha, a kind of head-dress, used by female deities and queens of certain classes of kings, 65.

Keśara, a class of single-storeyed buildings with front tabernacles in the centre, 49, 111; a class of three-storeyed buildings, 50, 111.

Keśaryādi-prāsāda, buildings of Keśari and other classes, 104.

Keśava, a name of Vishṇu, temple of, 189.

Keyūra, armlet worn on the upper-arm, 67.

Khaḍga, an octagonal type of building noticed in *Garuḍa* and *Agni Purāṇas*, 114, 115.

Khajurāho, the style of buildings at, 178, 179.

Khanana-vidhi, ploughing the soil of the site selected for a building, 96.

Khaṅjarīṭa, cage of, 70.

Khāta-śaṅku, wooden stakes posted in different parts of the foundation of a building, 37.

Kharvaṭa, name of a class of towns, 40, 143.

Kheṭa, name of a class of towns, 40, 143.

Kīla, axle-bolt, nail at the top of an object, 27, 60.

Kiṅkiṇī-valaya, bracelet fixed with little bells, 67.

Kinnaras, description of the images of, 80.

Kiraṇa-tantra, a treatise, the eight mouldings noticed in, 126, 127, 152; the five orders of columns described in, 150, 151.

Kirīṭa, diadem, crown worn by minor gods and certain classes of kings, 65, 67.
Kishku-hasta, small cubit, equal to twenty-four aṅgulas, a measurement, 35.
Kochchham, cane-bottomed chair, as stated in Buddhist literature. 16.
Kodrava, paspalum scrobiculatum, one of the ten kinds of cereals used for the foundations of buildings, 43.
Kola-(ka), a kind of fort, 42, 143.
Kolleru, lake of, 184.
Koṇa, a class of buildings noticed in *Kāmikāgama*, 118.
Kośala, in the valley of Mahānadī, conquired by Samudragupta, 184.
Kośāmbi, (see Kauśāmbi), city of, its architectural details, 9.
Koshṭha, a kind of walled town or fortress, 42.
Koshṭha-stambha, an order of columns, a pilaster, 45, 129.
Kośi, river of, 173.
Koṭṭur, hill forts of, 184.
Kṛishṇa-(lakshaṇa), image of, 107; the pose of, 86.
Kshaṇika, an idol for temporary worship, a class of phalli, 78.
Kshema, a class of buildings noticed in *Kāmikāgama*, 118.
Kshepaṇa, projection, a moulding, 74, 127.
Kshepaṇāmbuja, name of a moulding, 128.
Kshudra-kampa, name of a moulding, 128.
Kshudra-nāsī, vestibule, a moulding, 52.
Kshudra-padma, small cyma, name of a moulding, 128.
Kubjākāra, hump-backed, image of Agastya, 79.
Kubjaka, hump-backed, name of a class of towns, 143.
Kuḍmala, bud, the shape of the topmost part of the phallus, 74.
Kuḍya-stambha, pilaster, 45, 125.
Kukkuṭa, cock, cage of, 70.
Kukshi, navel, a part of the chariot, 60.
Kukshi-bandha, a class of bases, 128.
Kula-dhāraṇa, a type of pavilion for storing perfumes in, 54.
Kulāla, phasianus gallus, cage of, 70.
Kulattha, dolichas uniflorus, a cereal used for the foundations of buildings, 43.
Kumāra, one of the eighteen professors of architecture noticed in *Matsya-purāṇa*, 164.
Kumāra Gupta, reign of, 192.
Kumāra-sambhava, a jewelled ornament (muktā-kalāpa) noticed in, 67.
Kumbha, a class of nine-storeyed buildings, described in *Matsya-purāṇa*, 116; a moulding, 126, 127, 151.
Kumbha-bandha, a class of bases, 128.
Kumbha-karṇa, king of Medapāṭha, probably king Kumbha of Mewar, 103.
Kumbha-stambha, a column with jug-shaped capital, a type of columns, 45, 125, 126, 150, 151.

Kumbha-tala-(lakshaṇa), capitals of columns, name of a chapter in *Aṁśumad-bheda* of Kāśyapa, 92.

Kumuda, torus or astragal, name of a moulding, 127.

Kumuda-bandha, a class of bases, 128.

Kuṇḍala, a kind of head-dress, used by certain female deities and queens, 65.

Kuṇḍala, ear-ring, 67.

Kuṇḍika, water-pot, an attribute of Brahman, 71.

Kuñjara, a type of buildings noticed in *Bhavishya-purāṇa* and *Bṛihat-saṁhitā*, 116, 117.

Kuñjarāksha, elephant's eye, a particular kind of window, 53.

Kuñjarīya, cage of, 70.

Kūpa, wells, architectural details of, 97.

Kūrma, one of the ten incarnations of Vishṇu, temple of, 52.

Kushan, kings of, their relation with Samudra Gupta, 184.

Kūṭa-chakra, certain astronomical calculation made in connection with construction of buildings, 104.

Kūṭādi-lakshaṇa, finials and other objects at the top of buildings, 93.

L

Laghu-śilpa-jyotis-sāra, an example of works ending in *sāra*, 2.

Lakshmaṇa, image of, 108.

Lakshmī, goddess of fortune, her image described in detail, 74, 75, 98.

Lalita-vistara, a treatise, peculiar style of Sanskrit in, 213.

Lamba-māna, measurement along the plumb-line, a kind of linear measurement, 77, 121.

Laṅkā, architectural description of, 17.

Likshā, nit, a unit of measurement, 35.

Līlāvati, a work on astronomy, reference to important architectural matters from, 32, 172; author of, 165.

Limbs, defects of, 87.

Liṅga, phallus of Śiva, various classes and architectural details of, 72—74, 90.

Liṅga-lakshaṇoddhāra, unearthing of the phallus, 93.

Liṅga-purāṇa, references to architectural objects from, 21.

Liṅgodbhava-(lakshaṇa), revelation of the phallus of Śiva, 94.

Lion, vehicle of the goddess Durgā, 83.

Lokajña, one of the authorities on architecture mentioned in *Māna-sāra*, 165.

Lupā, an architectural object, details of, 47, 48.

M

Machine-room, as mentioned in *Ṛig-veda* together with some architectural details, 6.

Madhūchchhishṭa-vidhāna, casting of an image in wax, different processes and their details, 86-87.

Madhya-deśa, the middle country, topography and twelve-storeyed buildings of, 173, 174, 175.

Madhya-kānta, a class of twelve-storeyed buildings, once prevalent in *Madhya-deśa*, 50, 113, 173, 198.

Madhya-nīhāra, also called Madhyama-hāra, the third or middle of the five courts into which the compound of an edifice is divided, 51, 154.

Madhya-raṅga, the middle theatre, the enclosed quadrangular courtyard, 63-64.

Madurā, apparently southern variety of the name of Mathurā of North India, 180-181.

Madhurā (thura), city of, its architectural details as given in Buddhist literature, 9.

Magadha, its relation with *Daśa-kumāra-charita* and *Mānasāra*, 171, 167 ; topography and twelve-storeyed buildings of, 173, 175, 198 ; its relation with southern powers in Aśoka's time, 183.

Māgadha-kānta, a class of twelve-storeyed buildings, once prevalent in Magadha, 51, 113.

Mahābhārata, references to architectural objects from, 18-19, 81 ; description of the architect Maya's work in, 172.

Mahā-Govinda, an architect who built several cities and fortresses as noticed in Buddhist literature, 9.

Mahā-gopura, great gate house, of the fifth or last of five courts into which the compound of an edifice is divided, 52, 154.

Mahā-kāla, Śiva, temple at Ujjayini of, one of the best known phalli in India, 72.

Mahā-kānta, a class of eight-storeyed buildings, 50, 112.

Mahā-maryādā, the extreme boundary, the last or fifth court of a large compound, 51, 154.

Mahāmbuja, large cyma, a moulding, 128.

Mahā-nadī, the river of, the territorial boundary of the Northern style of architecture, 178 ; its valley was conquered by Samudra Gupta, 178.

Mahā-padma-(ka), a round type of building noticed in *Agni* and *Garuḍa Purāṇas*, 113, 114.

Mahārāja (or Adhirāja), one of the nine classes of kings, 57, 181 ; kingdoms, kingly qualities, strength, powers and other characteristics of 59 182.

Mahā-sudasana-sutta, some architectural objects explained in, 13.

Mahā-tantra, an authority on which *Mānasāra* was based, 165.

Mahā-vagga, references to architectural matters from, 10, 11, 13, 15, 16.

Mahā-vrata, a class of phalli, 72.

Mahendra (or Narendra), one of the nine classes of kings, 57, 181 ; kingdoms, kingly qualities, strength, powers and other characteristics of, 59, 182.

Mahendra-giri, the hill forts of, conquered by Samudra Gupta, 184.

Māhendrī, Consort of Indra, one of the seven mothers, image of, 75.

Māheśvarī, Consort of Śiva, image of, 98.

Mahī-(śakti), the earth-goddess, the image of, 74, 75, 76.

Mahotsava, a throne for great festivals, 62.

Majjanālaya, bath-room, 58.

Makara, crocodiles, their figures used as ornament for an arch, as well as for the ears, 63, 67, 78.

Makara-bhūshaṇa, car-pendant decorated with *makaras*, 67.

Makara-toraṇa, arches marked with crocodiles, 78, 63.

Mālā, garland or necklace, 68.

Malabar (or Keralas), the boundary of Drāviḍa country, 174.

Mālikā, a class of buildings, sub-divided into :—
Lāṅgala-mālikā,
Maulika-mālikā and
Padma-mālikā, etc., 25 ;
a round type of building, otherwise called Maṅika, 113.

Mālwa, apparently was known to *Mānasāra*, 171 ; Northern style of architecture in, 178 ; a fictitious king, Mānasāra, of, 197, 198.

Mālyaja, a type of pavilion (*maṇḍapa*), 53.

Māna, a kind of measurement, the length of an image from foot to top of the head, 76, 121.

Māna-bodha, an authority on architecture on which *Mānasāra* was based, 165.

Māna-kalpa, an authority on architecture on which *Mānasāra* was based, 165.

Mānāṅgula, a kind of finger measurement, a unit of measurement, 77 84, 122.

Māna-saṁgraha, system of measurement, name of a chapter in *Agastya*, 100.

Mānasāra, the subject matters of, 1 ; the other titles of, 1-2 ; ambiguous title, implying a treatise, an author, and a class of Professors of architecture, 2-3 ; mentioned in *Daśa-kumāra-charita* as a fictitious King of Malwa, 3-4, 170-171 ; seems to be implied in *Agni-purāṇa*, 4, 20, 169, and in some inscriptions, 4, 171 ; plan of Ayodhya correspond to the town-plan given in, 17, 18 ; compared with *Kāmikāgama*, chapter by chapter, 24—28 ; with *Suprabedhāgama*, 28 ; as in *Rāmāyana* and *Uttara-rāma-charita*, the engineer, Nala, is recognized as an architect in, 32 ; division of compound in, 33 ; Summary of the contents of, 34—88 ; compared with *Mayamata*-chapter by chapter, 89—91 ; with *Aṁśumad-bheda* of Kāśyapa, 92—95 ; with *Viśvakarma-śilpa*, 96—99 ; with *Agastya*, 100-101 ; with *Sanat-kumāra*, 102 ; with Maṇḍana's *Śilpa-śāstra*, 103—105 ; quoted in a compilation,

106; oldest and complete extant record on architecture, its position among *Śilpa-śāstras*, 109; various architectural divisions described in, 110-111; ninety-eight types of buildings classified under twelve-storeys, 111—113; its position among *Purāṇas* including *Bṛihat-saṁhitā* and *Agamas*, 110, 119-120, 131—133, 162—169; details of measurements described in, 121—124; columns and mouldings described in, 125—129; three main styles of architecture recognized in, 130-131; compared with Vitruvius, 134—159; compared with *Bṛihat-saṁhitā* by chapter and verse, 161—162; the authorities on architecture recognized in, 165; its relation with Astronomical treatises in regard to orientation of buildings, 172-173; significance of its ten geographical divisions of twelve-storeyed buildings, 173, 175-176; and three geographical divisions of of the styles of architecture, 176, characteristic features of these styles, 176, 177—181; the geographical divisions indicate an empire, 181—183; nine divisions of royalty, 181; the extent of this empire, corresponding to the Gupta Empire, 183—185; prevailing religion at the time of, 185—190, identical with that prevailing in Gupta times, 190—191; state of all things jointly point to the Gupta times, 191—195; 197-198; examples of the ungrammatical Sanskrit used in, 199—210; similar language met with elsewhere, 211—213; history of the origin of such language, 213-214.

Mānasāraka (? Manasāraka or Malasāraka), according to (the rules laid down in) *Mānasāra*, 16).

Mānasarpa (? for Mānasāra), an architect, 171.

Māna-sūtrādi, on measuring strings, etc., name of a chapter in *Aṁśumad-bheda* of Kāśyapa, 93.

Mānava-sāra, another title of the work *Mānasāra*, 2.

Māna-vid, an authority on which *Mānasāra* was based, 165.

Mañcha-bandha, a type of bases, 128.

Mañcha-bhadra, a type of pedestal, 128.

Mañcha-kānta, a class of four-storeyed buildings, 50, 112.

Maṇḍaleśa, a class of kings, 57, 59; palaces, thrones, crown etc. of, 181; relative position of, 182.

Maṇḍana, architectural treatise of, 103, 104; historical importance of, 104-105.

Mandara, a square type of buildings as noticed in *Agni* and *Garuḍa Purāṇas*, 113; a type of twelve-storeyed buildings as noticed in *Matsya-purāṇa*, 115; a type of ten-storeyed buildings as noticed in *Bhavishya-purāṇa* and *Brihat-saṁhitā*, 116, 117; another type noticed in *Suprabhedāgama*, 118.

Maṇḍapas, open-roofed sheds, as referred to in Buddhist literature, 11; pavilions used as council halls, inns, etc., 30; for bath, bed, assembly, horses, cows, musicians, dancing girls, etc., 52, 97; four classes of, 119; connotations of, 155; architectural details of, 179; noticed in various treatises, 90, 93.

Maṇḍi, a moulding, 126, 151.

Mandira, a class of buildings as noticed in *Garuḍa-purāṇa*, 114.

Maṅgala, a throne for the first stage of coronation, 62.

Mañjūshā, basket, chest, box, architectural details of, 68; made of timber or iron; square, rectangular or circular in shape; three kinds: *parṇa-mañjūsha*, 2; *Taila-mañjūsha*, *vastra-mañjūshā*, 69.

Maṇi-bandha kalāpa, jewelled ornament worn on the fore-arm, 67.

Maṇi-bhadra, a class of pavilions, 119.

Maṇika, an oval class of buildings having nine varieties as noticed in *Agni* and *Garuḍa Purāṇas*, 113, 114.

Manonmanī, goddess of love, her image described in detail, 75, 76.

Mānopakaraṇa, elements and system of measurement, 24, 89, 93, 137.

Mantarāja, his kingdom conquered by Samudragupta, 184.

Manu, a puzzling name, 4; one of the four heavenly architects, 35, 165; one of the several authorities on which Sanat-kumara's *Vāstu-śāstra* was based, 102; and the architectural portions of *Bṛihat-saṁhitā* were taken from, 163, 165; fourteen in number, 166; a generic name, 167; surname, 171; condition of the country at the time of, 183.

Manu-saṁhitā, references to architectural measure from, 122.

Manu-sāra, a possible (correct) reading for *Mānasāra*, 4.

Mānusha, a class of phalli, 73.

Mānya-kheṭa, Rāshṭrakuṭas of, 191.

Marāla, goose or duck, architectural details of the cage for, 70.

Marcus Vitruvius Pollio, the full name of the author of the treatise known as Vitruvius, 158.

Mārkaṇḍeya-purāṇa, the time of, 194.

Mars, temples of, 146, 147.

Māsha, phaseolus radiatus, used as a material for foundations of buildings, 43.

Masūraka, entablature in connection with *Madhya-raṅga*, 64.

Mathurā, Fa-hien's reference to monastries along the road to, 192; Jain inscriptions from, 212; architectural details of the ancient city of, 9.

Mātrāṅgula, a unit of measurement, 77, 122.

Matsya, one of the ten incarnations of Vishṇu, 52; king Virāṭa's capital, 174.

Matsya-purāṇa, architectual matters described in, 19, 114—116, 121, 126; identical with *Bhavishya-purāṇa*, *Bṛihat-saṁhitā* and *Kāmikāgama* in respect of certain matters, 22, 23, 115—118, 125, 126-127, 150, 152, 163; *Śilpa-śāstra* of Maṇḍana acknowledges the authority of, 103, 104; comparative study of, 110, 114—118, 119, 160, 164-165, 167, 168, 169, 170; details of twenty types of buildings given in, 115-116, 119; architectural and sculptural measures given in, 121—123; five orders and eight component mouldings described in, 125, 126-127, 150, 152; eighteen authorities on architecture recognized in, 164-165; age of, 194, 198.

Matsyākāra, eyes are stated to be shaped like fish, 84.

Mauli, a kind of head-dress, used by the love-goddess Ratī, 65.

Maulika, a type of pavilion (*maṇḍapa*) of six faces, 54; a class of halls (*śālā*), 55.

Maushalya, an authority on architecture, 107.

Maya-(Asura), recognized as an architect in *Mahābhārata*, 17-18, 166, 172; one of the four heavenly architects, as stated in *Mānasāra*, 85, 165; the architectural treatises attributed to, 89—90; Viśvakarma's treatise based on, 97; Agastya's relation with, 101; Sanat-kumāra's treatise was based on, 102; recognised as an authority in *Saṁgraha*, 166, in *Bṛihat-saṁhitā*, 163, 165 and in *Matsya-purāṇa*, 164, 165; seems to be a generic name, 167.

Maya-mata, treatises ascribed to Maya, 2, 89, 128; compared with *Mānasāra*, 89—91; its relation with other treatises, 99; as mentioned in *Saṁgraha*, 106.

Measuring-string (rajju), its relation with other units of measurement, 35.

Megha-kānta, a class of ten-storeyed buildings, 50, 112.

Megha-varṇa, king of Ceylon, 191.

Mekhalā, belt, girdle, an ornament, 68.

Mercury, temple of, 146.

Meru, a type of building mentioned in Maṇḍana's treatise, 104; in *Agni* and *Garuḍa Purāṇas*, 113; in *Matsya-purāṇa*, 115; in *Bhavishya-purāṇa*, 116; in *Bṛihatsaṁhitā*, 117; in *Suprabhedāgama*, 118; in *Kāmikāgama* (as Meru-kūṭa), 118; in *Mānasāra* (as Meru-kānta), 50, 111; further reference to, 168, 169.

Meruja, a type of pavilion used as a library-room, 54.

Meru-kānta, a class of three-storeyed buildings, 50, 111, 168, 169.

Meru-kūṭa, a class of buildings as mentioned in *Kāmikāgama*, 118.

Meru-tuṁga, a Jain author, 211.

Mewār, king of, 103.

Milanda-panha, possible identity with the Questions of Menander, 159.

Minerva, temple of, 141, 146, 147.

Mīrābai, queen of Mewar, patron of Rāja-vallabha-Maṇḍana, 103

Miśra, a kind of pillars which are made of two materials, 116; a classification of buildings based on building-materials, 110, 118.

Miśra-durga, mixed fort, 40, 143.

Miśraka-lakshaṇa, a chapter in Maṇḍana's treatise, 103.

Miśra-kalaśa, a chapter in Maṇḍana's treatise, 104.

Miśra-kalpa, a kind of ornament, made of leaves, jewels, etc., to be used by gods, Chakra-vartin and other classes of kings, 67.

Miśrita (or Śubhaṅkarī), the Composite order of India, 153 125.

Mithilā, city of, meagre architectural details from Buddhist literature, 9; from *Māhābhārata*, 17; capital of Videha, 173.

Monasteries (*maṭha*), as described in a chapter of *Kāmikāgama*, 27; stated to have been visited by Fa-hien along the road from the Indus to Mathura, 192.

Monopteral, a circular type of building, 147.

Mṛich-chhakaṭika, a drama, architectural details from, 32, 52.

Mṛiga, one of the deities to whom offerings are made in connection with building a house, 38.

Mṛiga-nābhi-biḍāla, musk cat, architectural details of the cage of, 70.

Mṛiṇāla (mṛiṇālikā), name of a moulding, looking like the stalk of a lotus, 127.

Mṛit-saṁskāra-(lakshaṇa), process of casting images in earth, 97, 100.

Mudga, phaseolus mungo, one of the materials of which foundations of buildings are built, 43.

Mukha-bhadra, its meaning, 48, 49.

Mukta-prapāṅga, open quadrangular courtyard connected with a tank, its description, 63-64.

Mukulī, a round type of building as mentioned in *Garuḍa-purāṇa*, 114.

Mukuṭa, a kind of head-dress, 65.

Mūla, the root, a lower member of the phallus, 78; a moulding, 127.

Mūla-bera, principal idol in a temple, 77.

Mūlikā, a material used in casting an image, 86.

Mūrdheshṭaka, brick at the top, an ornament upon the dome, 93.

Mūrdhikā, a moulding, 126, 151.

Mūrdhnīshṭaka, ornamental brick at the topmost parts of buildings, 26.

Mūrti-kānta, a class of five-storeyed buildings, 50, 112.

Mushṭi-bandha, a moulding, 126, 127, 151.

Mushṭika, an octagonal type of building as mentioned in *Garuḍa-purāṇa*, 114.

Myron, a sculptor, 141.

N

Nabhasvān-bhadraka, a type of chariots, 61.

Nāga-bandha, a type of window, 53.

Nagara, a class of towns, 40, 89, 93, 143.

Nāgara, one of the three styles of architecture, others being Drāviḍa and Vesara, 24, 48, 110, 118, 119; 130, 131; characteristic features of, 176; a square type of chariots, 61; a type of phallus, 78; the territory covered by, 180; identification of the territory, 181, 182, 183; geographical division of, 198.

Nāgara-khaṇḍa, a portion of *Skanda-purāṇa*, stated to have been named after the Nāgara Brahmins, 180.

Nāgarānandana-pura, stated to have been the home-country of the Nāgara-Brahmins, 180.

Nāgdā, style of architecture at, 178, 179.

Nagnajit, an architect, mentioned in *Bṛihat-saṁhitā*, 131, 163, 165; in *Matsya-purāṇa*, 164, 165.

Nakshatra-māla, an ornament, a necklace of twenty-seven pearls, 68.

Nakula, mongoose, cage of, 70.

Nala, hero of the famous episode of Nala-Damayantī, references to lofty balcony described in this connection in the Epics, 18; son of the architect Viśvakarman and engineer of the bridge connecting India with Ceylon, 32; one of the thirty-two architects mentioned in *Mānasāra*, 165.

Nāla, drain, details of, 64, 92, 106.

Nālikā-garbha, rectangular halls, as stated in Buddhist literature 11.

Nalīnaka, a type of building, as mentioned in *Suprabhedāgama*, 118.

Nandana, a square type of buildings, as mentioned in *Garuḍa-purāṇa*, 113; called Nandika in *Agni-purāṇa*, 113; a type of seven-storeyed building as mentioned in *Matsya-purāṇa*, 115; another type mentioned in *Bhavishya-purāṇa*, 116; and *Bṛihat-saṁhitā*, 117.

Nanda-vṛitta, a type of pavilions (*maṇḍapa*), 119.

Nandika, a square type of buildings as stated in *Agni-purāṇa*, (elsewhere called Nandana), 113.

Nandīsa, one of the eighteen architects mentioned in *Matsya-purāṇa*, 164.

Nandi-varddhana, a square type of buildings as mentioned in *Agni* and *Garuḍa Purāṇas*, 113; seven-storeyed as stated in *Matsya-purāṇa*, 115; another type as mentioned in *Bhavishya-purāṇa*, 116; and *Bṛihat-saṁhitā*, 117.

Nandyāvarta, a class of villages, 39, 143; a kind of wood joinery, 47; a class of six-storeyed buildings, 50, 112; a kind of windows, 53; a type of buildings, 118; a type of pavilions (*maṇḍapa*), 119.

Napuṁsaka, a neuter class of buildings, 118.

Nārada, an architect under whose supervision some chariots are stated to have been built, 20; one of the sources on which *Mānasāra* was based, 34, 165; an architectural treatise of, 107, 140; one of the eighteen Professors of architecture mentioned in *Matsya-purāṇa*, 164.

Nārada-purāṇa, references to architectural matters from, 21.

Narasiṁha-gupta-Bālāditya, religion of, 192; political position of, 195.

Nārāyaṇa, architectural treatise of, 107; temple of, 189.

Narendra, one of the nine classes of kings, 57; qualities and court, etc. of, 59; palace, throne, crown, etc. of, 181; rank of, 182.

Narochchatā, height of man in different ages, 98.

Nāsi, nose, a moulding, 127.

Nasik, style of architecture at, 179.

Nāsikā, nose, wings of buildings, 98.

Nāṭaka, a moulding, 127.

Naṭeśvra, Śiva, image of, 100.

Nava-kamma, new work in constructing a Buddhist monastery, 11.

Naya, one of the thirty-two authorities on architecture recognized in *Mānasāra*, 165.

Nayanonmilana, chiselling of the eye of an image, 34, 88.

Nīḍa, nests, for domestic birds and animals, architectural details of, 68.

Nigama, a kind of fort, 40, 148.

Nīla-kaṇṭha, peacock, cage of, 70.

Nīla-parvata, otherwise called Nishadha, a class of buildings, as mentioned in *Suprabhedāgama*, 118.

Nimna, drip, a part of the pedestal, 74; a moulding, 127.

Nirukta, references to architectural matters from, 33.

Nishadha, a class of building, as mentioned in *Suprabhedāgama*, 118.

Nishadaja, a kind of pavilion (*maṇḍapa*), 53.

Nishpāva-bīja, bean, nose to be shaped like, 84.

Nityārchana, throne for use in daily worship, 62.

Nityotsava, throne used for ordinary festivities, 62.

Nivāta-bhadraka, a class of chariots, 61.

Northern style, identification, territory and features of, 180—181.

Nṛitta-lakshaṇa, image of dancing Śiva, 106.

Nṛitta-maṇḍapa, pavilion in front of a temple where religious music is performed, 119.

Nṛitta-mūrti-lakshaṇa, image of Śiva in dancing pose, 97.

Nṛi-siṁha, temple of, 189.

Nūpura, anklet, an ornament, 6

Nymphs of fountains, temples of, 147.

O

Offerings, to deities in connection with building a house, 38.

One-peaked building, as mentioned in Buddhist literature, 11.

Orders, Indian and European, 150.

Ornaments, of the body, details of, 66—68.

Ovolo, a moulding, 127, 152.

Oxus, Samudragupta's diplomatic relation with kings who ruled on the banks of, 184.

P

Pachanālaya, kitchen, 58.

Pāda, trunk of the ornamental tree, 64; column, 89.

Pāda-bandha, a kind of throne for a class of kings called Astra-grāhin, 63.

Pada-(devatā)-vinyasa, ground-plan, 89.

Pāda-jāla-bhūshaṇa, net-like ornament worn on the feet, 68.

Padma, a type of pavilions (*maṇḍapa*) for storing flowers, 54; a moulding of the pedestal, 74; a round type of buildings mentioned in *Agni* and *Garuḍa Purāṇas*, 113, 114, three-storeyed as stated in *Matsya-purāṇa*, 116, another type as mentioned in *Bhavisya-purāṇa* and *Bṛihat-saṁhitā*, 116, 117; a moulding, 127, 152, 153.

Padma-bandha, a kind of throne, 62, 63; a type of base, 128.

Padmaka, a class of village, 39, 143; a type of pavilions used as temple-kitchens, 54.

Padma-kampa, a moulding, 128.

Padma-kānta, one of the five Indian orders of columns, 45, 125, 126, 150, 151; a class of six-storeyed buildings, 50, 112.

Padma-keśara, a kind of throne for gods and kings, 62; a type of base, 128.

Padmāsana, lotus seat, a kind of throne for gods, 62.

Pādukā, foot-wears, 97; a moulding, 127.

Palaces, with thousand pillars and gates as stated in *Ṛig-veda*, and *Atharva-veda*, 6; as described in *Harsha-charita*, 30; as given in *Mānasāra*, 57-58; the storeys of, 42.

Palakka, Samudragupta's conquest of, 184.

Pālikā-stambha, a pillar edged like a measuring pot, a type of column, 45, 125, 126, 150, 151.

Pallaṅka, bedestead, as described in Buddhist literature, 15-16.

Pāñchāla, a class of twelve-storeyed buildings, 50, 113, 198; topography of, 173-174; comparative size of the buildings of, 175.

Pāñcha-janya, conch-shell, one of the attributes of Vishṇu, 71.

Pāṇḍyas, independent of Magadha at Aśoka's time, 183.

Pāṇini, the famous Sanskrit grammarian, references to architectural matters from, 33; its position in literature, 133; certain rules of, 211.

Pañjara, a class of seven-storeyed buildings, 50, 112; cages of various descriptions, 68, 69-70; a kind of couch, 36.

Paṅka-durga, clay-fort, 40, 143.

Pāpanāth, style of architecture at, 177.

Paramāṇu, atom, the lowest unit of measurement, 35.

Paramārtha, a Buddhist author, 192.

Parama-sādhika, one of the thirty-two ground-plans, 38, 56, 58.

Parārtha, for others, a type of phalli used for public worship, 73.

Pythius, the architect of the temple of Minerva at Priene, 141.

Parāsarīyaka, one of the thirty-two authorities on architecture mentioned in *Mānasāra*, 165.

Parāvata, turtle dove, cage of, 70.

Parimāṇa, a kind of measurement, 77, 121.

Parimit, cross-beam, 6.

Parivāra-vidhi, attendant deities, their temples, etc., 93.

Pāriyātra, a type of pavilion (*maṇḍapa*), 53.

Parjanya, a plot in a ground-plan, a quarter, 189.

Pārshṇika, a kind of height, 41; a class of kings, 59, 181, 182.

Parvata, a type of building, as mentioned in *Suprabhedāgama*, 118.

Paryaṅka, couch, six varieities of, 36, 61-62.

Pāśupata, Śiva, a class of phalli, 72, 94, 100, 107.

Pāṭali-putra, Patna, king Rājahaṁsa of, 171.

Patra-kalpa, one of the four classes of ornaments, with foliated decoration, 67.

Patra-paṭṭa, a kind of head-dress used by the Paṭṭa-dhara class of kings, 65.

Patra-toraṇa, foliated arch, 63.

Paṭṭadakal, temple of Pāpanātha at, 177.

Paṭṭa, turban, a kind of head-dress, of three kinds, foliated, jewelled and floral, 65; a moulding (fillet), 127.

Paṭta—bandha, a type of bases, 128.

Paṭṭa-bhāj, a class of kings, 59, 181, 182.

Pattana, a type of town, a big commercial port, 40, 143.

Paṭṭa-dhara, a class of kings, 59, 181, 182.

Paṭṭikā, a part of the pedestal, a moulding, 74.

Paulastya, an architectural treatise of, 107.

Paushṭika a kind of height 41, 55, 124; a type of two-storeyed building, 50, 111.

Pavana-bhadraka, a class of cars and chariots, 61.

Pedestal (*upapīṭha*), details of, 43-44, 74, 128.

Peripteral, a circular type of building, 147.

Peripteros, a type of building, 147.

Phalaka, a leaning board, 16.

Phalakā, a sort of screen for windows, 53; planks, 92; a moulding, 126, 127, 151.

Phalakāsana, a type of couch, 36.

Phallus, an emblem of god Śiva, 21, 25, 91, 98, 108; installation of, 26, 27; various classes and architectural details of, 72—74.

Pillar (*stambha*), of the Vedic age, 6; of Budhist age, 13; of Paurāṇic age, 19, 125—128, 150-151; of Āgamic age, 25, 125-128, 150 151; different classes and measures, etc., as described in *Mānasāra*,—44 46; as also in other works, 125—128; comparative study of, 149—153.

Pishṭa-pura, capital of Kaliṅga, conquered by Samudragupta, 184

Pīṭha, pedestals, 27, 90,91; different measures and varieties of, 43-44, 128; of the phallus of Śiva, 74, 94.

Pīṭhikā, cushioned chair, 16; pedestal, 97.

Pliny, his mention of Vitruvius, 134.

Plumb-lines, details of, 85.

Polycletus, a sculptor, 141.

Pompey, the theatre of, 160.

Potikā, a moulding, 126, 151.

Prabhnajana-bhadraka, a class of cars and chariots, 61.

Prabhava, a rectangular type of building as mentioned in *Agni-purāṇa*, 113.

Prabodhaka, one of the thirty-two authorities mentioned in *Mānasāra*, 165

Prāg-vaṁśa, an architectural object mentioned in *Harsha-charita*, 30.

Prāhāraka, a class of kings, qualifications of, 59; details of their palaces, etc. 181, 182.

Prājāpatya-hasta, a cubit of twenty-four *aṅgulas* (finger-breadth), 30.

Prākāra, rampart, 11; one of the five courts, 33, 49, 51, 90, 93, 154; of the Dravidian temples, 177, 197.

Prakāśāditya, a king of the Gupta dynasty, 195.

Pralamba-phalaka, an instrument to ascertain the plumb-lines for the purpose of sculptural measurement, 85.

Pralīnaka, a class of buildings, 118; a type of pillar, 125, 126, 150, 151.

Pramāṇa, measurement of breadth, 76; a kind of linear measurement, 121.

Praṇāla, canal, drain; a part of the Pedestal of the phallus of Śiva, 73.

Prapā, alms-houses, 17; drinking-house, 30.

Prāsāda, one of the five classes of buildings as stated in Buddhist literature, 10-11; palace, 18; buildings in general, 92, 97, 111—118.

Prāsāda-Maṇḍana-Vāstu-śāstra, a treatise on architecture, synopsis of, 108.

Prashṭar, one of the thirty-two authorities mentioned in *Mānasāra*, 165.

Prastara, a class of villages, 39, 143; entablature, its different varieties, 46, 106, 149; 25, 89, 92; a moulding, 127.

Prathama (or janman), a moulding of the pedestal, the plinth, 74.

Prathamāsana, a throne fit for the first stage of coronation, 62.

Prathameshṭaka, the first brick, the laying of the foundation-stone, 43, 92.

Prati (also Pratika), a moulding, 127.

Prati-bandha, a moulding, 127.

Prati-bhadra, a type of pedestals, 44, 128.

Prati-krama, a type of bases, 128.

Pratima, a moulding, 127.

Pratimā, images in general, 90, 100, 101, 107.

Pratimit, prop, 6.

Prati-vājana, a moulding, 127.

Prati-vakra, a moulding, 127.

Prayāga, modern Allahabad, the boundary of Madhyadeśa or middle country, 173.

Priene, temple of Minerva at, 141.

Pṛishada-bhadraka, a class of cars and chariots, 61.

Pṛithivī-dhara, an oval type of building as mentioned in *Agni* and *Garuḍa Purāṇas*, 113 114.

Priya-darśana, an order of columns, 125, 126, 150.

Projections (*nirgama*), of pedestals, 44.

Pronaos, as described by Vitruvius, 155.

Proserpine, temple of, 147.

Prostylos, temples of a particular form, 147.

Pseudodipteros, temples of a particular form, 147.

Pulasti-pura, buildings at, 14.

Puṁ-liṅga, masculine type of buildings, 111, 118, 119.

Puṇḍarīka, a class of seven-storeyed buildings, 50, 112.

Pura, a class of towns, 143.

Puragupta, a Gupta king, 195.

Purāṇas, treatment of architectural matters in, 19—22; compared with *Āgamas* 23; mere compilations, 109; five orders of columns and their mouldings as described in, 125, 126, 127—129, 151; types of buildings as described in, 113—117, 119, 131; measurements mentioned in, 122-123; ages of, 161, 194; comparative study of, 163, 168; architectural authorities mentioned in, 164; provenance of, 175; pantheon recognised in, 191.

Purandara, an authority on architecture as stated in *Purāṇas*, 164.

Pura-sūtra, a chain worn round the chest, an ornament, 68.

Purusha, a masculine type of building, 49.

Pushkala, a type of two-storeyed building, 50, 111.

Pushkara, a class of buildings as mentioned in *Kāmikāgama*, 118.

Puspha-bandha, a bunch of flowers, a particular form of window, 58.

Pushpaka, a rectangular class of buildings comprising nine types, mentioned in *Agni* and *Garuḍa Purāṇas*, 113, 114.

Pushpa-mālya, flower-wreath, a kind of head-dress used by the Prāhāraka and the Astra-grāha classes of kings, 65.

Pushpa-maṇḍapa, flower-pavilion, 58.

Pushpa-paṭṭa, a kind of head-dress used by the Paṭṭabhāj class of kings, 65.

Pushpa-pushkala, a type of base, 128.

Pushpa-toraṇa, floral arch, 63.

Pushya mitra, reaction against Buddhism by, 193.

Pūtanā, a demoness, offerings in connection with house-building to, 38

Pycnostylos, a kind of temple, 147.

Q

Qualifications (of architects), as given in *Mānasāra* 35; compared with those given by Vitruvins, 138 –141.

Quinarian measure, stated to have first introduced by Vitruvius, 134.

R

Raivata, one of the fourteen Manus to whose name several architectural treatises are ascribed, 66.

Rāja-gṛiha, city of, built by Bimbisāra, 9.

Rājadhāni, a class of towns, 40, 143.

Rāja-haṁsa, king of Pāṭaliputra, 3, 4, 171, 197, 198.

Rāja-śekhara, a Jain author, 211.

Rāja-taraṅginī, chronicle of Kashmir-rulers by Kalhana, references to architectural matters from, 30, 31, 73.

Rāja-vāhana, the chief of the ten princes of the *Daśa-kumāra-charita*, 4, 171, 197.

Rāja-vallabha-Maṇḍana, an architectural treatise, its synopsis, 103-104; references to architectural measurement from, 122.

Rāja veśma, royal palaces, 90.

Rajju, ropes, a measure, 35.

Rajju-bandha-lakshaṇa, binding of rope, 94.

Rajju-bandha-saṁskāra-vidhi, repairs in connection with binding of rope, 101.

Rājputānā, style of architecture in, 178

Rākshasī, a demoness, to whom offerings are given in connection with the building of a house, 38.

Rāma, hero of *Rāmāyaṇa*, 18; image of, 108; temple of, 189; his capital stated to have been built by Manu, 166.

Rāma-Lakshmaṇa, image of Rāma and Lakshmaṇa, 108.

Rāmayaṇa, references to architectural matters from, 17, 122.

Rampart, its architectural details from Vitruvius, 145-146.

Rām Rāz, 13, 184.

Randhra (corrupt form of Andhra), a style of architecture, 130.

Raṅga-mukha, a class of buildings mentioned in *Kāmikāgama*, 118.

Rāshṭra-kūṭas, reign of, 185; period of, 190, 191.

Ratha-dhūli, a measure, equal to eight *paramāṇus*, 35.

Ratha-durga, chariot fort, 40, 143.

Ratha-lakshaṇa, details of chariots, etc., 60-61.

Ratha-nirmāṇa, construction of chariots, 107.
Ratna (compounded with kampa, paṭṭa, and vapra), composite mouldings, 127.
Ratna-bandha, a type of bases, 128.
Ratna-kalpa, a kind of ornaments, made of flowers and jewels, and used by gods, and the Chakravartin, Adhirāja and Narendra classes of kings, 67.
Ratna-kampa, a moulding, 128.
Ratna-kānta, a class of six-storeyed buildings, 50, 112.
Ratnāṅgulīyaka, jewelled finger-ring, 67.
Ratna-paṭṭa, a kind of jewelled head-dress used by the Pārshṇika class of kings, 65; a moulding, 128.
Ratna-toraṇa, jewelled arch, 63.
Ratna-vapra, a moulding, 128.
Rauchya-daiva-sāvarṇi, one of the fourteen Manus (to whose name several architectural treatises are ascribed), 166.
Raurava, a class of nine-storeyed building, 50, 112.
Repair (of broken images), as treated in *Śukra-nīti*, 30.
Ṛig veda, references to architectural matters from, 5, 6.
Ṛiksha-nāyaka, an oval type of building as mentioned in *Agni-purāṇa*, 113.
Roads and doors, (*Vīthi-dvārādi-māna*), as described in *Kāmikāgama*, 24.
Rod, (*daṇḍa*) a measure, 35.
Roga, disease, personified as a deity and worshipped in connection with the building of a house, 38.
Rohilkhand, identified with north Pāñchāla, 174.
Romaka-Siddhānta, a treatise based on a Roman astronomical work, 159.
Roofing, five kinds of, 13; other details of, 46.
Ropes (*Sūtra-nirmāṇa*), making of, 24.
Ruchaka (for Charuka in *Kāmikāgama*), a type of building, 113; one of the five orders of columns, 125, 126, 150, 151.
Rudra, a deity, 126, 151; temples, etc., of, 187.
Rudra-jaya, a quarter, 189.
Rudra-kānta, one of the five orders of columns, a sixteen-sided pillar, 45, 125, 150; a class of four-storeyed building, 50, 112.
Rudra-sāvarṇi, one of the fourteen Manus (to whose name several architectural treatises are ascribed), 166.
Rūpa-Maṇḍana, an architectural treatise, 103.
Ruskin, 18, 166.

S

Sabhā, assembly halls, as described in *Mahābhārata*, 18, 19.
Sabhāshṭaka, eight council-halls, 103.
Sadāśiva, a class of four-storeyed buildings, 50, 112.
Sādhaka-sāra-saṁhitā, one of the thirty-two authorities on architecture mentioned in *Mānasāra*, 165.

Sāgala, city of, 9.

Sages, images of the well-known seven ṛishis (Agastya, Kāśyapa, Bhṛigu, Vasishṭha, Bhārgava, Viśvāmitra, Bhāradvāj) are described, 79-80.

Śaiva, a class of phalli, 72.

Śaivism, its condition at the time of *Mānasāra*, 187, 188, 190.

Sakala-sthāpana-vidhi, installation of the images of *Sakala* (Iśvara and four other deities), 94.

Sāketa, city of, 9.

Sākiyas, the kinsmen of Buddha, who built the monumental dome about the same height as the dome of the St. Paul's, 15.

Śakra, one of the several architectural authorities mentioned in Sanatkumāra's *Vāstu-śāstra*, 102.

Śaktis, female energies personified, the leading female deities, their images described, 74—76, 71.

Śakuna-lakshaṇa, auspicious signs in connection with the building of a house, 104.

Śālā-griha (or Śālā-mandira), a rectangular type of building as mentioned in *Agni* and *Garuḍa Purāṇas*, 113, 114.

Śālagrāma, the stone-god, image of, 21.

Śālā-(vidhāna), halls, a kind of building, various classes and other details of, 54-55, 90.

Sālokya, a class of sages, description of their images, 80-81.

Śalya-(jñānam), some inauspicious things considered in connection with the building of a house, 97.

Sama, a rectangular type of building as mentioned in *Agni-purāṇa*, 113.

Sama-bhaṅga, equipoise of images, 86.

Sama-karṇa, a class of phalli, 72.

Samaya-vidhi, auspicious time for beginning the construction of a building, 96.

Śambhu-kānta, a class of eleven-storeyed buildings, 50, 112.

Saṁchita, a classification of buildings, 24, 49, 111, 118, 119.

Saṁgraha (also known as Śilpa-saṁgraha), a work on architecture, the synopsis of, 106—109.

Sāmīpya, a class of sages, their images described, 80.

Saṁkīrṇa, an object made of mixed materials, a kind of pillars made of more than three materials, 46; a class of building, 110, 118.

Saṁpūrṇa, a class of buildings, as mentioned in *Kāmikāgama*, 118.

Samudga (or Samudra), a class of buildings mentioned in *Bhavishya-purāṇa* and *Bṛihat-saṁhitā*, 116, 117.

Samudragupta, reign of, 185, 192; period of, 190; an all-sided development at the time of, 193.

Samudraka, a type of double-storeyed sixteen-sided buildings, as mentioned together with other details in *Matsya-purāṇa*, 116.

Saṁviddha, a kind of fort, 40, 143.

Sanat kumāra, an author on architecture, 2; synopsis of his treatise 102.

Sandhi-karma-(vidhāna), the joinery, various kinds and other details of, 47, 89.

Śaṅkha, a round type of building as mentioned in *Agni* and *Garuḍa Purāṇas*, 113, 114.

Śaṅku, a gnomon, finding out the cardinal points by means of a gnomon, its details, 37, 97.

Śāntika, a measure of height, 41, 55, 124.

Sapta-mātṛi, seven mothers (Vārāhī, Kaumārī, Chāmuṇḍā, Bhairavī, Māhendrī, Vaishṇavī, Brahmāṇī), their images, 75, 93.

Sāra, a class of buildings, as mentioned in *Kāmikāgama*, 118.

Sārasvata, a treatise on architecture, its synopsis, 108.

Sarasvatī, goddess of learning, consort of Brahmā (?), 71; description of her image, 75.

Śarkarā, gravel, one of the nine materials of which idols are made, 70.

Saro-rū(ru)ha, a class of six-storeyed building, 50, 112.

Sārūpya, one of the four classes of sages, description of their images, 80, 81.

Sarva-kalyāṇa, a class of buildings, as mentioned in *Kāmikāgama*, 118.

Sarva-kāmika, a kind of measurement, also known as Dhanada, 41, 55, 124.

Sarvato-bhadra, one of the eight classes of village, 39, 143; a kind of joinery, 47; a type of window, 53; a class of halls (*śālā*), 55; a quadrangular type of building, 113, 114; another type of five-storeyed building, 115; another type, 118.

Śata-patha-Brāhmaṇa, references to *aṅgula* measure from, 122.

Satra, inn, as mentioned in *Harsha-charita*, 30.

Śatruñjaya, the style of architecture at, 178, 179; language of inscriptions from, 211.

Sattaṅgo, sofa, as mentioned in Buddhist literature, 16.

Satya-kānta, a class of eight-storeyed building, 50, 112.

Saugandhi, a kind of fragrant grass used as a material for foundations of buildings, 43.

Saukhyaka, a pavilion (*maṇḍapa*) on the banks of a sea or river, 54.

Saumukhya, an order of columns, 125, 126, 150, 151.

Saumya, a class of buildings, as mentioned in *Kāmikāgama*, 118.

Saumya-kānta, a class of gate-houses (*gopura*), 52.

Śaunaka, one of the eighteen professors of architecture mentioned in *Matsya-purāṇa*, 164.

Saura, one of the thirty-two authorities on architecture mentioned in *Mānasāra*, 165.

Sura-kānta, a class of nine-storeyed buildings, 50, 112.

Sāvarṇī, one of the fourteen Manus (to whose name several architectural treatises are ascribed), 166.
Sāvatthi, city of, 9.
Sāvitrī, consort of Brahmā, her image, 71; one of the chief female deities, description of her features, 74-75.
Śayana, a type of temple, 24, 111; another type, 49; recumbent posture of images, 86.
Śayanādhikāra, a chapter dealing with bed-steads, 90, 61-62.
Śayanālaya, bed-chamber, 58.
Śayana-vidāna, a chapter dealing with couches, 61-62.
Sāyujya, a class of sages, their images described, 80-81.
Śayyā, beds, bed-steads, 96, 97.
Scotia (or trochilos), a Græco-Roman moulding, 127, 152.
Selection of site, (Bhūmi-saṁgraha), different tests, 36-37.
Seraphis, temple of, 146.
Seven Mothers, detailed description of their images, 76.
Seven-storeyed buildings, as described in Buddhist literature, 14; in *Mānasāra*, 50, 112; in *Mātsya-purāṇa*, etc., 116.
Shapes (of buildings), masculine, feminine, neuter, as described in *Mānasāra* and *Āgamas*, 24, 49, 111, 118; square, rectangular, round, oval, octagonal, and sixteen-sided as stated in *Purāṇas*, 113-116, 117, 118.
Shoḍaśa-bhūmi-vidhāna, description of sixteen storeyed buildings, 93.
Shoḍaśa pratimā, sixteen images, 100.
Śibi(vi)kā, palanquin, a conveyance, 36; a rectangular type of building as mentioned in *Agni* and *Garuḍa Purāṇas*, 113, 114.
Śibira, a kind of fort, 40, 143.
Sioha, a pavilion (*maṇḍapa*) used as an ordinary kitchen, 54.
Siddha, a class of two storeyed buildings, 50, 111.
Siddhānta-śiromaṇi, references to architectural matters from, 82, 122, 165, 172.
Siddhas, semi-divine beings, their images, 64.
Side-halls (or ante-chambers, Paksha-śālā-vidhi), description of, 25.
Śikhara, steeples, 17, 18, 177, 178, 179, 180, 196; a class of gate-houses (*gopura*), 52; erection of, 89; description of, 92.
Śikhā (or danta), axle-hand of chariots, 60.
Śikhā (or chūḍā-maṇi, crest-jewel, 67, 85.
Śilā-nyāsa, laying the foundation stone, 97.
Śilpa-dīpaka, a treatise, references to architectural matters from, 140.
Śilpa-ratna, a treatise, references to architectural matters from, 123.
Śilpa-saṁgraha, a compilation on architecture, its synopsis, 106—109, 172.

Śilpa-śāstra, used in the sense of Vāstu-śāstra (science of architecture), 1, 19, 20, 23, 24, 26, 27, 30, 32, 34, 133, 157, 158, 159, 178, 187, 193, 194, 195, 196, 199, 211; title of a manuscript of *Mānasāra*, 2.

Śilpa-śastra of Maṇḍana, synopsis of, 103-104.

Śilpa-śāstra-sāra, a treatise on architecture, 2.

Śilpi-lakshaṇa, qualifications of an architect, 85, 137—141.

Siṁha, a class of building, as mentioned in *Garuḍa-purāṇa*, 114; in *Matsya-purāṇa*, 115; in *Bhavishya-purāṇa*, 116; in *Bṛihat-saṁhitā*, 117.

Siṁhāsana, throne, different varieties and other details of, 62-63, 78, 98.

Sindhuka, a class of building, as mentioned in *Kāmikāgama*, 118.

Śiraś-chakra, a head-disc, ornamental nimbus put on by Vishṇu, 71.

Śirastraka, a kind of head-dress used by the Pārshṇika class of kings, 65.

Śiro-vibhūshaṇa, a head-ornament, 67.

Site, selection of, 24; ploughing of, 24.

Śiva, a type of pavilion (*maṇḍapa*) for unhusking corn in, 54; a member of the Triad, image described, 72; a class of building as mentioned in *Kāmikāgama*, 118; an order of columns, 126, 151; position of the deity in *Mānasāra*, 188, 189; position at the time of the Guptas, 191.

Śiva-bhāga, upper part of the phallus, 73.

Śiva-kānta, pentagonal pillar, 45; a column with five minor pillars, 46; an order of columns, 125, 150.

Śivāṅka, a class of phalli, 72.

Śivikā-garbha, square halls, as stated in Buddhist literature, 11.

Śivikā-veśma, a rectangular type of building, as mentioned in *Agni* and *Garuḍa Purāṇas*, 113, 114.

Skanda, a deity, his image, 107, 108; an order of columns, 126, 151.

Skanda-gupta, possible connection with *Skanda-purāṇa*, 171; last emperor of the dynasty, 190, 195; religious faith of, 192.

Skanda-kānta, a type of hexagonal pillar, 45, 125, 150; a column combined with six minor pillars, 46; a class of gate-houses (*gopura*), 52.

Skanda-Purāṇa, references to architectural matters from, 19; associated with Skandagupta, 171, 180; age of, 194.

Skanda-tāra, a type of single-storeyed buildings with hexagonal spire and necks, 49, 111.

Skandāvāra, a kind of fort, 40, 143.

Snapana-maṇḍapa, a kind of bath-room, 119.

Soil, examination of, 24.

Soma, a deity, image of, 107.

Somāskanda, the combined image of, 100

Somanātha, one of the best known phalli in India, temple of, 72.

Sopāna, stairs, as described in Buddhist literature, 13; in classical literature, 32; in *Mānasāra*, 51.

Śphaṭika, crystal, a material of which idols are made, 71.

Sphū (Gu)rjaraka, a class of twelve-storeyed buildings, 51, 113, 173, 174, 175.

Śreṇī-bandha, a type of base, 44, 128.

Śrī-bandha, a type of base, 44, 128; a kind of throne, 62.

Śrī-bhadra, a kind of throne fit for the Adhirāja and the Narendra classes of kings, 62; a type of Pedastal for the phallus, 74.

Śrī bhoga, a class of seven-storeyed buildings, 50, 112; a type of base, 44, 128; a kind of gate-houses (*gopura*), 52.

Śrī-dhara, Vishṇu, temple of, 189.

Śrī-jaya, an oval type of building as mentioned in *Agni* and *Garuḍa Purāṇas*, 113, 114.

Śrī-kaṇṭha, an octagonal type of building as mentioned in *Agni-purāṇa*, 113.

Śrī-kānta, classes of three and seven-storeyed buildings, 50, 111, 112; a type of base, 44, 128.

Śrī-kara, classes of one and two-storeyed buildings, 49, 50, 111; an order of columns, 125, 126, 150, 151.

Śrī-mukha, a type of throne fit for the Maṇḍaleśa class of kings, 63.

Śrī-varta, a type of building, as mentioned in *Suprabhedāgama* 118.

Śrīvatsa, a symbol on the image of Vishṇu, 71, 78; a square type of building, as mentioned in *Agni* and *Garuḍa Purāṇas*, 113.

Śrī-viśāla, a class of gate-houses (*gopura*), 52; a type of thrones, 62; a type of Pedestal for the phallus, 74; a class of single-storeyed buildings, 49, 111.

Śrī-vṛiksha, an octagonal type of building, as mentioned in *Garuḍa-purāṇa*, 114.

Śriyā-vṛitta, a type of pavilions (*maṇḍapa*), 119.

Sruk-sruva, small sacrificial ladles, characteristics of Brahma image, 71.

Stambha, pillar, as mentioned in *Vedic* literature, 5-6; in *Purānas* 19; in *Āgamas*, 25; in Grammars, 33; in *Mānasāra*, 44—46; in other *Śilpa-śāstras*, 89, 92, 96; comparative study of, 125—128, 149—153, 167-168.

Stambha-toraṇa-vidhi, arches on columns, 92.

Stana-sūtra, chain worn round the breasts, 68.

Sthānaka, a class of building, 24, 49, 111, 119; a posture in which images are carved, 85.

Sthānīya, a kind of fort, 40, 143.

Sthāpaka, master of the ceremonies, 56.

Sthapati, chief architect, his genealogy, staff and qualifications, 35, 107, 165; his leading part in house-opening ceremonies, 56, in carving images, 86; compared with Roman architects, 137-141.

Strī-liṅga, a feminine type of buildings, 49, 111, 118.

Strī-māna-madhyama-daśa-tāla, intermediate type of ten *tāla* measures referring to female images, 84

Stūpikā, pinnacle, 47, 48, 87.

Stūpi-kīla, pinnacle-staff, 47, 48.

Styles, three main styles of architecture and sculpture (49), 73, 110, 118, 130-132, 155, 176-181.

Subhaṅkarī, auspicious, an order of columns, 125, 126, 150, 151.

Śūchiyo, cross-bars, 13.

Śuddha, pure, an architectural or sculptural object made of one material, 46, 110, 118, 119.

Sudhā, stucco, one of the materials of which idols are made, 70, 82.

Śuka, parrot, details of the cage of, 70.

Śuka-nāsā, parrot's nose, gargoyles, 169.

Sukhālaya, a class of three-storeyed buildings, 50, 111.

Sukhāṅga, a pavilion (*maṇḍapa*) for a guest-house, 54.

Sukhāsana, a sitting posture of an image, 94.

Śukra, one of the eighteen professors of architecture mentioned in *Matsya-purāṇa*, 164, 170.

Śukrāchārya, the author of the *Śukra-nīti*, 170.

Śukra-nīti, named after its author, 2; references to architectural matters from, 29-30, 169-170.

Śūla-lakshṇa, the pike for images, 94.

Śūla-māna, measurement of pikes (for images), 101, 107.

Śūla-pāṇi-lakshaṇa, image of Śiva, 94

Śulva-sūtras, references to architectural matters from, 7-8, 122.

Sundara, a class of six-storeyed buildings, 50, 112.

Suprabhedāgama, synopsis of, 27-28; method of first casting of image, in, 87; comparative study of, 110, 119, 160; types of buildings described in, 118, 131, their details from, 121; *aṅgula* measure as given in, 122; *tāla* measure in, 123; five orders of columns as given in, 125, 150, 151, their component mouldings, 126; bases as described in, 128.

Suprati-kānta, a class of nine-storeyed buildings, 50, 112.

Sūrya-siddhānta, a treatise, references to architectural matters from, 32, 172, 173.

Sūtra-dhāra, a class of architects, his qualifications, 137, 138; see Takshaka, 35.

Sūtradhāra-Maṇḍana, a treatise on architecture, its synopsis and historical importance, 103—105.

Sūtradhāra-pūjā, offerings to architects in connection with building a house, 104.

Sûtra-grâhin, draftsman or designer, a class of architects, his genealogy and qualifications, 35, 137, 138, 165.

Suvarṇa-kañchuka, golden cuirass or bodice, 68.

Suvarṇa-sûtra, gold chain worn round the breasts, 68.

Svarga-kânta, a class of eight-storeyed buildings, 50, 112.

Svârochisha, one of the fourteen Manus (to whose name several architectural treatises are ascribed), 166.

Svasti-bandha, a class of single-storeyed buildings with octagonal finial, 49, 111.

Svastika, a class of villages, 39, 148; a kind of joinery, 47; a class of two-storeyed building, 50, 111; an octagonal type of building, 113, 114; a type of window, 53; a class of hall (*śâlâ*), 55, 118; a class of phalli, 72.

Svasti-kânta, a class of six-storeyed building, 50, 112.

Svastika-khaḍga, an octagonal type of building as mentioned in *Agni-purāṇa*, 113.

Sva-vṛiksha, a round type of building as mentioned in *Agni-purāṇa*, 113.

Svayaṁbhû, self-revealed, a class of phalli, 73.

Svâyaṁbhuva, one of the fourteen Manus (to whose name several architectural treatises are ascribed), 166.

Systems of measurement, both architectural and sculptural, details of, 35-36, 81, 84, 89, 121—124.

Systylos, a class of temples where the columns are not thickly set, 147.

T

Taḍāga, tank, architectural details of, 97.

Taittirîya-saṁhitā, references to architectural matters from, 17.

Takshaka, a class of architects, genealogy and qualifications of, 35, 98, 165.

Tala, storey, 49, 50, 111, 112; a moulding, 126, 151.

Tâla, a unit of sculptural measure, equal to the length of the face or the distance between the fully stretched thumb and middle finger, 123, 78, compared with Grecian Télcios, 157.

Tāla-māna, sculptural measures, 19, 26-27, 78, 84, 93 123, 124.

Talon, a moulding, 127, 152.

Tâmasa, one of the fourteen Manus (to whose name several architectural treatises are ascribed), 166.

Tamil, the territory of the language of, 174, 180, 185.

Tāmra-patra, copper-leaf, its use in connection with the casting of images, 86.

Tanjore, temple (*vimāna*) at, 82; the Nagore port at, 181.

Tapas-kânta, a class of eight-storeyed building, 50, 112.

Tâpti, river of, the southern boundary of the territory of the Indo-Aryan style of architecture, 178.

Târa, measurement of breadth, 77.

Taruṇâlaya-(vidhi), a special kind of building, 8.

Taru-tantra-vidhi, certain rules regarding wood used in houses, 102.

Tâṭaṅka, a kind of ear-ornament, 67.

Tâṭikâ, a moulding, 126, 127, 151.

Telugu, territory of the Vesara style, 130, of the script of, 180; same as Andhra country, 184.

Testing of soil, for the purpose of building, 36, 86, 142.

Tetrastylon, one of the five courts of Vitruvius, 154.

Testudinatum, one of the five courts of Vitruvius, 154.

Thambhâ, posts or banister of stairs as stated in Buddhist literature, 13.

Theatre, its details as given in *Mânasâra*, 63.

Throne, its details as given in *Mânasâra*, 62-63.

Ties (of various sorts), used in constructing straw-houses at the time of the *Atharva-veda*, 6.

Tila-pushpâkṛiti, shaped like the sesame flower, ideal nose of images, 84

Tirhut, stands for a part of ancient Janaka country, possessing once a type of twelve-storeyed building, 178.

Tîrthaṅkaras, Jain apostles, their images, 185.

Tittiri, francolin partridge, details of the cage of, 70.

Titus, time of his reign, when the Roman architect Vitruvius might have lived, 160.

Tod, author of the *Annals of Râjasthân*, 103.

Todas, huts of, 6.

Toraṇa, arched-gateway, 18; details of arches, 63, 61, 92.

Torus, a moulding, 127, 152.

Town-planning, in the time of the *Vedas*, 8; of the Buddhist literature, 9; of the *Epics*, 17; of the *Âgamas*, 25; of the *Artha-śâstra*, 29; of the *Mânasâra*, 40, 143, 144, and other *Śilpa-śâstras*, 89, 93, 97; compared with the Roman systems, 143—147.

Trambaka, an instance of the popularity of Vaishnavism at the time of *Mânasâra*, 187.

Trayodaśa-tala-vidhâna, thirteen-storeyed buildings as mentioned in *Amśumadbheda* of Kâśyapa, 93.

Triad (Trimûrti), images of Brahmâ, Vishṇu and Śiva, 70—72; other details of, 23, 188.

Tri-bhaṅga, having three flexions, a pose of images, 86.

Tri-bhûmi, three-storeyed buildings, 50, 90, 106, 111.

Tri-dhâtu-śaraṇam, three-storeyed dwelling, as mentioned in *Ṛig-veda*, 6.

Tri-kaliṅga, identified with Telugu country, the territory of the Vesara style of architecture and sculpture, 130, 176.

Tri-kânta, a column combined with three minor pillars, 46.

Trinity, their comparative position in *Āgamas* and *Purāṇas*, 28.

Tri-pura-mūrti-lakshaṇa, image of Śiva in the pose of killing the demon, Tripura, 94.

Tri-purāntaka, Śiva, his image, 100.

Tri-purī, image of (Śiva), 108.

Tri-vishṭapa, a class of octagonal buildings comprising nine types as stated in *Agni* and *Garuḍa Purāṇas*, 113, 114.

Tulā, balance, 68; a moulding, 126, 127, 151, 152.

Tumburu, a heavenly musician, his image used as a decorative device on arches, 68.

Tuṅga, a moulding, 127.

Tuscan, an order of columns, 125, 149, 150, 151, 152, 154.

Tvashtar, one of the four heavenly architects, 35, 165.

Tuscany, country of, 126.

U

Udaipur, style of architecture at, 179.

Udara-bandha, girdle worn round the waist, 68.

Udaya-giri, cave temples at, 196.

Udbhūta, self-revealed, a class of phalli, 73.

Udyāna, garden, architectural details of, 97.

Ugra-dṛiś, of a terrific appearance, feature of the Garuḍa image, 82.

Ujjeni, city of, (in the Buddhist period), 9.

Unhīsaṁ, an architectural device on stairs, 13.

Unmāna, a kind of linear measurement, 77, 121.

Upādhāra, a kind of support upon which the structure of the chariot rests, 60.

Upakānta, a class of six-storeyed building, 50, 112.

Upamāna, measurement of inter space, 77, 121.

Upamit, a kind of pillar, as mentioned in Vedic literature, 6.

Upāna, a moulding, the plinth, 128.

Upānaha, shoes, architectural details of, 97.

Upapāda, minor pillar, 46.

Upapīṭha, pedestal, its different varieties and other details, 43-44, 89, 92, 101, 106, 107, 149; of the phallus, its details, 74.

Upari-prāsāda-tala, upper flat surface of a house, 14.

Upāsaka, devotee, details of his house in the Budhist period, 11.

Upasaṁchita, a classification of buildings, 118 (see *Asaṁchita*, 49, 111).

Upatulā, a moulding, 127, 152.

Uraga-bandha, a type of bases, 128.

Ūrdhva-padma, a moulding of the pedestal of the phallus, 74.

Ushṇīsha, head gear, 28; the protuberance of the skull of Buddha image, 79.

Ushṇīshī, a round type of buildings, 114.

Uttambha, a rectangular type of building, 114.

Uttara, a moulding, 44, 126, 128, 151.

Uttaroshṭha, lower-lip, a moulding, 127, 152.

Uttara-Rāma-Charita, a drama written by Bhavabhuti, references to architectural matters from, 32.

Uttarīya, upper garment, 71.

V

Vāhana, riding animals of gods, images of, 81, 82-83; a moulding, 127, 152

Vāhinī-mukha, a kind of fort, 40, 143.

(Vai)jayantika, a class of single-storeyed building with round spire, pinnacle and neck 49, 111.

Vaikhānasāgama, references to architectural matters from, 28, 123.

Vaira, an octagonal type of building, as mentioned in *Garuḍa-purāṇa*, 114.

Vairāja, a classification of the square type of buildings comprisings nine varieties as mentioned in *Agni* and *Garuḍa Purāṇas*, 113, 114.

Vaishṇavī, one of the seven mothers, her image described, 75, 76.

Vaishṇavism, its leading position at the time of *Mānasāra*, 185, 188, 190, 193.

Vaivasvata, one of the fourteen Manus (to whose name several architectural treatises are ascribed), 166.

Vājana, a moulding, fillet, 64, 74, 126, 128; 151.

Vajra, a class of phalli, 73; an octagonal type of building, as mentioned in *Agni-purāṇa*, 113; an order of columns, 125, 126, 150, 151.

Vajra-bandha, a type of base, 128.

Vajra-kānta, a class of eleven-storeyed building, 50, 112.

Vajra lepa, cementing and white-washing, 22.

Vajra-paṭṭa, a moulding, 128.

Vajra-svastika, an octagonal type of building as mentioned in *Agni-purāṇa*, 113.

Vakra, an octagonal type of building, as mentioned in *Garuḍa-purāṇa*, 114.

Valabha (Valabhī), a moulding, 128.

Valabhī, a rectangular type of building, as mentioned in *Agni* and *Garuḍa Purāṇas*, 1 3, 114; a moulding, 128.

Vālāgra, hair's end, a measure, 35.

Valaya, armlet, 67; a round type of building, as mentioned in *Agni* and *Garuḍa Purāṇas*, 113, 114.

Vallabhi-chchhandaka, a type of five-storeyed building, as described in *Matsya-purāṇa*, 115.

Valli, a type of window, 58.

Vāma, a class of phalli, 72.

Vāmana, Vishṇu, popularity of, 189.

Vaṁśa, bamboo cane, used for roofing in the time of *Atharva-veda*, 6.

Vaṁśaka, territory of the *Vaṁśa-kānta* type of twelve-storeyed building, 50, 113; its topography, 173, 175, 198.

Vamśa-kānta, a class of twelve-storeyed building, 50, 113.

Vana-durga, mountain fort, 40, 143.

Vana-mālā, garland of wild flowers, 68, 71.

Vāpī, cistern, its foundations, 42; tanks, 97.

Vapra (Vapraka), a moulding, 128.

Vapra-bandha, a type of base, 44, 128.

Varāha-mihira, author of *Brihat-saṁhitā*, 22, 28, 160, 162, 163, 164, 165, 169.

Vārāhī, one of the seven mothers, her image, 75, 76.

Varāṭa (Virāṭa), a class of twelve-storeyed building, 50, 118.

Varddhanī, a round type of building, as mentioned in *Agni-purāṇa*, 113.

Vardhaka (or Samṛiddha), a kind of fort, 40, 143.

Vardhaki, one of the four classes of architects, his special branch of study, genealogy and qualifications, 35, 157, 188 165.

Vardhamāna a class of halls (*śālā*). 55, 118; a type of phalli, 72.

Varṇa-lepana-medhya-lakshaṇa, colouring, details of 94.

Varṇa-saṁskāra, preparation of colours, 94, 100, 101, 107.

Vartula, a class of building, its description as given in *Matsya-purāṇa*, 116.

Vasanta-senā, palace of, 52.

Vasishṭha, an authority on architecture, as mentioned in *Bṛihat-saṁhitā* 163, in *Matsya-purāṇa*, 161.

Vasishṭha-Saṁhitā, references to architectural matters from, 140.

Vāstu, its definition, classification and other details, 86.

Vāstu-bodha, one of the thirty-two authorities on which *Mānasāra* was based, 165.

Vāstu-homa, sacrificial offerings to the presiding deity of the site of a building, 92.

Vāstu-lakshaṇa, (see Vāstu), characteristics of architectural objects, 103.

Vāstu-maṇḍana, an architectural treatise, 103.

Vāstu-mañjari, an architectural treatise, 103.

Vastu-nikshepa-maṇḍapa, a store-house, 58.

Vāstu-pradīpa, a treatise, references to architectural matters from, 140.

Vāstu-prakāra (see Vāstu), classification of architectural subjects, 89.

Vāstu-prakaraṇa, (see Vāstu), definition and classification of architectural objects, 141.

Vikramorvaśī, a drama by Kālidāsa, references to architectural matters from, 82

Vāstu-purusha, the presiding deity of the site for a building, description of, 38 96

Vāstu-ratnāvali, a treatise, references to architectural matters from, 140.

Vāstu-sāra, an architectural treatise, 103.

Vāstu-śāstra, science of architecture, objects treated in, 1; its mythical origin, 84; treatises bearing the title of, 102, 103, 125-126, 140.

Vāstu-vidyā, a treatise, references to architectural matters from, 122, 128; name of a chapter of the *Bṛihat-saṁhitā*, 22, 161.

Vâstu-vidyâpati, one of the thirty-two authorities on which *Mânasâra* was based, 165.

Vâsu-deva, Vishṇu, his image, as described in *Agni-purâṇa*, 21; one of the eighteen professors of architecture, as mentioned in *Matsya-purâṇa*, 164; popularity in the time of *Mânasâra* of, 189.

Vasu-bandhu, a preacher of Buddhism at the time of Narasiṁha-Gupta-Bâlâditya, 192.

Vâtâpi, early Châlukyas of, 191.

Vatsa, kings of, 173.

Vâyu-purâṇa, references to architectural matters from, 21; age of, 194.

Vedas, references to architectural matters from, 5—8; their knowledge necessary for architects, 35, 138; a type of pavilion (*maṇḍapa*) for an assembly-hall, 54.

Vedânta-sâra, an example of treatises ending in *sâra*, like *Mânasâra*, 2.

Vedi-bhadra, a class of pedestal, 44, 128.

Vedi-(kâ), altar, 87; platform, railing, 61, 92.

Vedika-chatushṭaya, four platforms, 103.

Vedi-kânta, a class of four-storeyed building, 50, 112.

Vengi, the territory between the Kṛishṇâ and the Godâvarî, conquered by Samudragupta, 184.

Venus, temple of, 164, 147.

Vesâli, city of, 9.

Vesara, a style of architecture and sculpture, 24, 48, 110, 118, 119, 130-131, 179, 198; characteristic features of, 176; a circular type of cars and chariots, 61; a class of phalli, 73; the territory of (the Telugu scripts), 180, 182, 183.

Veśman, residential buildings, 41.

Vidâri-(kâ), a demoness, offerings made to, at the time of constructing a building, 38.

Videha, the territory of the Janaka type of twelve-storeyed building, 173.

Vidyâ-dharas, semi-divine beings, their images, 64, 80.

Vighneśa, a deity, temple of, 99.

Vihâras, Buddhist monasteries, one of five classes of buildings described in Buddhist literature, 10, 30.

Vijaya, a class of two-storeyed building, 50, 111; an octagonal type of building, 113, 114; another type, 118; types of pavilions (*maṇḍapa*), 53, 54; a kind of throne, 62

Vijaya-râja-deva, the language of the inscription of, 212.

Vikalpa or Saṁkalpa), a classification of buildings, 41, 48, 110, 118, 147; a class of phalli, 73; a type of doors, 155.

Vikramâditya, king of Ujjain and stated to be the patron of Kâlidâsa, Varâhamihira, etc., 23, 161.

Village, its plans and other details (see Grâma and Nagara), 30, 144

Vimāna, pavilion, 17, 18; buildings in general, 47-48; a square type of building, as mentioned in *Agni* and *Garuḍa Purāṇas*, 113; other types as mentioned in *Bhavishya-purāṇa*, and *Bṛihat-samhitā* 116, 117; Dravidian temples, 177.

Vimāna-chchhanda, a class of eight-storeyed building, as described in *Matsya-purāṇa* and in *Bṛihat-samhitā*, 115, 117.

Vimāna-vatthu, a Buddhist treatise, references to architectural matters from, 9.

Vināśana, the eastern boundary of the territory of the *Madhya-kānta* type of twelve-storeyed buildings, 173.

Vinatā, the mother of Garuḍa, 81.

Vināyaka-lakshaṇa, image of Gaṇeśa, 93.

Vinaya texts, Buddhist scriptures, references to architectural matters from, 11, 14.

Vindhya, the range of mountain between North and South India, 173, 174, 180.

Vipula, dimensions (of buildings), 42.

Vipulākṛiti-(ka), a class of six-storeyed building, 50, 112.

Vipulāṅka, a class of six-storeyed building, 50, 112.

Vīra, a kind of throne, 62.

Vīra-bhadra, image of, 108.

Vīra-kaṇṭha, a kind of column, 45; a moulding, 126, 151.

Vīrāsana, a type of pavilion (*maṇḍapa*), 119.

Virāṭa, a class of twelve-storeyed building, 50, 113, 198; topography of the country of, 173, 174, 17*.

Viśāla, a rectangular type of building as mentioned in *Agni* and *Garuḍa Purāṇas*, 113, 114; another type as described in *Kāmikāgama*, 118; a type of pavilion (*maṇḍapa*), as mentioned in *Suprabhedāgama*, 119; one of thirty-two authorities on which *Mānasāra* was based, 165, also perhaps the architectural portion of *Matsyapurāṇa*, 164.

Viśālāksha, one of the eighteen Professors of architecture mentioned in *Matsya-purāṇa*, 164.

Viśeshārchana, a kind of throne for special worship of a deity in, 62.

Vishṇu, description of the image of, 71; the deity of, 74; an order of columns, 125, 126, 150, 151; origin of the science of architecture ascribed to, 34, 165; popularity of his worship at the time of *Mānasāra*, 187—189; temple of, 191; in the time of the Guptas predelection for, 194-195.

Vishṇu-bhāga, middle-part of the phallus, 73.

Vishṇu-gupta the author of *Artha-śāstra*, 170.

Vishṇu-kānta, an order of octagonal columns, 45, 125-126, 150-151; a column combined with twelve minor pillars, 46; a class of four-storeyed building, 50, 112; a type of gate-houses (*gopura*), 52

Vishṇu-purāṇa, age of, 1 4.

Vishṇu-saṁhitā, references to sculptural matters from, 87.

Viśva bodha, one of the thirty-two authorities on which *Mānasāra* was based, 165.

Viśvak, references to architectural matters from, 140.

Viśva-kānta, classes of five and nine-storeyed buildings, 50, 112.

Viśva-karman, one of the four heavenly architects from whom came the four classes of earthly architects, 35, 166; synopsis of the treatise of, 96—99; comparative study of, 101, 102, 163, 164, 165; further references to architectural matters from, 107.

Viśva karma-prakāśa, one of the several treatises ascribed to Viśva-karman, 96.

Viśva-karma-śilpa, a treatise on architecture, its synopsis, 96—99.

Viśva-karma-vāstu-śastra, one of the several treatises ascribed to Viśva-karman, 96.

Viśva-karmotpatti, origin of Viśva-karman, 98.

Viśva-kāśyapa, one of the thirty-two authorities on which *Mānasāra* was based, 165.

Viśveśa, one of the thirty-two authorities on which *Mānasāra* was based, 165.

Viśva-sāra, a treatise, references to architectural matters from, 108; one of the thirty-two authorities on which *Mānasāra* was based, 165.

Viśveśvara, one of the best known phalli in India, his temple at Benares, 72.

Vitasti, span, a measure, 35.

Vitruvia. the family of which Vitruvius, the Roman architect, was born, 160.

Vitruvius, references to architectural matters from his treatise, 87, 172; origin of columns as given by, 126; his treatise compared with *Mānasāra*, 134—159, (references to several editions of his treatise, 134—136); similarity in number and titles of chapters, 137; in training of architects, 137—141; in preliminary chapters, 141—143; in town-planning, 143—147; in forms, species and foundations of buildings, 147—149; in columns, 149—153; in courts, 154-155; in doors, 1.5-156; in sculptural measures, 156—157; in language and title, 158-159; his identity and age, 160, 198.

Vivṛi(vṛa)ta, a class of nine-storeyed building, 50, 112, 168, 169.

Vrihaspati, one of the eighteen professors of architecture mentioned in *Matsya-purāṇa*, 164.

Vrihi, rice, one of the several materials of which foundations are made, 48.

Vṛiksha-saṁgrahaṇa, collection of wood for building, 94.

Vṛisha, a class of two-storeyed building, as described in *Matsya-purāṇa*, 115; other classes mentioned in *Bhavishya-purāṇa*, 116, in *Bṛihat-saṁhitā*, 117.

Vṛishabha, bull, oval types of buildings mentioned in *Agni* and *Garuḍa Purānas*, 113, 114; description of the image of, 82.

Vṛishabha-vāhana, bull, the riding animal, image of, 94, 100, 107.

Vṛita, one of the thirty-two authorities on which *Mānasāra* was based, 165.

Vṛitta round, types of building mentioned in *Bhavishya-purāṇa* and *Bṛihat-saṁhitā*, 117, 168, 169; an order of columns, 125, 126, 150, 151.

Vṛitta-kumbha, a moulding of the Pedestal of the phallus, 74.

Vṛitta-sphuṭita-(lakshaṇa), an architectural matter, as described in *Aṁśumadbheda* of Kāśyapa, 92.

Vulcan, temple of, 146.

Vyāghra, tiger, architectural details of the cage of, 70.

Vyājanā, fan, an article of furniture, 68.

Vyāsa, one of the several authorities on whose works the architectural treatise of Sanat-kumāra was based, 102.

W

Watch-towers, provided for the surrounding walls, 40.

Water-channel (nāla), description of, 49.

Waterways (and drains), construction of, 25, 39, 40.

Wood-joinery, varieties and other details of, 47.

Y

Yajamāna, worshipper, the height of the image of a deity is determined according to the height of, 77–78, 121, 124.

Yajña-kānta, a class of five-storeyed building, 50, 112.

Yajñopavīta, Brahmanical sacred thread, 98.

Yajur-veda, reference to architectural matters from, 15.

Yakshas, semi-divine beings, their images described, 61, 80.

Yama one of the several authorities on architecture, on whose works the architectural treatise of Sanat-kumāra was based, 102.

Yama-kānta, classes of five and eleven-storeyed building, 50, 112

Yāna, conveyance, including *ādika*, *syandana*, *śibikā*, *ratha*, 36, 60, 62, 90.

Yantra, machines, details of, 103, 137.

Yūkā, louse, unit of measurement, 35, 122.

Yantra-gṛiha, a bathing place for hot sitting baths, a room, 11.

Yard-stick, a measure, preparation of, 35.

Yāska, author of *Nirukta*, references to architectural matters from, 33.

Yava, barely corn, a unit of measurement, 35, 122.

Yoni-dvāra (also known as Praṇāla), a moulding of the Pedestal of the phallus, 73.

Z

Zend-Āvesta, Ahura-Mazda of, 166, 172.

Ziggarats (of Chaldæa), details of, 14.